ANCIENT
MIRRORS OF
WOMANHOOD

ANCIENT MIRRORS OF WOMANHOOD

A Treasury of Goddess and Heroine Lore from Around the World

MERLIN STONE

Illustrated by Cynthia Stone

BEACON PRESS *BOSTON*

Copyright ©1979 by Merlin Stone
First published by Beacon Press in 1984.

Originally published by New Sibylline Books, Inc.
Beacon Press books are published under the auspices
of the Unitarian Universalist Association of
Congregations in North America,
25 Beacon Street, Boston, Massachusetts 02108
Published simultaneously in Canada by
Fitzhenry and Whiteside Limited, Toronto

(hardcover) 9 8 7 6 5 4 3 2 1
(paperback) 9 8 7 6 5 4 3 2

Library of Congress Cataloging in Publication Data

Stone, Merlin.
  Ancient mirrors of womanhood.
  Reprint. Originally published in 2 v.: New York:
New Sibylline Books, c1979.
  Bibliography: p.
  Includes index.
  1. Goddesses. 2. Women and religion. I. Title.
BL325.F4S76 1984   291.2'11   83-73164
ISBN 0-8070-6718-0
ISBN 0-8070-6719-9 (pbk.)

CONTENTS

CONTENTS

ANCIENT MIRRORS OF WOMANHOOD

Preface

Nothing would be more interesting in connection with the WOMAN'S BIBLE *than a comparative study of the accounts of creation held by people of different races and faiths.*

CLARA COLBY—COMMENTS ON GENESIS
THE WOMAN'S BIBLE 1895

There has been an ever growing consciousness of the advantages of being able to personally identify with positive images and role models, in developing the self-esteem that encourages the fulfillment of individual potential. This consciousness has made us increasingly aware of the general lack of strong and positive images of women, in the literature and traditions, both sacred and secular, of our own society. In reaction to these realizations, some of us have been searching in the obscure records of the last few centuries, reclaiming the histories of important women who have been all but ignored. Others have been developing fantasies of the future, inventing new images of woman, in the hope that they will be there for the women of today and tomorrow. These efforts and contributions are of immense value to the building of a body of positive female role models, but is this truly all that is available to us, as we search for role models and inspiring images of womanhood?

The hopeful request quoted above, made by Clara Colby, editor of the nineteenth century *Woman's Tribune,* was written as women were initially confronting and challenging the gender biases, and roles of women, in the Hebrew Scripture (the Old Testament), and the New Testament—and the negative effects that various aspects of these religious scriptures have had upon women. With just a slight knowledge of Mexican, Scandinavian, and Algonquin beliefs, Clara Colby observed that images of womanhood seemed to be somewhat different in the religious lore of non-Judeo-Christian cultures, and thus suggested that a further exploration of this lore might produce some valuable insight and information.

Yet many women of today suspect, or even firmly believe, that a study of the religious accounts "of different races and faiths" would probably only result in finding that womanhood has always been perceived and portrayed as secondary to manhood. Statements, some even by well educated feminists, often convey the idea that if actual accounts from societies that regarded woman as powerful, as supreme creator, or as important culture heroine, ever did exist, such information is now buried in the dust of prehistory— a Goddess name here or there all that is left to ponder.

The gradual formation of these attitudes has been accomplished in various ways. One has been to confine grade school and high school studies primarily to what has existed in relatively recent, generally Caucasian, male-oriented societies. Another has been through reassurances by university teachers, and texts, that if some cultures had viewed woman as supreme deity, or that an accompanying female clergy had deeply influenced moral and social structure, indication of this occurs only in the scantiest (and therefore inconclusive) of references. A more subtle factor at work has been the rejection of all things 'religious' or 'spiritual', by many who might agree with the need for finding positive images of woman, but would prefer not to discover them in other than secular sources—thus ignoring the power and influence that contemporary male-oriented religions have upon even the most atheistic or agnostic of women today. Though stemming from an almost antithetical set of values, the above attitude manifests itself in a manner that is almost identical to that of the orthodox or devout Catholic, Jew, Protestant, or Muslim, who chooses to ignore any information that might bring long held religious beliefs into question. An even further buttressing of these attitudes has been provided by the few scholars who were aware of a wider body of knowledge on the subject of Goddess reverence, and/or female

2

clergy, in a particular period or area, but continually referred to this material as 'mythology' — thereby relegating it to a topic closer to fairy tale or fantasy, than the religious beliefs of a particular society. These factors, along with several others, have combined to quite efficiently smother the fires of motivation to search. After all, it is pointless to look for something that one has been taught to believe does not exist, is sinful, or is not especially pertinent or meaningful to 'real' life.

Just casually scanning *ANCIENT MIRRORS of WOMANHOOD*, the reader cannot help but observe that assurances of non-existence, or very minimal existence, of information about woman as deity, as clergy, or as important culture heroine, were simply not true. Though widely scattered in brief, often fragmentary, references, a large body of detailed information about woman as deity, often as supreme, omnipotent deity, has long existed in the written literature of many cultures, and in the oral traditions of many others. Perhaps, in our contemporary quest for role models and positive images, the accounts of woman as Goddess, or as culture heroine, that reveal portraits of woman as strong, determined, wise, courageous, powerful, adventurous, and able to surmount difficult obstacles to achieve set goals, may be of even greater interest and value for women of today. Yet nearly all of the information included in this volume has been completely ignored in our educations, and in popular literary themes, while in the few, usually obscure, texts that do include any information, it is most often covered in the most cursory of references.

Gathering the material presented in this volume has required many years of patient gleaning of fragments of information, from an enormous number of archaeological and ethnological studies, and literature as diverse as the Prose Edda to the Shan Hai Ching. Thus each of the fourteen sections in this volume is the result of lengthy research, and correlation of information, about images of woman as Goddess and culture heroine, as they have been known in various cultures. It is these generally unfamiliar images, these proud portraits of womanhood, discovered and brought together as a body of information, that comprise *ANCIENT MIRRORS of WOMANHOOD*.

For those like myself, who suspected the existence of this material (although to be honest, I never expected to discover so much), this volume will affirm those suspicions — and I hope bring joy at the reclamation of these treasures of our woman heritage, that belong to all women. For those who believed that such images had perhaps once existed, but had been lost to us forever, I hope that this volume will bring the satisfaction of having long lost possessions returned. For any who had been convinced that images of woman, such as the ones included here, could only have existed in contemporary feminist fantasy, it is my hope that the spiritual wisdom, inherent in many of the accounts, will be of help in coping with the rear-rangements of basic realities that such readers might need to make.

Writing this preface as the final pages, before this manuscript is sent off to be printed, I admit to feelings similar to those of waiting to watch loved ones open presents for which they had yearned — but never really expected. Although it has taken some eighty-five years to finally fulfill the hopeful request of Clara Colby, I type these last lines with thoughts of those courageous and perceptive women, who dared to confront Judaic and Christian thought, as it negatively affected the lives of women — the twenty three who were responsible for *The Women's Bible* — and dedicate this book to their memory.

Introduction

The ancient Akkadians wrote that the Goddess known as Mami pinched off fourteen pieces of clay, and making seven of them into women, making seven of them into men, She placed life upon the earth. The Dahomeans said that the Goddess known as Mawu built the mountains and the valleys, put the sun in the sky, and placed life upon the earth that She had made. Chinese texts record that the Goddess known as Nu Kwa patched the earth and the heavens, when they had been shattered, and thus restored harmony and balance to the universe. Mexican records reveal that the Goddess known as Coatlicue lived high upon a mountain, in a misty cloud, and there She gave birth to the moon, the sun, and all other deities. Hesiod wrote that the Goddess known as Gaia gave birth to heaven, and mating with heaven, She brought forth the other deities. Sumerian texts tell us that the Goddess known as Nammu was called upon as the mother who gave birth to heaven and earth, and that She supervised the creation of all life by Her daughter Ninmah. Australians explain, that it is to the Goddess known as Kunapipi, that our spirit returns upon death, thus remaining with Her until the next rebirth. Indian records state that if the Goddess known as Devi were to close Her eyes even for a second, the entire universe would disappear. In Egyptian hieroglyphics, it was written that the Goddess known as Au Sept was the oldest of the old, She from whom all becoming came forth. Navajo people know that Changing Woman is sacred Nature, in all that She unfolds.

These are just a few of the images of woman as deity, primal force of existence, as they have been known in various cultures. Can it be completely coincidental that the multitude of accounts of female as deity have been classified as 'mythology', rather than as sacred and religious scripture? It seems that there are few people, in contemporary western societies, who are able or willing to perceive the creation stories and accounts of deities, that were written on the clay tablets or papyri of ancient cultures, as truly 'religious' concepts, and even fewer who are willing to regard the beliefs of the tribes of Dahomey in Africa, the Toba of Argentina, or the Chinese of ancient Chi' province, as anything more than interesting mythology, or intellectual curiosities.

Writers, with psychological concerns, often approach the spiritual beliefs of other cultures with scholarly interest, believing that they can discover patterns, observe universal archetypes, or analyze the underlying meaning of symbols—all the while referring to the accounts as curious, intriguing, creative—but nonetheless, mythology. Yet the accounts of deities of other cultures, separated from western religious thought by chronology, geography, or levels of technological development, are obviously much more than mythology, as we generally comprehend the term. They reveal spiritual contemplations, and religious concepts, that developed within various cultures, just as the stories in Hebrew Scripture developed within early Hebrew society, The New Testament within early Christian society, and the Koran within early Islamic society. Some claim that it is a 'primitive' quality, an 'irrationality', in the events and images, that define an account as myth, yet how many of the people who make these claims or definitions would refer to the Genesis account of creation, the account of the opening up of the Red Sea, or Jesus walking upon the water and feeding five thousand people with five loaves of bread and two fish—as mythology?

The reader might ask, 'What is wrong with referring to these accounts of other cultures as mythology, since Webster's Unabridged Dictionary defines myth as "A story of great but unknown age which originally embodied a belief regarding some fact or phenomenon of experience . . . " and as " . . . an ancient legend of a god, a hero, the origin of a race . . . ", while mythology is simply defined as "The science which treats of myths . . . "

My reply would be that Webster (1913) goes on to define mythology as " . . . the collective myths which describe the gods of a *heathen* people . . . " while at the same time defining the word theology as "The science of God or of religion; the science which treats of the existence, character and attributes of God, his laws and government, the doctrines *we* are to believe, and the duties *we* are to practice . . . " I might add that the more contemporary American Heritage Dictionary defines myth as " . . . a traditional story presenting supernatural beings, ancestors or heroes that serve as primordial types in a *primitive* view of the world", and offers as a second definition, " . . . *any fictitious or imaginary* story, person or thing.", while it defines theology as "The study of the nature of God and *religious truth.*" (My italics)

Aside from the so called generic usage of the male terms—gods, ancestors and heroes—and the differentiation implicit in the uses of upper and lower case G/g's for God/god, the inclusion of the words "heathen" and "primitive" make it quite clear that mythology is to be regarded as the accounts of *others,* while theology is to be viewed as "the doctrines we are to believe", and "religious truth". Nowhere, in these definitions of mythology, does the word religion even appear.

Though heathen literally means from the heath, as pagan is derived from the Latin *paganus,* a country person—both heathen and pagan are defined by Webster as *other* than Christian, Jew, or Mohammedan. It is in this way that the distinction between how we are to perceive the religious beliefs of those whose sacred accounts are classified as mythology, and those whose are to be considered as religious truth, is semantically structured, far from church, temple, or mosque. One might be tempted to ask if these three major religions have qualified as non-heathen simply because they happen to be in the small minority of faiths that revere no female deities within their beliefs, each having made overt efforts to suppress earlier Goddess reverence—and to wonder if, when so called primitive people of today are converted to Christianity, their acceptance of the New Testament then classifies that scripture as mythology?

Surely, in the midst of this semantic ethnocentricity, it is time to question these divisions, between what is to be regarded as mythology, and what are to be considered as sacred accounts and beliefs. We must begin to be conscious of the cultural blinders, the cultural static, that keep so many of us from acknowledging that the spiritual and religious beliefs of others, past and present, were or are as valid and integral a body of "religious truth" in their lives, as Hebrew Scripture, the New Testament, and the Koran, are to Jews, Christians, and Muslims.

For the many who have rejected all religious beliefs and literature, the semantic boundary lines between myth and religious accounts are perhaps not so clearly defined, but readers who may regard *all* religious literature as myth — and as such not worthy of serious interest, or careful examination — may be embracing yet another form of tunnel vision, one that is aware of little else but that which is directly in front of it.

In reading the following accounts, that are included in this volume, I ask that all readers attempt to approach the evidence of the religious beliefs of all cultures with as open a mind as possible. They provide a body of information that allows us to broaden our knowledge and comprehension of the vast diversity of human thoughts and ideas about origins and existence, and, of especial importance to us today, about the diversity of roles and images of woman, as perceived within many cultures — information that has for the most part been ignored in general literature and education.

The task of collecting information about each image of woman included in this volume — as Goddess or as heroine — is one in which I have now been involved for almost fifteen years. It has certainly been a long lasting task, but seldom an uninteresting one. Searching for the evidence of reverence for deity as female, and for accounts of legendary heroines, from nearly every area of the world, from people of every racial group, has been a treasure hunt with all the excitement, suspense, and pleasure, that such a term implies. Each clue, each lead to another source, each discovery of a specific fact, each additional fragment of knowledge about deified or heroic images of women, has been an ever refueling energy source, that has never run dry throughout my many years of research.

How could any woman, raised and living in a male-dominated, male-oriented society, fail to remain fascinated, while continually discovering gems of woman heritage such as: an account of a High Priestess of the Moon Goddess Jezanna from the Mashona people of Zimbabwe, explaining how she alone revised an important religious ritual; Chou and Han period texts of the Goddess in China, that describe Her role in structuring the harmony and patterns of the universe; an account of a welcoming ritual into the society of womanhood among the Cuna people of Panama—for young women reaching menarche; Egyptian records that describe the Goddess Maat as the very essence of the rhythm and order of the universe; Tantric Indian texts that explain Shakti Goddess power as that which causes all action to occur; a poem of the poetess Avvaiyar to her woman lover, written in the Tamil language in the city of Madura in the first century B.C. of India; or the text of an ancient ritual that included a temple gift offering of a vulva carved of the precious stone, lapis lazuli, for the Goddess Ishtar in Semitic Mesopotamia.

As I continued my research, the joy of finding accounts of images of woman as creator of the universe, provider and teacher of law, possessor and prophet of ultimate wisdom, initiator or inventor of important cultural developments, or as courageous warrior—continually enticed me to carry on with the search—ever on the edge of new discoveries of images of womanhood, that were far different from those generally familiar in our society. There was a gift for every woman, of every racial background, of every age, of every temperament, a proud heritage, precious mirrors of womanhood that I was gradually accumulating in the chest in which I stored my ever more numerous notes—until the day that this treasure would be shared with all women.

Many people of today, even many with university educations, think of Goddess reverence as having existed only in prehistoric periods (some doubting its existence at all). Yet archaeological evidence attests to the fact that at the initial period of the development of writing (the Jemdet Nasr period of Sumer—about 3200 B.C.), and for at least *thirty five centuries* after that development, that first brought us into the period of written history—the Goddess was not only revered, but honoured in *written* tablets and papyri. Written prayers, written descriptions of rituals, written titles and epithets, and religious scripture (generally referred to as epic legends), have been excavated from their long hidden burial places, to provide more than ample witness to Goddess reverence in *historical* periods. Although archaeological evidence almost certainly assures us that Goddess worship existed for many millenia prior to these historical periods, the erroneous belief, that worship of the Goddess existed *only* in prehistoric periods, must be laid to rest, in light of the mass of actual written evidence. We may want to question the possibility of racial bias, as well as gender bias, in the initiation and maintenance of the idea that the study of Ancient History should begin with Homer and Classical Greece, when writing had been developed, and in use, for over *two thousand years* before that time.. Perhaps, as with the perceptual division between myth and sacred scripture, the human mind is capable of intellectually absorbing factual knowledge— while at the same time avoiding full comprehension of that knowledge for various emotional reasons.

After about eight years of research on deified and heroic images of women, I began to write about what I had found, and was soon working on an introduction to point out the similarities, the differences, the influences and transitions within the context of historical data, and the effects of migrations and invasions, upon Goddess reverence. It was this 'introduction' that eventually became a volume in itself, originally published as *The Paradise Papers—The Story of the Suppression of Women's Rites* in London, later published as *When God Was A Woman* in the U.S. But I had already collected a vast amount of material, evidence of Goddess worship, and heroic accounts of legendary mortal women, from nearly every area of the world. This was the material that *When God Was A Woman* had initially been based upon, but only a very small portion of it had been included in the actual text (which rather organically developed into an historical analysis of the suppression of Goddess reverence in the Near and Middle East— the areas in which Judaism, Christianity and Islam first emerged).

After *When God Was A Woman* had been published, I returned to the problem of how to present all else that I had found—most of it discovered in fragmented and piecemeal bits of information. This problem of a mode of presentation was more challenging to me than all the years of research had so far been. How to best present each piece of evidence, each fact that pertained to a specific Goddess or heroine name—in a way that would share the overwhelming sense of a long hidden heritage—as well as the enormous number of specific details? In writing the introduction that eventually became a book, I had drawn upon methods learned during many years of writing college term papers and theses, replete with quotations and references. But how to structure such a mass of fragmented, diverse, and generally unfamiliar, bits of documentation, gleaned from such an enormous number of disparate sources? There were prayers and parts of prayers, rituals and parts of rituals, legends and parts of legends, titles, epithets, symbols, inscriptions—that had each been gleaned from: translations of cuneiform tablets; translations of papyri and carved inscriptions; ethnological and anthropological studies that included accounts of spiritual beliefs; and translations of the early literature of Mexico, Scandinavia, China, Ireland, Iran, Wales, Japan, India, Greece and Rome. In addition to this written information, there were my personal observations of sacred artifacts that I had studied at the museums of the U.S., Europe, and the Near and Middle East; as well as my personal observations of ancient temple sites. Each provided evidence of images of womanhood, that ranged all the way from the creation of the entire universe and all life—to the winning of a horse race, and giving birth to twins at the finish line.

Over my many years of research (which has never really stopped), I had begun to observe that most European and Euro-American presentations, of the religious beliefs of other cultures, were done as if the writers were describing a banana—still in its skin. Crescent, deep yellow tinged with green or brown, somewhat hard to the touch—perhaps useful as a prop for a still life painting, or brightening up a fruit bowl—but not truly known because it had not yet been peeled, and its inner fruit experienced by tasting and eating it. Yet it seemed that at the very moment one actually tasted, chewed, and swallowed, a piece of the banana, no longer was it considered possible for that person to describe the banana—objectively. Objectivity, emotional distance from subject matter, may be a viable method or approach for the study of certain subjects, but ignoring the spiritual or religious qualities of the *core* of religious beliefs—a deity—though it may be regarded as good scholarship, insures that at best, the subject will only be partially understood. Such objectivity, carefully avoiding the subjective aspect of the *sanctity* of the subject discussed, when the facts discussed were about religious beliefs, resulted in descriptions that may best be likened to the scholar having used a telescope or microscope with an inverted lens—one that viewed the subject as smaller than it actually was. It was also clear, after years of reading many texts on the spiritual beliefs of other cultures, that the initial choice of a topic, as a subject for examination and discussion, as well as what each scholar chose to include—and to exclude—were purely subjective decisions, thus negating the possibility of totally objective studies, even as they began.

It was with these observations in mind, that I began to reject the idea of a strictly academic presentation of the information that I had found. Having read several carefully footnoted studies of Egyptian beliefs, in which the Goddess as Isis or Hathor, was not even mentioned; and studies of Greek beliefs, in which Artemis and Hera were mentioned in two or three brief references, while entire chapters were devoted to Zeus and Apollo, it was obvious that to footnote biased emphasis of specific material—did not make it any less biased. Thus I openly admit to my own bias in choosing to study only female images, a form of bias that few male scholars have even considered, as they chose what was of interest to them, and wrote volumes with titles such as Gods and Heroes, or Man and His Gods.

It was also clear to me, that if I was going to present this material at all, I was going to do so with respect—the respect of seriously considering the religious ideas of others as more than intellectual curiosities. I was dealing with images and information about deities that people had prayed to, honoured, held as sacred. Could I do less than to try to regard and present these beliefs, and the evidence of them, with a feeling of respect and sanctity—the very qualities that had been carefully discarded, in the efforts to comply with the requirements of at least a superficial semblance of scholarly objectivity? I was determined to peel the banana and taste it—preferring an honest admission of subjectivity to a pretense of what passes for academic objectivity, when writing about the religious beliefs of others.

As a result of this inner debate with my years of academic education and conditioning, I began to consider the facts about each image of Goddess and heroine with what some might regard as a difficult, perhaps even impossible, point of view, for a person of western Caucasian background. Somewhat like actors, whose current roles begin to seep into their offstage lives, I spent long hours of every day considering the facts that I had gathered on each specific image of woman, as I imagined one who had actually lived in the culture that had held that specific woman image as sacred or heroic, might consider or describe it. I better understood why my mother had so often referred to me as a daydreamer, as I spent my days with my thoughts and feelings more in Buto, Erech, or Hattusas, or among the Buhera Ba Rowzi, the Kiowa, or the Chibcha, than in any current reality. Half consciously, I found myself writing the account of Sun Sister, of the Inuit (Eskimo) people, on a day that my room was chilled by a heavy midwinter snowfall; the story of Australian Lia, when the summer temperatures sizzled in the high 90's. Mother Nature seemed to be cooperating, for it rained incessantly during the week I wrote of the Zulu Rain Goddess, Mbaba Mwana Waresa.

Thoughts came to mind of the time I had glued the pieces of my grandmother's favourite serving dish back together again, when it had broken many years after she had died. As with my grandmother's dish, I could not bring myself to throw away the shattered pieces of an object that I had known and admired on her abundant table as a child, and as with the dish, I would not allow myself to add any extra pieces, though I confess to using a small tube of glue. Though truly saddened by its damaged condition, the reconstructed presence of the serving dish still provided me with nostalgic thoughts of a woman most dear to me, my emotional response to the repaired dish perhaps even heightened, by the consciousness that it would never be completely whole again—as I would never again be able to sit as a child at my grandmother's table. A visual reminder of the passage of time, in which joy and sorrow flow together. It was in much this same way, that I spent two years in piecing together the multitude of broken fragments of Goddess and heroine images, that are our heritage as women—with loving care, respect, and a deep concern for the integrity of using only what was truly a part of it.

Though somewhat hesitant about confessing to the following, throughout the process of organizing and writing of each of the many images of Goddess or heroine, I sensed, almost heard, the voices of women reciting the information that I had collected, read, and repeatedly reread, on the pages of my notebooks. Even as I typed, my mind was often filled with images of sitting around a campfire or on the bank of a lake or river, of being in an ancient temple or inside a communal tribal shelter—as if listening to the recitations of a story teller, hearing the pace, the pauses, the phrasing of each account, as if it were being told aloud. If I over romanticized such situations, I offer my apologies to any who may object, but I explain these experiences to any who may be puzzled by the form of writing that evolved. Years of having studied the translations of the ancient tablets of the Sumerians, Hittites, Babylonians, Ugaritans, and others, most surely affected my perceptions of how such information may have been initially orally conveyed. Added to this were the years of listening to parables told at various churches and temples, along with having long been intrigued by hearing a good yarn being spun along various waterfronts, or in the Irish pubs of London. Such was the strange potpourri underlying my feelings about story telling, as they evolved through years of telling bedtime tales to my daughters, and as they synthesized to pass along all that I had discovered about our heritage as women. Now, somewhat uncertain about just whose voice or voices told each account, I assure the reader that the events, actions, and conclusions, of each account, are as I found them. If I may again resort to an analogy with food, it seemed that with some of the primarily narrative accounts, it was as if water was being restored to the contents of packages of dehydrated soups. Having had the chance to compare the translations of many actual ancient tablets, to the brief summarized accounts of those same tablets in other texts, I was aware that as with the sanctity—the drama, the poetry, and the suspense, had also often been removed. It is my hope that having restored the 'water' to 'dehydrated' summaries, when there were no tablets available with which to compare them, has made it possible to relate each account in a form that is more in keeping with what is known about the traditions of oral recitation within so many cultures. If there are cultures who repeat their legends, of sacred and heroic figures, in as perfunctory and terse a manner as most of the summaries of anthropologists, historians, and ethnologists, I offer my apologies for assuming that all cultures would describe accounts of their own heritage with more respect and care.

I imagine there will be some who view my intentions and experiences, thus this form of presenting factual information, as not quite valid—just as Sir Arthur Evans' reconstruction of the temple of Knossos on Crete has been viewed as unacceptable by some archaeologists, who would have preferred that Evans had left the fragments of Knossian walls and pillars lying where he found them. It may offer some insight, into the nature of the academically critical mind, to realize that no archaeologist has ever suggested that Evans' removal of the piles of earth, that had for so long hidden the buried ruins — might in itself be tampering with the realities of the past. At any rate, chancing the criticisms, rather than produce a dictionary or encyclopedic volume of fragmented and dehydrated details, I too chose to reconstruct.

Now that I am better able to view this multitude of Goddess and heroine images, as other than hundreds of pages of fragmented pieces of information, I believe that the rich and diverse images of womanhood that they reveal, emerge above and beyond any of the weaknesses that may confess to my reassembling and restoration of the many broken and shrunken pieces. My hesitations, that these images of woman might be thought of as other than those of the many varied cultures included, fade away, as I am better able to grasp the immensity, the uniqueness, the ingenuity, of all that each culture has created. And viewing the study as a whole, it seems obvious that no one culture, certainly no one person, could have conceived of all that is included.

When all fourteen sections were completed, I realized that once again, as with the introduction that became a book, the amount of material during fifteen years of research had far exceeded my expectations. But it is my deepest hope, that all who read this volume, will be fully aware that each and every section is equally important to the true and complete realization of the immense richness of our heritage as women. The accounts of woman images, of each racial background, each culture, each section grouping, are each but a part of the whole. To read and become familiar with only a part, or a half, is to settle for a partial understanding — and therefore an inaccurate idea — of all that is our rightful inheritance. Each arc of colour may be lovely to behold, but it is the full spectrum of our woman rainbow that glows with the brightest promise of better things to come.

Once familiar with all the accounts of Goddess reverence, and legends of heroines, from so many cultures, the reader soon becomes aware that no simple archetype, or duality of archetypal aspects (e.g. Good Mother vs. Terrible Mother—as in Erich Neumann), or simple stereotype, or duality of stereotypes (e.g. madonna vs. whore), could possibly encompass all the images and perceptions of woman, as they have actually been known. It is in the rich diversity, the almost astonishing multitude of various traits and aspects—many often attributed to the same deity—that the consciousness of what images of woman have been, and what images of woman can be—emerges most clearly. I believe that it is this diversity, and the acknowledgement and celebration of it, that offers the firmest foundation for our growing strength—as we move ahead in our consciousness of ourselves as women, and of our potential as human beings on this planet. The dishonest canvas rips, the dishonest carved marble cracks apart—as we are each better able to declare ourselves as the unique, multi-faceted beings we each are—leaving behind all false or simplistic portraits, that were said to symbolize *all* womanhood.

Symbols such as the moon, the sun, the various stars and planets, volcanoes, caves, springs, rivers, lakes, ocean, lioness, serpent, heifer, mare, whale, heron, raven, vulture, dove, fig tree, laurel, corn, marigolds, meteorites, obsidian, Earth Mother, Sea Goddess, Queen of Heaven, the force of existence, the flow of existence, traits that appear to mesh, traits that appear to conflict— are each a part of the full and wondrous treasure. Images of the creator of the universe, the creator of life, the one who takes in death, the one in whom our twin spirits unite until we are reborn, provider of law and cosmic pattern, provider of herbs and healing, the one who is compassionate, the one who is wrathful, the essence of wisdom, the guiding holy spirit, Liberty, Victory, Justice, Destiny, Lady Luck and Mother Nature—all have been known in the form of woman. As anthropomorphic huntress, judge, warrior, tribal ancestress, inventor of writing, protector of animals, prophetess, inventor of fire, guardian of the celestial chamber of grain, teacher of carpentry and masonry, scribe of the tree of life— and as the more transcendental, metaphysical, female principle, that brought existence into being, and continues to cause all to occur—each known concept attests to images of womanhood that refute generalized archetypes, stereotypes, and simplistic dualities.

There are accounts: of mothers mating with their sons, such as in Bachue, Fire Woman and Inanna; of daughters both helping and defying their fathers, such as in Mella and Golden Lotus; of rituals for the Goddess including lesbian relationships, such as in the Mysteries for the Greek Goddess Gynacea and the Roman Bona Dea; of the Goddess choosing a mortal male for a mate and living happily ever after, such as in Mbaba Mwana Waresa; of the women of an entire tribe leaving the males to set up a community of their own, such as in Lia; of the worship of both Mother and Daughter as the sacred pair, such as in Lato and Artemis, Demeter and Persephone, Mahuea and Hina; of reverence for the Mother, two daughters and a grand daughter, such as in the Sun Goddess of Arinna. However one attempts to construct a mold, it will not fit them all.

Along with the pride of regained heritage, in becoming familiar with these many accounts of images of womanhood, we may also gain some insight into the various efforts made to suppress and alter these images, even to erase the very memory of them, by various male-worshipping groups. In the earliest periods there are the Sumerian transitions, from the most ancient Creator Goddess Nammu to the less powerful Inanna, and the loss of power by the Goddess Ereshkigal, through the trickery and violence of the male deity Nergal. Kuan Yin, whose image may be derived from the pre-Buddhism Creator Goddess Nu Kwa, is described as having once been a male boddhisatva, who decided to return to earth as Kuan Yin. The Arabian Goddess Attar, associated with the Semitic Ishtar and the Egyptian Hathor, is described in later South Arabian inscriptions as a male deity. The effects of early Judaism are noticeable in the accounts of the Goddess of the Semites as Asherah and Ashtart; Ashtart (Ashtoreth) used as a name of a demon in the Middle Ages, though the gender was also changed to male. Early Christians made the Goddess Bridget into a Catholic saint, but doused Her eternal flame at Kildare; while later Christians burned the holy books of the Mayans, but appropriated the Tepeyac shrine of the Goddess Coatlicue and dedicated it to the Virgin Mary as the Lady of Guadalupe. Long after St. Patrick destroyed the sacred cairn of the Cailleach Bheur in County Covan, missionaries in Hawaii encouraged converts to defy the Goddess Pele, by throwing stones into the crater that was sacred to Her.

17

Thus as we become familiar with images of womanhood that were once held as sacred, we also come to realize how various male worshipping groups degraded, and/or erased, their existence. For those who question just what effects these images might have had upon the status and perceptions of womanhood in the societies that had revered these images, we might in turn ask why the male-oriented religions were so anxious to hide or deny them by these various means — and why the once almost universal existence of female clergy, that accompanied Goddess reverence, is a precept that today draws ridicule and dissent from so many.

Perhaps it was some of the symbolism associated with ancient Goddess reverence, as various elements of nature, and at times the enactment of ritual in a natural environment, that led to the labelling of ancient Goddess reverence as a "nature cult." Along with the demeaning implications of the word cult, as compared to the term religion, when applied to any body of spiritual beliefs, it may also be time to challenge the type of thought process that automatically assumed that a nature cult revealed a lower level of spiritual development, than that inherent in the major religious institutions of today. Faced with the all too real threats of the continually escalating accumulation of nuclear weapons, poisonous pollution of land, sea, and air, and the complete extinction of many species of life on earth, perhaps even our own, we might do well to examine the rituals, parables, and symbolism, of spiritual beliefs that included regarding various aspects of nature as sacred — thus inviolable. Along with a reclamation of our heritage as women, we may gain from the spiritual wisdom inherent in many of the accounts. One cannot help but wonder, if polluting the environment was to be regarded as blasphemous to our deepest religious beliefs, and if our religious values were truly in focus with natural life and existence, such beliefs and attitudes might help to ensure the very survival of life upon this planet. As I explained, there are great diversities in both images and practices of Goddess reverence, as it has been known in various cultures. Yet a careful consideration, of some of the links between Goddess reverence and the sanctity of nature, may provide us with a useful understanding of why the even now familiar title, Mother Nature, has survived in societies that claim to reject Goddess reverence, and preach against so called "nature religions."

Upon the prompting of an editor several years ago, I had briefly considered the idea of dividing the evidence about Goddess reverence by specific types of symbolism, e.g. moon, sun, sea, agriculture, healing, warrior, serpent, bird, etc. I soon realized that such divisions inherently negated the actual multi-faceted dimensionality of many of the female deities, as they had been described and revered, by those of their own culture. Would I place the Egyptian Goddess Isis under stars (for Sirius), heifer, law, agriculture or magic? Would I place the Goddess Hina of the Polynesians under fire, water, moon, caves or agriculture; the Mexican Goddess Coatlicue under creator, volcano or serpent? In thinking about this, I became ever more convinced that my initial intention, of dividing the sections by cultural source, was the only way to retain the full integrity of the image of each Goddess and heroine.

As women, we are many, more than half the people of the world. We come from many diverse backgrounds, and many varied racial and cultural roots, even as we are each unique within our own racial or ethnic groupings. To strive for a sameness or classification of image, might mean to aim at a categorization that could smother and obliterate our precious differences. Perhaps just the knowledge that womanhood has been held as sacred, and/or heroic, among the Athapascans and the Anatolians, among the Chinese and the Chibcha, among the Irish and the Iroquois, among the Japanese and the Jicarilla, among the Egyptians and the Eskimoes, among the Mashona and the Mexicans, among the Semites and the Scandinavians, among the Zulu and the Zuni—helps us to begin to comprehend the enormity of what we have seldom been encouraged to know, about the diverse images of woman, as perceived by the human mind. (It may, in fact, be helpful to keep a world atlas or a globe near at hand while reading, to better understand some of the geographical connections).

A few years ago, I wrote and spoke at some length about the distortion of our perception of the events of the past, that is caused by our referring to all periods that occurred before the rise of Christianity as B.C. (Before Christ) or B.C.E. (Before the Common Era). At that time, I explained that such an arbitrary division of the passage of time not only forces us to count backwards, when discussing any period before two thousand years ago, but inherently encourages the idea of our separation from the series of events that led to society as we know it today, e.g. the development of agriculture, architecture, ceramics, textile making, metallurgy, wheeled vehicles, and methods of writing. By implying that those many millennia of cultural development (i.e. before One B.C.) were not in *our* era, we automatically place many millennia of Goddess reverence in those same B.C. periods, that seem to waft away into a vast emptiness of time that is not quite real — time that seems to move in reverse rather than towards today.

In reaction to this distortion of chronological perception, I suggested if we were to simply add the eight thousand years, that began in what we refer to as 8000 B.C. (a central date in the period of initial agricultural development), to the years that we then counted as 1977, we would arrive at the more logical date of that year as 9977 A.D.A. (After the Development of Agriculture). It is with apologies to those who *do* understand this temporal distortion, that I have reverted to B.C. ←——→ A.D. dating in these volumes. Given the choice of double dating all given dates, or confusing readers who have not read or heard my full arguments about this, I once again submit to this distortion of chronological perception, with some misgivings, and hope that my more enlightened readers will forgive this inconsistency.

As with *When God Was A Woman,* it was clear that to attempt to include specific footnotes to the sources of each of the enormous number of fragments of unfamiliar information, such documentation would have taken nearly as many pages as the text itself. The ancient prayers presented in the Semitic, Anatolian and Sumerian sections are composites of the various translations of the original tablets. In the Semitic section these are based upon the work of Robert Biggs, G.R. Driver, John Gray, Stephen Langdon, E.A. Speiser and Ferris Stephens; in the Anatolian section upon the work of Albrecht Goetze, O.R. Gurney, Hans Güterbock and C.H. Haspels; and in the Sumerian section upon the work of Edward Chiera, A.K. Grayson, Stephen Langdon and Samuel Noah Kramer. For those truly interested in doing further research on this subject, and I hope that my book will motivate at least a few readers in that direction (being all too aware that there is still much more evidence to be gathered), some primary sources are included in the introductory sections and in the accounts, and a full bibliography is included at the end of the book.

*   *   *

In considering the much more recent past, I want to acknowledge my appreciation to the many scholars whose work I have studied, and to those who have personally helped in this long project. My gratitude to Myrna, Alice, Batya, Fran, Z., Nancy, Ruth, Jean, Lenny, Charlene, Gloria, Judith, Marion, Linda, Buffy, Tracy, Susan, Elisa, Kay, Rory, Joan, Donna, Jill, Barbara, Roma, Carmen, Ursula and Yolanda. I especially express my appreciation to my two daughters, who first motivated me to present this information, precisely because they are daughters and deserved to know of their proud heritage as they grew into womanhood. In turn, I was rewarded, not only with their unflagging encouragement over the many years, but with Jenny's illustration for the section on Egypt, and with Cynthia's patient and knowing lines of hand and pen, that over the years began to flow with the ever-developing ability to create visual images of women that were non-sexist, non-racist and non-agist. This combined text and illustrations of mother and daughters was a dream we first had some ten years ago, and as with all other goals and hopes for these volumes, we hope that the positive woman energies of our working together on this will be shared by all women.

Just as Cynthia's and Jenny's contributions are important to me, it is my hope that the information about Goddess and heroine images, provided in these books, will motivate many women to absorb them into our culture, by using them as themes for drama, dance, poetry, fiction, song, painting, sculpture, and in any other form that will speak of our long hidden heritage as women — regained. Thus we offer this work not only as hopefully enjoyable and worthwhile reading, but as reference books to which the reader may repeatedly return for inspiration in the years ahead.

The knowledge of these images of womanhood, and old/new ways of perceiving ourselves as women of this world, is our inheritance, our legacy of pride and self-esteem. Whether atheist or minister, scholar or carpenter, avowed feminist or fence-sitter, nine or ninety — we can all grow stronger on these treasures of our worldwide heritage that have been kept from us for far too long.

A Gentle Omnipotence
China

he way of Mother Nature, ever moving, ever changing, ever beginning, ever ending, flowing calmly along, or rushing quickly by, yet never ceasing to flow—as the cycles of life continuously occur—is the essence of the image of the Goddess, as She was known among the ancient peoples of China.

Perhaps the best way to begin to understand the image and nature of the Goddess within the culture of China is to become familiar with a world view that appears in many early Chinese texts, a recording of mythic memories of a period long before—that of The Era of The Great Purity. In the *Chuang Tzu,* written in the third century B.C., the time of the Great Purity is described as the epoch in which people knew their mothers but not their fathers (29:1). Other texts speak of this period as a time when all people lived in a state of innocence, being genuine and simple, spontaneous and direct in their conduct. They were in harmony with the seasons and with the ways of nature; animals and humans did no harm to one another. The Chinese texts then explain that this paradise was destroyed by mining minerals in the mountains, felling trees to build houses, hunting, fishing, and even by learning to make and control fire. The period of the obliteration of this perfect life, and the loss of touch with the patterns of nature, was referred to as— The Great Cosmic Struggle. Nature had been defied and this was said to be the original cause of human discord and problems. Thus we may observe in very early Chinese thought, the very problems most of us regard as those of our own time—the struggle to preserve natural life on the planet as modern technology threatens to destroy it.

In an effort to better comprehend this ancient past of which the texts speak, let us take a look at human development in China, and the view of nature—the guiding essence of The Era of The Great Purity—and how it came to be associated with the female principle. The lands that we now know as China have been inhabited for at least 500,000 years. This is the time generally assigned to the scanty skeletal remains of about twenty-five pre-homo sapiens, described as Pithecanthropus Pekinensis, more commonly known as Peking Man—discovered some thirty miles southwest of Peking.

The development of full homo sapiens is attested to by the Ordos culture of the Upper Paleolithic period of about 25,000 B.C., a culture that developed along the Hwang Ho (Yellow River) between the provinces of Shensi and Shansi. The cave at Choukoutien near Peking, where pre-homo sapiens have been found, was also used by full homo sapiens whose skeletal remains reveal the beginnings of specifically Mongolian racial characteristics. By about 4000 B.C. small settlements were being made throughout the provinces of Kansu, Shensi, Shansi and Honan. Cultures such as the Yang Shao and Ts'i Kia P'ing are especially noticeable, their sites revealing ceramic work of well developed quality and design. Despite our pleasure in the esthetic and cultural achievements of these early peoples, we must also admit that it seems that The Era of The Great Purity had ended, or at least that the time of The Great Cosmic Struggle had certainly begun.

What of the spiritual beliefs of these ancient people of China? A form of hieroglyphic writing, that seems to have developed some time in the beginning of the second millenium B.C., is known to us from articles of bone, shell and bronze. Many scholars suggest that bamboo may also have been used as a material for writing, and although there is no actual evidence of this, the absence of it may well be the result of the natural deterioration of such a material. But on the more permanent writing surface of bone, a phrase written at Anyang in Honan Province tells the reader to "pray to Grandmother Yi for rain." This fragment of writing, using the term grandmother to designate a female being who was powerful enough to affect the weather, leads us to the probable origins of belief in the

Goddess—as Divine Ancestress. The worship of ancestors, a religious practice known throughout the world, is well attested in China. In a society such as that described in the Chuang Tzu—where people knew only their mothers and not their fathers—ancestor worship may well have been ancestress worship.

In the existent texts of the Chou period (about 1000 B.C.) and the later Han period, it was written that Nu Kwa created all people, thus revealing Her nature as the original parent or most ancient ancestress. But according to these texts, it was not only as the Mother of all people that Nu Kwa was revered. She was also described as the one who established harmony and the patterns of the universe, arranging the order of the seasons, and setting the stars and planets upon the proper paths. It is this more complex and omnipotent view of The Mother, not only as She who first gave birth to people, the Creator of human life, but also as She who arranged the workings of the universe, the patterns of nature—that reveals that the image of the most ancient ancestress was that of Nature Herself—the harmonious essence that was defied in The Great Cosmic Struggle.

Are the few accounts of the Goddess, the earlier ones of Nu Kwa and Hsi Ho, and the later ones of Kuan Yin and Tien Hou, all that remain of these ancient beliefs? I think not. A careful reading of the most basic book of Taoism, the *Tao Teh Ching,* believed to have been written at about 600 B.C. by Lao Tzu (which literally means Ancient Teacher), may be the mirror in which, to some extent, we are able to observe reflections of ideas and beliefs that may once have been the theological/philosophical core of ancient Goddess reverence in China. In the *Tao Teh Ching,* we do not find prayers to a concept of Goddess that is external to, or separated from, earth and ourselves, but rather the understanding of Nature as the maternal spiritual essence that is inherent in all that exists and occurs. It is a concept of Goddess that is also to be found in the texts of India, concerning the Goddess as Shakti or Devi, and in the texts of E-gypt, concerning the Goddess as Maat. It is this gentle omnipotence of She who is the essence of the patterns of the universe, all that is actually implied when we speak of Mother Nature, that appears to be the core of the wisdom and the way of the Tao Teh Ching.

Perhaps one of the most significant aspects of this understanding of Mother Nature is the light that it throws upon the concept of the female principle, *yin.* Contemporary interpretations by western writers often translate or define *yin* as that which is totally passive, unmoving, waiting to be acted upon by the male principle, *yang*. But the female principle of the *Tao Teh Ching*, as well as the accounts of the ancient Goddess, suggest that yin did not originally imply passivity, but rather a specific form of activity, as compared to that of the more aggressive yang. The wisdom of the activity of the water flowing around a great boulder, rather than repeatedly crashing against it, is the wisdom of Mother Nature— the female principle of following the strategy, that to some may seem passive, yet in the long run is most likely to assure a reaching of the destination. Thus the scriptures of the Goddess religion are to be read in the observation of the organic processes of Mother Nature. The concept of the Goddess is not that of a static being, but an omnipotence that is manifested in all of Mother Nature's constant workings.

Nu Kwa arranges the patterns of universal activities. She is Nature in action. The later image of the Goddess as Kuan Yin, though not imbued with attributes as all encompassing as those associated with the image of Nu Kwa, still retains the idea of gentle but consistent, determined action, that which succeeds in eventually overcoming each obstacle. Even in the story of the mortal heroine Gum Lin, we may observe the importance of the studying the natural way and pattern of each being. In this case, by knowing the natural patterns of the dragon, Gum Lin and the dragon's daughter are able to devise a plan of strategy that avoids direct confrontation—but achieves their ultimate goal.

The emphasis in these accounts of Goddess reverence among the ancient people of China is not on a passive acceptance of all that happens as the will of Nature, but on the advantages of studying the ways of Nature very carefully. It is this observation of all that Nature does, and how She does it, that seems to be the true study of the wisdom of the Mother Goddess. Continually ramming into a boulder that is in one's path simply leaves the body hurt and bruised, though it may wear the boulder down a bit. Flowing along as the river flows, rushing past on one side when the boulder blocks the other, making new paths when there are none available, gathering more speed and power as the volume of the waters increases—the student of Goddess wisdom understands the importance of an ever continuing observation of the way that all proceeds. Learning from the ways of Nature, She who has mothered all, we may learn how best to reach our goals, and perhaps to realize that the erosion caused by our constant rushing past the side of the boulder—will eventually wear it down to the size of a tiny pebble.

NU KWA

Reverence for the Goddess as Nu Kwa (Nu Kua) comes to us from the people of the northern provinces of China today known as Hopei and Shansi, the area once known as Chi'. The most detailed accounts of Nu Kwa's creation of all people, and Her repair of the universe, are from texts of the Han period (about 200 B.C.-200 A.D.). They appear in the writings known as the *Lieh Tzu,* the *Feng Su T'ung Yi,* the *Shan Hai Ching,* all from the Han period. There are less detailed remnants concerning the nature of the Goddess Nu Kwa that appear in the literature of the Chou period (starting at about 1000 B.C.), but according to Chinese tradition the story of Nu Kwa repairing the universe dates to about 2500 B.C., the time spoken of as the period of The Great Cosmic Struggle. The emphasis on the harmony and rightness of nature's patterns, in the legends of Nu Kwa, offers an interesting comparison to that same emphasis that is the core of the *Tao Teh Ching.* Visual images of Nu Kwa, with the tail of a fish, provide interesting parallels to Atargatis and Nina (see Semitic and Sumerian Sections).

To the valleys of the wide flowing Hwang Ho, came the Goddess Nu Kwa and there from the rich golden earth, She fashioned the race of golden people, carefully working the features of each with Her skillful fingers. But so arduous was Her task that She soon tired of making these individual creations and began to pull a string through the mud. In this way She made the others, though not as carefully formed, as She had made those of the golden earth, the ancestors of the Chinese people.

From the Kun Lun mountains, sweet western paradise whose summits reach the heights of heaven, Nu Kwa sent the great winds and the life giving waters, making the earth good for planting, pouring the excess waters into the Chihli Po Hai Bay—and then She filled it with fish so that all might eat to satisfaction.

But there came a time when all the universe was in great chaos; fires raged and waters brought floods. At this time, the pillar of the north, the pillar of the south, the pillar of the east, and the pillar of the west—all of these were destroyed. The nine provinces of the earth separated from each other and even heaven and earth were no longer suited to each other, for they had blown so far apart. Everything was wrong. Animals ate the people. Vultures seized and killed the elderly and weak.

Then Great Mother Nu Kwa saw what had happened and came to repair the damage, using coloured stones to patch the heavens. Seeing the ruins of the pillars, those which had supported the four corners of heaven, She took the legs of the great turtle and used them as columns, placing them firmly at the four compass points of the world. With Her mighty arms She smothered the blazing fires and when the burning reeds had turned to ash, She piled the ashes high enough so that the wild flooding waters came to repose where they are today. When all was once again in place—only then was Mother Nu Kwa satisfied to rest.

It was then that She looked upon all that She had done. It was a time of perfect harmony when all flowed in its course, each at its own pace. The stars followed their correct paths in the heavens. The rain came only when the rain should come. Each season followed the one before—in rightful order. Mother Nu Kwa had repaired the pattern for all that occurred in the universe, so that the crops were plentiful, the people were no longer the meal of the wild animal, vultures did not prey among the weak and old, nor were serpents harmful to them either.

Life was spent in nights of peace, undisturbed by anxious dream, and waking time was carefree and untroubled. It was the time of Mother Nu Kwa, She who established the patterns of existence, the order and rhythm of the universe, the sacred way of harmony and balance.

KUAN YIN

The Goddess Kuan Yin (Kwan Yin) is still revered in China today, but it may well be that Kuan Yin is a relatively recent reflection of the more ancient Nu Kwa. Both *Nu* and *Yin* mean woman, while the word *K'uai* means earth, and although the connection is not certain, both names may refer to a concept of the Goddess as Earth or Nature. Some of the accounts of Kuan Yin, still told today, describe Her as having originally been a male who had reached the state of Buddha being, but who then decided to return to earth as a Boddhisatva, a spiritual teacher—taking the form of Kuan Yin. This idea, that the Goddess was once a Buddhist devotee, can of course only have developed after the birth of the first Buddha, Gautama Siddartha (about 560 B.C.), and may reflect the influence of one set of beliefs upon the other, the newer concepts of Buddhism superimposed upon beliefs about the ancient Goddess. Images of Kuan Yin, riding upon a dolphin, may be related to the fish tailed images of Nu Kwa.

Holy Mother of Compassion who achieved ultimate enlightenment, yet chose to return to us when we called in times of trouble, though we are grown, to Her we turn in our moments of deepest need, and She heeds our childlike calls for help—the Merciful Mother, Most Holy Kuan Yin.

In the blazing pit of fire I called and She came to take me to the cool of the river waters. When thieves overturned my wagon and left me beaten in the mud, I called and She carried me to my home, there healing and soothing my wounded body. When cruel ones threw me from the rocky cliff, I called and She came and in Her arms I gently floated down to earth unharmed. When the scorpion and the tiger hissed their anger at me in the jungle, I called and so loud did She shout that they ran in fear, and I escaped to the safety of my village. When my beloved child lay lifeless upon her mat, I called and She came and sprinkled the water of life from Her sacred willow branch, until the child breathed again and rose in health. Truly She is the Merciful Mother, Most Holy Kuan Yin.

There once was a time when She came to live as the youngest daughter among three, watching Her elder sisters: marry a lusting warrior, marry a greedy merchant. At Her refusal to take a husband, asking only to be able to enter the temple of women, did Her father not arrange that the women of the temple should treat Her with cruelty—so that She would change Her mind and accept the bonds of marriage, as he wanted Her to do?

Difficult was Her life at The Temple of the White Bird, for those who feared Her father's wrath assigned to Her the most arduous of tasks, but when She worked while the others slept peacefully upon their mats: the serpent came and helped Her fetch the water; the tiger appeared and gathered the wood for the fire; the birds flew busily about collecting the vegetables from the garden; the spirit of the fire rose up and helped to cook the food; the peacock even used its elegant feathery tail to sweep the kitchen floor.

When news of these miracles reached the house of Her father, so angry was he that his plan had not worked, did he not then set fire to the shrine, willing to burn each and every woman who lived peacefully within, just to revenge the thwarting of his will? And when Kuan Yin came and smothered the fire with Her own hands, hands that did not burn nor blister, did he not then order that Her head be severed from Her body?

Was the astonishment of the headsman not great when he tried to follow the orders of Her father, only to find that his sword broke itself in two, rather than harm Her holy body? But was not the headsman's fear of Her father even greater than his fear of the message that his sword conveyed, for it is said that he then murdered Her with his own hands about Her throat—and tied Her lifeless body to the back of a tiger, setting it loose in the jungle.

Was it dark in the Land of the Dead when Her precious soul descended and did Her young girl heart feel fear? Yet we know, that even in the house of death, She sang sacred chants of goodness and mercy, relieving the suffering and pain of the souls that dwelled therein, until they kneeled about the hem of Her robe in gratitude and respect. This so infuriated the King of the Dead, he who delighted only in punishment and torture, that he could not bear Her perfect presence near him—and thus banished Her from his kingdom of death.

Once again alive on earth, compassion and mercy triumphant over cruelty, Her soul rejoined Her body. So it was that She made Her way to the island in the Northeastern Sea where She now lives in peace, but never has She forgotten us as there She chants and meditates for our well being, still listening for our cries when troubles overtake us, always coming to our rescue when we call upon Her name—Merciful Mother, Most Holy Kuan Yin.

HSI HO

These scanty references to the Goddess as Hsi Ho appear in the *Shan Hai Ching* and the *Huai Nan Tzu,* both texts of the Han period. In these writings, Hsi Ho is said to live beyond the southeastern waters, in an area referred to as the Sweet Waters, *Kan Shui.* Even more minimal remnants of information about the nature of Hsi Ho appear in the earlier Chou texts. The Fu Sang tree is generally thought to be a mulberry. Three hundred li is about one hundred miles. It may be completely coincidental, but it is interesting to realize that the concept of there being ten suns also appears in the beliefs of the Native American Shasta tribes of California.

Mother of the ten suns,
She who creates the heavenly bodies,
She who creates the calendar
of the ten days of the week—
She causes all to happen
by Her celestial design.

Each morning we may look upon
the Valley of Light,
watching Her bathe one of the suns,
the one that She has chosen for that day,
in the sweet waters of the Kan Yuan Gulf
and then watch Her place the sun
in the branches of the Fu Sang Tree
where it sits among the multitude of tiny leaves,
raised three hundred li into the sky,
until it starts upon its way
across the wide heavens
finally coming to rest
on western Yen Tzu Mountain,
only to return to Her again—
as each of us shall do
after our journey upon the earth.

TIEN HOU

This is a story that can still be heard around the area of the island of Meichow Tao, located off the central coastline of China. It is an account that appears to be about a young woman who might be considered to be a mortal heroine, rather than a Goddess figure, yet the mystical aspects of Her supernatural abilities and powers, and the manner in which they are used, transcend Her mortality. The evidence of shrines and statues of Tien Hou suggests that the image of Tien Hou was a long held religious image that, as with many other ancient Chinese beliefs, was later embroidered upon to explain the origin of Her existence.

On the ragged coastline of the province Fukien, on the easternmost end of Meichow Bay, sits the island of Meichow Tao, homeland of the maiden Tien Hou—She who is known as Protector of the Sea. Those who live along these coastal waters remember this young woman who lived in days so long ago, and often tell of the joyous day that she was born—to a mother who had given birth to four sons, and had prayed fervently, during the many months of her fifth child growing within her, that she might have a daughter.

While the four brothers of Tien Hou went off in the fishing boats, the daughter kept her mother company, delighted when they gathered shellfish on the beach, or wove baskets that they would trade for yards of cloth or bowls of clay. Sometimes sitting quietly together in their home, the mother told the daughter tales of the sea, tales that she in turn had heard from her husband and her sons. When still a growing child, Tien Hou was satisfied enough to listen to the stories of men's adventures on the wide sea, but as young womanhood arrived, her desire to experience for herself grew greater—until she began to wish that she might do something as important and exciting as the deeds of the men in her mother's stories.

A day arrived when Tien Hou's father and her brothers had been gone for half a moon, promising before they left to return with baskets full of fish. Tien Hou sat upon her mat, sorting the lengths of reed, when suddenly she felt a great pain in her head, gasped for breath as if there was not enough air in the small hut to fill her lungs, and slumped flat upon the ground—her eyes closed, her throat emitting the hoarse dry whispers of a dread fever coma.

Desperate with worry, the mother bathed the daughter's brow with cool well water, stroked her soft golden arms with mother tenderness, pleaded with Tien Hou only to hear her voice, to fight whatever strangeness had claimed her—to waken to let her mother know that all was as well, as it had been but moments earlier. Tien Hou felt her mother's tears and kisses upon her fevered body and finally revived, repeating as she woke, 'I should have stayed just a moment longer. I should have stayed just a moment longer.'

Little was said of this incident until the arrival of the fishing boats, and the father and the brothers return to the island—telling the strange story of how their boat had floundered in the waters, as violent storm and thunderous cresting waves had washed them from the deck. Each explained that somehow Tien Hou had come to pull them from the waters, flying down from the heavens as if she had the wings of a great bird. But once the father and three of the sons had been placed safely in the boat, Tien Hou had disappeared, and the fourth son had succumbed to the sea, unable to fight the raging waters without the help of Tien Hou.

'It was for this reason', Tien Hou explained, 'that I did not want to wake, yet I heard the frantic worry in my mother's voice and felt I could not stay any longer.' So puzzling was Tien Hou's account, so puzzling were the others, that little more was spoken among the members of the family, who mourned the loss of one of their own in silent confusion.

Only when the coma was repeated, only when the mind of Tien Hou once again seemed to leave her body, and when this time no one called to wake her, so that she breathed with life but did not wake, did the family remember aloud the miracle that Tien Hou had done. Trusting that she might again be flying over the wide sea, rescuing those in trouble, they cared for her body in its daytime and night time sleep.

Alive, yet not alive, Tien Hou lay upon her mat, tenderly cared for by her mother, while all about the islands of Nanjih and Haitan, even as far as Penghu Tao, those who fished began to tell stories of a young woman who flew from the skies—to pull them from furious waters, to push a boat of murderous pirates far away from their own, or even to hold a ship together, one that had been torn on jagged ocean rocks, long enough for all to swim to shore.

Grateful for the many lives that had been saved, families began to build shrines to honour the courageous Tien Hou. Even after life completely slipped from her small young body, still the people of the sea told of new miraculous rescues by the young one with the long black braids, who flew to their sides just when they thought life would soon be gone. Carving statues, now adorning the simple Tien Hou in robes of royalty, placing a stately crown upon Her head, they called upon Her as Queen and Protector of the Sea, as they kneeled before Her statues to pray for the lives of those who daily faced the dangers of the sea, and for the protection of the daring and compassionate Tien Hou.

MOTHER NATURE (TAO)

Tao is not generally regarded as a Goddess name but rather as a term most often translated as The Way or The Path. The reasons that I have included this adaptation of a few excerpts from the *Tao Teh Ching* in this volume is the continual suggestion, in the *Tao Teh Ching,* that the ways in which one may better understand Tao is to understand and follow the ways of Mother Nature—as well as the fact that the values, applauded in the book of the Tao, are those which are repeatedly referred to as feminine and maternal. This emphasis upon following the ways of Nature, and the image of Nature as Mother, suggests that this treasure of wisdom, in which philosophy and religion are inextricably entwined, may well be a most enlightening text in our efforts to better understand the true nature of ancient Chinese beliefs about the Goddess. Though I had long speculated about this possibility, as my knowledge of Goddess reverence grew, my decision to include this piece in this volume was encouraged by a recent reading of Ellen Chen's paper *Tao as The Great Mother and the Influence of Motherly Love in the Shaping of Chinese Philosophy.* Ms. Chen bases her reclamation of Tao as Goddess religion on her careful examination of the *Tao Teh Ching, Chuang Tzu,* and other early Chinese writings, in the original Chinese.

Nature, since it has mothered all, may be regarded as Mother Nature. Only those who understand Mother Nature, understand Her many children. If we choose to avoid mistakes and desire to have a wise guide throughout life, we should study the wisdom of Mother Nature's ways.

There is no way to truly describe Nature, for to describe Her completely, we would have to create a perfect duplicate—and this no one but Nature could do. We might try to explain Nature by saying that She is the ultimate source of all that exists, all that comes and goes, all that begins and all that ends, all that is and all that is not—but to describe Mother Nature as the ultimate source of all is only to use a few of Her sounds.

Mother Nature contains all natures, yet no matter how many natures come into being, Her supply is without end. We may learn from Mother Nature, as She reveals the way in simple lessons: those who try to reach beyond their reach by standing on their tiptoes, soon lose their balance; those who stretch their legs too far apart to try to walk more quickly, soon find they cannot walk at all; those who brag about themselves too much, soon find themselves more ignored than others; those who push their views most heavily upon others, soon find that fewer people will agree with them; when people claim credit for what they have not done, they soon find that they do not even receive the credit they have earned; the more one is filled with arrogance and pride, the further the fall when humiliated; the longest journey beings with the first step; the tallest tree starts as a small seed; the highest tower starts with the first brick.

Learning from the ways of Mother Nature, one continually discovers how best to proceed.

GUM LIN AND LOY YI LUNG

The tale of Gum Lin is another that is still remembered in China. Although its central theme is that of hardship and drought, certainly real enough problems in the life of people in some parts of China, it is also the legendary memory of a young woman who was so concerned about the people of her village that she would not be swayed from her goal of helping them, even when tempted by personal comforts and riches. The portrayal of the mortal Gum Lin is all the more interesting, as it is interwoven with the somewhat supernatural image of another young woman, Loy Yi Lung, the daughter of the dragon. As the story proceeds, it is clear that only by the cooperative efforts of the two young women can the difficulties of the people be overcome. The interpretations of this legend, and its possible underlying morals or messages, may be numerous, but the sense of self-esteem offered to girls growing up on such stories is certainly clear enough.

Young and old, the women gather and walk slowly to the foot of Tai Ma Shan—Great Horse Mountain. There they stand side by side in the light of the waning moon, the third moon of the new year, and by the flowing waters of the the river that wash the foot of the mountain, the riverbank lit by the twenty-one day old moon, they send their voices across the waters. Soft and loud, high and deep, the voices float off together into the night air—carrying with them the most wondrous of tales, the story of Loy Yi Lung, the dragon's daughter, and of the girl who had once lived in their village in times long ago, the brave and loving Gum Lin—Golden Lotus.

At first there is a sadness in the voices of the women, as they sing of the time of the dryness of the land, when the water was so scarce that the rice would not grow, when the bamboo withered and died in the drying mud of the gullies that had once been the beds of flowing streams. They sing of Gum Lin, when she was not yet a woman, and how she had gone about her work, her small hands cutting the reeds, her small fingers tying them together, making bamboo brooms, making bamboo mats—and selling all that she had made to help to feed her family:

As the land grew dryer and more barren, further and further from home did Gum Lin have to wander, searching for a few stalks of bamboo, when all that had grown close to the village had been stricken by the thirst of their roots. Miles from home she walked, into the deep forest thick with trees, making her own path between the great rocks, until far beyond the tall trees, at the foothills of the mountains, she saw what seemed to be an image in a dream. Thickets of bamboo, tall and yellow green, bent gently in the soft wind, clustering along the edges of a clear blue lake, a secret bowl of water in the mountains, one that she had never seen before. Gathering all that she could carry, Gum Lin returned to her village with her precious bamboo treasure.

All through the long night She tossed upon her sleeping mat. So much water in the forest where few can drink. So little water in the village where thirst was part of every day. The slender reeds of dream wove in and out through her restless sleep, until they wove themselves into a channel, a canal that the water could pour through—a canal in which the waters of the forest lake could find their way into the thirsty village, there filling up the muddy ditches where other waters had once run.

In the light of the early morning, a shovel and a pick-axe balanced upon her small shoulder, her long black hair braided tightly to last the rigours of the hard day's work ahead, Gum Lin started on the way that led to the clear blue mountain lake. There she planned to dig a pitcher spout on the rim of the reservoir of water, so that it would pour from the foothills of the mountain, into the thirsty gullies of the village from which the rice and bamboo had once been free to drink their fill. But arriving at the water's edge, she noticed a thick grove of trees on one side, and rocky ledges and boulders along another. By the rim of the great cup that held the deep, gathered, mountain waters, Gum Lin walked and looked, hoping to find the right place—until, just a few steps before her, in a place where she had thought she might dig, she saw a great stone gate.

She pulled upon the door of the gate, but it would not open. She picked and pried with the tip of her axe, but the door was very thick and tightly bolted. Stopping for a moment to catch her breath and to think of what to do, Gum Lin was surprised by a strange voice, and turning to see from where it came, all she could see was a wild grey swan that had made its way almost to where she stood at the edge of the lake. Again she heard the voice. Could it be the red ringed throat of the swan that was saying, 'These waters are yours, once you find the key to the stone gate.' There was no one else in sight, but by the time she thought to ask the wild swan if it had been speaking, and if so, where this special key might be found—the graceful wild bird had already made its way far across the wide lake.

Needing time to solve the puzzle, Gum Lin wandered back into the forest, winding her way between the cypress trees, thinking about the strange gate, wondering about the key to its latch. She had hardly noticed the three brightly feathered birds perched up high on the branch of a gnarled cypress, until voices, that seemed to come from where they sat, sang out in perfect chorus, 'The daughter of the dragon. The daughter of the dragon.' But just as Gum Lin was about to ask the birds if they had truly spoken, three pairs of wings of brilliant colour slid into the air, waving as if in farewell. Gum Lin would have been more puzzled yet, had she not taken notice of the tail of a peacock, as it spread out against a tall pine, fanned open as wide as it could be. Suddenly the peacock shook its tail into a blur of blues and greens, and in the sound of the rustle of the feathers, Gum Lin heard these words, 'Go to the edge of Ye Tiyoh, Wild Swan Lake. Stand upon its banks and sing the songs of your people. Make your voice loud and clear, so that the daughter of the dragon may hear you, and if your songs please her, she will come to you.' And then the peacock folded its fan of eyes into a long tail, that followed behind its soft round body, and walked further into the dark woods.

The small legs of Gum Lin, still carrying the weight of pick and shovel, moved as fast as they could, back to the water's edge. Standing her tools beside her in the dirt, she leaned upon the handles, breathed deeply in, and then chanted out in a voice that was as clear as the blue lake water. She sang songs of the snow on the mountains, of the peaks that one could see from the village, of grass as green as that which she had been told once grew, of the loveliness of flowers that she had never seen—but though she sang song after song—nothing happened. The daughter of the dragon had chosen not to listen.

Determined to follow the peacock's instructions, Gum Lin thought of every song she knew. When she had finished the songs of the loveliness of nature, she began to sing the songs of the people of her village, of those who worked in the flooded fields of rice, of those who could not work now that they were dry. She sang the songs the women sang, as they wove the reeds, or as they repaired family huts after strong winds had blown them apart, or as they tried to feed the small but hungry mouths of new existence. They were proud songs, of people who did the best they could, but they were not the pretty songs of grass and flowers and snow capped mountains. Surely if the other songs had not brought the dragon's daughter forth, these songs would please her even less. Still Gum Lin sang.

Singing of the hardships of her people, of the loving kindness that they gave to one another, when there was little else to give, tears came to the dark brown eyes of Gum Lin, blurring her vision of Loy Yi Lung, the daughter of the dragon—as she emerged from the waters of the lake. Wiping the tears from her cheeks, Gum Lin soon remembered why she had been singing and called out to the daughter of the dragon, 'The key. Please may I have the key? My people are dying of hunger. They work very hard but without water they have no food, without water the rice cannot grow.'

38

'The key is in my father's cave on the deepest floor of the lake.', Loy Yi Lung answered. 'There he guards it, as he jealously guards all his worldly treasures—and would destroy anyone who might dare to intrude—even his own daughter.' Then growing from a moment of further thought, a scheme was devised by the daughter of the dragon, who knew the dragon as well as he could be known. 'Often when I sing just outside the cave, my father crawls closer to the entrance to listen to my song. Perhaps if we sang together, our voices would bring him to the entrance, and while I continued to sing, you could slip past him and search for the key.'

All proceeded just as the two had planned, but when the brave young Gum Lin found herself in the darkness of the cave, she was overwhelmed by the sight of trunks and vessels piled high with golden coins and precious gems. For a moment she thought to stuff her pockets with the jewels and gold, for with them she could move her family to better land, but then remembering the others of the village, the hungry crying infants, the weakened grandparents, those who still searched daily for any rice plant that might have survived the drought, she knew that she could not leave the cavern until she had found the key to the waters. Just at that moment, the edge of her shoulder upset a small ivory box that sat upon a rocky ledge. As it fell, it tumbled its contents out upon the watery stone floor—and there before her lay the key, golden and glowing, a carefully formed swan at its top, swimming in a sea of pearls that had long nestled against it in the box.

The key safely tucked inside her pocket, Gum Lin swam quietly past the dragon's side, and reaching the place where Loy Yi Lung still sang, she grasped her hand in joyous triumph. Side by side they swam to the edge of the mountain lake, to the place where the stone gate stood. Loy Yi Lung watched from the water, as Gum Lin climbed back upon the bank, and slipped the key into the long unused lock, turning it this way and that, pulling upon the handle of the door with all the strength of her small arms—until suddenly the door flew open as if being pushed from the other side! It was in this way that the water that had pressed upon the door rushed forth upon the grassy lakeside, digging deep into the ground—carving its own canal.

The water swam until it reached the dry waiting stream beds of the village. It sped along, diving over rocks, thinking only to quench the thirst of the ground where the rice and bamboo had once grown.

It danced joyfully about the ankles of the few remaining plants, and tenderly bathed the seeds and ailing saplings, tucking them in their moist bed to rest, humming lullabies of how tall they would grow as it bubbled by. It tunnelled beneath the earth to leap inside the stone walls of wells, pouring itself into the cups of the thirsty. Ye Tiyoh Lake had stretched out its merciful river arm, spread its blue palms and fingers open in offering, to share itself with the people in the village of Tai Ma Shan.

Gum Lin walked along the river banks, following the path that the water had chosen into the village, as Loy Yi Lung swam alongside, relieved that the angry bellowing of her dragon father was quieting with the distance. The broad river provided directions to a stream, that now flowed by the small home of Gum Lin, and in the fresh new mountain waters, there the dragon's daughter made her home. By that stream Gum Lin would sit upon the grassy edge, and spend the hours of her days tying the bamboo and visiting with Loy Yi Lung, both singing as they had by the entrance of the cave, the perfect mating of their voices ringing as celestial chimes throughout the village.

It was this ancient tale that the women of the village sang, as they stood upon the banks of Ye Tiyoh, Wild Swan River, at the foot of Tai Ma Mountain, their voices finally waning in the dark night, as the moon waned in the sky and the great starry dome of night filled with silence. But it was then that they heard the most marvelous music of all, though the women of the village made not a sound—two women's voices, joined in perfect harmony, rang out from beneath the deep blue waters.

and there before her

lay the key

Mighty in Magic, Enchantment and Divination
Celts of England, Ireland, Scotland, and Wales

As part of our exploration of the nature of the Goddess among the Celtic peoples, those whom we know best from Ireland, Scotland, Wales, Cornwall and Brittany today, we must first be aware of the vast geographical areas that the Celts once inhabited, and of the great number of quite separate tribes that formed the group we refer to as the Celts. In the third century B.C., large numbers of Celts were spread across Europe, from the mouths of the Danube in Roumania to the western coastlines of France. The Classical Greeks referred to the Celts as Keltoi; the Romans knew them as Galli or Gauls. Galicia in Poland, and Galicia in Spain, were once Gallic/Celtic areas. Perhaps most surprising is the evidence of Celtic tribes living in Turkey, forming the nation/state of Galatia, so well known from St. Paul's epistle to them in the New Testament.

Excavations of the Hallstatt culture of Austria (800-500 B.C.), and the La Tene culture of Switzerland (500-50 B.C.), reveal that these sites had once been Celtic settlements. Celtic tribes such as the Brigantes, Belgae, Helvetii, Sequani, Parisi, Boii, Iceni, Cornovi, Bellovaci, Trinovantes, Osisimi, Treveri, Silures, Demetae, Domnonoii, Cantiaci, Novantae, Aquitani, Remi, and many others, lived upon the European mainland until migrating or fleeing from Romans and/or Teutons, and finally settling in their current homelands. Those who had settled in Britain were driven even further west by later Teutons (Angles, Saxons, and Jutes). From these Celtic tribes, European place names such as Paris, Belgium, Helvetia, Carnac, and Reims, still survive today.

Many archaelogists identify the homelands of the earlier Proto-Celtic people with the sites in France and Germany of the Bell Beaker culture (2000-1200 B.C.), and the Urnfield culture (1200-650 B.C.). These cultures may account for a great many of the Proto-Celtic people during these periods, but quite possibly not for all. Celtic references to very early Celtic settlers of Ireland, as Danaans, have raised questions and theories concerning possible links between the Celtic Danaans and the Greek Danaans of Homer's account who participated in the Trojan War in Turkey. There are further speculations on links between the Celtic Danaans and the early Danes, as well as with the Danuna, a tribe thought to be from Adana, Turkey, listed among the Sea Peoples who raided in the Mediterranean areas in the twelfth century B.C. These possible links, between the Celts and groups of Greece and Turkey, are further supported by a Welsh account that Celtic Llundein (London) had first been settled by a man named Brutus, described both as a worshipper of the Goddess as Diana, and as a Trojan from Anatolia (Turkey).

Though the possibility, that some Proto-Celtic groups may have been living in Greece and Turkey during the second millenium B.C., may be difficult to reconcile with our knowledge of the Celtic people of today, we should keep in mind that tribes speaking Indo-European languages did live in the southern regions of Russia, and that some of these tribes entered Turkey, Iran, and India, during the second millenium B.C. One current hypothesis suggests that Celtic society was the result of the merging of the Bell Beaker culture of Europe and the Indo-European Battle Axe culture of southern Russia. Although this theory is too complex to discuss here, for those interested, further study on these possible connections may provide answers to some of these puzzling links. To even further complicate the matter, there are the statements by Arrian, that the Celts of Galatia paid homage to Artemis, and by Strabo, that Gallic representatives attended a religious council in the sacred centre of the Anatolian Goddess Kybele (the city of Pessinus) in the second century B.C. This in turn brings to mind, although probably coincidental, that the castrated clergy that served Kybele in Turkey were known as *Galli*.

Since there is no written material from the Celts until the period of their arrival in their current homelands, the nature of the Goddess, as revered among the Celts, is drawn primarily from Irish, Scottish, and Welsh tradition and literature. This does not mean that these beliefs were not held by the Celts in earlier periods, but suggests that up until the time they were recorded, they were probably preserved through tradition and oral recitation.

One of the major themes found in the accounts of the Celtic peoples is the association of the Goddess with a particular body of water—usually a river, but at times a spring, a lake, or the ocean. The Divine Ancestress of the Celtic Boii tribe was known as Boann, and linked with the River Boyne in Ireland. The Divine Ancestress of the Sequani tribe was Sequana; the River Seine of France, once known as the Sequana, named in Her honour. A healing shrine dedicated to Sequana stood at the headwaters of the Seine near the modern day city of Dijon. There has been some hypothesis that the Sequani were also linked to the River Sankarya of Anatolia, the river that was known as the Sangarius to the Greeks, and cited by Homer as an area in which Amazons had lived. Sequana's name was later linked with the River Shannon of Ireland. The most ancient Goddess name on Celtic record is that of Danu, Mother of the Danaans. Her name is usually associated with the Danube (Donau and Dunava in areas of eastern Europe). There is some speculation that in Proto-Celtic periods, the name Danu had been linked with the River Don in Russia, Don also used as a river name in Celtic Scotland.

This association of the Goddess with various bodies of water, in turn appears to be linked with the Celtic reverence for the Goddess as The Great Mare. The white breakers of the ocean were described in Irish legend as the white mane of The Morrigan's head. The equine Goddess Macha, whose colt 'returned to the sea', is at times referred to as the The Daughter of the Sea. Epona, a name of the Mare Goddess in Celtic Europe, was at times linked with Neptune (Poseidon) in Roman festival. The connection is interesting in that Poseidon was regarded not only as a deity of the sea but described by Greeks as the inventor of horse racing. An account of Poseidon mating with the Goddess, as Demeter, both in the form of horses, may have been influenced by this Celtic imagery.

Though at first glance it may seem that the symbolism of the mare has little to do with the symbolism of river or ocean, it may be worth noting that both are important in transportation and mobility. The double imagery of horse and water may well be compared to that of a figure known as the Submarine Mare, in the accounts from India. This image of the Mare from India was said to have a divine fire in Her mouth, and to have lived in the ocean—to avoid burning up the world. This connection of sea and horse might help to explain the double use of the word mare, meaning sea in Latin and Russian (and the root of the English word marine), while at the same time used to designate a female horse. Both meanings of mare may have been derived from the same initial Indo-European source word, possibly the Sanskrit *mah* meaning mighty. This word may also be the foundation of the Goddess names—The Morrigan and Morgan—the roots *gan, gin* and *gen* meaning birth, as in genesis and begin.

Another prominent aspect of the nature of the Goddess, as revered by the Celts, is the ability to assume various forms and identities. In the material in this section, The Morrigan becomes an eel, a wolf, a heifer, a raven, and several diverse images of mortal women. Cerridwen transforms Herself into a greyhound, an otter, a hawk, and a hen, while Macha, the Caillech Bheur, and Rhiannon, take the form of horses. This shapeshifting aspect of the Goddess is one that recurs repeatedly in Celtic accounts, and unless it is to be viewed as purely poetic metaphor, which the texts do not really suggest, it may well have encouraged those who revered the Goddess to treat all animals with respect and caution. It seems to be this aspect of the nature of the Goddess that most insistently remained as Christianity gained power in Celtic society, this ability then transferred to the more acceptable image of Faerie Queens.

A less documented image of the Goddess among the Celts is the figure of the Goddess of Victory, invoked by Celtic Queen Boadicea as Andarta or Andrasta, a name quite similar to one applied to Egyptian Isis, that of Adrastea. The Goddess name of Tailltiu is mentioned briefly in some texts, as the mother of the god Lug. Tailltiu was honoured at the Feast of Lugnasadh (Lammas), August 1st, though at the period of the early Irish literature, as a secondary figure to Lug. Yet Her name was especially linked with Tailltean Games played during Lugnasadh, and the town of Tailltenn. There has also been some speculation that the famed prehistoric mounds of New Grange were at one time associated with the Goddess name of Grainne. This New Grange site that lies along the coast between Dublin and Belfast, just a few miles west of Drogheda, has been attributed to peoples as diverse as very early Celts—to Phoenician colonists.

Celtic accounts of legendary women as governmental and/or martial leaders, and soldiers, are found in the descriptions of Scathach, Aife, Medb (Maeve) and the nine Gwyddynod of Gloucester. Actual historical records of the powers and actions of Boadicea (Boudicca), Queen of the Iceni tribe, who personally led a rebellion against the Romans in 61 A.D., and Cartimandua, Queen of the Brigantes, who made the decision to sign a peace treaty with Claudius of Rome, suggest that the more legendary figures were based upon historic realities.

Along with these records of the martial prowess of Celtic women, Plutarch wrote that Celtic women often acted as ambassadors in battles and rivalries between the Celtic tribes, and sat upon peace councils when disputes were discussed. *Banfathi* (prophetesses) often accompanied troops into battle, and were relied upon for advice and strategy. Plutarch's account of women travelling with German troops, in much this same capacity, explains that the German women based their advice upon listening to the sounds of streams, and studying the eddies and currents of the waters. It seems quite possible that these methods were also used by the Celtic banfathi, who regarded rivers and streams as possessing the essence or spirit of the Goddess.

Mention of groups of Druidesses, in early Irish literature, appears to be connected to the references to women's islands, especially to those off the western coast of Brittany, such as the Druidesses of Sena on the Isle de Sein (just west of Pointe du Raz). Although no specific Goddess name is mentioned, early Christian tradition at Chartres Cathedral included the idea that Chartres had been built in the very place that was the major religious site of Druidic beliefs, its underground passages not unlike those of Mont Saint Michel's lower levels still dedicated to Notre Dame Sous Terre, Our Lady Beneath the Earth, while those at Chartres were remembered as the holy places of The Black Virgin.

DANU

Evidence of this most ancient Celtic Goddess, as Divine Ancestress of the Tuatha de Danaan (literally, tribe of Danu), is found primarily in the Irish *Lebor Gabala* (Book of Invasions), dated at about 1000 A.D. In the Welsh *Mabinogin,* Her name is given as Don. This image of the Goddess among the Celts is one that probably originated during the periods that Celtic tribes inhabited the mainland of Europe, the reverence for Danu being closely linked with the River Danube (Donau). As mentioned in the general introduction, the Celtic Danaans may have been related to the Danes, the Greek Danaans, the Danuna, or even, as some have speculated, to the tribe of Dan in Canaan. Considering the widespread movements of the Celts, any or all of these associations may be correct, but until further research is done, none can be stated with certainty. There is also the question of possible links between the name Danu, the name Dione as a Goddess name in Greece, and the Goddess name Diana, as known by the Romans. The name Danu may mean wisdom or teacher, as in the English word don, or giving, as in the root of the word donate.

Goddess whose spirit lives in the mighty waters that flow from snow capped Alpen mountains into the darkness of the Black Sea, ever flowing, ever giving, She is Donau, Dunav, Danube, Mother of all Celtic peoples. She brought the dawn of being for those who dwelled upon Her banks so that they understood that it was Danu who gave them sustenance and life.

The tribe of Mother Danu, the Tuatha de Danaan, most ancient of the Celts, those who were once spoken of as Gauls when they lived upon the lands that stretched from the coasts of the Atlantic to the triple mouths of the Danube, kept the memory of Mother Danu deep within their hearts and when fleeing from their Gallic lands, they carried Her with them to the British Isles.

Finally pressed by Teutons and by Romans to the lowlands of Cornwall, to the highlands of Scotland, to coastal western Wales where The Mother was called upon as Don, Her memory was also taken for safekeeping to the Isle of Erin where She was spoken of as Danu, Mother of the Tuatha de Danaan and long remembered as the most ancient Mother of the Celtic peoples.

In the twilight of the day whose light lingered longer than any other, there were prayers for abundance on Midsummer's Eve, the holiest of Danu's holy days. Worshippers carrying windblown torches of blazing bundled straw tied upon long branches made their way up the mountainsides, blessing the new cattle and the newly planted seed, explaining that they were commemorating the very day that the children of Mother Danu had first set foot upon the Irish soil.

THE MORRIGAN

The Morrigan is a major figure in the Irish epic *Tain Bo Cualgne*. The narrative of the epic makes it clear that The Morrigan's loyalties are with the Tuatha de Danaan and the Celtic tribes that had settled in the area of the large nation/state of Connacht. Though at times there is a tendency on the part of some to attribute a triple nature to Goddess images from all cultures, even when there is a complete absence of evidence of triplicity, there is no doubt about the triple nature of The Morrigan. This concept of the threefold nature of the Goddess among the Celts may also be seen in the Goddess as Bridget, as well as in the Three Matrons or Mothers who were often depicted in Celtic art, sitting side by side. But unlike the more sedentary images of The Mothers, The Morrigan was extremely active, even aggressive, and certainly always acting with a comfortable self assurance.

Triple imaged Morrigan, triple named Morrigan, Mighty Queen, Badb and Macha—it was She who protected the Tuatha de Danaan by cover of fog and rain and cloud so that the people of Danu could land safely upon the coast of Ireland. Those who say that She was three parts in one, say many things about Her: some say She was the three phases of the silver moon, waxing, full and waning, while others speak of the Three Mothers, The Divine Matronae who sat side by side with cornucopias of abundance upon their laps; some explain that The Morrigan was Maiden, Matron and Crone, saying that The Holy Trinity was once the Daughter, the Mother and the Grandmother.

Some saw Her as a vengeful crone, chortling in delight at spilled blood upon a battlefield, drowning enemy princes beneath Her white waves, battling against the Fomorians and the Fir Bolgs to protect those of the tribe of Danu. To others, She appeared as a young woman dressed in brightly coloured cloths embroidered with threads of glistening gold. Changing shape and form was but play to the mighty Goddess—and poetry and prophesy Her natural tongue.

Loud was Her war cry when She took the form of Badb; sharp were Her spears; powerful were Her enchantments; true were Her grim prophesies—as She flew across Celtic battlefields black as the sleek raven, making Herself visible only to those whose life would soon be over, Her raven caw filling hearts with dread, as death's call slid from Her widespread wings. And as The Mighty Queen, She took Dagda's body into Her own while Her feet were firmly planted upon opposite banks of a wide flowing river, from this joining giving birth to Mecha who had three serpents in his three hearts.

How filled with anger was The Morrigan when the lad named Odras used Her sacred bull to mate with his cow. Gathering up both bull and cow, She took them through the oak woods of Falga and brought them to the cave at Cruachan, not far from the River Shannon, where one might enter into the Otherworld. Desiring to retrieve his cow, Odras followed as fast as his legs would move but the fleet footed Morrigan, even with the burden of bull and pregnant cow, soon outdistanced the exhausted fellow—arriving at the cave of Cruachan while Odras was still far behind. When She later came upon him in the woods, his eyes closed deep in the sleep of his fatigue, She laid a magic spell upon him so that he changed into a pond, his spirit captive in the water of the oak woods of Falga until this very day.

But it was the warrior of Ulster, the arrogant Cu Chulainn, who most aroused the anger of The Mighty Morrigan. Some say that Her feud with him first began on the day that She had watched him bathing by a river bank and upon seeing his bared body, desired to lay him down beside Her. It was then that She approached him in Her finest robes, embroidered with all the colours of the rainbow. Though all the other soldiers could hardly look upon Her, so filled were they with awe and admiration, Cu Chulainn refused Her suggestion that he lie with Her in love, claiming that he was too weary from the day's battle.

Still, it was not this refusal that angered The Mighty Morrigan, who showed much patience and concern for the man that She desired, for She then suggested that She would help him in the battle and with the energy that he would save by Her conquests in the fighting, he would be able to accept Her offer of a loving bed. But this second offer was responded to with great disdain at the very idea of a woman helping in the battle and it was this reply that aroused the wrath of The Morrigan—thus making Cu Chulainn an enemy of the powerful Daughter of Eternity.

So it came about that on a morning when Cu Chulainn still lay fast asleep, he was wakened by a noise so loud and startling that it caused him to tumble from his bed on to the floor and to then rush half asleep through the door without a stitch of clothing. Jumping into his battle wagon, naked and unarmed, the mist of sleep began to clear and Cu Chulainn soon realized that although his intent was to ride to a battle, he did not know in which direction he had meant to go.

Sitting there in naked puzzlement, he saw another wagon approach, that one drawn by a single bright red horse that walked upon three legs and pulled the vehicle behind it by a pole that ran directly through its body—the tip of the wagon pole emerging from between the horse's eyes. Alongside the horse walked a footman, a forked wand of hazel in his hand. And upon the high seat of the wagon sat a woman whose hair and thick brows were the colour and brilliance of flame, Her long cloak of blood colour spread out about Her—as if She sat upon a throne.

Ever more puzzled and confused, Cu Chulainn asked their names and purpose. But he found that the riddles that he received as answers were far beyond his ken. As he added questions to his questions, the riddles grew in sarcasm so that his confusion soon became frustration. Just as he realized what a fool he must seem, sitting naked and unarmed in his own wagon, puzzled by words of his own language, holding the reins but ignorant of his intended destination—all disappeared except the woman, who suddenly became a great black bird, cawing in laughter at his plight as Her wings slid off into the morning air.

But Morrigan was not satisfied to have shown the man a fool. When next the warrior Cu Chulainn fought upon a battlefield, She gathered fifty white heifers and linking them together with a perfect silver chain, She took the form of a heifer without horns, thus leading the herd across the fields and waters—until the confusion they had caused among the troops of Cu Chulainn gave the advantage to his enemy. The Morrigan then made Herself into a long black eel and twisted about the arms and legs of Cu Chulainn so that he was unable to move in the waters but just as he was almost able to pull the eel from his body, She became a sharp toothed wolf, cutting deep and painful gashes on his arms. In this way they battled, until the dark of evening began to cover all. Then She left him on the battlefield—knowing that he would make his way towards home to heal his cut and broken body.

The Morrigan too had been badly hurt, especially about the face and eyes. Realizing that She could best be healed by the one who had caused the wounds, if She could win three blessings from him, She soon devised a plan. So it was that at the next noon, She became an old woman with a milking pail, sitting with a cow by the side of the road, the path that Cu Chulainn would have to take upon his journey to his home. When he came along the road, as She knew that he must do, his body as dry and tired as She suspected, She called out the offer of a cup of milk, suggesting that it might be pleasant to feel the wetness upon his throat. Not knowing who the woman was, he came gratefully to Her side and drank the creamy liquid from the cup, blessing Her for Her kindness as he took the empty cup from his mouth. When She poured a second time, again he drank and blessed the woman and yet a third time did he do the same until—thrice blessed—The Morrigan was healed.

Cu Chulainn was startled as The Morrigan then spread Her raven wings and more so when the old woman disappeared and the large raven that took Her place perched itself upon a nearby bramble. It was then that he heard the shrill cawing prophesies of a future grim and short in time, and watched as the wide black wings of The Morrigan disappeared into the distance—as he stood earthbound and fearful of Her wrath and magical powers.

MACHA

The name of Macha (literally meaning mighty) is given as one of the three aspects of The Morrigan, but in several accounts Macha appears almost as a separate deity. Thus we may regard the following material, primarily from the Irish *Noinden Ulad*, as the acts of Macha, while at the same time consider them to be the actions of one of the aspects of The Morrigan. Macha appears to be the embodiment of the equine imagery of the Goddess, suggesting a relationship to the Celtic Mare Goddess known in Europe as Epona. Two sites in Ireland's county of Ulster still bear the name of Macha, one an ancient capital of Ulster known as Emain Macha, literally Twins of Macha, the other, Ard Macha, the present day city of Armagh. The story of the curse that Macha laid upon the county of Ulster is one that might well linger in our minds upon considering the tragic plight of that county today.

In the days when dense forest still covered the earth, the mighty Macha came with Her great axe and cleared the land—so that the cattle could graze, so that the wheat could grow.

Again She came in the days of the two brothers, of Cimbaeth who was evil, of Dithorba who was cruel. Saviour of the people, She drove the brothers from the land and then ruled upon their throne for seven years. But the sons of Dithorba challenged Her rights; five lads lay claim to one throne, yet no better were they than their father had been and mighty Macha caused them to flee beyond the borders of the province.

When rumours gained entrance to the court that the sons of Dithorba made camp in the forest nearby, living for the day that they could defeat the mighty Macha and dominate the land as their father and uncle had done, Macha left the court, disguised as a leper. Deep in the damp green of the woods She spied the campfire, the wild boar roasting for dinner—and the five brothers who sat about it, plotting Her destruction.

Though the sight of the leper woman hardly pleased them, they allowed Her to stay at the edge of the warmth, uncomfortably withdrawing to the other side of the blazing logs to return to battle talk and brew. Four dry logs had been brought to the fire when the youngest thought, despite Her apparent disease, to use Her in the woods. Thinking Her a simpleton, he suggested a stroll but upon reaching a great oak, he fell upon Her with violent force—only to find himself tightly bound against that tree and left alone in the forest.

Returning to the campfire, Macha explained his absence by telling of the shame he must have felt for lying with a leper, until a hearty laugh was had by all, but soon the second youngest thought to do the same. Just as with the first, he was left in the woods secured to a great oak, not far from the one that held his captured brother. This time Macha told of the second lad's shame, yet it was not but the burning of another log before a third was tempted, and thus the fourth, and thus the fifth—until it came to pass that the five sons of Dithorba found themselves bound captives in the forest.

With Her magic She had tied them. With Her magic She then taught them, so that each became a faithful servant of the mighty Goddess. It was in this way that the five sons of Dithorba came to build the temple of Emain Macha, serving Her there for the rest of their lives.

Many years later, Macha took the form of a poor young peasant woman and after wandering through the forest, She entered the small wooden house of Crunnchu, a widower yet not much past a lad. Making Her way about the cabin, She soon fit it to Her liking. When She was satisfied with what She had done, She beckoned to the fellow—who was more than pleased to find such a woman in his home.

For moments that seemed as eons, for eons that passed as moments, so pleased was Macha with Her life that She made the life of Crunnchu one of joy and abundance—until his only wish was that children might enter into such bliss. In this way it happened that Macha, the mighty Macha, grew great with life.

It was not without a bit of surprise that Crunnchu glimpsed this mother-to-be darting about between the trees, so swiftly that Her feet seemed never to touch the ground so that when a time soon came that Crunnchu happened to be in Ulster and chanced upon the men of the Ulster Court, he told them of this wonder, of a pregnant woman who could run faster than the king's horses. Of course they laughed, with insinuations that the man was daffy, but Crunnchu continued to insist until the men of Ulster grew so angry that they cried, 'blasphemy that anyone should dare to so insult the name of the king by saying that his wife, full with child, could run faster than the steeds of the royal stable'.

'Blasphemy!', they cried and swore to take his head—and then relented just enough to let him try to prove the truth of such an absurd claim. So it was that upon his return to the mother of the yet-forming child he had desired, Crunnchu told Her of his days in

She sprang off so lightning quick

Ulster and insisted that She must save his head by proving that his claim was veritable truth. He looked upon the swelling roundness in which the child lay, never suspecting that the woman was other than mortal, yet so worried was he for his own head that even when She begged for time—at least until after the birth—saying that to run now might endanger the babe, perchance kill the mother, he ruled that they must go. Perhaps the men of Ulster, seeing Her so filled with new life, might see fit to postpone the challenged race—but go they must, for his head was in peril.

Almost in disbelief of Crunnchu's willingness to chance Her life for his, Macha arrived at the court of Ulster to be greeted with jeering cries of blasphemy, doubt and challenge. Nowhere, in the hearts of the crowd that had formed, was there anything that might keep them from watching such a race. Already the king's steeds pranced about, nipping at their reins, anxiously waiting for the moment that they would be set loose. The noise of the gathered crowd was thunderous. How dare a man claim that his wife could best the finest horses of Conchobar, the King of Ulster?

Right up to the starting line She tested their hearts as they thought to test Her legs. Not a 'stop' was to be heard among the thousands, though they swarmed by the place where the great horses waited, watching, as She stood for a moment to pull the pins from Her braided bun, watching, as hair coloured with the glow of burning embers blew behind Her as a mane in the wind. Then She sprang off so lightning quick that it seemed that She flew over the horses and pulled ahead with such a speed that the royal steeds were hardly to the halfway mark—when She calmly made Her way across the finish line.

But this is not the ending of this story, for the mighty Macha, as quickly and easily as She had run, then brought forth the set of twins that had grown in Her womb and took one up under each powerful arm. No one made a move. The air was dense with quiet as thrice victorious Macha, Her new born babes held close to Her sides, stood before the now frightened men of Ulster. With the resounding echo of prophetic words that will never be forgotten, Her voice rang out into the silence. Thus She cursed them for their pride and for the cold blood in their hearts and warned them that misery and suffering as painful as the labour of childbirth was to be Her punishment of Ulster for nine times nine generations. And with these words, Macha took Her twins and left the land of Ulster.

CERRIDWEN

The name of Cerridwen has been translated both as Cauldron of Wisdom and Fortress of Wisdom, *caer* meaning fortress, *cerru* meaning cauldron. Although references to Cerridwen occur as fragments in several texts, most of the information about Her is to be found in the work of the Welsh Elis Grufydd done in the sixteenth century A.D. Grufydd relied upon oral traditions and earlier texts in compiling his treatises on ancient Celtic literature. The powers attributed to Cerridwen, who was described by Grufydd as a witch, reveal Her nature as one imbued with great wisdom, prophetic foresight and magical shapeshifting abilities. This account, of the theft of these powers by the male Gwion, may offer some insight into the otherwise puzzling accounts of Merlin's capture by The Lady of the Lake (see Morgan le Fay and The Lady of the Lake).

Mighty in magic, enchantment and divination, the ancient Cerridwen lived upon an island in a lake, some say on the waters of Llyn Tegid in Penllyn in County Caernarvon in Wales, while others say that it was on the island of the Sidhe, the place known as The Land Beneath the Waves.

It was on the island that a son was born to Cerridwen, a boy that She named Morfran, because he was as black as a raven. But some called him Afagddu saying that his darkness was ugly, so that the dark Cerridwen worried that the life ahead of him would not be one of ease or pleasure. Thus Cerridwen decided to give Her son a birth gift of the magical powers that She knew so well, hoping that this might make Morfran's years on earth easier for him to live. For this reason She began to prepare the Cauldron of the Deep, the cauldron known as Aven, from which three drops of liquid providing foresight and magical powers could be given to Her son.

Some say that She followed the Books of Pherylt. Some say that She followed those of Vergil. Yet none say that the magic cauldron Aven was not Hers. Into it, She poured the water of prophesy and inspiration and then carefully observing the movements of the moon, the sun and each and every star, She was able to add each herb, each root, even the foam of the ocean, at the proper planetary moments. As the ingredients began to boil, cress and wort and vervain simmering in the waters, She arranged for a blind old man to keep the fire burning, and for a young lad named Gwion to stir the contents of the cauldron.

Nine women stood close by, just as the nine women of Bridget tended the ancient fire at Kildare. Some say that those at the cauldron of Cerridwen were the Druidesses of the Isle of Sein, sacred island off the coast of Brittany, lived upon by women who could take the form of any animal, ban filid who could blow the seas into a rage with their perfect poetry, ban fathi who could heal all wounds and illness and foretell the events of the future. All agree that the nine women breathed upon the magic cauldron as it boiled night and day for one entire year.

But a year and a day was the time the formula required. When the day finally came in which the three drops would be ready, Cerridwen placed young Morfran by the cauldron to receive the legacy that She had prepared for him. Then in fatigue, after all that She had done, Cerridwen fell asleep in the woods nearby. But young Gwion, seeing that the year and the day were drawing to a close and that Cerridwen was still asleep in the forest, shoved the child Morfran to one side and scooped the three precious drops on to his own fingers, which he quickly thrust into his mouth—as the poisonous remainder of the waters split the very sides of the cauldron apart and poured out upon the ground.

The thundering noise of the cracking cauldron woke Cerridwen from Her sleep. Soon realizing what had happened, She moved to punish Gwion who used his new gained powers to change into a hare and hop off as quickly as his legs would take him. Cerridwen took the form of a greyhound and followed in swift pursuit until She was just about to catch the lad—when he changed into a fish and slipped into a nearby river. Cerridwen then took the body of an otter and diving into the water She was soon close to the tail of Gwion, who in terror that he might be caught, changed into a bird and flew off into the sky, only to find that Cerridwen was still close behind him—in the form of a great hawk.

Fearing more than ever that the time of his punishment and death were growing near, Gwion noticed a pile of wheat upon the land below and changing himself into the tiniest of grains, he dropped upon the pile. Cerridwen's sharp eyes saw what he had done and taking the form of a black crested hen, She pecked at the grains until She found and ate the seed that had been Gwion—thinking that would be the end of him.

But the tiny grain of Gwion took root inside Her womb and soon began to grow. Cerridwen swore the nine months long that on the day that Gwion would be reborn, She would destroy the infant, yet upon the day of birth She relented, hesitating to strangle the new born child. So it was that with the intention of leaving him to his fate, She placed him in a leather sack and threw him into the raging waters—two days before the first of May.

* * *

The ancient poet Taliesin, spoken of by many as the wisest and most profound of Gaelic prophets, claimed that he had once been Gwion, born from Cerridwen's womb. Saying that his leather sack had been fished from a lake on All Hallow's Eve, holy Samhain when dead souls rise, Taliesin also claimed that he had once been the wizard Merlin, thus making it most clear that Celtic wisdom, poetry, magic and foresight, the riddles beneath which divine knowledge lies, had long ago been stolen from the cauldron of the ancient Cerridwen.

MORGAN LE FAY AND THE LADY OF THE LAKE

The image of Morgan le Fay is generally thought to have been derived from earlier Celtic beliefs in The Morrigan. Although Morgan le Fay and The Lady of the Lake are most often described and presented as two quite separate figures, the many curious links between them, that I have described here, suggest that they may both have been derived from a single, earlier, concept of the Goddess. Again we will want to remember the widespread habitation of the Celts in Europe, as we read of Morgan le Fay in England and Wales, Morgain la Fée in France, and Fata Morgana in Italy. Along with similarities of mystic isles, secret lakes and castles on crystal mountains, the events surrounding the Celtic accounts of Arthur, and the sword Ex Calibur, should lead us to a more careful exploration of the connection between these two figures, whether as Goddess or Faerie Queens. In exploring these connections, it may also be helpful to consider the other Goddess images associated with specific bodies of water; Sequana

of the River Seine, Boann of the River Boyne, Danu of the Danube,
Cerridwen of Lake Llyn Tegid and the magical Caer who lived on Loch Bel
Dragon. (The lake of Caer may offer some insight into the traditions
surrounding Loch Ness in Celtic Scotland, the Loch Ness 'monster' said to
have been 'subdued' by the Christian missionary St. Columba at about 550
A.D.) The stories of the male wizard Merlin, being captured by The Lady
of the Lake, may be the result of the confusion caused by transitions of the
powers of the earlier images of the Goddess to a male, as more clearly
described in the accounts of Cerridwen and Taliesien/Gwion.

Queen of the mystic isle of Avalon, Morgan le Fay, was woven
with delicate haunting threads into the tales of Celtic Britain, yet
was She not still remembered by those who lived upon the continent
where tribes of Celts first made their home and there spoken of as
the magical Morgain la Fée, the Queen of Faerie? And does Her
memory linger in the one they described as Faerie Queen Melusina,
She whose spirit was said to come forth from the bubbling springs
in the Forêt Columbiers while memories of the Faerie Queen in
Celtic Germany told of a wondrous palace upon a crystal mountain
on an island in a lake where flowers bloomed throughout the year, a
perfect paradise—inhabited by ten thousand women, yet visible to
very few.

Celtic memories of the great Queen Morgan also lingered in
Italian lands, where tales were told of Fata Morgana who lived
beneath the waters of a lake. But Bojardo wrote that the powerful
Fata Morgana was but another name for the holy Goddess
Fortuna, She whose shrines once graced Etruscan towns where
omens of the future bubbled forth from underground springs. And
there are those who say that Fata and Fortuna were but other
names for The Three who were known as The Fates, for are not
Fata, Fay and Faerie simply other ways of saying Fate?

Some claim that Morgan le Fay was sister to King Arthur, and
that it was She who took his body upon Her holy barge to the island
of Avalon when he lay close to dying, yet some speak of the Faerie
Viviane, She who was known as The Lady of the Lake in the Forest
Broceliande in Brittany, and say that She too made that fateful ride.
Many claim that it was The Lady of the Lake who gave the sword
Ex Calibur to Arthur, that martial sceptre that allowed Arthur to sit
upon the throne, yet they also claim that the sword of rule had first
been forged in Morgan's Avalon. Still we hear that at the moment
before Arthur's death, he returned the sword to The Lady of the

Lake, who thrice brandished it in the air, before Her hand, reclaiming the sword of sovereignty, slipped into the deep waters of Her home.

Tales there are aplenty of how The Lady of the Lake tricked the wizard Merlin into teaching Her his store of magic knowledge, just as he was said to have taught Fata Morgana. Yet he who is said to have been the cornerstone of Arthur's victories through his wealth of magic powers was later imprisoned by The Lady of the Lake, who supposedly made use of what She had learned, to capture the wizard Merlin. But Taliesin claimed that he had once been Merlin, as he had once been Gwion, thus confessing that the powers and the knowledge had been stolen from the cauldron of the wise Cerridwen. Was this why it was said that the shape changing Merlin at times took the form of a woman, as people still remembered the one who first held the knowledge of enchantment: remembering the powers of the mystical Morgana, Queen of the Isle of Avalon; remembering the powers of the ancient Cerridwen, Lady of the island of the Sidhe folk, Lady of the Land Beneath the Waves; remembering the powers of The Morrigan whose mane was seen in the foamy breakers of the ocean? For had Merlin's powers truly been the greater, why then was it said that he was captured by The Lady of the Lake—while She was ever free to roam?

There are many who still search for Avalon, the island ruled by Morgan le Fay, and upon hearing that it was an isle of glass, believe it to be Glastonbury, though memories of snow capped Alps of the ancient Celtic homeland may live in images of castles upon glassy crystal mountains reflected in deep blue mountain lakes—as ancient Britain's name of Albion reflected the whiteness of Alpen peaks. And there are those who follow brooks and streams or listen for the bubbling whispers of a spring in Brittany as Gallic priestesses may once have read the omens of the future in the eddies and the windings and the flowing speech of running waters. But those who search for Avalon remember that it was known as the land of Avalloch and looking for the home of mighty Morgan, they also search for the dwelling place of The Lady of the Lake.

Where to hunt for Celtic Avalon, or the island of a castle upon a crystal mountain that may be deep beneath the waters, for is not that island always to the west, ever rich with blossoming apple trees, reminiscent of the Greek Garden of Hespera sometimes described as the homeland of the Amazons? But perhaps the island is not to be found in England, France or Germany, nor in Switzerland or Italy, nor in Libya or Greece and not even in Ireland, Scotland or Wales, or off any coast upon the earth where islands may hover grey in the distance—but in those mystic waters where lie the Isles of the Blessed or the island of the Sidhe folk—where Celtic souls were said to go when they departed from mortal bodies, as Arthur went to Morgan's Avalon when life left his body.

Perhaps it is the Heaven Loch, eternal isle haven upon eternal waters and no matter how far to the west one goes, the island is yet further to the west, forever lit by the glow of the setting sun. For is it not there that the Mighty Regina, Morgan, Mistress of Avalon, waits for each of us to one day sail to Her—there to learn that beyond the setting sun is the Morgan that is morning.

BRIDGET

The transitions in the status and nature of the Brigante Goddess Bridget, whose powers were celebrated at the Celtic ritual of Imbolc on February 1st, help us to more clearly understand the continual process of the Christianizing of early Celtic deities. In the case of the information on Bridget, we are fortunate enough to have both the accounts of Bridget as the supreme Goddess of the Brigantes, as well as accounts of the later canonization of Bridget as a Christian saint—said to have been the midwife to the Virgin Mary. The fire at Bridget's shrine in Kildare, originally tended by priestesses, was later cared for by Catholic sisters—until the decree of a Bishop declared it to be pagan, and ordered that the fire be extinguished in 1220 A.D.

Across the lands that lie between the town of Nottingham and that of Leeds, nearly all the lands that now comprise the province of Yorkshire, the Gaelic Brigantes, driven from the shores of Gaul, called upon the name of the Great One, the Mother who was known as Mighty—as Brigantia, Briginda, Brigidu and Bridget, Divine Ancestress of the Brigantes who had given them so much for which to be grateful.

Some say that Bridget was born exactly at sunrise, and that a great tower of flame reached from the top of Her small head all the way into the heavens—thus signalling the birth of a holy babe. It was this very same fire that was tended by the Daughters of the Flame, the nine who are Ingheau Anndagha, those who lived inside the fence of Bridget's shrine and could be looked upon by no man, to insure that the purity and sanctity of the fire would be protected.

It was through these sacred women that the wisdom of Bridget was spread among the people, spoken by the priestesses to the women of the village, those who brought them food, and in this way heard of the healing herbs and which would cure what ailment. It was in this way that women also learned of the sites of the healing springs which became known about the countryside as Bridget's wells of healing, for the water of these wells could cure the leper or make the impotent husband able to join his wife in bringing children into their lives.

Bridget's wisdom reached the smithy, so that he learned how to forge the iron that would soften in the heat of the fire, and even how that fire might best be built and kept. And from Bridget came the tales that none had known before, and the Gaelic trick of painting pictures with words. With Her wisdom She revealed that sounds might be turned into written marks, so that another, though many miles away, could hear them with their eyes. Some poets call upon Her yet, inviting Her to speak inside their heads with her tongue so sharp and sweet.

One story is told—perhaps She came Herself and told it to the speaker of the tale, for she knew much about the sacred well, the one so filled with grey stones that it was no longer used to heal the ill. 'It was Ostrialoch, son of Indoch', she said, 'who so despised the well that he destroyed it, for in it his enemy, a son of Bridget, had been cured when he lay dying.'

Yet another tale about a well has crossed past many lips, the story of a time that a man, dying of leprosy, asked of Bridget that he might die owning a cow, a richness that he had never known since birth. But Bridget proposed a greater gift, and once agreed upon, his long ill body was made well with the touch of the well's waters from Bridget's own fingertips—so that the man kneeled in promises of everlasting gratitude. Two more, stricken with the leprous skin, heard rumours of what had taken place and travelled far to ask for Bridget's help. By the well of healing waters, She instructed one to bathe the other until that other watched his skin grow well before his very eyes, while he who had helped this to happen still lived with the disease. Turning to the one now cured, Bridget bade him to do the same as had been done for him, but now, repulsed by the disease he had once suffered, the healthy one refused to help the one who had bathed him—and upon his refusal was once more stricken—at the very moment that his friend was healed. Thus Bridget taught compassion.

Bridget's fire, carried from the land of Brigantia upon the British Isle to Hibernian Kildare not far from Dublin, burned brightly with the caring of the Daughters of the Flame—and even later when it was tended by sisters of the newer Christian faith who called upon the Goddess as St. Bridget. But there finally came a time when its flames were extinguished by those of the church who knew of its beginnings and spoke of it as pagan. How dark it was after the dousing of the ancient fire.

CAILLEACH BHEUR

Folk traditions of the Cailleach Bheur are found primarily in Ireland, though closely associated with a very similar figure, sometimes known as Mala Liath (Grey Mare), in Scotland. The name Cailleach is alternately translated as hag, crone, or wise old woman. Yet it is clear from the accounts of Cailleach's ability to move mountains, and to have carried the massive stones of the sacred circles and cairns in Her apron, that She was viewed as far more than a mortal woman. The accounts explaining that it was the Cailleach who created the many stone monuments in Celtic areas may once again cause us to suspect the origins of the attributes credited to the wizard Merlin, one of which was that he alone had brought the stones to Stonehenge, and built the great monument himself. The images of both the Cailleach, and Mala Liath, as a grey mare, provide possible connections to the images of the Irish Macha and the Welsh Rhiannon, and we may once again look to the ancient Mare Goddess Epona for their origins.

The Old Woman of Bheur, Daughter of the Moon, ran with the wild animals of the woods, yet threw thunderbolts from the heavens, raised and calmed the winds and sometimes set the forests of Scotland and Ireland on fire, if the people aroused Her anger. Still, She cared for Her herd of deer with tenderness, as they roamed along the rockiest of western beaches, and even brought fish and seaweed to feed them when they could not find enough food for themselves.

She might take the form of an eagle or a sleek black cormorant to fly across the waters but whatever shape the Cailleach would take, She would carry her magic wand that brought frost and snow to the land, when its tip grazed the earth. It was a branch of such immense power that many tried to steal it or to gain possession of it by trickery but none succeeded, for the Cailleach easily outwitted all who dared.

Some speak of the Cailleach as Mala Liath, saying that She dwells in Scotland and that Her giant being can be seen along the most deserted beaches, while others claim that She makes Her home in Ireland—and pointing to her sacred site in County Covan. they tell of the time that Patrick destroyed Her cairn. Some claim that these circles or mounds of rocks had been poured out from Her apron on to the hills of Meath, pointing to the sacred stones at Knowth. Still others claim that She moved the mountains and the islands off the coast of western Kerry and that it is from the peninsula of Berre that She takes Her name, explaining that the rocks that She dropped upon the earth had been carried in Her creeling basket and that it was upon Berre that they first fell—yet those in Limerick say they know the Cailleach best, for She is none but the Queen of the Faeries of Limerick.

Nearly always appearing in some disguise, She takes all shapes and forms and might become a great grey stone or a pale grey mare, so enormous that She leaps from mountaintop to mountaintop. One can never be certain that any person, any animal, any rock, is not filled with Her being. One tale they tell of the Cailleach is about the three brothers who sat by their fire in the woods of Scotland at the end of a day's hunting, eating the catch that they had roasted on the spit. It was at that moment that an old and unkempt beggar woman came out of the woods, pleading for a bite to eat and to sit by the warmth of the fire. When the eldest ignored the old woman's requests, the woman turned to the next in age but was this time met with flat refusal. Before the woman even had a chance to ask the youngest, the lad stepped forth and offered the poor woman what meat he had left and made a place for her by the fire. When the time for sleeping came, the youngest brother worried that the old woman might freeze in the damp night air and thus offered half his blanket—and the place beside him on his bed of soft pine needles. They say that it was in this way that the youngest brother of the three came to spend the night with the Cailleach, the Queen of the Faeries—never regretting for a moment that he had been so kind.

But another story is of a man who did not fare as well, for when he chased a wild boar, determined to kill it for his dinner, he of course was unaware that it was the Cailleach, enjoying romping in the forest for the day. As the day went on, Her anger grew with each arrow that She diverted, but when the sun began to set and the man continued to give chase to the boar who had outwitted him all day, the Cailleach filled with rage and caused a thorn of poison to prick his foot—so that by early evening, it was that hunter who lay dead in the forest.

MAEVE (MEDB)

The image of Maeve is a somewhat unusual combination of a Faerie Queen and a martial leader of troops (see Scandinavian Section—Freya). Maeve's appearance in the *Tain Bo Cualgne* is as a mighty queen, and general of the army of the Irish county/state of Connacht. Both Her husband Aillil and Her lover Fergus rode alongside Her in battle, Maeve clearly leading the way for all three. In the *Fled Bricrenn* of the *Lebor na L'Uidre,* Maeve was portrayed as a judge of protocol and status among the Celtic peoples. As Queen of the Faeries, Maeve's tomb was said to be a cairn overlooking Sligo Bay, in an area that was once part of Connacht. Later images of Maeve as the Shakespearian Mab, Queen of the Faeries, were based upon these ancient traditions of the Celtic Medb or Maeve, as they remained in Anglo-Saxon England.

Tales of the mighty Queen Maeve still linger in memories of Celtic lands, some saying that She is the Queen of Faerie and that those who truly know Her, speak of Her as the magical Mab, the Queen of Elfhame. Others say that She was a mortal queen of County Connacht and wore the purple robes of royalty, Her sceptre a massive iron sword—yet upon the shoulders of this queen of mortal body, they say there perched two sacred golden birds whose magic voices whispered wisdom into the ears of Maeve.

Owner of the Sovereignty of Ireland, the throne was Hers alone, for only when Maeve chose a new lad for Her bed, might he then claim the title of a king. There are many who remember that until Maeve had slept with the fellow, even Cormac was not a king of Ireland, and that when She led the troops of Connacht to retrieve Her brown bull from Conchobar of Ulster, it was yet another husband, Aillil, who rode at Her right side, while Her lover Fergus rode at Her left.

Whether Faerie Queen or General, the spirit of Maeve still rides through the woods along the upper Shannon and floats heaviest in the mist near the cave at Cruachan, the cave to the Netherworld, the cave not far from the town called Elphin, the place where the words that She spoke when Ireland was but young may still be heard echoing through the trees:

If I married a selfish man
our union would be wrong
because I am so full of grace and giving.
It would be wrong if I were the more generous,
yet I would not want to take more than I offered.
I would not want a timid man
for I must admit that I thrive upon action
and believe that any couple must be equal in spirit.
It would be wrong if I married a jealous man
for never have I been with one man
without another waiting patiently in his shadow.

The spirited courage of warrior Queen Maeve rides through the recollections of the many battles that ancient Connacht had with Ulster—just as many Celtic women warriors linger in other memories: the mighty Scathatch who lived beyond Alba, said to be a genius in both weaponry and prophesy; the courageous Aife who some say lived as far to the east as Greece; the Gwyddonod of Gloucester, the nine of them remembered as crones, warriors, prophets and witches; the Iceni's Queen Boudicca who burned the town of London down to defy the Roman army and then offered gratitude to the holy Andrasta, Iceni Goddess of Victory, revered upon the land where Norfolk now stands; Brigante Queen Cartimandua who decided upon a peaceful treaty with Claudius of Rome and so put aside her husband who opposed her decision— choosing to rule the people of Bridget as sole sovereign of the tribe. Was it the ban filid, the poet/prophetess Fedelm, she who carried a golden weaving rod, saying that she was a student of vision and verse in Alba when her wagon chanced to pass Maeve's chariot upon the road, who wrote so many tales of the mighty Maeve? And was it the poetess Fedelm, she of the yellow hair and ebony brow, she who looked out upon the world with triple irised eyes, who told of Maeve leading the Connacht troops in battle and of how many fine children Maeve had brought forth from Her womb—and how Maeve assured them of Her mother strength by saying, "I can best thirty men a day—on the battlefield or on the bed."

RHIANNON

The name Rhiannon was derived from an earlier name for this image of the Goddess among the Welsh, Rigantona, literally translated as Great Queen Goddess. The importance of the pale-white horse of Rhiannon, and the magical bag of abundance that She possessed, both suggest that the image of Rigantona was in turn derived from the Mare Goddess Epona. Epona was often depicted at Celtic sites in Europe, carrying a similar bag or pouch, inscriptions beneath Her image carrying the epithet—Regina (Queen). The assertive wit, tinged with a bit of sarcasm, that is noticeable in the words attributed to Maeve, is also found in several of the passages of the *Cyfranc a'r Mab* of the *Mabinogin* that are concerned with Rhiannon. One passage records that as Rhiannon rode upon Her magical horse, a prince of Dyfed made many attempts to catch up with Her, each in vain. After several days of trying, always finding his horses slower than Hers, the prince finally called out, asking Her to wait. Rhiannon turned to the prince, still far behind Her, agreeing to his request, but not hesitating to add, ". . . and it would have been far better for the horse had you asked long before this."

ANCIENT MIRRORS of WOMANHOOD

The Great Queen Goddess, Rigantona, Regina, Rhiannon, rode upon Her pale white horse, canwelw coloured mare, ambling at a steady gait, seemingly as slow and aimless as the clouds that drifted by, yet no steed or stallion in the country could reach or overtake Her.

Within the holiness of Rhiannon live even older memories of Divine Epona, Her most ancient images carved in stone across the wide Gallic continent—woman sitting proudly astride the magic mare, in Her hand the bag of abundance, Her spirit and the animal as One, Her gentle foal close by Her side. This trinity of Woman, Mare and Colt, seen across the lands from France to Austria, was taken south into Rome and as far west as Uffington upon the British Isle. And wherever this triple image went, there the divinity of The Mighty Mare echoed as Regina, Queen, among the Celtic people, Her yearly feast a joyous celebration in expectation of the Winter Solstice.

Though some say that Rhiannon's home was near the magical mound of Arberth, not far from St. Bridget's Bay in Wales, and that Rhiannon was often seen there riding by in golden silk brocade; others say that Her home was on the island of the Sidhe folk where the souls of the dead resided and that it was there that She truly dwelled with Her three sacred birds that perched upon Her shoulders—as the perfect sound of their song lulled the living to death, woke the dead to life and healed all sadness and pain.

So clear and sweet were the voices of Her birds, so great their power over life and death, that many tried to capture them to keep them for their own. Thus the giant Buddaden ventured upon the island, to steal the birds from Rhiannon, but chancing upon their nest, he greedily ate the eggs the magic birds had lain so that when the Goddess came upon him, She saw feathers sprouting from his pale leathery skin. The sight was so ridiculous that Rhiannon bellowed with hearty laughter until Buddaden grew scarlet with embarrassment, and in his shame he felt the need to hide the absurdity of his feathered body. So it was that the giant Buddaden fled from the island of the Sidhe, forgetting all but his own foolishness.

Often taking Her pleasure in the woods, ever exploring and playing among the trees and in the meadows, in the form of any animal that She cared to take for the hour or the day, Rhiannon knew well the tiniest of roots to the greatest of oaks. Hopping as a hare across the bushy lowness of a field, a hunter one day spied Her playful pace and thought to kill Her for his dinner, thus setting his dogs upon Her scented trail. So it happened that when the lad Cian saw a hare jump frightened at his feet, and saw many dogs in close chase behind it, he lifted the hare to his chest and carried it over a nearby creek. Upon reaching the far side of the waters, he was astonished to see the Goddess Rhiannon standing there before him, while the hare was nowhere to be seen.

Pleased with the lad's compassion for a small animal fleeing for its life, Rhiannon thought to honour his kind heart by welcoming him to join Her on the island of the Sidhe, for never was there a place more beautiful, air more clear or colours more brilliant. Thus Cian went to live upon the magic isle, passing his days in perfect hours, passing his months in perfect days.

Many moons had waxed and waned, and many hours had Rhiannon strolled with Cian, hearing always of his joy and pleasure in living upon such an idyllic island—until the day that the Goddess decided to enjoy the solitude of a long familiar grove bathed by thin streams of gold that pierced through the tree tops. So filled with peace did She feel that when a man crept silently up behind Her, and then tried to force his body upon Her own, She could hardly believe that such a thing was happening. Turning to see who had dared to attack Her in this way, She was more than shocked to see the face of Cian!

Anger rose from Her usually gentle being, wrath at the arrogance of such an act, a cowardly attack—without even the honour of a warning that any enemy warrior would give before engaging in a battle. Her rage doubled at the feeling of betrayal of the kindness and concern that She had shown him all those months. As if from the power of the anger, Rhiannon took the form of a great mare, whinnying with Her rage, stomping Her hooves upon the ground, until She raised a massive leg against Cian's body and splintered his thigh bone with her powerful hoof. So it was that Cian limped in pain for the remainder of his life—never able to forget either the kindness or the wrath of Rhiannon.

The Oneness That Lies Beneath All Dualities
Central and South America

As Mother of the corn and earth, shining as the moon yet found in the sacred caves of mountains, Her essence known in both eagle and serpent—Goddess images in Middle and South America are as rich and diverse as the many varied cultures in which they have been known and revered. But we can scarcely attempt an exploration of the nature of Goddess reverence in these areas, without first realizing that the people who settled in the more southerly areas of the two continents of the American hemisphere, originally came from the same area of northern Asia as the Native Americans of North America.

Examinations of prehistoric sites throughout the two American continents, and in Siberia, suggest that the many waves of migrations of the Mongolian peoples who crossed the Bering Strait into Alaska, and gradually moved southwards, may have begun as early as 40,000 B.C. If recent studies at Fell's Cave are correct, some of the groups that crossed over from Siberia, from there making challenging and courageous treks over many thousands of miles, appear to have reached the southernmost tip of South America by 11,000 B.C. More conservative scholars state that this most southerly point was inhabited by at least 6000 B.C.

Although we have long been encouraged to regard the Native Americans of North America as quite separate from the Native Americans of Middle and South America, the archaeological and anthropological evidence suggests that early Native Americans traversed the two continents with quite different perceptions of the land than those accompanying contemporary views of national borders. It is somewhat ironic for U.S. citizens, especially those descended from Caucasians, whose ancestors lived in Europe until just a few centuries ago, to regard a Native Mexican or Native South American of today, one who is descended from people who had lived in and made their way through North America over a period of so many thousands of years—as an alien in North America. It is equally ironic that the Rio Grande River (at one time, a major route for those who had lived in what is now known as Colorado and New Mexico to the land that is now known as Mexico) today comprises such a major portion of the U.S./Mexican border.

It was long believed that most of the groups that had settled in the southerly areas of the western hemisphere had continued to subsist on food gathering, fishing, and small game hunting, until shortly before the arrival of Columbus and the Spanish conquerors. Now, several studies, such as that of the Tehuacan Valley of Mexico, reveal that there was an understanding of agricultural methods in this area, perhaps as long ago as 6000 B.C. Early cultivation of beans, maize, squash, and chili peppers, have been noted at several sites, suggesting that agriculture in the 'New World' developed relatively shortly after it did in the Near and Middle East—and prior to its development in northern and western Europe.

Although the dates of origin are as yet uncertain, the cultures of Mexico and Guatamala had developed a form of glyph writing that appears on stone carvings, and on accordian folded bark paper made from the fibers of the *copo* plant. Surviving fragments of this writing reveal that the peoples of this area possessed an extremely complex knowledge of mathematics and astronomy. Accounts, of Europeans from the sixteenth century, state that upon their arrival to this area, they were surprised to find that most major villages and cities kept archives of many books. Though some of the original writings have survived, much still undeciphered, the majority of them were destroyed. Unfortunately, most of the earliest sources of evidence about these cultures are accounts written by Catholic friars who accompanied the soldiers at the time of the Spanish conquests. Biased attitudes, towards the beliefs and customs of the people of Mexico and Guatamala, were made clear

THE ONENESS THAT LIES BENEATH ALL DUALITIES

in the writing of Spanish Franciscan Bishop Diego de Landa who referred to the holy books of the Mayans as " . . filled with superstitions and lies." He ordered a mass burning of all Mayan books in 1562. Though he also recorded, " . . . we burned them all", several books survived, later surfacing in Europe, probably as a result of having been kept as souvenirs by Spanish soldiers.

Alongside evidence from the writings mentioned above, numerous Goddess images have been discovered at sites at least as old as 2000 B.C. Even older images may still lie buried in the vast areas of South America that have never been explored for archaeological remains. Though we have no written records of names, or information on the nature, of Goddess reverence in the earliest periods, one of the more ancient concepts of the Goddess may be that later embodied in the Goddess as Chantico. This Goddess of Fire, both of hearth and volcanic eruption, was included as a minor deity in Aztec beliefs. She may have been worshipped at the pre-Aztec open air altar, set upon a high adobe mound, built to face the volcanic Ajusco range of Mexico. Though little is known about Chantico, other than Her primary attribute of volcanic fire, She may have been the source of some of the symbolism associated with the Mother of All Deities as known among the Aztecs. Images of the Goddess as Mother Coatlicue, Her altars of cooled lava, Her birth of a child that was described as volcanic obsidian, and Her home upon the peak of a high mountain always covered with a dense cloud—each suggest volcanic symbolism in the worship of Coatlicue. Though it is certainly plausible that such imagery would naturally develop among people who lived in such a heavily volcanic area, comparisons with the Goddess as Mahuea in New Zealand and the Goddess as Pele in Hawaii, are difficult to avoid (see Oceanic Section).

The multiplicity of names, that we today identify with Goddess reverence in Mexico and Guatamala, may be partially the result of various languages and dialects, as well as of the many titles and epithets of the deities. Coatlicue literally means Lady of the Serpent Skirt. Tonantzin simply means Our Mother. Toci means Our Grandmother. Tonacacihuatl is the word for Goddess. Teteu Innan (Teteoinan) is translated as She Who Gives Birth, a title not unlike that of Coatlicue as Mother of All Deities. This last title is also applied to the Goddess as Tlazteotl—known to have received confession, absorbed the sins of the guilty, and to have thus purified all worshippers.

75

The Goddess known as Chicomecoatl was most closely associated with the growing of maize (corn), known to the Aztecs as *zea mays*. Ilamatecuhtli was known as Old Princess, symbolic of the maize at the time of its full ripening. The early stages of the maize crop were symbolized by the young Xilonen. Both Goddess images, Ilamatecuhtli and Xilonen, are aspects of Chicomecoatl, revered as The Great Corn Mother. The use of the word *coatl,* meaning serpent, in the names of Chicomecoatl and Coatlicue, suggests a possible linking between these two images as well.

Ideas, similar to beliefs about The Corn Mother of Mexico, may have been shared by those who settled in and around the Andes Mountains. Although in most studies of ancient Peru, the male Viracocha is named as the supreme deity of this area, along with the claim of his singular importance, it is often more casually added that Viracocha was the supreme deity of the ruling Incas, but that the worship of a Goddess of the crops, Pachamama, was the most common form of religious belief among the general farming population. Along with this reverence for the Goddess of the farming people, those who lived along the coastal areas also revered a Goddess of the Sea, whom they spoke of as Mamacocha, and envisioned as a great whale. The similarities of the names Mamacocha and Viracocha (*cocha* meaning sea), along with a prayer to Viracocha that begins, "Viracocha, Lord of the Universe, whether female or male, at any rate guardian of the sun and the making of new life . . . ", suggest that the deity of the sea may once have been regarded as a gynandrous being. Gynandrous, and closely coupled deities, were not uncommon in Middle and South America. The supremacy of the male aspect among the ruling Incas, while only the female aspect was called upon by the coastal population, may even reveal a complete change of gender by a clergy closely associated with the male dominant Inca regime. The moon was also revered as a Goddess image among the ancient Peruvians, Her name, Mamaquilla, translated as Golden Mother.

Although it is generally accepted by most scholars that the primary route by which Native Americans of both continents entered the western hemisphere was by way of the Bering Strait, there is some evidence of possible contact between the people of Central and South America and Polynesian groups. Extreme similarities in the construction and scaling of music pipes, the widespread use of the word *kumara* for sweet potato, feather mosaics, and specific weaving and dyeing processes, all point to possible connections. A minor strain of Australoid skeletal structure, common among Polynesians, has been noted in the Americas.

The general attitudes towards these links have been to believe that they are purely coincidental, or to assume that the people of Polynesia, even Asia, must have influenced the 'New World'. This last conjecture was supported by the drifting of a boat from Osaka to southern California in 1815. But it is just as possible, if these developments were indeed connected, that at least some of the knowledge may have travelled in the direction of Heyerdahl's raft, drifting from Peru to the Tuamoto Islands (northeast of Tahiti) in 1947. The nature of the Goddess as Chantico, and the imagery of the Goddess as Coatlicue, may certainly be compared to beliefs about the Goddess as Pele in Hawaii, the Goddess as Mahuea in New Zealand, and the Goddess as Fuji among the Ainu of Japan, while the cave of the Goddess of the Cuna of Panama may bring the rituals of the Australian Kunapipi to mind. But statements made about direct influence, and especially the source of that influence, would at this time be hypothetical at best.

Perhaps the truth to be gained from an exploration of the Goddess in Mexico, Central, and South America, is that travelling from one side of the planet to the other has been in vogue for some 40,000 years. Developments that were not the result of contact, or direct influence, may help us to better understand the astonishing similarities and ingenuities of the human mind, in relating and responding to specific environmental situations. The reverence for the Goddess as symbolized by maize, rain, moon, and volcano, are perhaps not too surprising. But the theological concepts embodied in the Goddess of the Cuna in Panama, who welcomes each girl into sacred womanhood, and the joyful Chibcha Huitaca, who beckons us from the chastity and sobriety demanded by Bochica—to sing, dance and rejoice in Her moonlight—may be images of Goddess that most deeply touch that elusive essence that we refer to as our souls.

MU OLOKUKURTILISOP

Knowledge of the puberty rituals for young women, and the reverence for the Goddess, of the Cuna peoples of Panama, is drawn from anthropological field studies done during this century, especially the work of Dr. Clyde Keeler. The painting of the red juice of the saptur fruit upon the face of the initiate, as a symbol of the menarche, is echoed in menarche rituals among the Navajo. The cave, as the burial place of the dead, offers an interesting parallel to the womb/cave of the Goddess as Kunapipi in Australia (see Oceanic Section).

Deep in the sacred caves of the mountain Tarcarcuna, overlooking the deep waters of the Gulf of Darien, the spirit of the Goddess Mu, Giant Blue Butterfly Lady, still lingers lovingly, protecting the women of the Cuna tribe.

In the days before the world began, Mu gave birth to the sun and taking Her sun as Her lover, She gave birth to the moon. Mating with her grandson Moon, She brought forth the stars, so many that they filled the heavens. Then mating with the stars, the sacred womb of Mu once again stirred with life so that in this way She brought forth all the animals and plants. It is for this reason that Cuna people remember that Mu Olokukurtilisop gave birth to the universe—created all that exists.

The first Cuna people made their homes in the caves of Tarcarcuna but even when they wandered as far as the Chucunaque River, still they brought their dead back to the caves of the mountain, there to rest in the womb of Mother Mu, the protective womb from whence all people came.

Close to the caves of Tarcarcuna, stands the sacred grove of saptur, trees whose fruit contains the juice of the menstrual blood of Mu. And close to the grove is the sacred hut of the Inna, the shrine of female puberty that each young woman enters at the time of her new womanhood, the time she celebrates the ceremonies of the Inna. On the ground near the Inna shrine, the young one lies being as one with the earth, as the older women toss the sacred soil upon her. Gathering in a circle about her, they sit on the benches to form the Ring of Protection, smoke rising from their pipes as incense invoking the spirit of Mu. Then removing the covering of earth, the women take the young one and paint the red juice of the saptur, the menstrual blood of Mu, upon her face—chanting their blessings on her life, honouring her with the dance of new womanhood.

Into the sacred Inna shrine, the young woman is escorted and there the black ribbons of her hair fall upon the earth, as her childhood falls from her in the woman shrine that no man has ever entered, the holy place of Mother Mu. Emerging from the Inna shrine as a full grown woman, her golden brown face glowing with red saptur is now framed within her small black satin cap of woman hair—as she awaits the time of the omens.

One sacred saptur tree is felled by the women as a gift of Mu to the initiate. Carefully studying the cross grain of the tree, the women read each and every line, foretelling the events of the new woman's life. Only now that the woman blood has begun to flow, only now that she is one with the earth, only now that the menstrual blood of Mu has brightened her face, only now that her head is free from the weight of the hair of her childhood—is the young woman dedicated to the Goddess Mu Olokukurtilisop, brought into the sacred fold of womanhood and provided with her secret Cuna name that she will tell no others to the end of her days on earth.

AKEWA

This unique account of women's arrival upon earth, from the Toba people of Argentina, is one that may linger in the minds of many women, as we struggle to comprehend the senseless violence of both rape and war. Though images of the Goddess in many cultures of Central and South America is as the moon, the Toba reverse the situation, regarding the sun as the Goddess, the moon as male. The ability of Akewa to grow young, as well as old, may be compared to the Navajo concepts of Changing Woman (see Native American Section). For those fascinated by theories about spacemen arriving on this planet, this account, and the account of the origins of Ishtar (see Semitic Section), suggest that if such an event ever oc-

79

curred, it may well have been spacewomen, rather than spacemen, who stopped by to visit or settle earth.

Who has not heard of that most ancient time when women descended from the heavens, climbing down the great rope that hung from the sky to walk upon the earth, searching for new plants and roots that they might carry back to their home in the heavens?

And who has not heard that when the women arrived the men were still animals, their bodies covered with fur, walking upon their hands as well as their feet? So it was that chancing upon the rope whose end touched the brown soil, the animals jumped at it and snapped it with their sharp teeth—so that the women from heaven were forced to remain upon the earth. It was in this way that the women of heaven and the male animals of earth began to live side by side and upon their mating with each other, they brought forth the people who now live upon the Toba lands.

Yet one woman still lives in the heavens for each day we see the fiery Akewa as She climbs from the lowest part of heaven to walk across the wide skies, bringing us Her golden light and warmth, giving us the gift of Her brilliant being—until She travels so far to the other side that She slides into the abyss at the end of the world, leaving us for the night. Just like any other woman, Akewa grows old and tired so that She walks across the heavens slowly. At that time the days are very long for Her brilliant light moves as She walks along but unlike any other woman, Akewa also grows young and in Her youth moves quickly, so that when She is young, the hours of daylight are few.

When Akewa leaves the sky each evening and the world grows dark with night, out comes an old man, one with a potbelly too full of food. Although his belly glows with a silver light, when he lays down for the night he turns from side to side—but he has never found just the right position in which to keep the huge belly, so that he may sleep in comfort.

In the vast spaces of heaven, the Jaguar also dwells, always wanting to eat Akewa and the moon man. Thus Jaguar attacks the moon each month for the moon is fat and cannot run, but Akewa fights with metal weapons so that Jaguar seldom catches Her—except for the few times that Akewa was hidden in the middle of the day and all were filled with fear that beloved Akewa was being killed and that the world would end. For who could live without the nurturing warmth and light of Akewa?

80

HUITACA

This wonderfully rebellious, light hearted image, of the Moon Goddess Huitaca, from the Chibcha people of Colombia, is surely a unique and delightful concept of deity. Since Bochica is regarded as a teacher of spinning and weaving, both activities done by Chibcha women, ideas about Huitaca's role may have developed in reaction to an emphasis upon industry, chastity, and sobriety, that threatened the more relaxed pleasures of a woman's life. It is tempting to assume that these pleasures had once been quite acceptable before the arrival of the ever wandering Bochica.

Wonderful Huitaca,
wild and lovely Goddess,
appearing in the night,
some say as an owl,
some say as the silver moon,
leading us into merriment,
encouraging us us to drink
the juices of intoxication,
encouraging us to feel the wonder
of the touch of our bodies against another,
until the time Bochica spoke against you,
saying that life must be completely serious—
and that the joys that you offered
must be seen as wrongs.

This joyless Bochica,
who some call Nebterequeteba,
walked throughout the countryside,
preaching that the good drinks were bad
and pleasure from our bodies even worse,
crying out that to follow your ways
was a great mistake
but just as the people of the villages
began to consider his ideas,
you appeared, laughing and happy,
teasing the unsmiling one
so that his anger rose
but all who watched and listened

soon laughed along with you,
calling you Chie and Jubchas Guaya,
Mother of Joy—
and though Bochica frowned and glowered—
we danced about the moon
and called your name.

COATLICUE

The Goddess as Coatlicue, Mother of all Aztec deities, was associated with Aztlan, legendary homeland of the Aztecs. Current day conjecture, on a possible location for Aztlan, ranges all the way from just north of Mexico City to areas in New Mexico and Colorado, the latter suggestions supported by the linguistic affinities between the Aztec language and that of the Hopi tribes of the southwestern U.S. Aztec accounts describe the mountain upon which Coatlicue lived as being surrounded by water. Such a description may summon up images of Pacific islands, rather than any area on the mainland of the two American continents, but the area surrounding the two volcanoes located on Ometepi Island, in Lake Nicaragua, may deserve some careful exploration. This is further suggested by the names of a pair of deities, female and male (at times depicted as one gyandrous being), who were regarded as original creators of life and the universe by the Aztecs (a role also attributed to Coatlicue). Their names were Omecihuatl and Ometecuhtli, suggesting their possible connection to Ometepi Island. It is interesting that although the Aztec word *ome* simply meant two, in the Hopi language *oma* means cloud, and *omic* means high or up. The repeated relationship of serpent to fire, and serpent to cloud, among many groups in Mexico, may be derived from the image of Coatlicue as Lady of the Serpent Skirt living upon a high mountain peak, revered at altars made of volcanic lava. Such an image of the Goddess may or may not have a connection with the volcanic Goddess imagery of the Oceanic peoples, but the similarities certainly provide interesting comparisons.

In the most ancient days of the peoples of Mexico, Mother Coatlicue hid Herself in a misty cloud upon a mountaintop in the homeland of Aztlan, while Her serpent servants lived within the mountain's caves. From this sacred home She brought forth both the moon and the sun, and all the stars in the heavens.

It was Coatlicue who gave all life and took again in death, the necklace of skulls that She wore about Her neck or those She sometimes wore as headdress, reminder of the certain time that each would return to Coatlicue, for each was the child that She held above Her altar of molten lava. Was She not the source of all being, the One who made the earth quake, giver of the goodness of life, She who enfolded the dead in Her bosom when their life on earth was done? Was it not into Her lava altar that each would one day melt again with Her, while in Her mirrors of cooled obsidian She would reveal what the future held?

It was upon Her sacred mountain in the land of Aztlan that Coatlicue had nurtured yet another new life deep within Her holy womb, some say from the swallowing of an emerald, while others claim that a ball of soft furry feathers fell upon Her and in this way She knew that another child was to arrive. Thus the warlike Huitzilpochtli was said to have been born, though some gave his name as Tezcatlipoca and said that a son of obsidian, a smoking black mirror, was born to Coatlicue, Mother of the Deities.

Upon learning of the expected birth, the older children of Coatlicue are said to have grown angry, fearing that the new one might replace them in the heavens. So it came to pass that soon after the birth the warlike son went forth, murdering each and every star, the many holy children of Coatlicue. But when Huitzilpochtli pressed his knife blade of obsidian to the throat of Coyolxauqui, the fairest daughter of Coatlicue, the one the Mother called Golden Bells, Coatlicue broke down in grief. Recovering the severed head of the daughter who had brought the Mother's greatest joys, the daughter who had tried to protect Coatlicue from the anger of the others, Coatlicue set the golden head in a most honoured place in heaven so that daughter Coyolxauqui would never be forgotten—as Her round and radiant face lit the night time skies—from that time until now.

Still the daughter Xochiquetzal lived. They say that it was She who brought the knowledge of the spinning and the weaving; the gifts for the eyes of the painting and the carvings; the gifts for the ears of the pipes and the drums. Especially was She remembered and honoured by the women who lived as they pleased, for they say it was Xochiquetzal who taught the goodness of woman's sensuality and that when a woman felt the pleasures of her body, it brought special joy to Xochiquetzal.

From Xochiquetzal they learned the message of the marigold, the petalled book of the cycles of life, of seed to leafy stem, of leafy stem to bud, of bud to flower fully open to the sun, of flower to drying petals that housed the womb pocket of new seeds, seeds that would take root in the earth and grow again. From Xochiquetzal's teachings the people came to understand the flow of life eternal, unchanging in its ever changing, as images of Xochiquetzal on the ocelot, quetzal bird feathers rising from Her head, two flowers set in Her long black hair, thin chains of glowing jewels stretched across Her golden cheeks, provided visions of this daughter of Coatlicue.

From Xochiquetzal's mouth came words like sweet flowers. From Xochiquetzal's mouth came words as sharp as the blade of a knife. Both emerging from Her bejewelled lips, She was called upon as the Obsidian Butterfly, soft and mobile as the bright winged being that was once the hidden unmoving chrysalis, while at the same time hard as the glassy black obsidian that had once been glowing, flowing, molten lava. And was it the knowledge that Xochiquetzal was the spirit of changing, the oneness that lies beneath all dualities, that caused the people to speak of Her as The Ruler of the Land of the Dead—for it was the statues and the temple sites of Goddess Xochiquetzal that were honoured on the Holy Day of the Dead Ones, pilgrims heaping sacred marigolds upon Her perfect feet.

Yet a third daughter came from the womb of Coatlicue, She who was known as Malinalxoch. This daughter was so filled with the powers of Her Mother that the wildest animals of the jungle grew docile in Her presence—as did the humans who revered Coatlicue. Yet was it not this daughter that Huitzilpochtli spoke against, envious of Her great powers, jealous of Her ease in leadership? So it was that he told the Aztec troops he led to leave all thoughts of Malinalxoch behind—as they marched and conquered the villages of Mexico.

So long had Coatlicue been known as Mother to the people, that great statues and temples had been built in Her honour. Upon Her sacred hill of Tepeyac on the western banks of Lake Texcoco, some came to call upon Her as Tonantzin. Thus when the arriving priests of Spain noticed the great importance of the ancient holy site that was each year visited by pilgrims who brought rounded cakes of corn to honour the ancient Mother on the twelfth of December, just before the rains were due, they claimed that the site belonged to Mary. It was in this way that the ancient shrine of Coatlicue became known as the shrine of the Black Madonna, La Virgen Morena, and some began to tell of sightings and miracles of Mary at the temple of The Lady of Guadalupe Hidalgo—while the spirit of She who gave birth to the sun and the moon still lingers about the sacred site of long ago.

CHICOMECOATL

The Aztec image of Chicomecoatl was primarily that of The Great Corn Mother, revered by many peoples of the southwestern U.S., as well as in Mexico. Although Her name is literally translated as Seven Serpents, *coatl* meaning serpent, the word coatl is also known among the Pueblo people of North America—as a digging stick used to plant seeds. The connection with childbirth, as well as the sun on the shield, both suggest an association of Chicomecoatl with the Goddess as Teteu Innan.

Along the path of the valley village, the young girls danced in gay procession, following the three who had been chosen as Corn Maidens for the year: the youngest with her hair cropped short as image of the newly rising sprouts; the second whose hair fell upon her shoulders as image of the corn half grown; the oldest and tallest of the three, her waist long hair tied into a braided bun, as image of the full grown crops. Each wore the opalescent glow of fish scales painted as discs upon her golden cheeks; each had brilliant scarlet feathers thonged to golden arms and legs—as they walked proudly along the path to the temple of Mother Chicomecoatl.

The first walking of the temple way was to bring the baby sprouts of corn, to lay them at the feet of Chicomecoatl. The second walking of the temple way was when the maize had grown half way to harvesting. Yet a third time did they go, on the day when the corn waved highest in the fields, the bundles of seven ears wrapped in tissue red coverings, carried upon the backs of the holy three, as mothers might carry their children. Thus were the seven ears presented to the Goddess, the Mother of Corn, She whose spirit had made it grow.

Feasting and celebration were accompanied by deepest gratitude from those who knew the true sanctity of the corn and regarded it as a gift from Chicomecoatl. They knew this was a time for thanksgiving, the time to take the seven ears that had been blessed and store them in the granaries until the days of the sowing would come again and the dried kernels of the blessed ears would be pressed into the earth—to fulfill the sacred patterns of the Goddess.

The corn was sometimes spoken of as Cinteotl, or known as Xipe Totec, the son of Chicomecoatl. Some said that it was his spirit that lived within the ears of corn after they had ripened, his body dismembered, his skin flayed—just as the kernels were taken from the cob, yet each year reappearing in the plants that grew.

As Chicomecoatl watched over each harvest, so too did She linger protectively over all women who died in childbirth. Such women, spoken of as heroes and warriors by the people of the valleys of Mexico, having given their life for a life, their very own life's breath extinguished in the battle of labour—were especially honoured and cared for by Chicomecoatl who kept watch over their souls that resided in the highest heaven.

Some say that this ancient Mother, Her skirt covered with white flowers, Her face covered with red ochre, Her shield emblazoned with the sun, the knife of obsidian in Her hand—was the First Mother of the people of the valley of Mexico. They tell of the time that She was known long before the Tenocha Aztec tribes arrived and that it was Her spirit that was called upon at the most ancient council meetings, for it was remembered that it was Chicomecoatl who had first taught the knowledge of the ancient temple ways and that the highest priestess, Snake Woman, had once attended the mighty Corn Goddess whose essence was in the Seven Serpents of Her name.

Still She lived in heaven, even after the Aztec tribes had come, caring for the wondrous crops of corn, caring for the woman warriors as they hung as spiders upon silken spider threads, menacingly swinging from their webs in heaven, daily escorting the sun to its western destination. But there are those who say that the spiders are angry and that one day they will cause the sun and the moon to collide, crashing wildly against the stars—so that the world as we know it will end, the spiders then dropping from their celestial webs to feed upon the people of the earth, perhaps even to take life as it had once been taken from them.

TETEU INNAN

The somewhat sparse information on the Goddess as Teteu Innan (Teteoinan), from accounts of the Aztec period, portrays Her as a Goddess of childbirth, healing, and prophesy. The word *innan,* meaning birth, may be related to the title of the menarche rituals of the Cuna, the *Inna.* Teteu Innan's skirt of shells perhaps reveals a connection with the Pueblo concept of White Shell woman, the youthful manifestation of Changing Woman.

Holy Mother of Birth and Healing,
Matron Spirit of all Midwives,
Goddess of the sacred totoixitl herb,
Teteu Innan wears the skirt of many shells,
as the sky wears many stars,
a golden disc in proud display upon Her shield,
appearing in glowing visions
to those who call upon Her powers.

It is Teteu Innan who fills the wombs
of those who wish to bear new children.
It is Teteu Innan who empties wombs
of the women who do not,
remembering always to ease the pain of childbirth
for Her daughters upon the earth.
Yet Her sacred spirit also dwells
in the magic springs of healing,
rising in the steamy mist
in answer to the pleas of the ill,
providing the curing waters,
while in Her vast wisdom
She arranges the patterns
of the tossed kernels of corn,
thus making known Her will and Her decree
to all who care to read the prophesies
written in the chance falling of the corn,
offering glimpses of the future
that She will bring.

CHALCHIHUITLICUE

The account of the great flood, caused by the Rain Goddess of Aztec beliefs, may be compared to the inundation attributed to the Mayan Moon Goddess Ix Chel. The concept of past eras of civilization, that had ended in total destruction, suggests comparison with the beliefs of many of the tribes now living in the southwest U.S. Though religious ideas common to peoples in Mexico and the southwestern U.S. are possibly the result of a common heritage, it is interesting to note that texts of India refer to four ages, *yugas,* existing in each eon of time, and that the Greek Hesiod also wrote that there had been four eras of civilization, each subsequently destroyed, before the one in which he lived. The Aztecs believed that the age in which they lived was reigned over by the sun god Tonatiuh, the one to whom they offered their sacrifices, perhaps suggesting that many of the other deities, to whom they offered reverence, were adopted deities of other groups, or ones they had revered before arriving in the area of Mexico City (probably as late as 1300 A.D.). A ten foot high statue, now simply known as Goddess of the Waters, had long been revered not far from where the Aztecs settled—perhaps explaining the origins of the belief that Chalchihuitlicue had reigned during the age that preceded the reign of the Aztec Tonatiuh.

In the garden of heaven where mist fills the air, and as far as eyes can see flowers dot the ground with brilliant colour, where an arching rainbow never fades—there lives the Goddess Chalchihuitlicue, Mistress of the Rains and Waters. There She sits upon Her celestial throne in Her crown of Quetzal feathers, in Her skirt of the bluegreen of the lakes, waterlilies floating upon it, jade adorning Her perfect neck, discs of turquoise framed by Her ears, while raging whirlpools circle round Her feet and all manner of precious gems swirl about in those wild waters.

In the most ancient of days when only jaguars had inhabited the land, Ocelot had ruled—for this was the time of the First Sun. Upon the emergence of the Second Sun, Quetzalcoatl sat upon the throne until the time that all living beings turned to monkeys as awesome hurricanes swept away their lives. Then Tlaloc came to rule by the light of the Third Sun which finally dimmed and died in the holocaust of storms of fiery rain. Thus came the time of the Fourth Sun—and the Goddess Chalchihuitlicue took the seat of rulership.

So it came to pass that Chalchihuitlicue sat upon Her heavenly throne in the light of the Fourth Sun until the time the Goddess

while raging whirlpools circle round Her feet

could no longer ignore the wrong that was being done to some by others. Choosing those who had been careful not to impose their wishes upon others, She built for them a bridge so that the people that She had chosen to save might cross over from the land of the Fourth Sun to live on earth in the light of the Fifth Sun. When the bridge was ready and all whom She had chosen had safely crossed, Chalchihuitlicue sent constant rains, flooding the land of the Fourth Sun with Her raging whirlpools, sweeping away those She had rejected—so that they floated as fish in the ocean. She raised the waves so high that any still afloat in their canoes were tossed into the icy waters and crashed upon the rocks. Then when all was done, She calmed the wild waters until they were as smooth as the feathers of a bird at rest—so that all that had been destroyed lay invisible beneath the still surface.

Thus was the Great Chalchihuitlicue remembered by those She had saved, so that each year during the month of Etzaqualitzli they came as pilgrims to Her temples to place jewels upon Her image, lighting incense and sweet smelling herbs in Her honour, joining in joyous celebration, praying to the Goddess of Rains and Water to send the water for the crops—but asking Her to please remember not to send too much.

BACHUE

The lake, described as the place of emergence, and the later habitation, of the Chibcha Divine Ancestress Bachue, is located a few miles northeast of the city of Tunja in Colombia. The image of Bachue as the protector of agriculture, as well as the teacher of peace and order, appears to be a somewhat universal concept—a similar combination of attributes described in the accounts of the Goddess as Demeter in Greece, Isis in Egypt, and Ala in Nigeria. The portrayal of Bachue as a woman—and as a serpent in the waters—presents an image that may well be compared to accounts of the Goddess among the Semites, e.g. Atargatis, Asherah and Tiamat, as well as the Sumerian images of the Goddess as Nina and Nammu (see Semitic and Sumerian Sections).

From the clear blue waters
of a small lake
near the village of Iguaque,
emerged Mother Bachue,
who some call Fura Chogue—Kind Mother,
and with Her came Her son of three years,
holding tightly to Her hand.

Living in the forests,
She raised the lad to manhood
until the time She took him as a husband
to bring forth all who live
along the banks of the great river
and on the mountainsides—
teaching them
as She had taught Her son
that they must live in peace
and with loving concern for each other.

When She saw that all was well
and that Her great family
knew how to care for themselves,
She returned to the lake,
taking Her son/husband with Her
and assuming the form of water serpents,
they slid into the rippling home
from which they had first come.

It was by the waters of this lake
the people came to offer
the sacred smoke of forest resins
to honour the First Mother,
asking for Her help in making the food grow,
asking for Her ever present protection,
thanking the Mother Spirit of the Waters
for the very joy of life.

MAYUEL

Though the name of the Goddess, as Mayuel, might suggest that She was worshipped by Mayans, rather than Aztecs, the name is known only from Aztec accounts. The similarity of Mayuel to Maya may simply be coincidental, or our lack of evidence from the Mayans perhaps a result of the obliteration of nearly all of the Mayan writings. Though revered by the Aztecs as the Goddess of the intoxicating liquid of the *maguey (metl)* plant, this account of Mayuel's discovery of the drink portrays Her as a mortal peasant woman. Mayuel, like Coatlicue, is described as having four hundred breasts, and as having given birth to the four hundred stars of heaven. Evidence that the pulque and mescal, made from the maguey, were used to ease the pains of childbirth, along with an Aztec account that the first two people on earth were raised from infancy on the juice of the maguey, may account for the imagery of the four hundred breasts to nurse the four hundred stars—the breasts of Mayuel perhaps regarded as having been filled with the magical and sacred drink. Mescal, better known as tequila, is distilled from the fermented juice (pulque) of the maguey, the century plant of the Agave species.

Astride the Great Tortoise, Mayuel rides, Goddess of Four Hundred Breasts, Mother of Four Hundred Stars, seen by all who drink Her sacred brew and intoxicated by Her spirit, they tell of a time when Mayuel was a woman living upon the earth:

Across the fields of growing crops, Mayuel walked in the dimming sunlight, tired from a long day's work, going to fetch the water as the last chore of the day. Passing the great maguey plant that towered high above her head, she noticed a tiny mouse nibbling at the lowest growth, strangely unconcerned by her approach. Much to her surprise the mouse began to dance about, as if in festive celebration, while Mayuel saw the wetness of the place from which the mouse had eaten, sap still dripping from the stalk. Wondering if the juice of the maguey was the reason for the mouse's joyful dance, she placed her water pot to catch the draining syrup and when the pot was filled with liquid, she continued on her long walk home.

Along the way to her thatched adobe na, her curious fingers dipped into the pot, her curious tongue then licking the liquid from her fingers. Much to her pleasure, despite the fatigue that she had felt, Mayuel found that she was in the mood to skip and sing, feeling a lightness in her step that she had not felt since childhood. So delighted was she with the wonderful discovery that she shared it with her family until their tiny home filled with the song and dance and laughter that each had long forgotten.

So it was that even after the time that Mayuel had finished her life upon the earth, those who knew of the magic of the maguey saw visions of the woman Mayuel as they drank the precious liquid to ease the pains of childbirth or sipped its magic at sacred celebrations to better understand the workings of the universe— remembering always to offer gratitude to Mayuel, She whose spirit lives forever in the Goddess given juice.

IX CHEL

Especially revered among women, the Mayan Ix Chel was closely associated with the moon. There is some question about whether the account of the moon's experiences with the sun was originally attributed to Ix Chel, or to another name of the Moon Goddess in Mexico and Guatamala, Ix Actani. The shrine on Cozumel Island, just a few miles off the northeastern coast of the Yucatan peninsula, is definitely associated with the name of Ix Chel. It was customary for all women who were pregnant or wanting to be, to visit the shrine of Ix Chel on this island. The astral bodies mentioned in the account are Venus (Chac Noh Ek), The Pleiades (Tzab), and the constellation of Scorpio (Zinaan Ek)—which, incidentally, was known as Scorpions to Mayan astronomers.

Ix Chel, sacred silver disc of the darkened heavens, first woman of the world, graciously gifted the people of the Yucatan, Campeche and Guatamala, with the easing of childbirth and the knowledge of healing. Mother of all deities, it is She who causes the blood to gather so that it may flow with the passage of the month.

So powerful was Ix Chel that when it was the time of the Haiyococab, the flooding and remaking of the earth, it was She who sent forth the inundating waters. Some say that She sent great waves from the ocean that pounced upon the land and swallowed it, while others tell of a giant earthen vessel whose contents She poured down from the skies—so that the earth could be cleansed, so that life could start anew.

Crowned with the feathers of an eagle, eagle feathers carefully woven in intricate design into Her heavenly throne, Ix Chel was known as Eagle Woman and eagles were seen as messengers of Her moon essence. From Her home in the heavens, Ix Chel watched a spider carefully as it spun its gossamer web and in this way gave birth to Ix Chebel Yax, She who later taught the knowledge of the weaving to the women of the earth. Thus they say it was the wisdom of the spider that gave us the ways of the loom and the spinning of the cotton, this knowledge brought to Guatamala by daughter Ix Chebel Yax who also taught how to blacken the cotton with carbon, how to redden the cotton with the rust of iron, how to purple the cotton with the fluid of the prized purpura shell.

Coming to the mats of those who were ill, Ix Chel would appear at their feet, invoked by the sacred smoke of copal and tobacco, bringing with Her the finely ground powder of crab, the slowly brewed broth of turkey, guava tips and the haaz papaya, the sap of the rubber tree and the honeymead balche to quench the thirst of fever. And all the while, as Ix Chel stood by the mat of the one who was ill, She held the reed cradle in Her arms, signifying Her power over life.

Among the Mayan people, the tale was told that in the very beginning of time the heavens were filled by two great lights—for at that time the moon was as bright as the sun. Ix Chel, glowing in all Her radiance, fascinated the sun so that he became determined to win Her love. To trick Her grandfather, who guarded Her jealously, the sun borrowed the body of a hummingbird and in this form, the sun flew to the home of the gracious shining Ix Chel. Upon the sun's arrival, he was welcomed by the Goddess with a drink of the honey of tobacco flowers but sitting there, sipping upon the cool drink, the hummingbird sun suddenly felt the sting of a clay pellet that had been sent with the force of a blow gun, piercing deep into his feathered side.

Who could have done such a thing but my grandfather, thought Ix Chel, as She carried the wounded bird to the privacy and safety of Her own room. There She nursed it gently until it could once more spread its wings and fly about the room. But caring for the wounded bird had aroused a tenderness within the Goddess, a feeling that She had never known before and when the sun suggested that they fly off together, into the empty spaces of the great heavens, to escape the jealous grandfather—though somewhat reluctant, Ix Chel agreed.

Clear across the heaven flew the two luminous bodies. Finding a cedar log canoe, they slipped it into a marshy stream of heaven and began to paddle as fast as they could. But the jealous grandfather, bursting with rage, called upon Chac, he who controlled storm, to hurl a lightning bolt at the two who had defied him. In hope of some protection, Ix Chel jumped into the water and became a crab. The sun soon followed close behind Her, taking the form of a mottled turtle. But the strategy was to no avail as the lightning bolt aimed at Ix Chel found its target—and the Goddess lay dead in the slow moving waters of the reed filled stream of heaven.

The buzzing of heavenly dragonflies mourned hymns around Her body. Wings fluttered in ripples of grief. But lamentation transformed into action when the dragonflies prepared thirteen hollow logs and for thirteen days they hovered about the dead Ix Chel—so many dragonflies that no one could see what was happening, not even the sun. On the thirteenth night the logs broke open. Out of twelve crawled the great and awesome snakes of heaven but from the thirteenth, Ix Chel emerged—once again alive and brilliant in Her regained wholeness. The sun was overjoyed and this time proposed marriage to which Ix Chel agreed. Thus the pair set up their home in heaven, side by side.

But it was not long before there was trouble, for soon they had a constant visitor in their new home. The brother of the sun, the delicately beautiful Chac Noh Ek, stopped by all too often for the comfort of the sun, often lingering closer to the moon and quickly disappearing when the sun arrived. The sun grew hot with jealousy, accusing the radiant Ix Chel of encouraging his brother, accusing the glowing Ix Chel of succumbing to his brother's charms, finally accusing the Moon Goddess of making love with Chac Noh Ek. And refusing to listen to Her words of reply, in insanely jealous rage—the sun threw the moon down from the heavens!

Landing not far from the Lake of Atitlan, scarcely missing the peak of the nearby volcano, Ix Chel fell upon the grassy banks, Her frustration and hurt at unjust accusations changing to anger and defiance. Just at that moment a vulture came gliding down and landing close by, the vulture's compassion for the moon caused it to offer Her a ride to the high mountain peaks where the vultures made their home. It was in this way that Ix Chel met the King of the Vultures and in Her sorrow and confusion accepted his offer to stay there with him as his lover.

But the sun soon learned that far from suffering, his wife was now well treated by the handsome black bird and in his jealousy, he grew even hotter—until he finally devised a scheme to find the vulture's nest. Hiding in the hide of a deer, the sun waited for a vulture to spot the carcass. Even sooner than he expected, vulture wings swooped down upon the deer, whereupon the jealous sun hopped upon the vulture's back—and so was taken to the summit where Ix Chel now lived.

Once there, the sun begged, he pleaded with Ix Chel, poured out apologies like drops of water in a flooding river, spoke perfect pictures of all they had experienced together to first become husband and wife. In even deeper confusion than before, Ix Chel bade the handsome vulture farewell and flew back into the heavens with the sun—to resume Her celestial throne beside him.

Hardly had She settled back into Her heavenly home, when again the sun grew hot with jealousy. Angrily, he shouted at Ix Chel, 'Why do you move so close to Chac Noh Ek? Why do you allow Zinaan Ek to brush against you and why do you stay in the house of the Tzab? Everyone sees you embrace them before you part. How can I call myself your husband and still keep my pride before all the others of heaven? It is true that you are beautiful, lustrous and radiant, wise and gentle, but if I cannot have you for my own, no one else will have you as you are!' Thus shouting and raging, the sun began to beat his wife, trying to destroy the beauty of Her being, to scar Her so badly, no other would want Her. Ix Chel stood firm with defiance as the blows fell upon Her. But as Her brilliance dimmed with the severe assault, Her will inside grew stronger—until, finally, with an anger of Her own, She flew off into the night!

Never again did She marry another, though many offered marriage as She passed by. 'The sun is my husband', She would say, though She quickly disappeared whenever he arrived. Wandering alone in the dark night sky, She thought about the women of the earth, those who paddled miles in small canoes to pray at Her shrine on Cozumel Island, those who asked for Her help, those who truly needed Her, those who had loved Her always. Thus among the many gifts of knowledge that Ix Chel gave to the women who knew Her best at Cozumel, was Her example that a woman must be free to come and go as she pleases—just as Ix Chel comes and goes, even disappearing for days at a time. But women trust that Ix Chel will return, for no matter how often She leaves, She soon reappears in the night time sky, Her image most brilliantly reflected in the waters that caress the shores of Cozumel.

IAMANJA

Although this account of the Summer Solstice ritual for the Goddess of the Sea, Iamanja, comes to us from Brazil, it is one that is believed to have been brought to South America by enslaved African peoples. It is generally assumed that it was originally a custom of the Yoruba groups in Nigeria, though it may have developed in South America from the tragedy of having been kidnapped and enslaved in a foreign land, and long remembering the ancient homeland across the sea. These ceremonies, now incorporated into the customs of many people of varied ethnic and racial backgrounds, are still enacted annually along the coastlines of Brazil on the eve of the Summer Solstice.

>Your holy spirit floats
>along the cresting waves of the water,
>as we walk out upon the sands,
>night time closing on the longest day of the year,
>and join together in small circles
>around the sacred boats
>that we shall send you,
>each whispering our prayers to a flower
>that we lay upon the boat,
>for Iamanja, Holy Queen Sea.

Flames set to floating campfire logs
flicker on the mounting flowers,
as our boats of prayers are set afloat
upon the edges of your being,
your gently caressing waves
washing about our bared legs,
cleansing away our sadness and our troubles,
bathing away any wrongs that we have done,
and as we watch the sparks of dancing light
dimming in the growing distance,
we know that you are waiting
for the messages we send,
Iamanja, Holy Queen Sea.

Fire reflections in your gently rocking darkness,
light above, so light below,
chanting chorus keeping time
to the rhythm of your being,
I stand to one side
to watch the others
toss their last flower prayers upon the moving boats,
thinking that you have enough to do
without my adding to your work.
But just before the last boat
floats out too far for change of mind,
I too toss my flower upon the others,
with prayers for your health and long years
and that you may always be
just as we have known you,
Iamanja, Holy Queen Sea.

And from Chaos She Has Led Us by the Hand
Semites of Canaan, Mesopotamia, and Arabia

long the great rivers of the Tigris and Euphrates, and across the northern sands of Syria to the lands that lie along the Mediterranean's eastern waters, Semitic people called upon the Creator of Life as She who descended from Venus, yet emerged from the waters upon the shore at Ascalon. Whether the result of creative invention, or embroidered memories of the ancient beginnings of human life, the nature of the Goddess of the Semitic peoples has been made known to us by the many treasures Her worshippers left buried in the earth, upon which they had lived.

The evidence of Goddess reverence, presented in this section, is drawn from a vast number of translations of tablets and texts written in the Semitic languages of Akkadian, Ugaritan, Phoenician (Canaanite), Amorite, Aramaean, Hebrew, and Arabic. Becoming more familiar with the geography of the areas inhabited by early Semites, helps to clarify the religious beliefs, and helps us to better understand both the similarities and the differences in these beliefs, as they appear in different areas of the Near East. Much of the evidence, of the worship of the Goddess among the Semites, comes from the area that stretches along the eastern shores of the Mediterranean, lands now known as Lebanon, Israel, and Syria. This area is referred to as The Levant. The other major area, in which written evidence of the worship of the Goddess by ancient Semitic peoples has been discovered, is that of the north and central sections of present day Iraq, ancient Mesopotamia. Between The Levant and Mesopotamia lies the vast Syrian desert, as far as we know, largely uninhabited in ancient periods, except for a few settlements along the Euphrates River. The Euphrates, which is the major link between The Levant and Mesopotamia, starts in Anatolia, crosses the northern section of Syria, flows southeast across Syria, into and through Mesopotamia, until its waters pour into the Persian Gulf. Both The Levant and Mesopotamia reveal evidence of settled sites, and Goddess imagery, that date back to the earliest neolithic periods. (The Tabun Cave, on Mt. Carmel on the Levantine coast, is one of the most ancient sites at which full homo sapien remains have been discovered.)

The worship of the Goddess as Ashtart (Ashtoreth, Astarte), Atargatis, Asherah, Anat, and Shapash, was primarily known in Levantine areas. The worship of the Goddess as Mami, Aruru, and Ishtar, was best known in northern and central Mesopotamia. The images and nature of Ishtar may have been derived from, or influenced by, religious beliefs of Anatolia (Turkey). A larger body of evidence reveals that the worship of Ishtar was integrated with the worship of the Goddess known as Inanna among the Sumerians of southern Mesopotamia. The name of Ishtar eventually replaced that of Inanna at the Temple of the Queen of Heaven in Erech, a city not far from the Persian Gulf. While Semites of northern Mesopotamia had many links with Anatolia, and Semites of central Mesopotamia had many links with the Sumerians—Semites of the Levantine coast had access to Egypt, Cyprus, Crete, southern Anatolia, and the many islands of the Mediterranean. Ports all along the coast of The Levant—such as Ascalon, Sidon, Tyre, Byblos, and Ugarit—are especially noticeable in accounts of Goddess worship, and provide a great deal of information about Goddess reverence among the Semitic peoples, both in the Levant and throughout the Mediterranean area.

Under each Goddess name, I have included the material specifically associated with that name. The epithets and titles are from translations of carved or clay cuneiform inscriptions. Place names of shrines and temples, and specific information about them, are based upon the records of archaeological excavations. The prayers are from translations of cuneiform tablets, some combined adaptations, when I had access to two or more slightly differing translations of the same tablet. The narrative accounts are from translations of sacred epic poems found upon the clay tablets of ancient libraries and temple archives. Cuneiform, wedge shaped marks pressed into damp clay, was a method of writing almost certainly first developed by the Sumerians of southern Mesopotamia. Soon after its development, it was used by Semitic Akkadians, who adapted it to record their own language. After a long period of use and change, Semitic Phoenicians (Canaanites) of The Levant passed this knowledge of writing on to the Indo-European Greeks, who then further adapted it to record their own language.

I have tried to present as much information as possible about Goddess reverence among Semitic peoples, in a volume such as this, but this is by no means all that is known about each specific Goddess name. Connections and influences between the Semitic people and the Sumerians are discussed in greater detail in the Sumerian section. Connections between the Semites and the Anatolians (Turkey) are further examined in the Anatolian section. Although each Goddess name, and accompanying information, is presented separately, even within this section we cannot help but notice the overlapping concepts of certain religious customs and rituals such as: the presence of eunuchs who castrated themselves to serve in the clergy of the Goddess; the sexual rituals (more fully described and explained in *When God Was A Woman);* the sacred marriage rites; and perhaps most abundant are the translations of the legends and rituals surrounding the annual enactment, or commemoration, of the death of the son or brother consort of the Goddess. These connections may be observed not only within the Semitic accounts of Ishtar, Ashtart, and Anat, but also in those of the Anatolian Kybele, the Egyptian Isis (Au Sept), the Sumerian Inanna, and the Greek and Cyprian Aphrodite (see Anatolian, Egyptian and Greek Sections).

For far too long, psychologists, mythologists, philosophers, and theologians, have written and developed numerous treatises on the 'inherent' nature of woman, often basing their theories upon references to ancient Goddess imagery. Many of these theories have revolved about structured dichotomies of either good or bad. Reading over the actual prayers, narrative accounts, titles, and epithets, of the Goddess as She was worshipped by Semitic peoples, it is clear that theories of dualistic archetypes are not only simplistic, but actually in conflict with the multi-faceted nature of the Goddess, as She was known by those who revered Her.

Some scholars have referred to the Goddess of the ancient Near East as a fertility figure, the central figure of a fertility cult. Others have opened their eyes just a bit further (though categorizing all evidence of fertility attributes under the label Goddess of Love, rather than sexuality and creation of life) and have also mentioned the heroic or martial aspects of the Goddess of the Semitic people, by the additional label of Goddess of Battle. Most of those who bother to mention both of these attributes, often add a comment about this as a strange, or improbable, pair of traits, describing them as 'paradoxical'. This paradox remains a paradox only as long as the reader is unaware of all the *other* aspects attributed to the Goddess—such as prophesy, judgement, divine decree, law, divine guardianship of the right to rule or lead the people, creation of life, and concern for the oppressed and mistreated. It is as if one were to claim that Jehovah's creation of life as told in Genesis, and the leading of Joshua in the invasion of Canaan, as told in the Book of Joshua, presented a paradox, excluding mention of all other stated attributes and actions of Jehovah.

Only with a thorough familiarity with the actual texts available from ancient periods, can any meaningful or intelligent discussion of Goddess reverence in the ancient Near East even be initiated. There is a vast, diverse, and complex body of beliefs, about the ancient Goddess of the Semites, one that we simply cannot ignore, if we are to approach any analysis of the nature of womanhood through ancient Goddess imagery.

While reading of the various types of records and evidence, certain topics may present themselves as areas for further research and examination, beyond what I have been able to present here. One subject, that has been largely ignored, is that of the existence of the oracular shrines of the Goddess, wherein priestesses provided predictions and counsel, as interpretations of the word of the Goddess—thus influencing political and governmental issues, well into periods in which Goddess reverence was losing ground. Another is the nature of the *Ibratu* shrines, which are mentioned in various texts and proverbs, described as gathering places for women both in Sumer and in Semitic Akkad (Babylonia). The reader may be interested in a further exploration of the repeated mention of the sacred stones in the worship of Ba'Alat at Byblos and Al Uzza at Mecca, comparing these to the worship of the sacred stone of the Amazons at Colchis, and the one associated with the

Goddess as Kybele in the city of Pessinus — a stone considered to be so important that it was later brought to Rome at the decree of the prophetic Sibyls (see Anatolian section for these last two references). The claims that Ishtar and Her women had descended from Venus, and that Ashtart arrived as a fiery star that fell into the lake at the sacred shrine of Aphaca — alongside African beliefs about the star Sirius (see African section introduction), and the association of the Egyptian Goddess as Isis with Sirius — may provide topics for speculation for those with broader imaginations.*

Along with the material from Sumer, Anatolia, and Egypt, evidence of Goddess worship among Semitic speaking peoples is some of the earliest written material that we possess. Since Goddess worship in these areas both predates, *and* coincides, with biblical periods, this information allows us to examine statements about the religious beliefs and customs that surrounded the early Hebrews, later the early Christians, and even later the early Muslims. This more knowledgeable point of view allows us to examine the political and religious biases about so called pagan religions, and certainly to question the gender biases inherent in the biblical diatribes against the most ancient religion of all, that of the Mother as Creator.

*Current excavations in the area of northwestern Syria (in The Levant), have recently revealed the ancient culture of Ebla, and the name of the Goddess there as Eshtar. The Semitic language found on Ebla tablets, tentatively labelled Eblaite, appears to have been used at about 2400 B.C. The name Eshtar, in northern Syria, further links the worship of Ishtar of Mesopotamia with Ashtart of The Levant area.

MAMI ARURU

These two names of the Goddess, as Creator of Life, were most often used separately, but in the *Babylonian Theodicy,* an Akkadian discussion of theological concepts, the names Mami and Aruru are used interchangeably. The information on the Goddess, as known by these names, is rather minimal, but references found in several different texts of Akkadian Babylonia provide the information included here.

Aruru, Oldest of the Old
Creator of Life,
Mami, Divine Mother of All,
Womb that created all humankind
and still creates all destiny.
They kissed Her holy feet
and called upon Her
as Creator of Humanity,
Mistress of all Deities.

Sweeter than honey and date wine
was the ancient Mother,
for it was She who made all life
by pinching off the fourteen pieces of clay—
and laying a brick between them,
She made seven women
whom She placed to the left,
She made seven men
whom She placed to the right.
Forming them into people
She then placed them on the earth.

ISHTAR

There are several conjectural origins of the worship of the Goddess as Ishtar. The site of Arpachiyah, from the Halafian culture of about 5000 B.C., was situated on the Tigris, within a mile of where one of the most sacred centres of Ishtar, Nineveh, later stood. It may be of interest that other Halafian sites were in Anatolia, perhaps settled by descendants of the even earlier Catal Huyuk culture. Excavations of Arpachiyah have provided us, not only with very early Goddess statues, but a Goddess accompanied by images of doves, serpents, and the double axe—symbols that reappear repeatedly in later Goddess imagery. Since the son/lover of Ishtar, Tammuz, is almost identical with the Damuzi of the Sumerian Goddess as Inanna, it is also suggested that the symbolism, stories, customs, and rituals, associated with Ishtar, were derived from Sumerian beliefs. Whether these various aspects of the religion, known to have been connected with reverence for Ishtar, were derived from Anatolia, Sumer, or the Semites of The Levant (as the accounts of Ashtart might suggest), Ishtar became the most popular name and image of the Goddess, as She was known among the Semites of northern and central Mesopotamia.

Ishtar, Queen of Heaven, said to have descended from the planet Venus, thus arriving upon earth accompanied by the Ishtaritu, Ishtar's holy women, was revered as Mother by Semitic peoples who lived along the banks of the Tigris and Euphrates.

Many claim that Ishtar was one with Inanna, for when Semites went to Sumerian Erech, they called upon the Goddess of the ancient Erech temple as Ishtar, though Erech had long been known as the holy place of the Sumerian Mother. And it is true that at Telloh, Kish and Ur, the name of Ishtar replaced that of the Sumerian Inanna, but Ishtar's name had long been called upon in Nineveh, Aleppo and Arbela, in Assur, Mari and Ischali, and in the great city of Babylon at the temple known as E Kidurinum. Both Ishtar and Inanna were known as Queen of Heaven, but in ancient Sumer it was said that Inanna had eight Ibratu, eight smaller wayside shrines where women gathered daily for prayer and meditaton, or even to exchange the news of the day—while Ishtar had one hundred and eighty.

Images of Ishtar were known throughout Semitic lands: horned as the holy heifer of Egypt; armed with bow and arrow; wearing the tiara crown upon Her head; holding the double serpent sceptre; holding Her hands beneath Her breasts; standing upon the lion beneath Her feet; mushrusshu dragons by Her sides; riding in Her chariot drawn by seven lions; holding a bull by the horns; seated upon Her lion throne; riding upon the back of a large bird; holding the sacred branches in Her hands; brandishing sword or scimitar; priestesses sitting on the ground before Her—knowing Her as the most sacred eight pointed star, the guiding light of the planet Masat Venus, Star of Prophesy, Her holiness shining in the heavens.

Many were the sacred titles that She bore: O Shining One, Lioness of the Igigi; Mother of Deities; She Who Begets All; Producer of Life; Creator of People; Queen of Heaven and Earth; She Who Guides Humankind; She Who Holds the Reins of Royalty; She Who Possesses the Law of Heavenly Sovereignty; Guardian of Law and Order; Mistress of Ordinances; Ruler of the Heavens; Director of the People; Light of Heaven; Shepherdess of the Lands; Possessor of the Tablets of Life's Records; Source of the Oracles of Prophesy; Lady of Battle and Victory; Lady of Combat Who Carries the Quiver and the Bow; Exalted; Glorious; Heroic; Supreme; Malkatu; Gingira; Belit Mati—Queen, Lady of the Lands.

Across the ancient lands many carved inscriptions revealed the nature of the holy Ishtar:

Mother of the fruitful breast,
when at the front of combat She is seen,
She is a flood of light whose strength is mighty.

When at a quarrel She is present,
it is She who understands the matter.

It is Ishtar who renders all decisions,
Goddess of all that occurs,
Lady of Heaven and Earth
who receives our supplication,
who hears our requests,
who listens to our prayers.

It is Ishtar who is compassionate
because She loves righteousness.

She is Ishtar the Queen,
oppressing all that is confused,
holding full powers of judgement and decision.

106

AND FROM CHAOS SHE HAS LED US BY THE HAND

Prayers that passed across the lips of many people, prayers inscribed on stone and clay, still echo Her sovereignty as sacred songs in memory's ears:

Queen of Heaven, Goddess of the Universe,
the One who walked in terrible chaos
and brought life by the law of love
and out of chaos brought us harmony
and from chaos She has led us by the hand.

Woman of women, Goddess who knows no equal,
She who decrees the destiny of people,
Highest Ruler of the World,
Sovereign of the Heavens,
Goddess, even of those who live in heaven.

It is you who changes destiny
to make what is bad become good.
At your right side is justice,
at your left side is goodness.
From your sides emanate life and well being.
Ishtar, how good it is to pray to you;
there is concern in your glance,
your word is the light.
Please look upon me with affirmation.
Please accept my prayer.

With Ishtar there is counsel and wisdom.
The fate of everything She holds in Her hand.
Joy comes from Her very glance.
She is the power, the magnificence.
She is the deity who protects.
She is the spirit that guides.
Be it maiden or mother,
women remember Her and call Her name.

O Lady, glorious is Thy omnipotence,
Thy exaltation above all other deities.
Thou art the mighty One, the Lady of Combat,
strong enough to suppress the mountains.
Full judgement and decision are in Thy power
as are the ordinances of heaven and earth.
In Thy chapels, in Thy holy places,
at Thy sacred shrines,
we come to listen to Thee.

O Shining One, Lioness of the Igigi,
You stop the anger of all other deities.
You care for the oppressed and the mistreated,
each day offering them your help.
You are the One who gleams brightest
in the midst of all other deities.
You are the holy One of women and of men.

Praise Goddess, the mightiest of deities.
Let us revere the Mistress of People,
more exalted than all other deities;
Praise Ishtar, the mightiest of deities.
Let us revere the Queen of Heaven,
more exalted than all other deities.

O Ishtar, Sovereign Mistress of all people,
You are the light of heaven and earth;
heaven and earth move because of you.
All people pay homage to you
for you are great, you are exalted.
All humankind recognizes your power,
for you are the bright torch of heaven and earth,
the light of all living,
One who cannot be opposed,
whirlwind that roars against all that is wrong.

Her lips are sweet,
Life is in Her mouth.
When She appears, we are filled with rejoicing.
She is glorious beneath Her robes.
Her body is complete beauty.
Her eyes are total brilliance.
Who could be equal to Her greatness,
for Her decrees are strong, exalted, perfect.
Ishtar—Who could be equal to Her greatness
for Her decrees are strong, exalted, perfect.

All other deities seek Her counsel,
unique is Her position
for Her word is so respected,
it is supreme over them.
She is their Queen.
It is they who carry out Her decrees.
All of them bow down before Her,
receiving their light from Her.
Thus women and men hold Her in highest reverence.

AND FROM CHAOS SHE HAS LED US BY THE HAND

At Assur, at Arbela, at Mari, at Kalah, at Nineveh, at Kissuru, priestesses of Ishtar called upon Her wisdom at these shrines of divine prophesy, speaking of Her as The Lady of Vision, speaking of Her as The Prophetess of Kua, answering questions of life, deciding mortal problems whether great or small. Thus the names of priestesses were marked upon the ancient records of the oracles, names of the holiest of women who had spoken the words and decrees of Ishtar, names that resound with the echoes of the years—Belit Abi Sha, Ishtar Bel Daini, Sinkisha Amur, Urkittu Sharrat, Ishtar Latashiat, Baja and the woman known as Rimute Allate, priestess of the shrine of Goddess prophesy in the village of Darahuja in the mountains.

On the night of the full moon, the holy night known as Shapatu, special offerings of food and drink were made, as they were on the night of the new moon, when joyous celebration filled the temples. The sacred Qadishtu, the women who came to live as priestesses in the temple's Gagu quarters, took lovers in the Bit Ashtammi of the temple, expressing the sacredness of sexuality as the gift of Ishtar. Of these holy women it was said, "Respect and submission to a husband are not to be found among them." Men who joined in reverence of the Holy Mother offered their organs of maleness joyfully, in the midst of highest festive celebration, using razor, sword, or knife of stone, later wearing these upon their sash as symbol of their consecration to The Mother, thus joining the ranks of Kurgarru and Ishinu who served as eunuch attendants at the temples of Ishtar.

In the month of Tammuz, on the twenty-eighth day, the Day of the Sheepfolds, highest holy rites were celebrated by those who revered the mighty Ishtar—a vulva of lapis lazuli and an eight pointed star of gold placed upon Her altar—for was She not the star from whose vulva all life had come forth?

Those who called upon Ishtar knew well the story of Her son, he who had also been Her lover and Her consort, Tammuz, he who had died when but a youth. For it was Tammuz who was spoken of as keeper of the cattle stalls, leading goat of the land, tamarisk tree that could find no water, he who had been given the shepherd's staff by Ishtar, the one whom Ishtar had chosen for the sacred marriage rites celebrated during the holy days of the great Akitu festival, the one chosen as the shepherd for the year, after he had proven himself upon Her couch.

But the shepherd Tammuz was then removed from Her by death, causing sorrowful lament throughout the land, as flutes and drums accompanied dirging voices, as women mourned in sympathy for Ishtar, who grieved that Tammuz had been taken from Her—as Inanna grieved when Damuzi died, as Ashtart grieved when Tammuz died, as Isis grieved when Osiris died, as Kybele grieved when Attis died, as Anat grieved when Baal died, as Aphrodite grieved when Adonis died. But as the Goddess continued to rule upon Her throne in heaven, so did Her priestesses continue to convey Her word to those on earth, each year choosing a new Tammuz, each year celebrating the sacred marriage rites, each year mourning at the chosen shepherd's death.

In days when invaders conquered Ishtar's cities, Gilgamish prepared to take part in the rites of the sacred marriage, thus to gain the divine right to shepherdship, that which was bestowed by Ishtar—for knives and swords and spears are not the tools of the shepherd. But Gilgamish sought immortality, permanence upon the earthly throne. Thus the legend formed, the story of the changing of the rites, telling all that when the mighty Ishtar proposed to Gilgamish that he lie upon Her bed of pleasure; tempting him even further with promises of a chariot of lapis and gold drawn by the swiftest of storm demons; saying that all others would bow down before him; saying that tribute from field and orchard would be his—Gilgamish feared that his death might be included in the bargain, and that his life would end, as that of Tammuz had ended.

Thus Gilgamish challenged Ishtar with these words, "What mate would thou love forever? What shepherd boy would please thee always?", adding that each former mate of Ishtar had met a tragic end. Refusing to join Her in the sacred marriage rites, Gilgamish then killed Her bull of heaven, crying aloud that he wished that he could do the same to Her. Gilgamish, with warrior army behind him, defied the ways of those who worshipped Ishtar, the consort whose life ended with the year, so that the consort shepherd no longer met his death after a year of temple life. But those who then declared themselves as king, in deference to the ancient rites and customs, yearly had their hair shorn from their head, yearly had their royal insignias and jewels removed, yearly had their robes of royalty stripped from their bodies, as they were struck upon the face with a cord of seven knots and thrown into the river, afterwards walking about in the sackcloth of mourning for three days of lamentation—in memory of the time they would have died.

So it came to be that those who first gained kingship by sword, instead of shepherd's staff, gained seats of permanence upon a throne of rule. Still they continued to speak of themselves as The Beloved of Ishtar, the one who received the reins of royalty from Ishtar, the one who received the staff of shepherdship from Ishtar, the one who received the year of reign from Ishtar. In this way, the High Priestess of Ishtar was left with hollow symbols of power, as the new kings placed Ishtar upon a crumbling pedestal of worship—while they sat firmly upon the seat of rule.

Yet memory of the time, when the shepherd would have met his death, still lingered in the minds of many, who knew that the shepherd king was but a servant of the Goddess, the one who must convey Her wishes and decrees to keep Her love. Thus were the oracular priestesses still consulted for advice and counsel, as the word of Ishtar. And when the time of year arrived, the time that the shepherd would have met his death, the king was yearly struck by the cord of seven knots. In this way, all were reminded that the king must show humility, for it was said that if tears streamed down his face, all would be well—but if the signs of humble atonement did not come, Ishtar would lay evil fortune upon the land.

ATARGATIS

The name of the Goddess as Atargatis was especially associated with the temple at Ascalon on the Mediterranean coast, about 50 miles west of Jerusalem. This temple was famous for its dove cots, and as a shrine of oracular prophesy, yet the primary image of Atargatis was as a Goddess of the Sea, sometimes depicted with the tail of a fish. Her name and image were also connected to the Hierapolis temple on the Syrian Euphrates, a shrine that was said to have been founded after a great flood (see Ashtart). The association of Atargatis, not only with Ascalon, but with the Euphrates, and with the city of Nineveh on the Tigris, suggests a great antiquity for the fish tailed image of the Goddess, possibly connected to very early Sumerian images of the Goddess as Nina or as Nammu (see

Sumerian Section). It may be that this ancient portrayal of the Goddess led
to later accounts of mermaids, and sirens, and mystical islands in unknown
waters that were populated only by women (see Celtic Section). The
Goddess name of Attar also appears in Arabia, described as a male deity in
later periods.

Ancient Goddess of the Sea,
swimming in Mediterranean waters,
climbed upon the shore at Ascalon,
bringing Her infant daughter Shammuramat
and leaving her to the care of tender doves,
She slipped back into the sea,
there to live as Holy Mother.
Thus they honoured Her with sacred lakes
on whose shores were built Her shrines,
purity to be gained from Her holy waters—
while pilgrims swimming as the fish of the lakes
were touched by Her eternal presence.

Some say that it was Her earthly daughter
who founded the shrine for Her at Ascalon,
sacred site of doves of prophesy,
and that Shammuramat then made her way east
to build the city of Nineveh
along the waters of the Tigris,
while others claim that Atargatis had first been born
in the waters of the wide Euphrates,
Her priestesses upon the earth
offering fish upon Her altar
as Sumerians had done for Nina
by the waters of Euphrates at Eridu—
for the sign that meant Nineveh
was the same as the sign that meant Nina.

Thus was Atargatis honoured at Ascalon,
thus was Atargatis honoured at Hierapolis,
as Sumerians spoke of Nammu
as The Primeval Goddess of the Sea,
as Canaanites spoke of Asherah
as The Primeval Goddess of the Sea,
as Egyptians spoke of Nuneit
as The Primeval Goddess of the Sea.

ASHTART

The connections between Ashtart and Ishtar are obvious in the similarities of the names, as well as in the identification with Venus, and the title Queen of Heaven. The name of the son/consort of the Goddess, as Tammuz, occurs in worship of both Ishtar and Ashtart. The claim, by the people of Byblos, that the Goddess first descended to earth as a fiery star that landed in the lake at Aphaca (near Byblos), and that Aphaca was also the actual site of the death of the original Tammuz, made the area of Aphaca and Byblos one of exceptional importance, even to Egyptians. Byblos is in an area rich with human history: situated not far from the site of extremely early homo sapien habitation at Mt. Carmel; close to the Eynan site of the Natufians of about 9000 B.C.; and not far from the Ghassulian mural of the eight pointed star, dated to about 4500 B.C. Worship of the Goddess at Aphaca continued until about 300 A.D., when the shrine was closed by Christian Emperor Constantine, along with other Goddess temples of Syria, Lebanon, and Israel.

The worship of Ashtart on Cyprus, and many other islands and coastal cities of the Mediterranean, helps to explain the origins of many of the shrines that were later known as sacred sites of the Greek Aphrodite. The legend of Europa, being abducted from the Levantine city of Tyre and taken to Crete, may well be an allegory of the spread of the worship of the Semitic Goddess. The reverence for Ashtart in The Levant lasted well into biblical times, as Hebrew Scripture passages reveal. (see Sam. 7:3,4; Judges 2:13, 3:7; I Kings 11:5 and Jer. 44:15-19) It was during the Greek occupation of Syria and Lebanon that Ashtart came to be called Urania (Greek for Queen of Heaven), the title also used for Aphrodite, whose worship was initially derived from that of Ashtart. The Pyre ritual, described by Lucian at Hierapolis, appears to have been a synthesis of Greek and Semitic rituals, *pyre* being the Greek word for fire.

As many named Sovereign of Heaven, as Guiding Star watching over all, some say that Ashtart first came from an ancient homeland in Arabia, where children were once known only by their mother's clan. They say that there Her name was Amma Attar, Malkatu Ashar Amaim, or Allatu. But others say that Semitic people had long lived on the lands of Syria, and along the Mediterranean shores, suggesting that their ancestors were the Goddess revering settlers of neolithic Jericho, and perhaps even the community of Natufians, who lived not far from Nazareth some eleven thousand years ago.

Those who later lived at the port of Byblos, along the Levantine coastal waters, did not explain their own arrival on that land, but treasured a sacred stone that they said fell from heaven—

as they also said that the Goddess Ba'Alat Ashtart had descended from the heavens, as a fiery falling star. Byblians long remembered that it was in this way that the Mother of Deities had first arrived, spinning round like balls of fire in the sky, skimming over the peak of Mt. Lebanon, Her fiery mass then cooling in the waters of Aphaca. Thus they built Her most sacred shrine at the site of Aphaca—close by this holiest of lakes. The people of other towns and villages long honoured this sacred inland shrine, building the great Byblos temple some five thousand years ago, at the place where the waters from Aphaca flowed out to the broad sea. And there in this temple at Byblos, they kept Ba'Alat Ashtart's sacred stone.

Pilgrims from far off places visited Aphaca, to pay honour at the ancient holy site, casting jewels of gold and silver into the Aphaca waters, saying that the Aphaca shrine was doubly sanctified, for it was also the place where the son lover of the Goddess had died. Once paying their respects at Aphaca, the pilgrims then made their way to Byblos, following the westward waters of the river, until they reached the Byblos temple that looked out upon the waters of the Great Sea. And there in Byblos, they stood in the presence of the ancient stone that was said to contain the souls of all people, to heal upon the touching, and to whisper with the knowledge of all future events—for those who could understand Her words.

Egyptians said that it was to this port of Byblos, on the shores of ancient Canaan, that the grieving Goddess Isis travelled, while searching for the murdered body of Osiris, and that She discovered it there in the trunk of a tree, that had been used as a pillar in the Byblos temple. Yet Byblians claimed that when Egyptians sailed to their port so rich in timber, they came to know of the holy rituals for the dead shepherd Tammuz, and they then took these ancient rites back with them to Egypt. For do not even Egyptians say that Isis found the pillar tree, whose boughs and winding trunk had grown about the coffer of the dead youth, in Byblos of Canaan—Byblians adding that the pillar of the Byblos temple was a tree that grew on the hills of Lebanon.

It is true that Egyptians of most ancient days had wandered far into The Levant, leaving silent proof of their travels at Megiddo and Bethel, at Ugarit and Byblos, but it is also true that Ba'Alat Ashtart was often seen wearing the horns of Egyptian Isis upon Her holy head. The truth of the matter may never be ours to know, for all the way from Egypt to Canaan the Goddess was known as Queen of Heaven, Mother of Deities, Guardian of the Land, while images of Her upon Her lioness were oftimes simply marked with Her title—Quadesh—That Which is Holiness. But Isis was said to be seen in the light of the bright star Sept/Sirius, while Ashtart was looked upon as the light that some call Venus, The Eye of Heaven known as Masat, Prophetess.

Many were the images that conveyed the presence of the Mother of Semitic peoples. At Beth Shan and Beth Shemesh, at Beit Mersim and at Gezer, at Tir Dibba and Ain Shems, and at holy Byblos, sometimes known as Kepni or Gebal, images of Ba'Alat Ashtart were formed with the sacred serpent entwined about Her body, or emerging from Her perfect forehead, between holy heifer horns, that held the disc of the sun. At lonely Serabit El Khadim, upon the sands of Sinai, Semitic words were inscribed upon the walls, to Ba'Alat as the ancient Serpent Lady. At the Canaanite city of Sidon, Ashtart was known as Queen of Heaven with the Crescent Horns, while the name of the town of Ashtoreth Karnaim simply meant Ashtoreth of the Horns. In other towns of The Levant, priestesses of Ashtart sat upon thrones flanked with lionesses, or even sphinx, some inscribed with the words, "To my Goddess Ashtart,", while a stone carving of a doe, suckling her fawn, was marked with the inscription, "Ashtart is my strength."

*   *   *

In later times, Greek Lucian wrote of the holy city of Syrian Hierapolis, that stood by the waters of the Euphrates, not far from Anatolia. To this shrine too, pilgrims came from distant towns, to hear the oracles of prophesy at the temple that was said to have been built after the great flood—tradition claiming that a chasm had opened at that very spot, and the waters of the flood had poured into it and disappeared. As reminder of that eventful time, waters from the wide Euphrates were brought into the temple twice a year. And although the temple was dedicated to the Queen of Heaven, tales were told on holy days of the ancient Atargatis, She who had the tail of a fish, yet gave birth to an infant daughter who walked upon two legs. Thus was the Mother Ashtart, She who had arrived from heaven as balls of fire, linked with the Holy One of the sea. At the sacred lake of Hierapolis, pilgrims bathed close by an altar stone that emerged from the centre of the waters, fish glowing with golden lines swimming all about them.

On the first day of the month of Nisan, to welcome the event of the vernal equinox, the festival known as Pyre began at Hierapolis, celebrated among the trees that had been erected as a grove in the courtyard of the shrine. Just as in earlier times, priestesses still took lovers from among the pilgrims, but only on these holiest of days of Pyre. And males who chose to remain among the clergy, still made themselves as eunuchs at this time, offering their organs of maleness, donning only women's robes, to gain entry into the clergy of the Queen of Heaven.

There were many who simply cut their hair, placing the shorn locks in great silver vessels, and though not initiates to the clergy, they attended the rituals of Pyre that were held twice a day. The first was in silent mourning meditation for the dead son lover, whom they now spoke of as Adonis, the one who had been Tammuz—though there were those who whispered that Osiris was his name. The second was spent in joyful song and dance, to the music of flute and sistrum rattle, as they called upon the name of the mighty Queen of Heaven. So it was, Lucian wrote, that they watched the smoke of sweet smelling incense rise from Her altar, and ascend to the golden ceiling, later floating through the doors of gold that crowned the cedar steps of the Hierapolis temple of the Queen of Heaven.

Semitic people, spoken of as Canaanites or Phoenicians, those whom Philo said took the names of their mothers for they cared not who their fathers were, lived along the shores of the Mediterranean waters. Knowing well the ways of sails and oars, they wandered far from their Levantine home, carrying the memory of Ashtart in their hearts. To the northern coast of Africa, to Carthage and Sousse Djerba, to Rousadu and Rachgoun, they brought the name of Ashtart—where She came to be called upon as Tanit, perhaps in memory of ancient Libyan Neit, though Her priestesses took the names of Bod Ashtart and Abda Ashtart in Carthaginian towns, close by the site where the Lake of Tritonis was said to have been, site where some say Amazons once lived.

Phoenicians honoured Ashtart on the isle of Thasos, and on rocky Delos, where Hellenic Greeks later said Lato had given birth to Artemis—Phoenicians leaving inscriptions there 'To Ashtart of Philistia'. To the isle of Callista they brought Her, Thera of the fiery volcano, island that some claim gave rise to the memories of Atlantis sinking. At Phoenician colonies on Sicily, Her name was inscribed as Ashtart of Eryx, perhaps in memory of the famed

Goddess temple at Erech, temple that had long honoured the Queen of Heaven as Ishtar or Inanna. At Nora, Sulcis, and Tharros, on the island of Sardinia, Phoenicians left shrines and images of Ashtart. And touching upon the isles of Gul and Malta, once known as Ma Lata, some say that it was these Canaanites of the waters who built the great temples of Hagar Qim and Hal Tarxien, where massive stone images of Goddess permeated all.

Trading along the coast of Spain, at Almeria and Los Millares, Ashtart revering Phoenicians made their way past the Gates of Gibraltar, settling a colony at Cadiz. There are even some who say that Phoenicians reached the coast of Brittany, and from there sailed to the British Isles searching for gold and tin, perhaps bringing with them the sanctity of great stone circles, like those of Ghassul and Wadi Dhobai in The Levant.

Horned as the holy heifer of Egypt, was it Ashtart who was carried from Phoenician Tyre to Crete, for though some give the name as Europa, and claim that Zeus, disguised as a bull, carried Europa to Crete—sacred horns adorned Cretan shrines long before the followers of Zeus arrived. At Paphos, Kition, and Amathus, ancient towns upon the Cyprian isle, Ashtart was known among Phoenician colonies; while upon the sacred isle of Cythera, so close to Grecian shores, the Queen of Heaven was worshipped at a great Phoenician temple, until Greeks spoke of Her as Urania, the Greek way of saying Queen of Heaven. It was Urania that Greeks came to know as Aphrodite, explaining that the light of Venus was sacred to Her, and that Her Cythera temple had been built in ancient times by Phoenicians from Ascalon. Though memories of Atargatis had faded with the many years, Greeks remembered that Aphrodite had been born in blue Mediterranean waters, but said that She had climbed upon the land on the southwestern shore of Cyprus— island where Ashtart had so long been revered.

TIAMAT

The name of Tiamat, as a Goddess name of Mesopotamia, does not appear to have been used other than in the Babylonian epic legend, the *Enuma Elish*, the account of the *murder* of Tiamat as The Great Mother of the Sea. The imagery appears to be associated with the Goddess as Asherah, Atargatis, and the Sumerian Goddess as Nammu and Nina (see Sumerian

Section). The *Enuma Elish,* quite a favourite among scholars of the twentieth century A.D. (if we judge by the number of interpretations and references to it), is believed to have been written during the period in which Indo-European led Kassites conquered and controlled Babylon (about 1600 B.C.). The explanation in the epic that Anu and Enki (two male deities who were associated with the arrival of specific groups at Erech and Eridu in Sumer) had made previous attempts to dispose of Tiamat—and failed—while as the direct result of the successful murder of Tiamat, the male Marduk gained supreme power—certainly provides fertile ground for an exploration of the demise of the supremacy of the Goddess in Mesopotamia.

> Mother of all Mothers,
> She who gave birth to all,
> though known as Tiamat
> by those who rejoiced at Her murder,
> rippled as distant echo
> of mighty Mother Goddess Sea,
> Nammu, Asherah, Atargatis, Nuneit.
> Well remembered as Creator of all,
> first owner of the Tablets of Destiny,
> Her omnipotence sat as challenge
> to those who worshipped others—
> and thus both Anu and Enki
> were sent to depose The Great Mother.

> Cringing before Her powers,
> unable to complete the gruesome mission,
> Anu and Enki returned in defeat,
> until in Babylon under Kassite yoke,
> Marduk demanded promises
> of power and supremacy,
> if he succeeded in murdering The Mother.
> As Indra had murdered Danu,
> so Marduk took the life of Tiamat,
> proud and joyous in the matricide
> that allowed him to sit on heaven's throne,
> bragging of how he had pierced Her belly,
> split Her in two with his evil winds,
> and from Her mutilated body
> had made the heaven and earth—
> thus distorting memory's echoes
> of Goddess Sea's creation of heaven and earth.

ASHERAH

Biblical references to the Goddess as Asherah, and to Her sacred tree or pole symbol, known as the *ashera,* reveal that Asherah was still worshipped in biblical periods. (See I Kings 15:13; II Kings 13:6, 17:9, 21:3, 23: 4-15; Deut. 12:2,3 and Judges 6:30.) The name Asherah probably means Holy Queen, while Her title as Lat, Elat, Elath, or Allat, literally means Goddess. Though most of the information about the Goddess as Asherah comes from the tablets of Ugaritan Canaan of about 1400 B.C., in them Asherah is often invoked as the Goddess of Sidon and Tyre, cities that were also associated with the names of the Goddess as Ashtart and Ishtar, thus linking the reverence for Asherah to Ishtar/Ashtart. Evidence of a Goddess name of Ishara was found in northern Mesopotamia, while at the northern Mesopotamian city of Assur, the most ancient shrine was known as the Asheritu. Located some fifty miles south of the towns of Nineveh and Arpachiyah, this Asheritu was later known as a temple of Ishtar. The epithet of Asherah, as the Goddess Who Walks the Sea, repeated several times in the tablets of Ugarit, suggests possible links with the imagery and traditions of the Goddess as Atargatis.

F rom ancient settlements along the waters, the Tigris, the Euphrates, and the Jordan, Semitic peoples spread across the Levant, often calling upon the Holy Mother as Asherah, Highest Queen—knowing Her as Lat, Elat or Elath, Exalted Mother, Goddess. She was the Holy Lady Who Walked the Sea, remembered even in Arabia, and at Mesopotamian Assur, where the most ancient shrine was the sacred Asheritu.

Mother of all Wisdom, Her ancient oracles of prophesy renowned, She gave the knowledge to diviners, helping them to see far into the future, while they remembered that She alone gave birth to the Seventy Deities of Heaven. In Her sacred groves, they knew Her as She Who Builds, providing the timber of Her trees, teaching Her people the art of carpentry. On the flatness of the land, they knew Her as She Who Builds, providing the clay of the earth, teaching Her people the knowledge of the bricks. So it was that Asherah taught those who revered Her how to build shelters from the heat and cold, and how to build the sacred shrines in which they called upon Her name.

There were those at Ugarit who said that She was married to Thor El, though never did they say that She moved from Her home of the sea, and when they dared to say that Thor El had created creatures, never did they dare to claim that he had been the father of Her seventy holy children, the deities of heaven.

In the many temples that housed Her holy presence, even in Her temple at Jerusalem, Her dedicated women wove the woollen bands of mourning that were wrapped about Her tree, the sacred ashera—as the women of Anatolian Kybele wrapped the woollen mourning bands about the tree upon which Her son lover had died. Thus the sacred ashera tree stood by Her altars, Her holy fruit hanging upon its branches, Goddess symbol so threatening to Gideon and Hezekiah that they rejoiced in destroying it—as they tried to destroy the very memory of Asherah.

Israelite Queen Maacah tried to speak of Asherah to tell the people of Jerusalem that Asherah was The Mother, but for her religious beliefs she found herself evicted from her Judah throne— by those who said that only a father made life.

ANAT

Accounts of Anat (Anath) appear to have developed as a result of the diversity of ethnic groups living in the coastal port of Ugarit, just south of Anatolia. Most of the information about Anat comes to us from the Ugaritan tablets of about 1400 B.C., a time when this city had large populations, not only of Semitic Canaanites, but of Mycenaeans and Hurrians as well. This may explain the increased importance of the consort Baal in the accounts of Anat, as compared to the Tammuz known in the worship of Ishtar, as well as the introduction of the more patriarchal Thor El as a husband to Asherah in the same Ugaritan tablets. There may also have been influence from Ugaritan allies in Hittite Anatolia, and possible links to the image of the Goddess as Anait (see Anatolian Section— Anahita). There is still much scholarly disagreement over the origins and nature of the Hyksos, the group that appears to have introduced the name of Anat into Egypt. Some claim that the Hyksos were Indo-European, while others believe they were Semitic. They may well have been a combination of the two.

Mighty Lady of northern Canaan, infinite and varied was Her holy nature, for even as the accounts of Her power in battle were told in the city of Ugarit, still She was called upon as Mistress of the Lofty Heavens; Ruler of Dominion; Controller of Royalty; Virgin, yet Progenitor of People; Mother of All Nations; Sovereign of All Deities; Ba'Alatu Mulki; Ba'Alatu Darkati; Ba'Alatu Samen Ramen; Strength of Life; She who kills and makes alive again; She who makes union upon the earth, spreading love throughout the land; She who provides well being and increase, even as She carried spear and shield, even as She carried the arrow and bow of battle, even as the earth quivered beneath Her footsteps. And even as Her divinity and name were best known in northern Canaan—still Hathor horns adorned Her holy head, and the sacred symbol of life, the holy ankh of Egypt, was often shown in Anat's hand.

Though Her memory echoes strongest where Semites called upon Her name on the Mediterranean shores of Ugarit, naming cities holy to Her—Anathel, Anathoth, and Beth Anat, there are those who say that She was one with Anahita of the Iranians, with Anait of the Anatolians, with Anatu of the Sumerians, and even with Athena of the Greeks. Pointing out these many connections, it is said that the legends of Her mighty feats, in the town of Canaanite Ugarit, had been embroidered upon by invading northern tribes—still Her most ancient sacred images revealed Her Hathor nature, and declared Her oneness with the Mother of Egypt.

It is true that Mycenaean Greeks from Crete lived in the town of Ugarit, as did their Hurrian cousins, settling as immigrants and merchants in this cosmopolitan trading post. And it is true that they may have brought Her Athena nature with them, for Anat sometimes wore the battle helmet—still She also wore the horns and disc, the wings and headdress of Egypt's Holy Mother, and there are many who say that She was also one with Ba'Alat Ashtart, ivory carvings of Her features reflecting Canaanite images of the Queen of Heaven, as She was known in The Levant.

To confuse the matter further, most claim that it was the Hyksos, the mysterious shepherd kings who invaded Egypt in horse drawn chariots, that brought Her Anat name to Egypt, where it was inscribed in the temple of Denderah, as yet another name for Hathor. So it was that Ramses II and Seti of Egypt called upon Anat's name in battle, while Thutmose the Third spoke of Her as The Strength of Life—even after the Hyksos were expelled. Centuries later, at the Egyptian city of Elephantine, Hebrews prayed to Anat-Jahu, some saying that Jahu was the consort of Anat.

There are those who claim that Anat was the daughter of Asherah, yet it was Anat who pleaded for a temple for Her brother consort Baal, Anat jealous because Asherah and Her kin had many sacred courts of worship, while Baal had none at all. And was it not Anat who predicted that Asherah would rejoice when Her brother Baal was murdered? Though it was written, in the texts of Ugarit, that Asherah entered the Field of Goddesses with Her daughter, to perform the holy rites, there steeping a kid in milk seven times over, the tablets do not speak of the daughter as Anat—but call upon the daughter of Asherah by the name of Rahmai.

Though some prefer to say that Thor El was the leader of all the deities revered at Ugarit, surely we cannot forget the time when he heard Anat approach his home, and in fear and apprehension, he hid himself in the innermost chamber of his house. Nor can we forget that when Anat discovered him, in his place of hiding, She threatened to trample him like a lamb, swearing to turn the grey of his beard red with his own blood—if a temple was not built for Baal.

Great were the powers of Anat, for when She heard of the slaying of brother consort Baal, he who had quaked with fear at the approach of threatening Mot, then met his death at Mot's hands, it was Anat who was strong enough to punish Mot. So it was that Anat seized Mot in Her two great hands, cleaved him in two with a blade, burned him with fire, ground him with a millstone, and threw his remains into a field. Yet Anat's gentleness was seen in Her sorrow at Baal's death. Her grief was said to be as a cow grieves for her dead calf, as an ewe mourns for her dead lamb. And Her revenge against Mot was not without purpose, for soon after Her battle with Mot, Baal was reborn, returning to kneel before Her in a field, admiring Her horns of strength, saying how pleased he was to again be able to look upon them.

Mighty Anat, Mother of Nations, annihilated the god River, muzzled the great dragon, slew the crooked serpent, vanquished fire and flame, and conquered the waters of the flood. When the men of the sunrise, and the men of the seashore, invaded the sanctity of Her temple, Anat hurled chairs and footstools at them, killing those who dared to challenge Her, with the perfect aim of Her bow. And when the battle was over, Anat laughed aloud with the joy of victory, bathing Her hands in the blood of battle, and then in the sacred oil of peace—washing them yet again in the fresh dew of the morning sunrise.

Perhaps as warning, for those who might dare to challenge the powers of the mighty Anat, the story was told of the youth Aqhat, and how Anat had once coveted his bow. Upon the request of the

Goddess to purchase his bow with gold or silver, Aqhat challenged Anat, by asking what need a woman would have for a bow. Thus Her wrathful anger was aroused, Anat swearing to meet him in his path of arrogance, to challenge him in his path of presumption, to hurl him down at Her feet in humility—for suggesting that his marksmanship would surpass that of any woman. Turning to leave Aqhat in the woods, the ground quivered with Her footsteps, as Her words floated sweetly, yet with warning threat in Her farewell, to "my darling he-man."

It was then that She arranged with Her assistant Yatpan, for Yatpan to fly as an eagle over Aqhat's head, and to swoop down from the air to snatch the bow from Aqhat's hands. But the plan did not go well, for as Yatpan descended upon Aqhat, Yatpan's eagle wings struck him so hard that the youth soon died from the blows. Sorrowing at the accident, for Anat had only meant to teach the lad a lesson, Anat hesitated to use the bow of tragedy, and snapped it in two, as symbol of Her mourning—as Aqhat's life had been broken by his lack of humility and respect for the powers of the Goddess.

Reverence for the Goddess as Anat found its way to the island of Cyprus, where Anat was called upon as Lady of Idalion, yet also spoken of as Anait on inscriptions that were later built into the walls of a Cyprian Christian church. Still other stones of Cyprus spoke of the Goddess as Anat-Athene, and Anat-Artemis, while the worship of Anait flourished in the towns of Zela and Ascilicena in the land we know as Turkey, the land once known as Anatolia—perhaps in honour of the invincible Anat.

ALLAT, AL UZZA AND MANAT

Our evidence on the names of the Goddess in Arabia is sparse, most of it coming from accounts of the final destruction of their shrines in the seventh century A.D.—upon the introduction of Islam. Herodotus referred to Allat as the primary Goddess of the Arabians, giving Her name as Alilat. The name Allat is cognate with the title of Asherah as Elat in Canaan. Al Uzza, though most often associated with the planet Venus, was at times described as the star Sirius, sacred star of the Egyptian Goddess as Isis. The name Al Uzza may be connected to the name of the pre-dynastic Egyptian Cobra Goddess, Ua Zit, who was closely linked with the image of Isis, especially at the site of Buto (Per Uto), on the Egyptian Delta.

Along the western coastline of Arabia,
the holy three were known:

Allat, Goddess who glistened
with the brilliance of the sun,
long had Her altars stood in Ta'if
where Her name was called upon as Mother,
until the day Her holy places were destroyed—
and Her ancient Mother being
was all but forgotten.

Al Uzza's light was seen
as the Morning and the Evening Star,
The Mighty One of Mecca,
Her strength emanating
from the Black Stone of the holy Ka'bah shrine,
stone said to be from heaven,
set into the Ka'bah wall
in the heart of sacred Mecca.
As the treasured stone of Ashtart at Byblos,
as the treasured stone of Kybele at Pessinus,
were revered as holy relics of the Goddess,
so too was the Black Stone of Mecca,
visited by pilgrims from far places,
who, naked, walked around it seven times,
kissing or stroking its sacred surface,
then making their way to Hill of Arafat,
to offer holy sacrifice at Mina.

Holy Manat spoke the words of destiny,
deciding fortunes, whether good or bad,
giving life and health as She saw fit,
taking in death when She declared the time.
Thus Her images were kept
upon the altars of each home,
so that all within might call upon Her name,
asking for safety and protection.

HOKHMA

Hokhma (Chokhma, *ch* as in the Gaelic *loch*) is the Hebrew word meaning wisdom. The following piece is adapted from excerpts of *In Praise of Wisdom*, from *The Wisdom of Solomon* in the *Apocrypha* of *The New English Bible*. The Apocrypha contains many texts that were removed from the main body of *The Bible*, the word apocrypha literally meaning hidden. We may want to question why this particular piece of writing, dated to the period of Israel's Solomon (about 900 B.C.), was not included in *The Bible*, in light of the exalted and powerful image of Wisdom as female. Even within *The Wisdom of Solomon*, as it appears today, we may observe possible evidence of attempts to alter the role and status of Hokhma. Such attempts may be the cause of the puzzling sixth paragraph of *In Praise of Wisdom*, which starts out by Solomon explaining that, "wisdom is under God's direction", and "He himself gave me true understanding of things as they are", but ends the long list of all that he had learned with, " . . . for I was taught by her whose skill made all things, wisdom". Throughout the piece, wisdom is repeatedly referred to in anthropomorphic terms, even described as seated by the door. Thus I have taken the liberty of capitalizing the name of Wisdom, whose role may be compared to that of the Egyptian Goddess known as Maat (see Egyptian Section).

Wisdom, She who knows all, shining bright and never fading, is recognized by all who love Her, quick to make Herself known to any who seek to find Her, for She is often seated upon the doorstep, just waiting to be invited in. The prudent will set all their thoughts upon Her, for to lie awake at night, with thoughts of Her upon the sleepless mind, is to find peace of mind more quickly—as She wanders about seeking out those who search, appearing with kindly intention, always meeting each halfway in their purpose.

That which comes from loving Her is the keeping of Her laws, the first of which is to forego pale envy, for from envy there is spite. Wisdom will not make Herself known to the spiteful, but only to those who realize, that compared to Her, all the gold in the world has the value of the sand upon the desert, and compared to Her, all the silver in the world in as common as the clay of the river bank. Her brilliance is greater than the sun, for She never disappears from view, but following Her to each place that She leads one may find riches greater than gold or silver, yet riches beyond count—and that which may comfortably be shared, for always She is there, to lead to more.

It is She who teaches the knowledge of the structure of the world, and of the constant changes of its elements: of the beginning and the end of eras, and the path of going from one end to the other; of the solstice and the equinox; of the changing of the seasons; of the patterns of the years, as the stars create their designs in the heavens; of the natures of animals and beasts, of the wild winds, and of the thoughts of people; of the many wondrous plants, and the purpose of each root—for whether visible or hidden, Wisdom teaches of all that She had made.

Wisdom is the Holy Spirit. She is one and yet She is many, so loose and free moving, so subtle and so light in touch that She is like the mist of the air, moving as easily as motion itself, loving what moves as easily as Herself, beneficence and kindness—as She permeates all with Her ethereal essence. Though they say that She is the brightness that comes forth from the eternal light, and that She is but the flawless mirror of the active power of God, they also say that it is She who continually renews all, as Her power spans the universe and Her kindly orders are always fulfilled; that She decides what God shall do, and that She is the cause of all that occurs.

Temperance and thoughtfulness, justice and strength—these are Her teachings. It is well worth listening to Her advice for She knows all that has happened in the past, as She also knows what is yet to come, and can thus explain the solving of all problems and the settling of all conflict, providing us with the knowledge of what to do through Her many signs and omens. If one follows to each place that She leads, each time doing as She suggests—afterwards there is rest with Her, rest without bitterness or pain, rest with only gladness and joy.

To begin to know Her is pure delight, to become with Her as family is the gaining of immortality. Understanding and eternal honour are won by those who hold converse with Her. Though they say that She sits by throne of God, and that She is his to give or to withhold, yet they also say that She was there in the beginning, at the time of the creation of the universe, and that She is the Holy Spirit that has since stood by us in our needs, forever teaching what would not otherwise be taught.

LILITH

The name of Lilith appears in several Sumerian tablets: in one text as 'the hand of Inanna'; in another as a female figure forced to flee from her home in a tree on the bank of a river. The Sumerian accounts may be linked to the Goddess as She was known in the Sumerian city of Nippur—as Ninlil (see Sumerian Section). Later Babylonian references describe a Lilitu, as a demon of the night air, again suggesting a link with Ninlil, whose name literally means Lady of the Air. The Lilitu texts occur at about the same period as the *Enuma Elish,* the account of the murder of the Goddess as Tiamat, and may be another manifestation of the suppression of Goddess worship. Accounts of Lilith, as the first wife of Adam, appear in the *Talmud* and the *Kabbalah,* but may well be based upon the Babylonian Lilitu—and in turn, a distorted version of the Goddess Ninlil.

How the many reflections of Lilith flicker upon the layered mirrors of time. Her name was once known as the hand of the Goddess Inanna, the one who brought the men of the fields into Inanna's holy temple at Erech. Yet they say there was a Lilith who lived within the huluppu tree, around which a serpent did entwine, until Gilgamish cut down its mighty trunk, from the bank of the river where Inanna had planted it.

Was the woman essence, that we've come to know as Lilith, taken from the ancient holy Ninlil, Goddess who gave the gift of grain, keeper of the divine Dukug grain chamber of the heavens, She who birthed the moon, in the darkness of the Netherworld, She who chose the lad at the holy Tummal shrine in sacred Nippur, Ninlil alone appointing him as shepherd?

Still they give the name of Lilith as the first wife of Adam, saying that she had been made of the dust of the earth, as Adam had been made, but that she left to live a life of her own, when Adam insisted that she lie beneath him—for she refused to be regarded as one inferior to any other. Angered by her independent ways, they then spoke of Lilith in her long absence, deriding her decisive woman strength, her insistence that she would have love only with mutual respect, or would not have love at all, by then saying that it was Lilith who came as a demon of the night, encouraging men to spill their sperm, defying their ideas of the legitimacy of each child who was born. So, into the Kabbalah it was written, that Lilith encouraged children to be born outside of marriage contract, to tug upon the father after he was dead, demanding an inheritance. And though they said that it was the father of such a child who was to bear the pain, they said that it was Lilith who was to blame.

Looking deep into the layers of Lilith mirrors, I see an ancient Goddess, She who brought the gift of agriculture, transformed into a demon; the image of woman as strong and independent degraded for her strength—thus distorted into a temptress of men—even as they admitted that she had chosen well between oppression and freedom.

SHEKHINA

The Shekhina does not appear in *The Bible*, or in the *Apocrypha*, but is regarded as part of Hebrew lore, as described in the *Talmud* and the *Kabbalah*. The Shekhina, which may literally mean being, is used almost synonymously with the figure known as The Bride of the Sabbath, the divine woman image that is to be welcomed on the eve of the Hebrew Sabbath. The word sabbath is derived from the Semitic Akkadian word *shapatu*, meaning the night of the full moon, though some would relate it to a seldom mentioned Sun Goddess known as Shapas, who was entitled Torch of the Deities in Ugaritan texts. Although Shapas was described as a Sun Goddess, the Akkadian Shapatu rituals were held on the night of the full moon, later on both full moon and new moon. The concept of The Shekhina appears to be a combination of a desire for the return of a divine female image within Judaism, while simultaneously embodying the hopes for better days for the Jewish people.

Holy Shekhina,
perfect reflection of woman being
whose image appears upon seeking the highest holiness,
too long has She been in exile,
too long have Her people
sorrowed at Her absence,
for since the burning of Her sanctuary,
She has been seen at the wailing wall,
clad in black and weeping.
Yet She may be found
in the field of holy fruit trees,
Her orchards ever sacred in memory—
and thus She is begged to return.

Perhaps She is one
with the Queen of the Sabbath,
Shabbat Bride of the Kabbalah,
perhaps once known as Shapatu
and seen in the silver of the moon,
for was She not once welcomed by Semitic peoples
and honour paid to Her sacred being
when first She arrived
as a thin young crescent
in the dark heaven,
and again, when in Her full glory,
Her perfect glowing roundness
cast silver flecks upon the leaves
of Her sacred grove?

Still the candles are lit,
still the sacred braided loaf is baked,
in hopes that Her ancient Sabbath spirit
will enter each home—
filling it with the Mother love
that is the very presence of the Shekhina.

Remind Them of the Sekpoli
Africa

I f any area of the world was to be regarded as the true home of the Goddess as The Mother of people, the extreme antiquity of human development on the continent of Africa must give highest priority to this area. Among the lakes and snow peaked mountains of Tanzania and Kenya lived the ancient ones who were the foremothers of the human species. Whether She was called upon as Mawu, Ala, Songi, Mbaba Mwana Waresa, Bomu Rambi, Jezanna, Mboze, Ngame, Nyame, Nuneit, Niachero, Amauneit, or Neit—it seems quite certain that it was on the soil of Africa that life came forth from the first human mother—the Divine Ancestress of all people.

In reading the accounts of reverence for the Goddess, and the legends of heroines from Africa that are included in this section, it is important to keep in mind that Africa is a vast continent. It stretches over five thousand miles from east to west and over five thousand miles from south to north. The material included here is but a small representation of the religious lore of the many diverse cultures that inhabit the African continent today. Perhaps even more significant is the fact that Africa has a history of human habitation (of homo sapiens and pre-homo sapiens) longer than any other area of the world. Since the accounts to which we have access are those which have been recorded over the relatively recent period of the last two centuries, it seems only reasonable to assume that they have probably undergone considerable transitions since their initial development; yet within them may be the core of very ancient traditions and beliefs.

Evidence of pre-homo sapiens in Africa takes us back several million years—to the hominids of Olduvai Gorge in Tanzania and Kafuan in Kenya. The earliest human made tools, so far discovered anywhere on earth, were made in these areas. The members of the Lower Paleolithic culture known as Abbevillian, which originated in central Africa, are generally regarded as descendants of those most ancient hominids. It was the Abbevillian culture that spread across Africa, eventually introducing the concept of toolmaking into Europe and the Near and Middle East.

Some scholars suggest that later groups from Africa may have influenced the Upper Paleolithic Age of France and Spain, the era of cave paintings and Goddess Venus figures of about 30,000 to 15,000 B.C. These suggestions are based upon the evidence of paintings and incised drawings found in caves of southern Africa, Zimbabwe, parts of Morocco and Libya, and around the Sahara. The characteristics of the bone structure of skeletal remains found in Europe, such as the burial at the cave of the Grotte des Enfants in Grimaldi which show definite black African characteristics, support these hypotheses. The Grimaldi burial was of an elderly woman and a young male, both richly decorated with necklaces, while the woman had worn a skirt and headdress ornamented with shells. The combination of the very early Abbevillian entry into Europe; the evidence of later skeletal remains; and similarities between the cave art of Africa and that of France and Spain, suggests the need for a more careful examination of the role that groups from the African continent played in the cultural development of both the Lower and Upper Paleolithic periods of Europe.

In considering the following accounts, we are then aware that we are discussing many widely separated, extremely diverse cultures, some apparently of exceptional geographical stability. Thus it is not too surprising to find that the images of the Goddess, and the actions and symbolism attributed to Her, vary from the exalted position of the Goddess Mawu as Creator of the world and life among the people of Dahomey, to the Goddess as the Moon in the accounts of the Mashona and Buhera Ba Rowzi people of Zimbabwe, while the Zulu of Natal and the Woyo of Zaire both regard the Goddess as She who sends the rain. Still, we may do well to keep in mind that these were the attributes and symbols stressed in the accounts as they have been recorded—most often by people of Caucasian European heritage—and do not necessarily provide us with a full picture of the Goddess as She was actually known by each group of people.

A theme that seems to thread its way through these particular accounts is that of a testing of human values. Nsomeka was unique in her helpfulness at home and in her independent fortitude. Mella was endowed with similar qualities with the addition of exceptional courage and perseverance. Notambu, High Priestess of the Moon Goddess Jezanna among the Mashona, trusted her own inner sense of morality and challenged the very structure of her own religious beliefs—to find that she alone had truly understood and properly interpreted the wishes of the Goddess. Men were not exempt from this testing. The chosen mate of Mbaba Mwana Waresa, Goddess among the Zulu of Natal, was tested to assure the Goddess that his values would allow him to perceive the difference between what is important and what is superficial. Awe, and the brothers of Mella, found that bragging and stealing were not acceptable to those who revered the Goddess. The concept of being tested by divine powers may be observed in the religious beliefs of other cultures, such as in the account of the near sacrifice of Isaac by his father Abraham, as recorded in the Bible, but in the accounts of the Goddess in Africa the test is usually in connection with an explanation of a moral truth, rather than a test of the blind obedience of a worshipper. In this context, the story of Notambu is all the more interesting in that the inner sense of morality is held higher than the following of structured religious ritual.

As in the spiritual or religious imagery of many cultures, the dwelling place of the Goddess in Africa was often described as being much like the shelters or environments of those who revered Her. Thus the Goddess may live in a small house, such as Mbaba Mwana Waresa or Songi, or in a jungle in heaven, the description of the home of the mighty creator Mawu. But the audience or reader of such descriptions soon realizes that these dwellings were understood to be endowed with qualities beyond the worshipper's earthly home—Mbaba Mwana Waresa's with an ever glowing rainbow on the roof, Songi's filled with a strange light.

Another point of perspective, on the antiquity of the cultural heritage of the African continent, may be gained from the accounts of the worship of the Goddess in ancient Egypt (see Egyptian Section). Quite a few references in Egyptian texts associate the worship of the Goddess as Hathor, especially in the form of a lion, with the land of Nubia. The Goddess as Hekit, well known to the Egyptians, was described as having come from Nubia. Connections between Egypt and the lands surrounding it should not be overlooked. Few people realize that the name Libya, mentioned repeatedly in Classical Greek texts, did not always indicate just the land we know as Libya today. At about 450 B.C., Herodotus wrote, "As for Libya, we know that it is washed on all sides by the sea except where it joins Asia." (Book 4). Herodotus explained that a ship sent by the Egyptians, though the crew was Phoenician, left from the Arabian Gulf, sailed " . . . around the tip of Libya . . . ", and re-entered the Mediterranean by sailing eastwards into the Straits of Gibraltar. In Book 2, Herodotus wrote, "The Nile flows from Libya . . . ", adding that "nobody knows anything about the source of the Nile because that river runs through a part of Libya which is uninhabited and desert." Thus, according to Herodotus, Libya (with the exception of Egypt) was the name for *all* of Africa to the extent that it was known to the Greeks.

Once aware of this ancient use of the name Libya, the accounts of Diodorus Siculus, that the Amazons of Anatolia had originally come from Libya—as well as the many other Classical references to Libya—may be seen in a different light. Nineteenth century accounts of the woman warriors of Dahomey, and of women warriors among the Lunda and Gager tribes of Zaire, should be examined more carefully. Any exploration of Amazons in "Libya" might do well to include the account by Apollonius, that Amazons lived and worshipped the Goddess in the area of Colchis. Although Colchis is located on the eastern end of the Black Sea, Herodotus recorded that the people of Colchis had come from Egypt. This ancient definition of Libya may also be of interest in studies of accounts of the origins of the Goddess as Athena, who was said to have been *born* on the shores of Lake Tritonis in *Libya*. It may be significant that Greek accounts mention Libya as the name of a female figure linked to the tale of Europa, the woman who was taken from the city of Tyre in Canaan to the island of Crete, a legend that has most often been explained as an allegory of the migration of the worship of the Goddess from Canaan to Crete. The woman named Libya was described as Europa's *grandmother.*

In many areas of Africa, carved ceremonial figures of the Goddess reveal the widespread reverence for Her, though various names, attributes and legends may be described. Studies among the Ashanti of Ghana reveal their reverence for the Goddess as Nyame, a name closely related to the Akan of Ghana's worship of the Goddess as Ngame. The matrilineal descent patterns among the Ashanti, known as the *abusua,* results in the special importance attached to the birth of female infants among them.

One intriguing sidelight, of the exploration of Goddess reverence among the many peoples of Africa, is the association of religious ritual with the bright star Sirius by the Dogon peoples of Mali. Sirius (Sept) was regarded as the sacred star of the Egyptian Goddess Au Sept (known as Isis to the Greeks). The reverence for Sirius brings to mind the accounts of the Semites of Mesopotamia, that the Goddess as Ishtar had descended from the planet Venus, along with Her retinue of holy women. The connection of the Goddess with a star is also to be observed in the Semitic account from Canaan—that the Goddess had descended as a fiery falling star that landed in the lake of Aphaca, near Byblos in Lebanon. This lake was later regarded as sacred, and an important shrine was built nearby. The Alur people of Zaire also have an account of a divine woman descending from a star. Niachero, known as 'The Daughter of the Star', was said to have arrived upon earth near a great mountain, later returning to heaven by standing upon the mountain peak. These concepts may also be compared to the Goddess in India as Tara, Tara meaning star.

The sacred lake, the Davisa, that was so inherent a part of the worship of Jezanna among the Mashona, offers an interesting parallel to the sacred lakes of the Goddess among the Semites. The recurring image of the Goddess as a being of the waters, or emerging from the waters, lake, river, or ocean, exists in cultures as diverse as the Woyo of Angola, the Chibcha of Colombia, the Sumerians of southern Mesopotamia, the Peruvians of the Andes, the Semites of Canaan and Mesopotamia, the Tantric groups of India, the Greeks of Cyprus and Greece, and the Celts of western Europe. The relationship of the star to the sacred lake appears specifically in the accounts of Semitic Aphaca, but Egyptian texts from Hermopolis, describing the original creation as occurring on a flaming island in a lake, may be linked to the Aphaca accounts. One cannot help but be reminded of an epithet often applied to the later Virgin Mary of Christianity, Stella Maris, Star of the Waters.

Whatever the original meanings or intended symbolism of the imagery of star and waters, it is perhaps the human values of honesty, courage, and concern for others, that emerge most clearly in the accounts of the Goddess on the continent that saw the dawn of human life.

MAWU

The powers of Mawu are those of the omnipotent creator of all life. But the accounts of Mawu also reveal specific theological concepts that are an integral part of the belief in Mawu among the Dahomey peoples of western Africa. The concept of the *Sekpoli,* which may best be defined as soul, goes beyond western theological contemplation of the soul in the explanation that it is because of the existence of the Sekpoli, as a *part* of Mawu in every person, that aggression and fighting are wrong. The account also makes it clear that although magic may be useful or impressive, it is insignificant in comparison with the overwhelming powers of Mawu. So important is the emphasis on human humility, and acceptance of the fact that it is the Goddess Mawu who holds supreme power, that when the miracle of new life is not enough to convince the unbelieving, death is then added as further proof. The account of Awe challenging the powers of Mawu may bring to mind the recent efforts to gain control of the birthing of new life, a desire that has apparently been on the minds of some men for a long time. We may want to consider why the fertilizing of an egg (from a woman) in a test tube (then returned to the womb of a woman to gestate for nine months) has been hailed as such a marvelous and astounding feat, while the daily repeated miracles of pregnancy and birth have been so trivialized in our society. If Awe is once again throwing his balls of thread into Mawu's heaven, what results will his challenges bring this time?

Riding high in Aido Hwedo's mouth, as if on the back of an elephant, Mawu, Mother of All, Mawu, created the mountains, the valleys, the rivers. She created all, all, all! Do you sometimes wonder why the mountains curve? Why the valleys dip? Why the rivers twist and wind as they flow? These are the paths that Mawu took as the primeval serpent, the faithful Aido Hwedo, slithered over the earth, carrying Mawu in its giant reptilian jaws.

At first it was dark, so very dark that one could hardly see. Then with Her magic, Mawu made the fire, great wondrous light that brings each day, and set it in the heavens, high over the earth— so that She might better view all that She had made. In the light, Mawu saw the vastness of Her works, felt the joy of Her creation, tingled with the pleasure of contemplating the beauty She had made. But soon She worried about how much weight the earth could hold and thus She spoke to Aido Hwedo, 'Crawl beneath the earth. Curl yourself up as round as a reed mat and like a platter that holds the food upon it, hold up the weight of the earth so that it shall never fall. I have created massive mountains, heavy hills and tall trees, elephants and giraffes, lions and zebras. The earth is heavy with my creation and you must hold it up.' Thus Aido Hwedo crawled beneath the earth and lies there still.

Mawu called to a monkey as he sat upon a branch and these words She spoke to him: 'Out of the clay I have formed you, breathed life into your earthen body; carefully did I shape your fingers and now the time has come for you to use them. From the clay you must form other animals. They may be of your own design, with feathers or with fur, with two legs or with four. I shall return to breathe the breath of life into each. When you have completed your task, you shall be rewarded well for I shall help you to stand as erect as the humans I have formed, so that your hands shall be free to use, even as you walk.'

But when Mawu returned to see the work that the monkey had done, the monkey was not there. She stood before the pile of clay. Not a leg, not a feather—the clay remained as clay. The monkey had scampered off to brag to the other animals in the jungle of his great fortune-to-be. What use are hands, Mawu wondered, to one who only cares to twine his tail about the leafy branches and to boast to all his neighbors of what he has not yet accomplished? What use are hands, Mawu wondered, to one who has allowed his chance to aid in the Creation to slip by unfulfilled? Forever shall he remain a monkey and use his hands to walk. So Mawu then decreed—and so it has been for monkeys until this very day.

Gbadu, Holy Daughter Gbadu, She who Mawu made first, sat upon the tallest palm guarding Mawu's work. Up She looked and saw the heavens. Out She looked and saw the sea. Down she looked and saw the earth. Everywhere, Gbadu saw sadness and turmoil, fighting on the earth, fighting on the sea. The people of Dahomey had forgotten the teachings of Her Mother, the divine words of Mawu. Thus Gbadu spoke to her children, 'Your Grandmother Mawu has made the people. She has given them life and the earth on which to live it—but they have forgotten Her wisdom. You must go and teach them as I have taught you, as Mawu once taught me. Remind them of the Sekpoli, that essence of life that is the gift of Mawu—so that to fight with another is to fight with another part of Mawu.'

Then Gbadu spoke to Her own eldest daughter, 'Minona, you shall be known upon earth. You shall be holy among women for teaching the omens of the palm kernels so that the people may know what is to come and who is to die and who is to be born. She who learns to read the palm kernels shall gain the knowledge of the unfolding of each day and thus will Mawu's word be known, so that the people of Dahomey will be wise once again.'

The children of Gbadu wandered the lands of Dahomey, teaching of Mawu and the Sekpoli, Minona teaching of the omens, until the wisdom of Mawu was known by nearly all. But Awe, boastful braggard Awe, said that he was as great, as great as Mawu, as powerful as the Mother of All and that he too could make life, as everyone believed that only Mawu could do. Soon the others began to listen to Awe, for he made miracles and strange magic. 'Can Mawu's magic be superiour to mine?' he asked. 'I shall stand before Her in heaven and prove that I am as mighty as Mawu!' Awe challenged the powers of Mawu. Awe challenged the powers of Mawu. Was Awe as great?

Into the sky Awe threw two balls of thread. The others stood and gasped as the threads of cocoon silk rose further and further into the heavens until Mawu's great hands reached out and easily caught the balls of thread whose ends still touched the earth. Truly Awe was great, they said, for who else could throw so high and with the same astonishment, they watched as Awe climbed the silken threads up through the clouds until he reached the heaven of Mawu. And there, in the highest heaven of all—Awe challenged the powers of Mawu. Awe challenged the powers of Mawu. Was Awe as great?

In the jungle of heaven, Awe chopped down a fine round tree. Back and forth with a sharp rock, Awe made the branches leave the tree and in the trunk that was left, he made eyes, he made a mouth, a belly, arms and even fingers. Awe was making a person. When Awe had finished down to the toes he looked up at Mawu and said, 'I have created a person.' Only Mawu could make a person. Was Awe as great?

'Why does Awe's person not smile? Why does Awe's person not walk? Can it dance and chant for you?' asked Mawu. 'Breathe into it Awe. If you are truly as great as Mawu, give it the breath of life. Give it a Sekpoli.' Awe took a deep breath so that his chest grew large and then he breathed out so hard that the leaves of heaven quivered for miles—but his person still lay upon the ground, not moving. Again he made his chest great and again he blew. This time his breath made such a wind that the statue stirred. But when the wind calmed down the person of Awe lay as lifeless as ever.

Two more times he tried, then bent his head in shame and defeat. Awe had failed. He had to admit that only Mawu could make life. But Mawu was wise. She knew that boastful, braggard Awe would soon forget his shame and once returned to earth, his boasts would be bigger than ever. Those who listened might again be deceived. Thus Mawu cooked a meal for Awe. First planting a seed in the ground, the instantly sprouting wheat was made into a bowl of cereal for Awe and Awe ate until the bowl was empty—not knowing what he had eaten.

In his porridge had been the seed of death.
Awe had eaten the seed of death.

His belly filled with the cereal, Awe began to descend the ladder of threads to return to the earth below. It was then that Mawu told him of the seed and why She had fed it to him. 'Remind them', She said, 'Remind them that you may use your human charms and potions, that you may make your amulets and magic but only Mawu, only Mother Mawu, can breathe the breath of life into each—and will suck it out when She chooses.'

So it happened that Mawu, Mother of All, sent the first seed of death down to earth with Awe so that people would never again doubt Mawu's omnipotent power. Thus those who are wise, treasure the Sekpoli in each and know that it is from Mawu, *only Mawu,* that we receive the gift of the breath of life.

ALA

Though the information that I was able to find on the Goddess of the Ibo people of Nigeria is scanty, it does reveal several major attributes of the nature of Her importance. Ala is both the provider of life and the Mother who receives again in death, both attributes revealing Her high position among the people who revere Her. It is also Ala who proclaims the law that is the basis for all moral human behaviour. In this last attribute, we may see a concept of the Goddess such as that found in the images of Demeter and Isis as providers of the law, or perhaps the understanding that the Mother of all explains the law through Her works, a theological concept close to that found in China. Most interesting is the custom of having life-size images of Ala sitting on the porch of a small wooden house in the village, visible to all who pass by. This custom may well be one that grew from the worship of the Goddess as ancestress or grandmother, Her image and spirit still dwelling in the village.

Holy Mother Earth,
She who guides those who live upon Her,
She whose laws the people of the Ibo follow,
living in the honesty and rightness
that are the ways of Goddess Ala;
it is She who brings the child to the womb
and She who gives it life,
always present during life
and receiving those whose lives are ended,
taking them back into Her sacred womb,
"the Pocket of Ala".

Along the Benue River
where the waters slide into the mighty Niger
and through its many fingers,
flow into the sea,
the women and the men
join in building the Mbari,
sacred houses where Goddess Ala
may sit upon the porch,
child upon Her knee,
sword sometimes in Her hand,
looking out upon the Ibo world
as the Ibo look upon Her—
glad that She dwells close by.

JEZANNA

The practice of human sacrifice appears in accounts of many ancient peoples, in cultures as diverse as the Celts to the Carthaginians. Here we have the sacred narrative of how this ritual came to an end among the Mashona people of Zimbabwe. The ritual of mourning, for the one sacrificed, invites interesting comparisons with the ritual mourning ceremonies of Sumer, Egypt, Babylon, Anatolia and even the Christian Easter. What is of particular interest here is the reverence for the Goddess as The Moon, and that the primary representative of the Goddess on earth is Her High Priestess. In considering the concept and purposes of the sacred lake, the Davisa, we may find interesting parallels in the Near East, especially among the worshippers of Ashtart (see Semitic Section).

Among the elders of the proud Mashona people, lingers the oft told memory of times so long ago, of the holy woman Notambu, High Priestess of the glowing Jezanna, She who shows Herself as the golden moon. Standing by the waters of the sacred Davisa where golden Jezanna's image dwells at night, the women and the men gather by the shore and listen as they have listened so many times before, to the ancient story of Notambu and how she gave Jezanna's wisdom to the great Mashona people:

In the quiet rippling waters, filled with the darkness of the night, the wetness of Notambu's body glistened in the moonlight, her skin as wondrous dark as the sky, her voice as soft as the gentle cresting of the sacred lake, as she recited the prayers of the Mashona, asking Jezanna for abundant crops, plentiful cattle, healthy children. Notambu knew Jezanna's answers when She joined Notambu in the waters, Her perfect circle being glistening close to where Notambu stood.

When the time for the holiest of festivals arrived, that which would pay Jezanna greatest honours, when each would say their prayers of gratitude and ask Jezanna for one more year of blessings, Notambu readied herself for her role in the procession. It was she who would lead the rest, she who would conduct the sacred ceremonies, that which she had never done before, for only seven moons ago had Notambu been chosen as High Priestess to Jezanna.

142

As Notambu made her preparations, the Nganga too made ready for the ancient rites. Watching for the fullness of the moon, the one that preceded the roundness of the full moon of the festival, the Nganga entered the jungle when Jezanna's light glowed brilliantly in the heavens, to live there for the full month's time—eating only the meat of the crocodiles, sitting in silent meditation, hearing no human voice, not even his own, thus purifying his body and his mind.

The ceremonies began in the sunshine as the people gathered in the village clearing, each finding their place in the line that was forming. Young ones, old ones, women with children at their breasts, followed the lead of the Nganga, who, knees bent, danced from side to side, shaking and swinging the zebra tail switch, his high piercing wail spearing into the brightness of the day. He in turn, followed the holy Notambu whose body stood as the straightest tree, whose head was held high as if her graceful neck might reach the heavens, the golden disc upon her forehead glistening in the sun, as she led the long procession along the path that wound its way to the Davisa.

The mournful cry of pipes of reed mingled with the shrill sound of the Nganga, while sobbing drumbeats fell upon the earth, as the heaviest of fruits cry out when they fall from mother tree. Voices sympathized with instruments of sorrow, singing the familiar hymns of the child that would die for others, the holy child, the perfect child, bright and healthy, with the promise of the future gleaming from its deep brown eyes. And there were songs of the sadness of the mother, whose tears of grievous lamentation would bring the tears of the very heavens to rain upon the planted seeds—so that the crops would grow and bountiful abundance would be ensured for the Mashona.

As Notambu grew closer to the waters of the Davisa, her vision of the mother and the child, standing in solemn silence at the shore, grew larger, ever larger, until the mother's size was as her own in closeness. Halting the procession where she stood, the eyes of Notambu touched those of the mother and the child. The pipes and drums and voices made a sudden silence that was louder than any sound that she had ever heard before. She watched the Nganga as he reached to take the child's hand, laying her down on the flat rock altar, drawing out his sacred knife, an act that once again raised the sound of the drums, beating even louder, even faster than before.

143

Notambu remembered other years and other tears but never had she been so close, as her eyes locked with the eyes of the little one who lay upon the flat grey stone, shining brown circles of terror betraying the calmness of her mouth. Questions rose in Notambu's heart for who knew Jezanna better than she and knew that the gentle light which had joined her in the sacred lake so many times, could never, would never, have asked that this child's life be taken to make the lives of others better. From Notambu's throat, where holy sacrificial chant was expected to rise, no sound came forth— but to Notambu's body came the message that she must speak with her arms.

Quickly sweeping the child from the altar, she held its shaking smallness to her chest. Notambu's strong brown arms wrapped about the little one in defiant gesture as the Nganga shrieked his anger, wildly waving his zebra tail in menacing threat to any who would dare to defy the ancient ritual. Notambu took not one step forward. Notambu took not one step back. But those who stood close by saw her look up into the afternoon sky and heard her whispered plea, 'Jezanna! Jezanna!'

Deep breaths of astonishment, backward steps of awe, rippled among the villagers, those who had now gathered about the empty altar, while in the sky where the sun still shone, the holy circle of the moon, glowing as the flames glow, marvelously luminous and large, suddenly appeared in the heavens, closer than Jezanna had ever been before. As Notambu raised her face to the scarlet moon, the disc upon her forehead reflecting Jezanna's fire, a gentle smile formed across her mouth and in the stillness of the moment, Notambu's voice came forth as clear and as gentle as the ripples of the sacred lake.

'Listen. She speaks to us. Jezanna tells us that the child must live—that never again should the life of any child be taken for our own comfort and abundance. These are the wishes of the great Jezanna.' As Notambu's voice floated over the waters and echoed back again to all who were gathered by the banks of the sacred lake, she set the child down to stand upon the earth. It was then that she saw that the terror and the anger that had covered the Nganga's face just moments earlier had been replaced by a surprising relief at Jezanna's word.

Ceremony turned to joyous laughter as those who had sung in lamentation now clapped their hands and moved about in a dance of exultation, gratefully rejoicing at Jezanna's decree. The little one stood close by Notambu's side until the darkness of the evening sky crept in from the east and when Jezanna saw that all was well, She floated back up into the heavens, Her fiery redness calming to a distant glow, Her satisfaction with the Mashona people sparkling like diamonds in Her radiant being.

Some say that when the little girl grew old, long after Notambu had been laid to rest, it was she who was the grandmother who saved the cattle of the tribe from the flames of the great fire. Others say that when the moon is full, those who walk to the Davisa might still catch a glimpse of Notambu and the little girl bathing in the holy waters, while Jezanna, filled with pleasure, dances by their side. But all agree that what they once believed were tears of sorrow that rained upon the crops of the Mashona, must now be known as tears of joy, for no life has been taken since that time, yet rains still fall from heaven—and the crops of the Mashona grow even taller than before.

SONGI

The large nation of Bantu peoples are represented throughout central and southern Africa. The name Bantu (Ba Ntu) is actually a language distinction such as Celtic or Semitic. It literally means the people. The languages known as Swahili and Zulu are part of the Bantu groups. This account, of why the women of the Bantu peoples developed the custom of notching their teeth, is one that speaks on many levels. Not only does it explain the origin of the custom, and the beliefs associated with it, but we may also observe the emphasis on the correctness of Nsomeka's actions—why she of all the young women of the village was singled out for such a special mission. We may also observe the knowledgeable acceptance of the fact that when the women own the lands, the home, and the property, men are more careful to treat them with respect.

Making the porridge, grinding the grains—poor Nsomeka, tired Nsomeka. All the children have run off to play but in the home of her mother, Nsomeka makes the porridge, Nsomeka grinds the grains—poor Nsomeka, sad Nsomeka. The work is done; she looks about but they are gone—swift Nsomeka, fleet Nsomeka—bounds as a zebra across the yellow grass, like a bird she flies over the ferns of the jungle—the almost invisible path reappearing, disappearing, reappearing. Tired from the morning's work, she runs and runs and runs, hoping all the way for a glimpse of the last straggler of the friends who could not wait.

Deep in the jungle, there is someone—but not the friends she seeks. A tall woman, an old woman, stands in the middle of the path. 'What is the rush, Nsomeka?' the woman asks, 'What makes you gallop as if you were on four legs instead of two?' Grateful for the chance to rest, Nsomeka stops to take a deep breath into her small chest and asks the old woman if she has seen the children pass by.

It is the wrong path, the wrong path, Nsomeka thinks, noticing the small house by the side of the road, wondering if it was there when she first stopped running. The offer of a cool drink takes Nsomeka through the doorway, her eyes greeted by a strange glow, her feet greeted by the softness of a reed mat. 'I have been here all day and no one else has passed by', the woman tells her gently, and then as if Nsomeka had spoken her thoughts aloud, the woman adds, 'But this is not the wrong path. You have come the right way. You have come to the house of Songi—The Mother.'

Sipping upon a cool drink, Nsomeka hears the woman say, 'The path was yours, made by your swift feet and your good heart. Someday you will lead your tribe but there is work that you must do first. No more shall the husbands beat their wives; no more shall they order them about. No more shall the women cry. Songi will protect Her daughters, if Nsomeka will help. Come sit down, my child.'

As Nsomeka sets her eyes upon a basket, Songi lifts the lid, allowing a small spotted snake to crawl about Her arm. Nsomeka sits in silence as Songi takes her hand—and shoulder to shoulder, Songi presses Her great arm against the child arm of Nsomeka, the snake winding about to bind the two arms together and thus entwined they sit. Then taking a rough white stone from a small wooden box, Songi begins to file notches in the teeth of Nsomeka— brave Nsomeka, fearless Nsomeka.

what is the rush,
Nsomeka?

Making her way back to the home of her mother, once the notching had been done, Nsomeka takes her mother's hand, gently pulling her as the child pulls the one who has given them life. Nsomeka leading, they walk along the path to her grandmother's home. And calling to her mother's mother, soon all three, daughter, mother, grandmother, stand together in the field, the sun cut in half by the great western mountain, welcoming the arrival of evening. So it is that the three stand together in the darkening field and when Nsomeka says that they must sing—three voices sing in chorus.

Hardly has the evening star arrived, when from between the notches of Nsomeka's teeth come cattle, come chickens, come pigs, come goats. The three continue to sing. Great fruit trees pass through the notches and root in the ground before them. The three continue to sing. Large reed houses, tied well and strong, fly out through Nsomeka's teeth, landing near the trees that will shade them from the hot daytime sun—sweet voiced Nsomeka, perfect voiced Nsomeka.

In the morning when the sleeping villagers awake, they can not believe what they see with their eyes. Hearing that this great wealth has come from Nsomeka, the men begin to beat their wives for not having brought them such riches, but Nsomeka calls to the crying women, beckoning them to join her. Thus the women gather with her in the field, the field where the three had sung, the field now filled with houses and trees and livestock—listening as Nsomeka tells the story of Songi and how and why Songi notched her teeth.

From the oldest to the youngest, one by one, the teeth of the women are notched by Nsomeka, her mother and her grandmother—so that each will be marked with the sign of Songi's protection. Filling with uncontainable curiosity, one by one, the watching men begin to enter the women's field. It is then that they see The Notches of Songi and know that it is Songi's village. Here they can not beat their wives nor order them about but so great is the desire of the men for the houses and fruit and livestock, so much do they want to stay, that they promise to treat the women with respect.

So it is that to this day the Bantu women are grateful for the life of Nsomeka who brought them under the protection of the Great Mother Songi—sacred Nsomeka, blessed Nsomeka.

MBOZE AND BUNZI

This image of the Rain Goddess, as the daughter of the original First Mother and Her son, from the Woyo people of Zaire, suggests that this account may have developed to explain the name of Bunzi replacing that of Mboze. Yet the image of the rainbow serpent, as the deity of rain, may be extremely ancient. It brings to mind the Rainbow Serpent of Australia who helps The Mother by providing nurturing rain. There are also hints of the relationship between the serpent and rain in the account of Fire Woman from Borneo (see Oceanic Section). Though the likelihood is rather slim, it is tempting to wonder if the concept of the Rainbow Serpent may be as old as the period in which the Australoids of Africa, Australia and Borneo, were a more cohesive group of people. Fire Woman also takes Her son as a mate, but with less dire consequences.

First there was The Mother,
fertile nurturing Mboze,
who watched over the people
who lived at the mouth of the great river
where it mingled with the waters of the ocean.
Taking Her son Makanga as Her lover,
Mboze swelled with new life
but as She brought forth
Her sacred serpent daughter Bunzi,
Her husband Kuitikuiti,
he who had changed his black skin for a white one,
grew furious upon learning
that Makanga was the father
and beat Mboze with such violence
that She finally sought peace in death.

As Bunzi grew older,
She learned to do the work
that had once been Her mother's,
pouring the rain from the heavens,

causing the fruit and nuts to grow.
Her brilliance was seen
in the many colours of the rainbow
as it arched across the sky,
Bunzi watching joyfully
after She had sent the welcome rain.
Yet those who sing and dance for Bunzi
and call upon Her gracious gifts,
do so in the wondrous darkness of the night
when Bunzi can be seen in the reflections
upon the opalescent serpents of the river,
the rainbow shining upon their skin,
as Bunzi promises the rains of abundance.

MBABA MWANA WARESA

This account, from the Zulu people of Natal, of how the Goddess came to
take a mate, includes a detailed description of the careful preparations
made for a marriage among the Zulu peoples. But the theme of the
narrative is the testing of the abilities of the one chosen, to be able to see
through the superficialities of such elaborate preparations, thus explaining
the greater importance of recognizing what is truly valuable. This account
may offer us some insight into a system of basic human values that western
thought has either forgotten or has yet to learn.

Sacred Goddess of the light that streaks across the skies, sacred
Goddess who beats upon the drums of heaven, sacred Goddess who
pours the waters from Her heavenly home roofed with rainbow
arches, sacred Goddess who makes the forest green, filling the fields
with grass for grazing, making the crops grow ever taller, sacred
Goddess who taught us how to sow and reap, sacred Goddess who

gave us the gift of beer so that we might celebrate our times of joy—Holy Rain Goddess of the Heavens, Mbaba Mwana Waresa, how dear to our hearts you are.

In the roundness of the thatched hut, listening to the rain that falls upon the leaves, the story of the marriage of the Rain Goddess pours forth from the mouths of the elders who remind us of the time when the Goddess decided to take a husband and when none in heaven took Her fancy, She chose a mortal youth, the most beautiful, the most wise, that She could find upon the earth. Thus the holy ones of heaven arranged the marriage that would take place in his village, before they returned together to Her home in the heavens:

When the sun of the wedding day peered above the eastern mountains, the Goddess prepared for the ceremonies in a way that astonished those who lived in heaven, choosing to shave the feather soft black hair of Her head, choosing to smear Her perfect black body with pale grey ashes, choosing to cast off Her rainbow coloured skirt and to dress in the torn skin of a zebra hide—while the friend that She had chosen to be attendant at the wedding was dressed as a Zulu bride is dressed.

The finest cloths were wrapped about the body of Her friend, her hair was twined into delicate braids, each braid laced through with precious beads; gold and silver bands circled about her wrists and ankles; sacred dyes were painted carefully upon her cheeks and forehead; a beaded belt was tied about her waist; glistening stones hung on thin copper wires in the warmth beneath her arms to jingle gently when she moved; great golden hoops were hung upon her ears; and the sacred curving wombshell of life was hung upon her forehead.

When all was ready, the Goddess and Her friend began their heavenly journey that would lead them to the village where the lad that was the chosen one of Mbaba Mwana Waresa lived, waiting for the day that the Goddess would arrive. Suddenly the sky above his home grew dark with storm; sharp branches of lightning shot through the heavens; thunder crashed above his head—and in this way the anxious lad knew that She who was to take him as Her husband, would soon be by his side. Looking up into the darkened sky, the fellow saw two women approaching and as he stood and watched, filled with the wonder of his wedding day, the rains of plenty and good fortune fell cool upon him as he waited.

The lad bowed low with reverence as the two women finally stood before his home, while the women of the village, those who had been chosen as the earthly attendants of the bride, watched to see if he would know which of the women was to be his wife. So it was that smiles broke upon their faces when he put his hand out to the Goddess, though Her head was shaved, though ashes made Her body grey, though She wore the torn hide of a zebra, and he softly said, 'Welcome Mbaba Mwana Waresa, Holy Goddess of the Rain, you need no beads nor gold nor silver, nor fine soft cloths wrapped about your body, for in your sparkling eyes I see the richness of the earth, the fruitfulness of the growing land, the beauty of the joyous harvest, the power of the thunder and the lightning—how deeply I am honoured that you have chosen me.'

Thus the ceremonies filled the day, dance and food and drink of celebration surrounded the Rain Goddess as She stood upon the earth and when the wedding day had ended, She took the lad, whose wisdom was in seeing truth, back to Her home in the heavens and lives there with him still.

MELLA

Although the moon, as the Goddess Bomu Rambi, is mentioned tangentially in this account of the heroine Mella, this is primarily a story of the courage that grows from deep concern about a loved one. It is both the courage and the integrity of young Mella that allow her to succeed, while those lacking these elements of human character fail. This account of Mella may be based upon an oral history of the Buhera Ba Rowzi people of Zimbabwe, since Mella's later role as tribal leader is stated so specifically.

In a bright sunny clearing on the edge of a deep green forest, were the homes of reed and fiber in which the people of the village dwelled. On a mat inside one home was the father of Mella, lying close to death, while all the offerings and sacrifice, while all the

153

music of the pipes and drums, while all the magic of Nganga healers, could not rouse him from his weakness and his dying.

Into the forest Mella walked one night, stopping in the rich moonlit dampness of the ferns, her fingertips about the crescent amulet that hung about her neck, her young woman body holding thoughts of age and sickness in its heart. There she called upon the merciful Bomu Rambi, She who watched over the village, begging for any word of what she might do to help. The leaves above her trembled with the presence of the power of the moonlight as it shone upon them, until Mella heard these words echoing over and over within her head, 'You must go to the Python Healer. You must go to the Python Healer.'

Mella's heart beat quickened. Her body grew cold in the warm night air. Fear crept into her worried heart. Had not her older brothers sought the help of the Python Healer many moons before and had they not fled in terror from the entrance of the python's cave, returning to the village so shaken with terror that their voices had died within their throats when they tried to speak of their visit to the Python Healer?

Lying on her straw mat in the dark of that night, Mella's eyes would not close; Mella's mind would not rest as thoughts of the Python Healer crawled in and out of her thoughts. When the dimmest rays of the morning sun fell upon her wakeful eyes, Mella rose from her mat, quickly gathered roots and grains, putting them into a small sack of elephant hide, and set off for the place that she had never been, the cave of the Python Healer, the cave set into the foothill of a mountain in the covering of the deepest, thickest jungle.

Four times the sun disappeared from the sky. Four times the sun returned to cross the heavens. All this time Mella walked through ferns as high as her head, up and down the many rock strewn hills, making her way through wooded mountainsides, sleeping in unfamiliar groves, crossing streams whose currents challenged the expert balance of her body, crossing clearings high with yellow straw that felt both soft but piercing beneath her feet, all the while bravely singing songs while her thoughts roamed between the eyes of the animals whose paths she used and anxious worry about her father, lying still and weak upon his mat at home. Then all thoughts were pushed from her mind by the sight of the spiral carved upon the rock at the entrance to the cave of the Python Healer!

In the darkness of an early evening sky, lit only by a thin crescent of the moon, Mella tried to find the voice that seemed to have fallen deep into her chest and would not rise into her throat to reach her lips—until she reminded herself of the reasons for her long journey. Taking three deep breaths of evening air, she finally called out to the hollow in the rocky cave, 'I am Mella, sent to you by Bomu Rambi. I have come to ask your help, for my father has lain ill for many moons and his weakness is the weakness of my people.'

Waiting in the silence for an answer, Mella noticed that even the birds had stopped their talking. They too seemed to be waiting for an answer during the time that was passing, a time that felt longer than all the days and all the nights that she had walked. And then in the darkness at the entrance of the cave, she saw a pair of eyes in the dim moonlight, heard a voice as hollow as the cave, a voice as frightening as that of Bomu Rambi had been reassuring. 'The bravest of your people have fled in terror from my door. Does such a small young girl as you are have no fear that I might strangle you and leave your bones about my cave?'

'It is not a lack of fear that I possess,' replied Mella to the hissing voice that seemed to be without a body, 'but a love and a caring that is louder than my fear, a love and a caring for my dying father who has done no wrong, yet neither the Ngangas nor the spirits of the ancestors can rid him of the illness that lays upon him as he lies upon his mat. So deep in sorrow have I been that Bomu Rambi came in answer to my prayers. It was She who sent me to seek you out, to beg for your help if any can be given.'

'Your love and caring more powerful than fear of me?', Python Healer questioned in reply. 'Would you be willing to turn your back and let me crawl close to where you are standing?' Mella spoke no word but turned her back to the entrance of the cave, the pride of her people keeping her head high, though she saw only the jungle night. 'Your loving and caring more powerful than your fear of me?' the Python Healer repeated, the hollow hissing voice now close behind her heels. 'Would you let me twine myself about you as I might do if I chose to take you for my dinner?' Though the frantic cries of animals and birds pierced through the trees in worried, anxious warning, Mella allowed the python to wind itself about her body and when only the legs, the arms, the head, of what had once been Mella, could be seen apart from the many rings of the python that coiled about her body, Python Healer instructed Mella to begin the long walk home.

Still she held her head up high, despite the serpent's weight upon her, despite the fear she tried to quell, until from a depth of courage in her heart, a sound rose up into her throat and floated out as song into the air so that all the animals and birds that came to gape along the path on which the serpent laden Mella walked, watched in awe of her bravery, each uttering growls or chirps of deep respect along the way. In this way exhausted Mella arrived at the edges of her village—with the Python Healer still wrapped about her body.

When the members of the village saw the monstrous creature walk into the clearing between two houses, they ran for their arrows and their spears but Mella raised her arm and called aloud, 'It is Mella, inside the Python Healer! Do not harm us for I have travelled a long way to bring healing to my father.' Thus they walked into the door of Mella's home, where the python soon uncoiled itself, slithering down upon the earthen floor, making its way to the mat of Mella's father.

From the small scaled pouch that hung about its neck, Mella took the healing bark as the Python Healer instructed her to do. From the small deer horn that hung about its neck, Mella took the muchonga oil as the Python Healer instructed her to do. With it she made a fire that sent the vapours of the healing bark floating into the air of their home while the Python Healer recited holy chants of the Buhera Ba Rowzi people. And then to Mella's great astonishment—her father began to kneel upon his mat, then stood erect and tall and finally began to walk about the room, something he had not done for all these many moons of illness.

Though the father spoke with many words of gratitude, providing festive food and drink for Mella and the healing serpent, the voice of the Python Healer now was silent. Once again it began to wind about the body of Mella, so that she knew she must again repeat the walk to return the Python Healer to its cave. Once again reaching the spiral marking on the entrance, Mella sighed in great relief as the python crawled down from her exhausted body and moved in silence into the darkness of its home. But as she turned to leave, the Python Healer called out and invited her to enter the deep cavern in which it lived—as animals and birds again cried out in even louder warning.

So much fear had Mella faced that once again she chanced to trust the healer who had helped her father, and step by step she made her way into the granite darkness of the cave. Suddenly a light glimmered in the distance, glowing brighter as she walked. Though she dreaded seeing broken bones lying about the cavern floor, she opened her hesitant eyes and was amazed to see pots of gold and silver, baskets of ebony and ivory and precious jewels nestled upon soft silken cloths and woven tapestries. But more astonishing than all the unexpected treasures were the words that came from Python Healer. 'Take what you wish, for your courage and love should surely be rewarded.'

Mella's eyes lowered with embarrassment, thinking it was she who should reward the Python Healer, and in a voice not much louder than a whisper, she asked the Python Healer to do the choosing. From a great wicker box that sat upon the rocky ground, the python quickly took a golden chain into its mouth, upon whose links was hung a golden crescent of the moon, sacred image of the Buhera Ba Rowzi, holy Ndoro emblem that matched the one that Mella always wore, the one she had touched to call upon Bomu Rambi—thus she knew that Python Healer truly was a friend.

Returning to her village, Mella told her family of the treasure of the cave, proudly showing the golden Ndoro she had won but greed soon entered into the hearts of her brothers who began to plot the python's murder, so that they might steal the riches. Overhearing the quiet scheming voices, Mella ran quickly along the now familiar path to try to protect her friend who lived by the sign of the spiral, to warn the Python Healer of her brothers' plans—so that when the brothers arrived, they were greeted by bursts of hot, unpleasant smelling smoke, frightening thunderous roars—until they again fled in terror as they had so many moons before.

When the people of the village heard of what had happened, they sent the three boys from their home, to live alone forever in the jungle. And when in later years Mella's father died, the people of the village appointed Mella as their leader, thus honouring her courage, her honesty and her love. Mella led the proud Buhera Ba Rowzi for all the long years of her life, visiting the Python Healer as often as she could. So it came to pass that it was Queen Mella who arranged for the great wooden carving that stood in the center of the village, a perfect likeness of the trusted Python Healer, the one **who knew the magic of the Ndoro Crescent moon of Bomu Rambi—and cared for those who lived with courage, honesty and love.**

To Watch over the People of the Islands
Oceania

eep in the caves of the mighty volcano we may find the Goddess in Oceania, half of our spirit soul entrusted to Her for safekeeping while we are alive, the other half to return to Her when we die—so that we may rest with our spirit united before we are reborn again. Such is the essence of Goddess reverence among the Australoid people of Australia, and the Polynesians of the Pacific islands, as revealed in their rituals and sacred lore.

The Australoids, most familiar to us as the 'Australian Aborigines', are part of a larger group of people that not only live in Australia and some of the nearby islands, but also survive in southern India and the southern coastal area of Saudi Arabia, while remains of Australoids reveal their one time habitation in Africa. These racial connections between Australia, India, Arabia, and Africa, reveal extremely ancient ties between the Australoid people of these widely separated areas, and suggest the possibility of actual physical connections between some of these land masses at a very early period. Skeletal remains of Proto-Australoids, pre-human forerunners of the present day Australoid people, have not only been discovered in Africa, but also in Talga (Queensland, Australia), attesting to the extreme antiquity of migrations from Africa to Australia. The existence of Australoid people along the

159

southern Hadramaut coast of Arabia suggests that these people may have crossed the Red Sea long before Moses did—probably at the Strait of Bab El Mandeb.

In 1800, the Australoids of Australia were represented by some 500 different tribes. Over the last two centuries, Caucasians of European descent colonized the continent of Australia, most of them settling in the eastern sections where the land is most fertile and supportive of life. Much of the indigenous population was gradually pushed into the almost uninhabitable desert lands of the central sections. Many of the arriving Caucasians claimed that the original inhabitants of the land were at a lower level of evolutionary development than themselves, an arrogant and erroneous idea that often allowed them to treat the Australoid people as less than human. Primarily as a result of the Caucasian colonization, the estimated population of about 300,000 Australoids in 1800 dwindled to today's population of about 40,000.

Though regarded as 'primitive' and 'savage' by most of the arriving Caucasians, a few of them were curious enough to explore and record the social structure and religious beliefs of the Australoid people. They were astonished to discover that many of these so called 'savages' lived almost completely without war or group violence. Despite the physical evidence of Australoid people having inhabited Australia for many thousands of years, a surprising number of their sacred legends included accounts of their arrival from across the sea, suggesting many waves of migrations, perhaps over many thousands of years.

The rituals and sacred legends that were recorded, reveal the Australoid contemplation of their lineage, origins, spiritual concepts of birth, death, reincarnation, and ideas about the nature of the universe. Much of the theological contemplation was associated with images of The First Mother or Divine Ancestress, the survival of these beliefs most prominent in the area known as Arnhemland, the northcentral section of Australia. Religious rituals were often connected to sacred caves, the sanctity of the cave based upon the understanding that it was 'the doorway to the spirit'. Though most of the nineteenth and early twentieth century writers simply stated that the Australoid concept of the 'spirit' was of the 'spirit of the ancestor', and that it was 'ancestor worship' that was the foundation of Australoid beliefs, a few explained that entering the sacred cave was described as going into 'The Womb of The Mother'.

Churingas, sacred objects of stone and wood, incised or painted with religious symbols, were kept in the special caves, much as holy relics are kept in churches and temples of other cultures. Some of the caves in the western area of Australia had paintings on the walls of the caves, the Karadjeri people periodically repainting over the cave images as part of the ritual to honour and invoke the 'spirit' of the cave. This practice of repainting has been linked to caves in what is now France and Spain, the images on the walls of European caves painted and repainted in the Upper Paleolithic period. The Karadjeri custom of impressing a palm print near the entrance of the cave, to assure the right to enter, is also to be compared to the palm prints of the Upper Paleolithic caves in southern Europe.

It was understood among many of the Australoids, that upon death, the spirit of the dead person would enter the cave, there to join and remain with The First Mother until the time of the next birth or incarnation. This belief in reincarnation, among the Australoids of Australia, suggests the possibility of extremely ancient cultural connections to the Australoid groups of India. Though it is most often assumed that the concept of reincarnation arrived in India with the Indo-Aryan invaders of about 2000-1500 B.C., and that this important aspect of Hindu religion originated with them, it may well have been adopted from the indigenous Australoids of India, who comprised a major part of the non-Aryan Goddess worshipping Dravidians.

The migrations of the Polynesian peoples, (a combination of Australoids, Mongolians and possibly the Ainu people now living in northern Japan), to the many widely separated islands of the Pacific, have been linked with periods of great geological upheaval, and the sinking of land masses, as a result of earthquake and volcanic activity throughout the western Pacific area—especially between Indo-China and Australia, where there are a great number of volcanoes, and the ocean waters are relatively shallow. It may have been these vast changes in sea and land distribution that provided the basis for the legends of a sunken Pacific continent—referred to as Lemuria or Gondwanaland. Flood accounts and mythic memories of a most ancient ancestress crossing the seas to found a new tribe, as an explanation of tribal origins in a specific area, or on a particular island, offer interesting sidelights to these theories.

Among the Polynesian Maoris of New Zealand, there is the belief that they originally came from a place in the west known as *Uru* or *Irihia,* which some scholars link to an early Sanskrit name for India, *Yrihia.* In the Maori language *uru* literally means west. Though probably coincidental, *ur* or *ura* was the word for ancient among the Sumerians who lived near the Persian Gulf, and also wrote of an ancient homeland, Dilmun, which some scholars of the Sumerian culture conjecturally link with India. Memories of an ancient paradise, a land in the west most often referred to as Hawaiki, appear in the legends of Polynesians in many areas of the Pacific, the name Hawaii probably based upon ideas about this long lost homeland.

Though we may be tempted to speculate upon a specific location for an original homeland for the Polynesian peoples, the continual waves of their migrations across the Pacific, and the interweaving of their Australoid, Mongolian, and possibly Ainu ancestry, make this a truly complex area of study. Yet we may certainly go as far as noting the similarities between the languages of the Polynesians and the Malayans of Indonesia, the speech of both included in the same language group—Malayo-Polynesian.

The association of caves with ideas about the Goddess or First Mother, among the Polynesians, may be observed in the accounts of the Goddess as Mahuea in New Zealand. Mahuea is said to have given birth to Her Goddess Daughter Hina in a cave. This cave is specifically described as being in a volcanic mountain; Mahuea Herself is described in volcanic imagery. The connection of volcanoes to Goddess reverence, in Polynesia, is found in areas as far apart as New Zealand and Hawaii. Volcanic images of the Goddess do not appear in the accounts from Australia, at least not in the ones I have so far found, but the concept of the sacred cave may be related, as an adaptation in a land that does not have volcanoes. The more parallel concepts of the Goddess as Pele in Hawaii, as Fuji among the Ainu (see Japanese Section), and the volcanic imagery in the beliefs about the Goddess as Chantico and Coatlicue among the people of early Mexico, offer interesting comparative material, as do the accounts of the Goddess as Parvati in India, Her association with a luminous mountain in the Himalayas repeatedly mentioned, while in Her aspect as Kali, She is linked to the peak known as Blood Red Mountain (see Indian Section).

The rituals and sacred lore, of both the Australoid and Polynesian peoples, offer us some insight into the spiritual contemplations and images of the Goddess as Divine Ancestress among people whose life may seem simple or even childlike to many who perceive through the eyes of urban European-oriented cultures. Yet it is clear that a structure of values, perceptions, and spiritual beliefs—about birth, death, reincarnation, and the universe—have served the spiritual needs of the Oceanic peoples as fully and as well as those of the so called 'developed' cultures. We may even be moved to question the very concept of technological civilization as 'progress', in light of the evidence that many of the Oceanic peoples have survived in virtual peace for so long, a record that many more 'developed' cultures might well respect and study.

PELE

The worship of the Polynesian Pele is as the Goddess whose spirit inhabits the volcanic Mt. Kilauea on the island of Hawaii. The relationship of volcanic imagery to concepts of the Goddess in other areas bordering on the Pacific Ocean may be observed in the descriptions of the Goddess as Mahuea in New Zealand, as the Goddess known as Fuji among the Ainu people of northern Japan, and as the Goddess known as Chantico in Mexico. Earlier Polynesian beliefs associated Pele with the islands of Kuai, Oahu, Molokai, and Maui, many accounts explaining Pele's creation of various salt lakes, rock formations, and craters, on those islands—before She finally settled at Kilauea on Hawaii.

Often said to be seen as a woman shortly before an eruption, Pele was known to fancy handsome young chiefs, and to enjoy joining in the holua sled racing and other sports—Her wrath incurred if any rejected Her company. It was the angry stomping of Her foot that would cause the ground to tremble before a volcanic eruption. Her priestesses wore robes whose sleeves and hems had been burnt ragged by fire, and carried a wand or digging stick, in imitation of the *Paoa* staff that Pele had used when She " . . . first dug the volcanic craters".

Reverence for Pele was discouraged in the early nineteenth century when the missionary Reverend William Ellis of England converted Kaahumanu, the *kuhina-nui* (queen) of Hawaii, to Christianity. It was further discouraged when the converted Chieftainess Kapiolani, of the Puna District of Hawaii, defied the rage of Pele by throwing rocks into the sacred crater, daring Pele to punish her. Yet when Mauna Loa erupted in 1880, sixty-three year old Princess Ruth Keelikolani still knew the ancient chants of the priestesses of Pele. Courageously, she walked up to the edge of a lava flow that was threatening the city of Hilo, reciting the chants and offering gifts of silk cloth and libations of brandy (in memory of the ancient sacred *awa* drink) to the hot lava stream of Pele. The eruptions stopped the next day, before the town of Hilo had been touched. Again in 1955 when the village of Kapoho was threatened, villagers offered food and tobacco as gifts to Pele—and again the lava stream stopped short of the village.

For us you are the Goddess spirit
who dwells within the boiling glowing Halemaumau,
lava lake heart of Mount Kilauea,
woman energies of fiery liquid,
your angry mass of molten lava
shooting your hot bubbling cones
of red and black
high into the heavens,
furiously loosing fume and flames,
clouds of smoky steam,
crackling lightning sparks
and thundering forth raging geysers of melted rock
that burst beyond the rim
of your crater cup of being
to crash down upon that which holds you,
your freedom allowing you to cool into pahoehoe,
glassy crystal slivers of your hair,
sparkling satin smooth stone of your body,
as you form the earth about you.

There you sit upon the plain,
central core of earth and ocean,
reaching into the heavens
while guarding the sulphur world below,
always ready to make known your will,
to crack the earth apart when you are not pleased
with what you see going on about you,
to send your lavablood of life
pouring through earth's gaping wounds
to announce your rage and your displeasure
at those who will not listen to your quieter messages—
and then heal
with the black stone of your holy being.

Are you telling us
to look upon your obsidian mirrors
so that we may see ourselves in you?

MAHUEA AND HINA

These five accounts of the Goddess as Mahuea (Mahu Ika, Mahui I'a) and Her Goddess Daughter Hina are not found as a group in any one area of the Pacific Islands. The imagery and narrative lore surrounding Mahuea are primarily from New Zealand. Hina is known on New Zealand as the daughter of Mahuea, but is a major Goddess figure throughout the Polynesian islands. Like Borneo Fire Woman, Mahuea is revered as the one who discovered how to make fire. The volcanic imagery associated with Her, probably linked to Her role as the originator of control over fire, presents interesting parallels to the worship of the Goddess as Pele on Hawaii. The figure of the male Maui is well known in Polynesian lore, but the seniority of Hina, and the even greater seniority of Mahuea, perhaps reveal that the accounts of Maui were later additions to the beliefs about the ancient Goddess who brought fire. One account of Maui, describing *him* as the one who first taught the Polynesian people how to make fire, briefly explains that he gained this knowledge from his ancient Grandmother, Mahuea, who kept fire in the tips of Her fingernails. The account of Hina and the moon may be from an entirely separate body of beliefs. Although the source of this account is Hawaii, its concept and imagery appear to be quite different from the other accounts of Hina, and the legend may have been linked to Her name as a result of the name Hina becoming almost synonymous with the concept of Goddess.

1. Mahuea

To the land of Ngaurohoe, to the land of Ruapehu—whose insides boil with the molten lava of the innards of the earth; to the land of Wanganui, to the land of Waitiki—whose waters run to serve the ocean's constant thirst; to the land of Wanoka, to the land of Hawea—who catch the mountain waters and keep it in their deep laps—the ancient Mother Mahuea came. Great Mahuea, Kind Mahuea, brought the Maori people from the west, from the Uru Irihia, the ancient homeland, to live upon the two great lands, most beautiful in all the waters of the great ocean.

When the home of the Maori people was overrun by snakes, Mother Mahuea took Her digging stick to frighten one away, but driving it hard into the ground, the stick snapped in half—and from the splintered ends—a flame burst forth. Thus Mahuea first discovered fire and gave this gift to the Maori people. Mahuea, Guardian of Fire, taught Her people how to use its flames for warmth, taught her people how to use its flames for light, taught Her people how to use its flames for cooking—and how to bring the fire back if all its flames have disappeared—by rubbing a digging stick into a hollow tube of wood upon the ground.

Her flashing eyes could once be seen far across the islands, bright as the fires of Ngaurohoe and Ruapehu. Her teeth were as fine and sharp as the glass splinters of cooled lava. Her hair streamed from Her head, like the hot red melting rivers that sparked down the mountainsides. Her sacred body emanated brilliant fire and dazzling light, while Her gentle presence could be found deep in Her dark volcanic caves, especially where the cool wet rivers flowed along the ancient lava paths.

In just such a hidden cave, its entrance veiled by falling mountain waters that dropped from a high ledge, Mahuea nurtured a child within Her womb. Mahuea felt Her belly move with life wanting to exist. Mahuea gave birth to Her daughter, the Holy Goddess Hina.

2. Mahuea and young Hina

Nursed at the breasts of Mahuea, Hina grew tall and strong and soon walked along with Mahuea through the tall fern of the evermoist forests, learning which trees gave gifts of fruit, learning which roots were good to eat, and which plants were known to heal. To the waters of the nearby river, Mahuea brought young Hina, watching Her small brown body, laughing, kicking, splashing, in the water, until Hina learned to move as easily in the water, as She moved upon the land, soon chasing fish and tying them together to bring them home for supper.

Always watching Mahuea, who worked with the ease of many years, Hina learned to pound the pulp from the bark of the mamake, until it formed the tapa cloth. Though the great boulders, which held the corners of the tapa from blowing as She worked, sometimes fell to earth with the crashing noise of thunder, Hina learned to use the iakuko mallets, and learned the chants that helped to ease the tapa into perfect shape—so that the rolls of tapa that She kept in the heavens soon flashed as brilliant lightning across the skies.

3. Hina as a young woman

Of all the gifts of knowledge that Mahuea passed to Hina, the greatest was the gift of fire, and the making of the imu oven for the cooking of the food and the ceremonial fires, whose flames still beckon to Her holy being. As the imu fires are lit, there are some who still remember the story of days long passed, when the people of Hina found themselves with no food, and great hunger was swimming in the emptiness of their stomachs. In their time of wanting, Hina appeared before them, telling them how to build the imu oven and which stones must be used, asking for the wood of the koa tree to be brought for the making of the fire.

When the sacred oven had been built, the branches of the many armed koa began to burn until—in the intense heat of the imu—Hina's spirit left Her body. Three days and three nights, while the hungry people stoked the fire, Hina's spirit travelled beneath the earth, exploring the maze of caverns of the Underworld until She found the object of Her search, the cavern that contained the fresh spring waters. These She channelled upward through an opening in the earth, so that the precious saltless waters fountained forth, not far from where the imu stood.

Her spirit then returning to Her body, Hina directed the people who had patiently kept the fire blazing, to dig among the ashes of the imu. To their astonishment, they discovered yams and cocoanuts, bananas and fish, foods that their bodies had so longed for, tastily roasted by the fire of the imu, gifts of abundance from the Holy Hina—She who had brought the fresh saltless water so that the food could once more grow.

4. Hina and Maui

On the beach by the Great Sea, Hina gave birth to a son, but She found him to be as unruly and disrespectful to his mother as She had been loving to Hers. After many years of unfilial behaviour, son Maui decided to take his mother's life, thinking that upon Her death, he could add the years of Her life to his own. Some say that he tried to crawl back into Her womb and out Her mouth, to reverse the process of birth, and thus to cause Her death, but that he was crushed between Her thighs as She protected Herself from his murderous plot. Others say that Hina had heard of the plan, even before Her son had taken any action, and had decided to capture Maui's hau, the core of his life essence and being, that which could be obtained in a drop of Maui's blood.

Thus She called upon the butterfly and sent the lovely Kahukurra to steal the hau of Maui, but when Maui saw the winged creature approach upon its mission, he killed it in its graceful flight. When Kahukurra did not return, Hina sent the tiny Tuia gnat, hoping that its smaller body might slip by unnoticed, but even Tuia was seen by Maui's watchful eyes and put to death by Hina's son.

Hearing of all that had happened, Hina summoned Waroa the mosquito, instructing it to fly by night, so that in the darkness it might succeed in returning with the drop of blood. But as it landed upon the shoulder of the sleeping Maui, he awakened from the itch and slapped his hand upon his shoulder, killing Waroa as easily as he had killed the others.

Still Maui planned to murder Hina, to take the remaining years of Her life for his own. Still Hina hoped to capture Maui's hau, but could not find a way until She sent the loyal Manu, golden sandfly whose gauzy wings spread wide enough to carry her body in swift silence. In the darkness of the night, Manu flew to the grass hut of Maui, landed upon his forehead, drew the drop of blood, thus capturing his hau—and quickly delivered it to Hina. Placing a magic spell upon the hau, Hina used Her powers until the callous son could only do as She commanded. So it happened that Hina prevented Her own murder, continuing to live, and to watch over the people of the islands that rose above the vast blue ocean.

5. Hina of the Moon

In Her days of great age, Hina took a husband, thinking that he might help Her with Her work, but though She was willing to stay with him in a small grass hut among the palms of earth, She found that he spent his days doing nothing. He did not fish. He did not hunt. He did not even help to gather fruit, or search for roots, or pound the tapa bark. He said little that was pleasant to hear, and did little that made Hina feel glad that She had married.

In the sadness of a long unpleasant day, Hina's eyes fell upon the glow of a rainbow, as it formed a curving pathway across the sky. Memories of better places, happier ways to live, sent Her thoughts walking along the brilliantly coloured path, hopes leaping ahead even faster than thoughts—along the rainbow road of heaven.

To the brightly shining sun I shall travel, She decided, where I can start my life again. With this goal in mind, Hina set off on the path of the rainbow, hoping to reach the brightly shining sun, but as the day went on and Hina drew ever closer to the sun, She felt the blazing burning heat, saw only the blinding whiteness. Soon thinking that this might be even worse than the life that She was living, Hina made Her way back down the rainbow road, returning to hut and husband.

Though at first relieved, simply to be away from the intense heat of the sun, Hina once again began to feel the discomfort of the misery of Her life, once again began to grow angry at the laziness of Her husband, at the sullenness of his voice. This time, She thought I will travel to the moon, the softly glowing light of heaven, where I will be able to live in peace and comfort.

When the sky had darkened and the moon was clear and whole, it was time for Hina to begin Her journey, but searching for the rainbow road, Hina realized that She could not see it in the darkness of the night and had to feel along each step of the way, trying to remember where the colourful path had been. Slowly, carefully, She began to ascend, testing the invisible path before Her with each movement of Her foot, climbing ever higher, climbing ever closer to the moon.

Higher and yet higher She went, stars greeting Her along the way. Hina soon began to smile with the joy of regained freedom, as the warm night air brushed across Her golden cheeks. Then suddenly She heard the voice of Her husband calling out behind Her, begging Her to stop, shouting that he would change his ways, that he would try to please Her—if only She would return. Hina thought of the many times that She had heard him say such things, and of each time that he had forgotten all that he had promised. This time, more determined than ever to live as She wished—Hina continued to walk.

Turning back to look, hoping to see Her husband retreating from the path, Hina saw him running towards Her, now shouting that he would never let Her leave, drawing closer and closer yet. Though She ran to escape his threat, he was suddenly upon Her, throwing Her down on the slightly curving rainbow road, still invisible in the darkness. Struggling to free Herself of his determined grasp, and from the blows that fell upon Her, She pushed against him, pounding Her fists against his face and chest so hard that he inched back as they battled. But as he jumped back, to avoid Her kicking leg, he fell off the edge of the rainbow road— hurtling into the emptiness of the night time sky.

With tears that sought to wash away the horror of all that had happened, Hina again began to climb, feeling Her way along the rainbow road, until the moon sent out a brighter path, one so soft and light that She hardly felt the aches of Her bruised and beaten body. At last, reaching the glowing silver moon, She made Her home upon it and lives there still—remembered by the women of the islands as Hina of the Moon.

KUNAPIPI

In the area of Arnhemland in northcentral Australia, the reverence for Kunapipi as The First Mother still exists in the twentieth century. Much of the lore of this area of Australia recalls a time when The First Mother arrived from across the sea, settling in Arnhemland and establishing Her tribe. Those who call upon The Mother as Kunapipi consider themselves to be Her descendants. It is Her 'womb' that is entered in the sacred cave or the substitute crescent trench. It is believed that the spirits of the dead remain with Her until the next rebirth, while the 'twin' or 'double' spirit of each person stays with Her throughout the time one is alive. The ritual described here, in which the initiate enters the 'womb', swinging a bullroarer fast enough to hear the sound of Kunapipi's voice, is enacted only once in a person's lifetime.

> Great Mother Kunapipi,
> you who have travelled
> far across the vast oceans
> to bring your children to this new world
> from submerged Gondwanaland
> as it sunk into the sea,
> hoping that loved ones
> had perhaps found their way
> to the summits of Java and Sumbawa,
> as you brought us
> to Arnhem Land in the Arafura Sea,
> Mother, it is you we call upon,
> in life, as in death.
>
> Dear Kunapipi,
> Great Kunapipi,
> I do not forget you
> as I climb back into your holy womb
> to make contact with my spirit soul,
> crawling into the crescent vessel
> of your protection
> dug deep into the soil of your body,
> carved into the precious earth beneath me.
> I beckon to my spirit soul
> which lives within you
> until my time of finishing this life
> and though I leave your womb

at this initiation time,
though I choose to climb out
from your nurturing warmth,
to live my years of life,
I ask you to care for my spirit soul
until my return
so that after my passing from this life
my two spirits may be reunited in you,
before you send me forth again
to once more live on earth.
Dear Kunapipi,
no matter how far I wander,
how many lives I live—
to you I shall always return.

FIRE WOMAN

This account, from the Sea Dyak culture of southern Borneo, offers us an explanation of how and why the original ancestress of a particular tribe came to found Her tribe on the land on which they live. It is also an explanation of how the making of fire was first introduced, linking this event of human development with woman, as the one who first taught the method of rubbing wood to create fire. It is an account of the discovery of fire that provides an interesting parallel to that of the Goddess as Mahuea in New Zealand—the imagery of the mountain of Fire Woman perhaps to be linked to the volcanic images of Mahuea. The sanctity of the snake, and its connection with rain, may be related to the Rainbow Serpent of Australia.

Between the banks of the Dyak Rivers that flow into the Java Sea, the women and the children made their way through the thick fern mat of the jungle where little sun can enter, searching for a bit of food to appease their empty stomachs. Chancing upon a great snake, enough to feed them all, they pounced upon it with their sticks, until all life had fled from its thick trunk—and dividing it among themselves, they sat upon the damp green ground and began to eat their dinner.

No sooner had they raised their portions of serpent to their mouths, torrential rains began to press upon the highest branches of the upward stretching jungle growth. Great hard drops of water forced openings between the leaves, spearing their way between the branches, falling so hard and fast that the jungle soon submerged beneath the raging, rising waters, drowning all but one woman, who ran towards where the land was higher. Though she carried the weight of an infant in her arms, she made her way to the top of a nearby mountain—and there survived the great flood.

As darkness came, winds that visited the mountains brought such chilling cold that the woman thought to rub her shivering body against the bark of a high growing tree, hoping to dry and warm herself and the infant in her arms. So fast and hard were her movements, against the roughness of the tree, that suddenly sparks leaped forth, landing upon some dry leaves and twigs. Thus the woman saw, before her unbelieving eyes, the unfamiliar light, the unfamiliar glow—of the first fire—its unfamiliar warmth caressing her in the damp loneliness.

In the flickering light of these first flames, the motion of a rabbit caught the woman's eye, reminding her of the hunger that had almost gone from her mind during her flight for survival. Catching the rabbit with her stick, she roasted it over the fire, and ate her fill, until the hunger pains subsided and the milk flowed once again into her breasts. In this way the woman and the infant survived the great flood, as she watched the raging waters pressing close about their mountain sanctuary.

Living for years upon the mountain in the waters, finding the food that would satisfy hunger, learning to make the fire, each day quicker than before, the woman began to understand that the flood had been a punishment, for killing a snake that was holy. Over the many years, the waters grew lower, as the infant that became a young man grew higher, until the time that the flood finally subsided, and the woman and her grown son wandered back to the land she had once known when she was young—only to realize that all the others had disappeared, and the now dry ground was empty.

Thus it was that Fire Woman took her son as her husband, and along the now calm waters of the Dyak they raised children, passing on the gift of fire to the Dyak people they brought forth, but warning them always—that to kill or eat a sacred snake might bring another storm of destruction.

STAR GIRL

This simple but poetic explanation of how stars came to be in the heavens comes from the Australoid people of the Nullarbor Plain of southcentral Australia. Though Star Girl is spoken of as mortal, her act exhibits powers that reveal her nature as someone who was regarded as a quite special being. The idea of the sun and the stars as 'fire in the sky' presents a concept of the bodies of heaven not unlike that of the most advanced scientists of today.

> In the days
> when only the sun and the moon
> lived in the heavens,
> some nights would come
> when even the moon would disappear
> and all was dark,
> except for the light of a tribal fire
> on the dark open plain.
>
> It was such a night
> when Star Girl stood in the darkness,
> watching those who sat about the fire,
> wishing that the moon
> had chosen to arrive that night
> to brighten her view
> of the earth and the sky
> and looking at the blazing flames,
> she reached into the fire,
> grasping a handful
> of still glowing embers
> that had fallen from a log,
> and threw these pieces of fire
> high into the heavens—
> where they stayed
> to form a trail of light
> across the sky
> so that none could ever
> lose their way again,
> even when the moon was too tired
> to guide them through the night.

LIA

This thirst provoking account of the heroic Lia comes from the southeastern section of Australia now known as New South Wales. It is an account of the Gippsland Australians, who have been conjecturally linked with Ainu groups of Japan and the East Indies. It appears to have developed around two separate themes. One is to explain the origin of the Murumbidgee River, that flows west from the southeastern coastal mountain range; the other seems to be an explanation of the origins of a people who had once been part of another tribe. Though the area near the river is much more fertile and moist than many other sections of Australia, this story gives some insight into the extreme hardships of survival in the desert areas. The origins of the account are a bit puzzling, in that it would be somewhat unlikely that a group living near the river would be so aware of the difficulties of desert life, whereas a desert group would hardly be likely to develop an explanation of the origins of a river that was not especially familiar to them. The account may be based upon an actual rebellion of the women of a desert tribe, and a subsequent migration to the area of the Murumbidgee, though some readers may prefer to free their imaginations enough to read it as the literal truth.

Looking down from the heavens, seeing only dry cracked land where once there had been grass, seeing only mudholes where once there had been lakes, seeing only ditches and widening gullies, where once there had been river beds, Lia decided to descend to earth to live among the people of the Goanna tribe. How different were their lives from that which the Mother of Life had planned.

Living in the heat of the constantly blazing sun was far from easy, but Lia was determined to help with the work of the Mother—and thinking upon how best this might be done, she soon became the wife of the chief of the Goannas. Why was it, she wondered, that he was never dry, never thirsty? Why was it, she wondered, that all the men of the Goannas seemed freshly washed, comfortable in the intense heat, while the lips of each woman were dry and parched, the skin of each woman covered with the pale dust of the arid desert stretches?

As each day came, Lia stayed with the other women, as they wearily poked their digging sticks in search of roots, all carefully sharing the water of the one water skin, that Lia's husband had provided for them. The men said they had more important work to do, and from early dawn to dusk none could be found near the village. Only in the bright orange glow of the setting sun did the men return, once again bringing the gift of the one precious skin of water, to the dry and thirsty women.

In the dark of the night, Lia lay upon her mat, images of cool, clear, flowing water rippling through her thoughts. Finally, turning to the man who lay beside her, she said, 'How fortunate we are that each day you bring us water. Where do you find it?' Much to her surprise, the man beside her laughed; the chief of the Goannas laughed louder and louder, as if at some secret joke. Then from the side of his mat, he brought out a second water skin and raised it to his mouth, allowing precious water to trickle carelessly down his chin. When he had had his fill, he offered it to Lia, and laughing yet again, he told the heavenly Lia that it was only for men to know the source of the water. Did he not bring a water skin to the village each night? Was it not he who was kind enough to bring water to the women? Lia fell asleep, hot and dry and troubled.

In the morning light, the women walked wearily to the edges of the village, each carrying her digging stick. Each began to poke the dry land as she had always done. Though Lia's head was bent in concentration, as if her eyes saw only what she hoped to discover at the end of her stick, carefully she watched as each man left the village. Carefully she watched, as they walked towards the place where the great grey rocks were so tall that she could see no further.

When the sun was nearly overhead and not a man was left in the village, Lia called to the other women. 'We must find water for ourselves. One skin is not enough for all. The Mother had made water enough for everyone.' Long sleeping anger woke abruptly in each woman. Truly, it was not fair that they should dig all day for supper, in the burning heat of the sun, while the men were cooling themselves, drinking freely, yet bringing so little water home.

Lia pointed to the mountains, in the direction of the tall grey rocks, where the men had gone. 'Tomorrow we will look for roots, but we shall look for water as well. We'll start out alone, each with her digging stick, but we'll meet further down at the foot of the great grey rocks—and from there we will hunt for water!'

The plan went well, and after gathering at the base of the mountains, not far from where the men had disappeared, the women began to climb. They searched every crevice, listened in silence for any hopeful sound, the slightest trickle of moving water, but when the dusk began to settle in, the women were as dry and as thirsty as ever. More exhausted than ever before, they returned to the village, only to be severely berated by the men for returning so late, and with so few roots for supper. And when the men began to notice the telling brown dirt of the mountains, layered over the pale dust that usually covered their feet and ankles, they began such a shouting that even the birds and snakes were frightened away.

It was Lia's husband who made the greatest noise, blustering like the hottest summer winds, roaring as only animals roar, violent, menacing, thundering, about what Lia had done and how she of all women, the wife of the chief, must teach the other women to obey. 'We must leave the village for several days,' he boomed and then threatened painful beatings, even death, to any woman who went near the mountains during the absence of the men. The women cringed in dread, and by the time the men had disappeared in the morning light, each had decided it was safer to obey. One could live with the thirst and the dry parched lips and throat.

Only Lia had not been frightened from her plan. 'Dig the roots if you must', she said to the others. 'I will find water for all of us.' At this show of defiance, two others offered reluctantly to join her. Thus the three women set off for the mountains, but they were hardly to where the grey rocks began, when one felt the terror of a possible fatal beating, and with apologies to Lia, she returned to the village to search for roots. Hardly was the woman out of sight, when the second too grew fearful for her life—and left Lia to climb the mountains by herself.

Alone, Lia began the rugged ascent. Higher she climbed, here balancing herself on a small rock ledge no larger than one foot, there lifting herself up on a small determined sapling. So Lia made her way, until the sun had completed its arc in the heavens, and chancing upon the entrance of a small cavern in the mountain, just as the sun slipped into its crack in the earth, Lia crawled inside—gratefully laying her tired body on the cool stone floor. The feverish heat of the day, the exhaustion of the climb, had left her tongue thick and dry in her mouth. Slowly, she let her eyelids cover her tired eyes, as a mother might cover a sleeping child, and prayed that sleep would come quickly.

Was it an hallucination from the heat, from the fatiguing efforts of the day—or was there truly a tiny person standing near her feet? Raising her tired eyelids upon hearing an unexpected sound, she saw another—and another. The Tukonee, they called themselves, the little people of the cave. More of them poured forth, from the deepest hidden part of the small rock shelter, and as if in a dream, Lia heard them tell her to return to the village in the morning—and to once again bring all the women to the mountains. Together the women must climb to the top of the mountain, high enough to see the sea beyond. There in a place the little ones described, Lia was to drive her digging stick deep into a crevice of the rocks, deep enough to touch the heart of the mountain—and when the mountain's heart was touched, fresh water would be theirs. Then as quickly as the Tukonee appeared, they were gone, and in the dark grey granite silence, Lia slept more soundly than she had since she had come to earth.

So excited was Lia's voice, as she spoke to the women of the village; so certain was Lia's plan, as it was explained in the morning light—that there was no argument when the women began to climb the grey rocks this second time—though anxious prayer passed across blistered lips, and throats hoarse with lack of moisture reduced those desperate prayers to private whispers.

Standing at the place described by the Tukonee, the women watched with a monolithic disbelief, that cracked only slightly with the pressure of deepest hopes—as Lia thrust her digging stick into the jagged crevice of the highest boulder. Suddenly, the entire mountain shook. A thunderous noise enveloped them, a shaking of the very air, as the stick seemed to pull itself from Lia's grasp and to push its own way deeper, far deeper, into the rock—until all disbelief and doubts were washed away by a crashing cascade of crystal clear water.

The fierce flow of the water splashed upon the grey rocks, finding its own pathways along the ridges of the stones, until it formed itself into racing rivulets, that covered themselves with bubbly white foam and swiftly slid into wider brooks, hurrying into broader streams that bounded down the mountainside, meeting on the edge of a wide plateau, to plunge fearlessly through the air and fall upon the dry sands of the desert—where the waters spread into a broad blue band that became the Murumbidgee River.

Dusty faces filled with awe at the sight of so much water. Some kneeled upon the rocks and moistened long cracked lips on the ripples of its surface. Hot throats soon gulped its coolness. Hands splashed grey faces into a rich, dark brown. Wet brown legs, wet brown breasts, wet brown shoulders, soon began to glisten in the sunlight—as the pale dust that had covered them returned to the earth where it belonged.

Playful hands became scoops to toss the wetness upon a sister, upon a daughter, upon a mother whose skin had only known the painfully shrivelling heat of a mercilessly blazing sun. The air soon filled with gleaming droplets. Pale sandy hair regained its rich

dusty faces filled with awe

darkness, as the water continued to leap forth from the crevice that Lia had opened—pouring, racing, falling down the mountainside, ever fresh, ever clean, ever cool. It seemed that women laughed who had never laughed before. They embraced in exultation, together felt their jubilant success, as tears of pain and tears of triumph mingled upon their cheeks, and slid into the treasured water. Lia had brought them a miracle.

Wading along the pathways of the down hill streams, ankles hesitant to leave the coolness, the women finally reached the ground below. They rested upon the bank of the new river, as the descending sun touched the blue with orange, the coolness of the water flying through the air—to touch them still. The world of the Goanna women floated like a perfect dream.

Thus the women sat, until the moment that unexpected voices reached their ears. The men had returned to the village—and they were demanding their dinners! But the voices of the men echoed with a distance. They were on the other side of the river! The eyes of the women met in silence. The new river was wide. The smiles of the women met in silence. The new river was very wide. So it happened that on that day the women of the Goannas set off to found a village of their own, leaving the Goanna men to live by themselves for the rest of their lives—on the other side of the Murumbidgee River.

ARUNTA SUN WOMAN

The Arunta (Araunta, Araunda) now living in central Australia, just west of Queensland, are one of the larger and better known groups of the Australoid people. This account of Sun Woman not only reveals the Arunta association of the sun with fire, but also explains some of the ideas about life after death of the Arunta people. As with Akewa of the Toba of Argentina, Sun Sister of the Inuit, Amaterasu of Japan, Allat of the

TO WATCH OVER THE PEOPLE OF THE ISLANDS

Arabians and the Sun Goddess of the Arinna in Anatolia, the image of the
Arunta Sun woman confronts the erroneous stereotype of the sun as a
universally male image.

Sitting out upon the sandy plain,
we watch the fiery Sun Woman
as She returns each morning
to the people of the earth,
carrying Her glowing torch of fire
to bring us warmth
after the night time chill,
to bring us light
after the night time darkness,
rising higher and higher
above the earth,
Her torch growing ever brighter
as She reaches the summit heights of heaven
and as the wooden torch
slowly burns away
She slowly lowers Herself again,
finally sinking in the dimming light—
into the ground.

Beneath the desert sands, She descends,
welcomed there by those
who have passed from earth
as they form a line on either side
creating a path of ancient souls,
so that She might pass by
with honour and respect,
each night receiving from them
a bright new dress of red
and a new log with which to light
Her daytime torch.
Then bidding them farewell
She begins Her morning travels
as She raises Her firebrand high,
floats up on to the earth,
rises upon the sandy plain—
to once again light the day of the Arunta people.

While Amazons Danced an Armed Dance
Anatolia

ncient Anatolia, Asia Minor, the land we today speak of as Turkey, provides us with a body of evidence of Goddess reverence that spreads across some seven thousand years—from the neolithic sites of Hacilar and Catal Huyuk to the time of St. Paul's confrontation with Goddess worship in the city of Ephesus.

It was in the land we know as Turkey that the Goddess worshipping cultures of Hacilar and Catal Huyuk had once flourished, the excavated sites of these most ancient cultures revealing shrines and statues of the Goddess, as She had been revered between about 7000 B.C. until about 5500 B.C. The buildings and artifacts, unearthed at the site of the Catal Huyuk culture, may help us to better understand religious and social customs that began to grow not long after the initial development of agriculture in the Near and Middle East. The people of the culture of Catal Huyuk, burials suggesting a surprising majority of women, were short, somewhat stocky, and doliocephalic (narrow headed). Although this culture existed some eighty-five centuries ago (i.e. some *sixty centuries* before the rise of Classical Greece), murals of priestesses wearing vulture masks and wings; evidence of the dead being buried carefully beneath the homes, and hearths set in open courtyards of closely clustered houses built of mud brick—each give us some idea of the life style of these Goddess worshipping people who lived so long ago.

At about 5000 B.C., sites of the Goddess worshipping Halafian culture sprung up near the headwaters of the Tigris and Euphrates Rivers in Anatolia, spreading south into northern Mesopotamia. Although there are some similarities, no direct connections between the Halafians, and the earlier cultures of Catal Huyuk and Hacilar, have yet been made with certainty. One of the most significant factors of the Halafian culture was the use of the symbol of the double axe, in conjunction with statues of the Goddess (at the Halafian site of Arpachiyah in northern Mesopotamia). This Goddess symbol, later used repeatedly on the island of Crete, and often portrayed as a weapon of the Amazons in Anatolia, thus first appeared at about 5000 B.C.—at a site that was later known as a sacred centre of the Goddess as the Semitic Ishtar.

Little is known about the cultures of Anatolia directly after the Halafian period. This may be the result of the people of these earlier cultures leaving Anatolia, or a possible period of nomadic migration that would have left few remains behind. This lack of evidence may also be a matter of chance discovery of sites, many perhaps still lying deep beneath the earth, waiting to tell their stories, as Hacilar and Catal Huyuk were just some fifty years ago. Whatever the reason, so far there has been little evidence of settled and developed sites in Anatolia from about 4500 to about 2700 B.C.

Once we reach the middle of the third millenium B.C., we are again heir to a wealth of Goddess images, from sites such as Alaca Huyuk, Boghazkoy, Yazilikaya, Beycesultan, Kultepe, Tahurpa, Gavurkales, Fraktin, Arslan Kaya, Yarre, Magnesia, Erythrae, Kohnus, Pessinus, Samuha, Hurma, Kyme, Priene, Pitane, Gryneium, Toprakkale, Kios, Bandirma—and of course the well known Goddess site of Ephesus. The numerous marble Goddess figures from the Aegean Cycladic Islands (found both on Crete and in western Anatolia), and those of the larger island of Rhodes, just off the southwestern tip of the mainland, add to our body of information about the nature of Goddess reverence in Anatolia.

Probably earlier, but at least by 2000 B.C., tribes speaking an Indo-European language entered the area of central Anatolia, migrating southward from the Russian steppes and the Caucasus regions. Riding in swift, horse drawn, war chariots, these tribes eventually conquered the inhabitants of central Anatolia, and established themselves as the ruling class of royalty and aristocracy. From these Indo-European invaders, who then adopted a method of writing from the neighboring Semites, we learn that the indigenous population of central Anatolia had spoken a non-Indo-European, non-Semitic, language, known as *Hattili*. They had referred to themselves as the people of the Land of Hatti.

Through a misunderstanding of the limited evidence available at the time, early scholars of Anatolian archaeology dubbed both the invaders, and the invaded, as Hittites—and thus the name still stands. (The Hittite records reveal that the conquerors spoke of their own language as *Nesili* or *Nasili.*) Although the term Hittite is still used to refer to the entire culture, after the conquest in Anatolia, it most often indicates the invaders, who assumed the roles of royalty, government, army and clergy. Thus, when referring to the indigenous population only, the term Hattian is now used.

The Sun Goddess of Arinna, known as Wurusemu and Arinitti to the Hittites, was a deity originally worshipped by the Hattians; Her Hattian shrines were eventually appropriated by Hittite clergy. Evidence of the relationship of beliefs about the Sun Goddess to the precept of the divine right to rule, alongside the extremely important position of the High Priestess/Queen, raises the possibility that the invading Hittites may have adopted older Hattian customs to gain legitimization and social acceptance of their control over the Hattian peoples—control they had initially gained by well documented martial force.

From texts of rituals, found in the city of Tahurpa, we learn that several former High Priestesses of the Sun goddess had incorporated the name Nikkal into their own names. Since the name Nikkal was the northern version of the Goddess name Ningal (Great Lady), (best known from Sumer and generally associated with the moon), there is the possibility that the original Hattian shrines at Tahurpa and Arinna may once have been linked to the widespread reverence for the Goddess as Nikkal/Ningal. The site of the most sacred centre of the worship of the Anatolian Sun Goddess, the city of Arinna, has not yet been located. Hopefully, its eventual discovery and excavation may clarify the actual origins of the great Anatolian Sun Goddess, who was invoked as Mistress of Heaven and Earth.

Other names of the Goddess that appear throughout the inscriptions and texts of Anatolia, names such as Hepa, Hebat, Kubebe, Kupapa, Lilwani, and Ma—were used among various groups that were to the east, west, and south, of the centrally located Hittites. Some of these names, especially Hepa and Hebat, were used by Hurrian groups—people who did not speak an Indo-European language, but, like the Hattians, were ruled by people who did. The Hittites also knew of the worship of the Goddess as the Semitic Ishtar, and incorporated legends, customs and images of Ishtar into Hittite religious records.

The later appearing Goddess name of Kybele (Cybele) is often associated with Phrygian groups, who entered Anatolia from the north some time between 1200 and 1000 B.C. Though the Phrygians appear to have revered the Goddess, and may even have introduced the name Kybele, similarities of ritual and legend (especially of the son/lover, whose death was enacted annually, and the presence of eunuch attendants—known as Galli) reveal that the worship of Kybele was linked to legends, rituals, and customs, that had long been known in the worship of the Goddess as Ishtar and Inanna. What is perhaps most interesting, in the exploration of the reverence for the Goddess as Kybele, is that these legends, rituals, and customs, so closely associated with Goddess worship in Mesopotamia, were imported into Rome in 204 B.C. The sacred black stone of Kybele, long kept in the city of Pessinus in Anatolia, was brought to Rome at that time, and a great temple, built to house it, was completed in 191 B.C. The discovery of several tablets, found in Rome in 1608 A.D., by workmen repairing St. Peter's Church, raises the possibility that the Kybele temple was not far from, possibly beneath, where the Basilica of St. Peter's stands today.

Anatolia is also especially interesting in that accounts of Amazons were often linked to various Anatolian towns and cities, particularly those of the western coastal areas of the provinces of Lydia, Lycia and Caria. Diodorus Siculus traced the long and complicated path of a large group of Amazons from Libya into Anatolia, citing a mass migration, and a series of conquests, led by Amazon sister/queens, Myrina and Mitylene. Whether the use of the name Libya by Diodorus refers to the lands we now know as Libya, or to Africa in general, as the writings of Herodotus suggest (see African Section Introduction), this report of a Libyan origin for the Amazons of Anatolia certainly calls for further examination.

The temple at the city of Ephesus (in the province of Lydia), spoken of by Greeks as a shrine of Artemis, and later by the

Romans as a shrine of Diana—was described by both Pindar and Callimachus as a holy site first founded by Amazons. This shrine in turn links the Amazons to the island of Crete; an inscription found at Ephesus dedicated to the Goddess as—The Cretan Lady of Ephesus. Many writers of Classical Greece, including Herodotus and Pausanius, claimed that these areas of western Anatolia that were linked to Amazon accounts, had been settled by people of Crete. The two seemingly contradictory origins of the Amazons, Libya and Crete, are not necessarily in conflict, for the excavations under the guidance of Sir Arthur Evans, on the island of Crete, provided a good deal of evidence of links between Libya and Crete, as early as 3000 B.C. Still, we would do well to keep in mind that the double axe symbol appeared in association with Goddess imagery in northern Mesopotamia at about 5000 B.C. (at the Halafian site of Arpachiyah). Discoveries of *tholos* buildings (circular buildings with long rectangular corridors leading to them), on the Messara Plain of Crete, may indicate that people of the Halafian culture had migrated to Crete, bringing both the tholos design, and the double axe symbol, with them. Whether from Libya, or Halafian Mesopotamia, or both, Pindar wrote that Amazon steeds rode across the plains of Xanthos in Lydia, while the legend of Bellerophon describes him battling with Amazons in Lycia.

There is also some confusion concerning the name of the Goddess, as She was worshipped by the Anatolian Amazons. Though the name generally given in Classical accounts is simply the title, The Mother of Deities, various contemporary scholars have sought to link The Mother of Deities with Kybele, or with Artemis. After a great deal of study on this, I suspect that the name most often used may have been Lato, the Mother of Artemis. The name Artemis is certainly linked with the Anatolian Ephesus shrine, but all statues of the Goddess at that site were of a matronly image of woman. Lato, whose name appears to be derived from the most ancient Lat, Elath, or Allat, of Canaan, is known in Greek accounts, but is most closely associated with Anatolia and Crete. One of the most important Goddess festivals of western Anatolia was the *Latoia,* probably related to the Cretan festival, the *Hellotia.* And although Classical Greek accounts state that Lato gave birth to Artemis on the island of Delos, Ephesians claimed that Artemis was born in a cavern at the foot of a mountain near Ephesus. The Anatolian town of Lata Kaya, (Latakia, Laodicea of the New

Testament) claimed to possess the most ancient statue of The Mother of Deities in existence. A great temple for Lato was built high on the mountains of Crete, not far from the town known as Lato even today, while Cretan Goddess names such as Eilythia, Eleuthera, and Eleuthia, appear to be derived from the names: Lato, Lat and Elath.

The Amazons were not only closely linked to the western Anatolian provinces of Lydia, Lycia, and Caria, but also to several large Aegean islands just off the mainland. Samothrace was described by Diodorus as the island most sacred to the Amazons, one that they had designated as the site of their holiest rituals for The Mother of Deities. These rituals may have been the origin of those later described as The Mysteries of Demeter and Kore (Kore literally meaning Daughter, most often named as Persephone) as they were celebrated on the island of Samothrace—rituals perhaps once performed for The Mother and The Daughter, as Lato and Artemis. The major town on the island of Lemnos, an island mentioned in Greek accounts as one on which Jason found an all female population, was known as Myrina—the name Diodorus gave as one of the Amazon sister/queens. The major town on the nearby island of Lesbos is still known by the name of Myrina's sister—Mitylene. The island of Samos also has a major town named Mitylene. Samos lies just across the waters from the Anatolian city of Priene—a city that Diodorus included among those he listed as having been founded by Amazons. Hellenic Greeks described this Anatolian island of Samos as the *birthplace* of the Goddess known as Hera, though they portrayed Hera as the ever jealous wife of Zeus.

Settlements of Celtic peoples in Anatolia, in the third century B.C., resulted in the area of central Anatolia, including the eastern parts of Lydia, then being known as Galatia. It would be difficult to ascertain the degree of influence that Anatolian reverence for the Goddess may have had upon the Celts, but Strabo's account that Celtic representatives attended a religious council in the sacred centre of Kybele, the city of Pessinus, does suggest this as a topic deserving further exploration.

As a result of the enormous amount of often extremely fragmented bits of information, covering thousands of years: archaeological artifacts; written records from Classical Greece and Rome; connections between areas such as Libya, Crete, Canaan,

Mesopotamia, and the islands of the Aegean—it would be impossible to fully describe or discuss Goddess reverence in Anatolia in a book such as this. But perhaps the following accounts of some of the evidence about the reverence for the Goddess in Anatolia, may help to provide us with at least a partial view of the multi-faceted nature of the Goddess, as She was known and worshipped throughout the many millenia.

GREAT GRANDMOTHER
OF ANATOLIA

This piece is based upon the many statues and shrines of the Goddess that were discovered in excavations of the very early neolithic sites of Catal Huyuk (about 6500 to 5500 B.C.), and Hacilar (about 7000 to 5500 B.C.) Since writing had not yet been developed at the time these cultures existed, our knowledge of Goddess reverence from these periods is based solely upon the architecture and artifacts discovered. Murals of priestesses dressed as vultures, found upon the walls of the shrines of Catal Huyuk, invite comparison with the worship of Nekhebt, the later pre-dynastic Vulture Goddess of Upper Egypt. Some insight, into the symbolic importance of the vulture, may be gained from an examination of the still existent rituals of the Parsees of India. The Parsees place the bodies of their dead on decks in trees, to allow the vultures to clean the bones, so that they may be buried with respect and care. The horns, set in the altars of Catal Huyuk, also suggest comparison with later Egyptian symbolism, as manifested in the importance of the Holy Heifer of Heaven—as well as the horns of consecration, so familiar at Cretan sites (see Egyptian Section).

Mother with no name,
may I simply call you Great Grandmother,
you whose images were left lying
deep beneath the Anatolian earth
for some eight thousand years.
You are the ancient one
who sat upon the lioness throne
in the days when the planting of the seeds
was still a new idea
and small houses made of earthen brick,
entered through the roof by ladder,
were occupied by those who built
your many sacred shrines,
placing your images safe within them.

Deep beneath the earth at Catal Huyuk,
deep beneath the earth at Hacilar,
villages for which you had once cared
lay dark and silent waiting
to once again see the light of day,
obsidian mirrors void of reflections,
jewellry of copper, shell and marble
adorning ancient bones
that had been painted with red ochre,
and placed beneath the floors
of the homes where those who died
had once breathed and laughed and cried,
their spirits protected and protecting
those they had brought into this world—
embraced by your ever guiding presence.

Wall paintings of your priestesses,
dressed in wide vulture wing,
left visions of ancient ritual
of those who had trusted the sacred bird,
perhaps to prepare the dead for final burial.
Pairs of sacred horns
rise as upraised arms from your altars,
said to be those of wild bull or auroch,
yet resembling the long curved horns of heifers
that still roam upon the lands that you once knew.

Mother with no name,
Great Grandmother of Anatolia,
your silent mysteries are many,
as are the myriad shadows
of your eight thousand years
as they flicker across the obsidian mirrors
that had lain so long beneath your earth
and now cast reflections of reflections of reflections
of your most ancient Mother essence
on the many layered mirrored hallways
of the obsidian infinity of our minds.

SUN GODDESS OF ARINNA

The ancient Anatolian site of Arinna, the most sacred centre of the Sun Goddess, is known to us from the texts of Boghazkoy (the site of ancient Hattusas), and Tahurpa—but Arinna itself has not yet been located. The prayer included here is from tablets found at Boghazkoy, while the ritual, of the High Priestesses of the Sun Goddess, is from a text of the Nuntari-yashas Festival of Tahurpa. It is clear, from the evidence of many Hittite tablets, that the right to rule was regarded as being given by the Sun Goddess of Arinna. This ancient precept, of receiving divine right to rule from the Goddess, was also known and practiced in Babylon and Sumer, and was probably the origins of the later Christian idea that divine right to rule was provided by Jehovah—a precept that long remained the foundation of royalty in Europe, and still functions in England today.

Though She shines above us as bright as the Anatolian day, Her holiest city of Arinna, Her most sacred shrine of days long past, still lies dark beneath the earth, silently waiting to be found. Just "one day's walk from Hattusas" the ancient tablets say, but they do not tell us in which direction, or we might go to find the many secrets that She keeps in Arinna—far from the light of Her holy being.

As if to tantalize, a tablet written in Her honour, left in Hattusas, tells us that She was all, reciting from its markings in baked clay:

Thou Sun Goddess of Arinna
art most highly honoured.
Thy name is highest among names,
Thy divinity greater than all other deities.
Compared to Thee there is no other deity
as honoured or exalted
for it is Thee who is sovereign over all,
controlling all rulership
both in heaven and upon earth,
settling boundary disputes,
dispensing Thy mercy,
feeling compassion for all
who call upon Thy name.
Thou art the source of all warmth,
parent of the people of every land,
Thy worship most reverently remembered,
Thy righteousness and justice ever present,

even as Thou allottest the other deities their worship,
their rituals, their holy days, their sacrifices,
for they protect the gates of heaven,
respectfully standing to each side
as Thou passeth through each day
in all Thy shining, omnipotent glory.

Some called upon Her as Wurusemu, while others said Her name was Arinitti, and at the city of Tahurpa they remembered Her sacred daughters Hulla and Mezulla, and the youngest Goddess, She who had not yet grown Her breasts of womanhood, Granddaughter Zintuhi. At the yearly Nuntariyashas Festival, Her Tawawannas priestess performed Her rites, remembering with honour and respect the women who had served before her. Sacred images of those women stood upon the altar, golden discs haloing the heads of those who had once performed Her rites, each a High Priestess of the Sun Goddess at Her Tahurpa altar, each a queen of the Land of Hatti—women who had once guided the land, carrying out Her rules and wishes. Thus Her Tawawannas priestess dedicated a perfect lamb to each, calling upon each ancient High Priestess name, paying respect and honour to each who had joined the Sun Goddess in Her home in the heavens—then known as Sun Goddess themselves: Sun Goddess Walanni, Sun Goddess Nikalmati, Sun Goddess Asmun Nikal, Sun Goddess Dudu Hepa, Sun Goddess Henti, and Sun Goddess Tawawannas, said to be a most ancient High Priestess of the shrine at Tahurpa and a long remembered Queen of the Land of Hatti.

HEPAT

At Anatolian sites in the southeast, some quite close to the Euphrates as it runs through northern Syria, the Goddess was known as Hepat, Hepa, Hebat, Hebatu, Kubebe, and Kupapa. The prayer from Boghazkoy (ancient Hattusas) included here, written at about 1300 B.C., by Queen Pudu Hepat of Hattusas, reveals the queen's opinion that Hepat was the same deity as the Sun Goddess of Arinna. As a former worshipper of the Goddess as Hepat, there may have been some poltical intent in pointing out the connection, but it could hardly have been done if the reverence for the Goddess in each area had been for quite different images or attributes. The records of Hattusas reveal that Pudu Hepat took an important part in state and governmental affairs throughout her life.

Long revered at Aleppo and Samuha, shrines where Ishtar was sometimes said to live, Mother Hepat stands upon Her lioness on the great rock carvings of the mountain pass at Yazilikaya. Her tall cylindrical crown and long straight robes that touch Her shoes declare Her divine dignity, as the double circle symbol of deity grows from the blossoming flower that She holds in Her extended hand. There She has stood for many thousands of years, Her priestesses standing in close attendance behind the mighty Anatolian Mother.

When the princess of the city of Comana of the Taurus Mountains came to live as queen in Hittite Hattusas, young Pudu Hepat spoke her prayers, and then left them carved in stone for all to see, thus explaining that the holy Hepat glowed with the brilliance of Arinna's sovereign Queen of Heaven and Earth:

Sun Goddess of Arinna,
Mistress of the lands of Hatti,
Sovereign Queen of Heaven and Earth,
I, Pudu Hepat, have always been Thy servant,
a heifer of Thy stable since my childhood,
a strong cornerstone on which Thou can depend,
for Thou art the highest,
the most exalted of deities
and though all other deities bow down to Thee,
no mortal appeals to Thee in vain.
Sun Goddess of Arinna,
Queen and Ruler of all lands,
in the city of Hattusas
Thou art called upon as Sun Goddess of Arinna,
yet in the far country, that from which I come,
that which Thou created as The Land of Cedars,
I called upon Thee there as Hepat,
Mother of Deities.

HANNA HANNA

Hanna Hanna was the name of the Divine Ancestress, as known by a Hattian group called the Gulsas. This Hattian account also includes mention of other deities, such as Kamrusepa who presided over magic and healing, and the sisters Istustaya and Papaya who spun the threads of the future (perhaps the source of the Greek image of The Fates). The relationship, of the The Bee to Hanna Hanna, raises questions about possible links between this Hattian imagery and the title of the priestesses who served the Goddess as Kybele, Artemis, and Demeter—each known as Mellissae—Bees. The symbolic association of the Goddess, as Queen Bee, may well be the source of this imagery, as well as the symbolism intended in the depictions of Artemis surrounded by bees—on gold jewellry discovered at Camirus on the island of Rhodes. The symbolism of the evergreen tree, to invoke new growth and abundance, may offer some insight into the Winter Solstice tree later used in Europe, eventually incorporated into Christianity as the Christmas tree.

Holy Grandmother who brought life, Hanna Hanna, Goddess of all, guided Istustaya and Papaya who spin the thread of destiny for those who dwell on earth, as they sit by the spindle of fate, as they sit by the waterbowls of reflection, forming all future events. Hanna Hanna guided the gentle Kamrusepa, She who had the knowledge of the healing and thus could free those who were bound by the demons of illness. Grandmother Hanna Hanna, oldest and wisest of all, guided each of Her divine children as they carried out Her wishes.

To Her grandson, Hanna Hanna assigned the work of bringing the rains, of stirring up the storms, so that the fields of barley and emmer, so that the fields of peas and beans, so that the orchards of pomegranate and olive which grew on both sides of the Marassantiya River, might provide Her people with ease and abundance. Thus Zaskhapuna gained the office of he who makes storms, so that his angry outbursts might be harnessed into watering the crops. Then trusting that each chore would be done, by one or another of Her great and holy family, Hanna Hanna rested in Her home, as a grandmother might well deserve to do.

But there came a time when all was not well. Hot steam fogged the window openings. Homes filled with the smoke of logs that would not burn in the hearth. Though seeded with barley and emmer, the fields lay barren; even the trees of the mountains dried and died. No new saplings took their place. Wells and brooks no longer offered water. Thirsty cows and ewes rejected their own young, refusing to bring forth calf or lamb even when their bellies had seemed filled with life. But none of this was noticed by Zaskhapuna until he found that his own throat was dry, and then realizing that something was wrong, he laid the blame on Telipinu; he laid the blame on his own son.

Zaskhapuna complained, 'I appointed my son to do my work so that I might relax and feast in heaven. I gave him the lightning and the thunder. I gave him the clouds and the vessels of rainwater, but now he is not even to be found.' So it was that swift Eagle was sent out, the sharp eyed bird sent to find the youth to bring him back to do the work of his father. Eagle flew over the highest of mountains. Eagle swooped over the lowest of valleys, gliding slowly to see what could be seen. Even over the broad sea, Eagle hunted, but when Eagle returned to Zaskhapuna, no trace of the lad had been found and the world remained dry and thirsty.

Zaskhapuna went to his father. 'Is this my fault', he asked, 'that even the seeds in the field have perished in the drought? My son, your grandson, has not done the work. Whose fault is this?' Zaskhapuna challenged, hoping for a word of solace, a confirmation of his own innocence in the matter. But the weight of responsibility was laid firmly in his hands. For when his father heard what had happened, he replied, 'It is your fault. You alone must carry the blame for passing the work on to your son, when it was yours to do. If great damage has been done, it is your life that shall be taken.' So saying Zaskhapuna's father ordered Zaskhapuna to search for Telipinu, suggesting that his life might still be spared—if Telipinu could be found in time.

In despair for his very life, Zaskhapuna then went to the highest heaven, the place where Hanna Hanna lived, went to seek the advice of The Grandmother, She who possessed wisdom beyond wisdom—She who could solve problems that Her children did not even understand. Standing before Her, Zaskhapuna began to weep. Through his tears he spoke, hoping for the sympathy that his own father had not given. 'I left Telipinu to do my work', he explained, 'and he disappeared from view. But when I went to my father and told him of the problem, he claimed that it was my fault and that my life will be taken, if Telipinu is not soon found. What shall I do, Grandmother Hanna Hanna? I beg for your help.' And with these words, the man of violent, stormy temper once again lost his voice with weeping.

Hanna Hanna rose from Her resting place and looked at the frightened Zaskhapuna, knowing that he was old enough to have a grown son of his own; still She looked upon him as a child. Thus She reassured him that he need not fear, that She would handle the matter, that She would find the hiding place of Telipinu and return him to his post. Whether Zaskhapuna had done right or wrong, Hanna Hanna would help.

Even at these patiently forgiving words of reassurance, Zaskhapuna's mind was filled with doubts. 'How can you find him when I have already sent the swift and sharp eyed Eagle, the bird that goes everywhere and sees all, for Eagle says that Telipinu is nowhere to be found?' With grandmotherly calm, Hanna Hanna explained that She would send the Bee, dispatch Her sacred messenger, and that Bee would find the lad that Eagle could not find. 'But Eagle is strong', cried Zaskhapuna, 'Eagle's eyes are clear. A bee is weak. Its wings are small. How could it accomplish what even Eagle could not do?' Now irritated at his doubts, Hanna Hanna ordered Zaskhapuna to be silent, to hold his tongue so that Her thoughts would be free to arrange the search for the missing Telipinu.

Thus Hanna Hanna sent the sacred Bee, and it was not long before Bee caught sight of Telipinu fast asleep beneath a tree in a forest near the town of Lihzina. Following the instructions of Hanna Hanna, Bee stung the sleeping lad upon his fingers, sent its burning sting into his toes, so that Telipinu awoke in a frenzy. As he hopped about the forest in discomfort, Bee flew back to fetch Eagle, leading the large bird to the grove where Telipinu had been hiding. Following the sacred Bee, Eagle carried Telipinu back to Hanna Hanna.

Kamrusepa had been summoned to the temple. She who did the healing work of Hanna Hanna stood over the confused youth, soothing his still burning skin with seeds of grape and fig stirred into a bowl of cream and honey. Kamrusepa calmed the moaning Telipinu and called for the torches to be lit, saying that all confusion should now pass, saying that all angers should now be forgotten. And standing by the torches, Kamrusepa spoke these words:

The seven doors of heaven have been unbolted.
The seven doors to the Otherworld are open.
Behind each door is a cauldron of bronze.
Upon each cauldron is a handle of iron.

197

Lifted from each cauldron is the lid of aburu metal.
Let all anger and confusion fall into the cauldrons.
Let it not return.

So chanted Kamrusepa softly and with the last of Her words,
She ordered that the torches be extinguished. Anger and confusion
were safely in the cauldrons, forever deposited in the Otherworld,
from which there was no escape. So it was that despair was raised to
joy, as a feast of twelve rams appeared upon the table of the temple.
A tall evergreen was set in place in the courtyard of the holiest of
shrines. Upon the tree was hung the fleece of the ram; inside the
fleece was sewn the fat of meat; inside the fleece were sewn the seeds
of wheat; inside the fleece were sewn the seeds of grape; inside the
fleece were sewn the prayers for abundance, for days of health and
vigour. So it came to pass that Hanna Hanna presided at the table
of Her family of deities, once again knowing peace and satisfaction.

KYBELE

The numerous and varied associations of the Goddess as Kybele (Cybele),
with earlier Goddess names and images of Anatolia, suggest many possi-
bilities in considering the origins of the worship of Kybele. Her hat and
robe are not unlike those shown in carvings of Hepat, while the name
Kybele may be related to the southeastern Anatolian worship of Kubebe.
The sacred stories and rituals, most closely associated with Kybele, reveal
close connections with the Goddess in Mesopotamia as Ishtar and Inanna
(see Sumerian and Semitic Sections). This is most evident in the rituals
concerned with the death of Attis and the attendant eunuchs. Her title, as
Mother of Mt. Ida, may reveal some links with Crete, or may simply refer
to the Mt. Ida near Troy. The worship of the Goddess as Kybele, at times
geographically overlapped with the worship of Lato, and the title Mother
of Deities, may indicate some connection between the worship of Kybele
and Lato. Yet we should keep in mind that Kybele was never represented as
having a daughter, but most closely connected with the dying son, Attis.
    According to the accounts of Lucretius, the import of the sacred stone,
the worship, and the rituals, of Kybele into Rome, occurred shortly after
the Metaurus battle of the Roman war with Carthage, and was done to

carry out a decree of the prophetic Sibyls [There may well be a link between the name Kybele (softened to Cybele—as Kyprus became Cyprus) and the title of the oracular priestesses known as Sibyls.] The great Roman Spring Festival for Kybele, the Megalesia, was celebrated at least as late as 50 A.D., its title eventually changed to the Hilarion, the predecessor of the rituals we know as Easter. Inscriptions, believed to be from the Roman temple of Kybele, were unearthed when workers were repairing the Basilica of St. Peter's in 1608 A.D., suggesting the proximity of the great Kybele temple, that housed the sacred black stone, to the area now known as the Vatican.

Across the lands of Anatolia, at Pessinus and Priene, at Kohnus and Kios, at Malatya and Bandirma, at Carchemish and Yarre, at Aizanoi and Marrash, at Gavurkales and at Fraktin, and at the two Comanas, statues of the Magna Mater were called upon as Kybele. Mother of Deities, She sat upon Her throne, sacred cymbal in Her hand, flanked by lions in faithful attendance—Her great and guiding spirit watching over all.

Kybele was the Mother Lioness, riding proudly astride a lion's back or sitting upon Her lioness throne, while Her priestesses rode in splendid chariot, drawn by lions in the holy day procession. Yet was She not also the Queen Bee, mightier than any other, Her Bee Priestesses known as Mellissae, while the honey of the bee was used in sacred ritual, and bees especially protected by law in the land of Anatolia. Upon Her perfect head She wore the high cylindrical crown of Hepat, or the turret crown of city walls, revealing Her as the protector of all who dwelled within. Still, She was called upon as Mother of Mount Ida, sacred mountain name, known so well upon the islands of Crete and Cyprus, while the Anatolian Ida rose high into the heavens, close by ancient Troy, its peak visible from the offshore isle of Lesbos.

Eunuchs gathered about Her by the thousands, anxious to shed their maleness to wear the robes of Kybele's clergy, Galli trying to gain the image of Kybele's son lover, thus imitating the castrated body of Attis to declare their dedication to The Mother. Priestesses took lovers from among the strangers who came to pray from field or far off town, their children honoured more than those that had come from contract marriage—for did Strabo not write that an unwed mother in Anatolia was she who was closest to Kybele?

Various were the legends of Her son and lover Attis, youthful shepherd who played upon his flute as he cared for the grazing sheep. Although some tell the tale of Nana who ate the fruit of the pomegranate, and in this way gave birth to Attis; others say that he was the child of Kybele. And stories abound of how he died, tending his flock in the meadow, pierced through by a wild boar, or attacked by the monster Agdistus who tried to force itself upon him, and in the revulsion that Attis felt, Attis tore the genitals from his own body. Still others say that Attis, in fear of being unfaithful to the Mighty Mother, cut the maleness from his own body, thus bleeding to death beneath an evergreen tree, as violets sprang from the ground where his blood had spilled. Yet all agree that Kybele had found his lifeless body and wrapped it in the woollen mourning bands, taking the emasculated body, and the tree upon whose roots the lad had fallen, to the mountain cave in which She lived. Planting the tree by the entrance to the cave, burying his body in the earth beneath, each year at the time of his tragic death She performed the rituals of mourning at the site of burial—each year as the spring time came lamenting the dead shepherd youth.

It was this ancient Anatolian ritual that found its way to Rome. After twelve long years of the Roman war with Carthage, Sibyl priestesses, who gave the oracles of prophetic wisdom and decree, announced that the sacred stone of Kybele—the small black meteorite mentioned in the Sibylline Books, the holy heaven rock of Goddess then housed in the shrine of Anatolian Pessinus—must be brought to Rome, and a temple built to house its sacred essence, in honour of the mighty Kybele.

Thus the ship, carrying this sacred icon, made its way from the western coast of Anatolia to the mouth of the River Tiber. When it grounded there upon the rocks, and none could loose it to continue on its journey, though many sailors tried, the woman Claudia Quinta gently pulled upon its ropes, which she tied to the girdle about her waist, and easily brought it back upon the waters—to pass the rope to relay groups of women, who, each in turn, pulled the ship, carrying the sacred stone, to Rome.

On the fourth day of April, two hundred and four years before the time of Christ, Kybele's stone was placed in the Temple of Victory, on the ancient Palatine of Rome. That summer brought not only the most bountiful of harvests, but the final retreat of the enemy. On the tenth day of April, thirteen years later to the month, the great new temple had been built, and dedicated to Kybele as Matris Magnae Idaea, Great Mother of Mount Ida—as the marble walls glistened in the sunlight of springtime in Rome.

Each year following, as spring began in Rome, it was the time of the sacred Megalesia, the celebration of the Vernal Equinox, when the silver image of Kybele was carried in a chariot, drawn by lions through the city, followed by those who had come with Her from Pessinus. It was these followers who taught the Romans to cut down the sacred pine, and to wrap it in the mourning bands, hanging an effigy of Attis upon its branches, in memory of the time that Kybele had found the youthful shepherd when he lay dead beneath a tree in Anatolia. So it was that these sacramental symbols of tree, and image of Attis, were carried in solemn springtime procession to the temple of Kybele in Rome.

Around the temple doors stood those who lamented for the dying Attis, forbidden to eat of the pomegranate, while eunuch attendants wore pomegranates wound about their heads, or carried them in their hands. Male initiates joined in sacred dancing, cutting themselves in sympathetic sorrow. It was at this time that many dedicated themselves to the service of Kybele, by removing their organs of maleness—in imitation of Attis, the son lover of the Mother of Deities. Three days of sacred dancing passed; three days of solemn lamentation passed—as the blood of castrations seeped deep into the ground, some say, for penitence and for the sins of those who had offended the Goddess law. At the end of the third day, a light shone forth from deep within the temple tomb, where the effigy of Attis had been buried, and Kybele's son lover rose from the dead to great feasting and celebration—as those who worshipped Kybele cried out:

"Be of good cheer, neophytes, for Attis has been saved and so shall we in turn be saved."

The newly dedicated followers, those who had eaten no bread in deference to the memory of the broken body of Attis, those who had smeared their blood as sacrifice upon the altars and the trees, then carried the silver statue of Kybele in joyous parade about the city, until the long procession stopped at the banks of the River Tiber. There they bathed the image of Kybele, even bathing the chariot wagon in which She had been carried, adorning both with violets, before returning sacred image and wagon to the Roman temple of Mother Kybele—until spring would come again.

The worship of the Anatolian Mother, who some came to call upon as Kybele Rhea, thus honouring the name of the mother of Zeus, continued until a fire destroyed the temple. But when the temple was once again restored, Augustus, Emperor of Rome, ignoring those who condemned the rituals, joined in the Megalesia, declaring its importance in the city of Rome. And Roman Emperor Claudius, some fifty years after the birth of Christ, also joined in the rituals of the Megalesia, to lament the dead son Attis whose image hung upon the tree, and to pay honour to the mighty Anatolian Mother of Deities, Ma Kybele, Ma Rhea of Rome.

LATO

The information about the Goddess as Lato (Leto), most often regarded as a Goddess image of Greece, is not plentiful among the Greek records, but emerges more clearly in the evidence from Crete and Anatolia. Lato's name, generally believed to be derived from Lat (Elat, Allat)—a title that literally meant Goddess in Syria, Canaan, and Arabia—suggests that the name of Lato may have been carried to Crete from the Levantine coast, thus reaching the western areas of Anatolia by way of Crete. It was probably in this area of Anatolia that Hellenic Greeks first found the name of Lato, long remembering that She was the Mother of Artemis (see Greek Section). Later known by the Romans as Latona, Lato may be the source of the name of the area of Italy known as Latium, tradition often mentioning Troy of northwestern Anatolia as the origins of early settlers of Rome. Thus it may be, that from the ancient Lat of Canaan, the name of the language known as Latin was derived.

How shall we know Lato best, for Her name appears in many ancient lands, in Canaan, Arabia, Sinai, Egypt, Malta and Crete, but on the western coast of Anatolia, where Amazons once rode their noble steeds, echoes of Her image ride with the warrior women. Although Hellenic Greeks pretended that Lato was but a passing fancy of Olympian Zeus, still they spoke of Lato as the mother of the moon and the sun, and said that Her daughter Artemis, Holy One of the Anatolian Ephesus shrine that Amazons had founded, roamed free and independent in the forests—as Amazons were said to do.

How shall we know Lato best? As Ilat, Allat or Allatu, Great Mother of Arabia, who was known as the sun that gives the light of day? As the Great Goddess whose massive images lie upon the island of Malta, island that was once known as Ma Lata? As Lat, Elat, or Elath—of Ugarit, Sidon and Tyre, Holy Mother of the Sea, Goddess of northern Canaanite lands who was called upon as Mother of Deities—in the Levantine lands that came to be known as Latakia?

As Ba'Alat Ashtart of Canaan's Byblos temple, where Egyptian Isis travelled to find the body of Osiris, close by the lake at Aphaca where the Goddess was said to have arrived as a fiery falling star? As Ba'Alat of Serabit El Khadim, revered upon the sands of Sinai, remembered there in prayers inscribed to Ba'Alat as—The Ancient Serpent Lady? Perhaps even as primeval Cobra Goddess Ua Zit, predynastic Goddess of the marshes of ancient Buto, living there among the waz reeds and the lotus—on the ever floating island, where the Egyptian shrine of prophetic wisdom was later known as the holy place of Lato? As ancient Serpent Mother whose priestesses, entwined with serpents, called upon Her in the caverns of Crete, where double axes made of gold were kept as votive relics of The Mother? As Eilythia, Holy One of childbirth and destiny, who received offerings of honey at Cretan Knossos, and was honoured with small but sacred gifts at the Cretan coastal cave of Amnissos, where they say Odysseus once harboured—while Cretan people long remembered ancient Hellotia rites?

High upon Cretan hills, set between two rising swells of green, ruins of Lato's temple still mark the site where inscriptions to Her as Eilythia were left within the sacred precinct, as silent reminder of the Mother's many natures. Oaths were sworn upon Her name, invocations of The Mistress of Destiny, while some say that it was Eilythia/Lato who made the decisions for the future and gave them to the Triple Fates, just as Goddess Themis was said to do—while the village nearby the temple ruins bears the name of Lato to this day.

Greek Hesiod wrote that Lato was a Titaness, a daughter of Phoebe, the one who is said to have given the Goddess shrine of Delphi to Apollo, Hellenic Greeks pretending that the murder of Delphi's serpent by Apollo had been done to protect his mother Lato. But once the gruesome murder had been enacted, it was not to Lato that Apollo gave the shrine—but kept it for his own from that time on. Hellenic Greeks also claimed that it was on the rocky isle of Delos that Lato had pressed fleet footed Artemis from Her womb, saying that Artemis could be seen in the moon, but adding that a twin, a second born, had been the sun Apollo—though Arabian Allat had long brightened the day.

As if to further confuse memories of ancient times, and to erase the awesome omnipotence of ancient Lat, Elat, or Elath, Hellenic Greeks claimed that Eilythia had served as midwife to Lato, while at the same time claiming that newborn Artemis had aided in Apollo's birth. And, in the middle of the muddle they had made, Hellenic Greeks then said that Artemis *was* Eilythia, while some vaguely hinted at memories that Apollo had come from the land of the northern Hyperborean winds.

But Ephesians of Anatolia claimed that Mother Lato had felt the pangs of labour in the cavern at the foot of a great mountain, not far from the site of sacred Ephesus, and that it was there that Lato brought forth Her fleet footed Daughter Artemis. Thus the shrine of Ephesus had been built close by this most sacred site. Long known as the holy place of Artemis, and as a shrine first founded by Amazons, Ephesus was said to have been built around a holy tree, a xoanan, while Callimachus wrote that the image first revered was that of the Mother of Deities, thus singing of Ephesus:

A long time ago,
the warrior Amazons
set up an image
of The Mother of Deities
under the shade of a great tree
and there Queen Hippolyta offered sacrifice,
while Amazons danced an armed dance,
the shield dance of the sacred rattles,
beating time upon the ground in unison,
as syrinx flutes sang their songs.

Although they later spoke of Ephesus as the holy place of Artemis, they called upon Her as Mother, and Queen Bee; Mellissae Bee Priestesses serving at Her altar, images of golden bees held in deepest sanctity, while Megabyzi eunuchs stood by in attendance.

Not far from holy Ephesus stood the ancient shrine of Beycesultan, its double altars adorned with sacred horns, mirroring those known so well on Crete, altars perhaps dedicated to the worship of the Mother and the Daughter—while at nearby Anatolian Latakia, and at sacred Anatolian Hierapolis, priestesses took the name of Lato. It was in Latakia and Hierapolis that the great Latoia Festival was celebrated, as Cretan people had celebrated the Hellotia. But Anatolian Latakians claimed that *they* possessed the most ancient of ancient statues of The Mother of Deities!

Was it chance, or was it ancient memory, that laid the foundations of the Goddess shrine at Latakia not far from the most ancient site at Hacilar? Though probably buried deep beneath the earth, for thousands of years before the builders of Latakia arrived, there in the ruins at Hacilar lay the statues of the Mother and the Daughter, woman with braided bun, maiden with pigtails. Had one been found by the priestesses of Latakia, or were all the statues of Hacilar seeing only the darkness of millenia of settled earth, through their obsidian eyes? Yet Lato and Artemis were known not far from that most ancient site, where the Mother and the Daughter had been known some eight thousand years ago.

Even closer by the Ephesian shrine, yet another temple was built for the daughter of Lato, at the town of Magnesia. And upon the outer walls of the Magnesia temple were carved images of Amazons in battle, images that perhaps revealed the nature of Lato and Her Daughter Artemis—just as images ordered carved by Artemisia, Queen of Halicarnassos on the Lycian coast, were massive stone reflections of the valiant women warriors, those who may once have honoured Lato as the Mother of fleet footed Artemis, as Mother of Deities. And is it Lato's name that is remembered in that which is hidden—latere; in that which is worshipping—latreia; in that which lets life come forth—latus; in that which signifies that life returns to death—lethe; in that which is revered beyond all other reverence—laud; in that which means The Sacred Mother Lord—The Lady?

One of the seven wonders of the world, the site of Ephesus, where prayer to The Cretan Lady of Ephesus was to The Bearer of Light, was spoken of in Roman times as the holy place of Diana, She who was the Protector of Animals, glowing in the moonlight, as Artemis, daughter of Lato, had been known.

Yet it was this most sanctified of places, the holy site of Ephesus, the shrine first founded by Amazons, that Paul chose to visit when Romans ruled, causing silversmith Demetrius to cry:

The sanctuary of the great goddess Diana
will cease to command respect
and then it will not be long
before she who is worshipped by all Asia
and the civilized world
will be brought down
from her divine pre-eminence. (Acts 19:27)

Thus Ephesians shouted at Paul's approaching steps, 'Great is Diana of the Ephesians!' But all that they had feared, finally came to pass, as the ancient shrine at Ephesus was all but forgotten, and people learned to call upon a father and a son, forgetting the ancient Mother and Daughter who had been called upon for so long, in the land of Anatolia.

HECATE

Though known in Greece, the Goddess as Hecate is most familar to us from the western Anatolian coastal areas, and the island of Samothrace, both areas associated with Amazons. The worship of Hecate was known as far north as Colchis, on the eastern end of the Black Sea, the area in which Euripedes placed Medea as a princess and priestess of Hecate. Apollonius mentioned Colchis as an area in which Amazons venerated a sacred black stone. Though the connections are not certain, the Goddess as Heqit (Hekat) was worshipped in Egypt, known to Egyptians as a Goddess that was from Nubia and the northern Sudan. The appearance of Hecate's altars in Colchis is especially interesting, in that Herodotus described the Colchians as having originally come from Egypt. As a Goddess of witches and magic, the name of Hecate is associated with the 'dark side of the moon', in a sense a mirror image of Artemis, especially as Artemis Lycia, Artemis of the Light. At times Hecate is associated with the Greek Persephone, as Queen of the Dead, perhaps explaining why both names were linked with the sacred island of Samothrace.

Mother of the Heka, the magical power of the Word, She who holds the moon's magnetic reins on ancient magic spells, was known first in the Nubian tongue. Sacred Goddess Heqit, Ancient Goddess Hekat, Oldest of the Old, amphibian being that swims in the water, yet walks upon the dry land, was the magical essence of

even as the wind was sleeping

Isis, She whom all of Egypt called upon, summoning Her from the land of Africa to do Her wondrous works—for the emanations of the Heh Ka, the mighty energies of a million hearts, are contained within Her. Holy Enchantress, Mother who brings birth and rebirth, forever renews the cycle of existence—as the frog brings forth the tadpole, as the tadpole turns to frog, so Hekat guides the transformations, giving power to the spoken word of sacred incantation.

Those who knew Her powers and Her secrets carried them to Lycia, and Lydia, and Caria, even as far as the land of Colchis on the Black Sea's eastern coast, where mighty sorceror Medea—she who may have given her name to the Median lands of Persia, for some say she taught her magic to the Persian Magi—once kneeled before Hecate's altar at Her Colchis shrine. And though far from the land of the Nile, Herodotus explained that it was in Colchis that Egyptians dwelled. And there remembering Egyptian ways, the amulets of leather, of papyrus, of stone and wood, marked with the words of power; figures moulded from the wax of honeycomb; power filled potions of date wine and honey, they carefully recited incantations—protecting, defending, even weakening, the one whose secret name they spoke.

And was it not on the coast of Colchis that Amazons had venerated the sacred black stone, at a temple on a small coastal island, or so Apollonius said. And on the holy island of Samothrace, sacred to the Amazons, Hecate's name was called upon in Her Zerynthian Cave, where dogs were most sacred to Her. Was this in ancient memory of the Dog Star, the one spoken of as Sept in Egypt, the one spoken of as Sirius in Greece, the one that was sacred to Isis when She was called upon by Her true Egyptian name of Au Sept? Or was Hecate but another name for Artemis, called upon when the moon was gone—for Samothracian Mysteries were wound about the Daughter's descent into death, and Her ever recurring return to life.

Those who later called upon the magic of Hecate, spoke Her name in the woods of Thessaly and Greece, as magician and wizard, sorcerer and witch, followed Her ancient knowledge. There they used the sacred cauldron at the threefold crossroads, in the darkness of a moonless night, adding wine or milk or blood in which to stir the sacred herbs, only those that had grown by moonlight, adding sacred stones from the East, using the olive or the willow twig to stir the contents of the bubbling, boiling cauldron—as those who called upon Hecate circled thrice about Her altar, laying flaming twigs upon it.

Even as the wind was sleeping, as were all the others of the village, the magic women of Hecate addressed themselves to each planet of the sky, to each watching star in the heavens that grew brighter as they spoke, listening to the hounds that bayed their knowledge of Her holy presence. And when the chariot of Hecate descended to take them to unknown regions, it was drawn by winged serpents who carried them across the vast heavens of night, as they called upon the Holy One who comes and goes as Artemis, as Diana, as Cynthia, as Selene—as Hecate, The Hidden One, Mighty Queen of Witches, Mother of the ancient Heka magic.

ANAHITA

The adoption of the Goddess into later Iranian beliefs was probably the result of influence from Anatolia, and to some extent from Iraq (Mesopotamia). This particular account is based upon a hymn from an Iranian Yast (Hymnal) that may have been written as late as the fourth century A.D. The combination of Anahita's role, as one who watches over the universe, along with the statement that the male Ahura Mazda assigned this task to Her, is probably the result of foreign concepts of Goddess reverence being incorporated into the male-oriented religious structure of the Indo-Iranians. Tribes of Indo-European speaking peoples are believed to have entered Iran, from the Kirghiz Steppes area of Russia, possibly as early as the fourth millenium B.C. Linguistic connections reveal that the Iranians were related to the Indo-Aryans who conquered the towns of the Indus Valley of India at about 1500 B.C. To a lesser extent, the Iranians were also linguistically related to the Indo-European speaking people who conquered the Hattians and Hurrians of Anatolia.

To the followers of holy Anait, whose worship was renowned across the northern stretches of Anatolia, and in Armenian lands, Medes and Achaemenids spread their empires, thus bringing the worship of the Goddess back with them into the land of Iran. Calling upon Her as Aredevi Sura Anahita, or as Nana whose name was sometimes given as the mother of Attis—even as Creator Nana had been known in ancient Sumer—Iranians claimed that it was Ahura Mazda who assigned to Anahita the task of watching over the universe.

Yet do they not say that it is Anahita who is the Cosmic Ocean in which the stars do float, and Anahita who provides the rain, sending waters from heaven to the springs and rivers, protecting the flocks in the pastures, causing them to bear their young—as it is Anahita who fills the womb with life? How glorious She is as She rides across the heavens, Her chariot drawn by four white steeds named wind and rain and clouds and sleet, or as She rides on the back of a gliding eagle, or even upon a lion. Yet the wings of the eagle grow from Her own shoulders, as the eight pointed crown sits upon Her head, as golden as the eight petalled star of Ishtar—one hundred small stars shining upon it.

Thus in Sardis and in Susa, in Kangawar and Ecbatana, revelations of Anahita's holiness were inscribed to the Mother of Wisdom, Protector of Humanity, while at Istakhr, famed Persepolis, the eternal flame burned within Her shrine, and the words beneath Her image read:

I AM THE CONSCIENCE OF THINE OWN SELF.

From the Waters of the Indus
India

he thousand named Goddess who sits upon the thousand petalled lotus of the cosmos, source of all energy, She who holds the entire universe in Her womb—manifests Her existence in the many Goddess images of the land of India.

The exploration of Goddess reverence in India is a vast and complex undertaking, the following section able to do little more than skim the surface of the subject. In such a study, it is of paramount importance to realize that Goddess imagery, ritual, and reverence in India are the result of a confrontation and eventual blending of at least two quite different major racial/ethnic groups. The first are the people of the early Harappan culture of the Indus Valley, believed to be the ancestors of today's Dravidians. The second are the much lighter skinned Aryans who began to invade the Indus Valley at about 2000 B.C. To understand Goddess reverence in India, a knowledge of the historical events that encompass the Aryan conquests of the people of the Harappan culture, and the subsequent institution of the caste system in which Aryans appointed themselves as the highest caste, the Brahmins, is vital.

India had been inhabited long before and during the Upper Paleolithic period, producing such cultures as the Soan and the Madras. The neolithic period of agricultural development started in India at about 5000 B.C. By about 3000 B.C., the culture known as Harappan began to flourish. Well built houses of brick, some two stories high, reveal that the Harappan culture spread

211

out over some 950 miles along the banks of the Indus River and its tributaries. A form of writing, including over 250 symbols, was developed, but unfortunately this writing has not yet been deciphered. The religious beliefs of the Harappans are known to us from the enormous number of Goddess statues unearthed at Harappan sites, many quite similar to those found in Mesopotamia

At about 2000 B.C., bands of nomadic Aryans, probably from the Kirghiz Steppes of Russia, descended upon and conquered many of the cities and villages of the Harappan culture. Accounts of these invasions and the massacre or enslavement of much of the indigenous population were recorded in the *Vedas,* the earliest written material from the Aryans of India. The Vedic writings reveal the extreme patriarchal orientation of the early Aryans, while explaining that their religious beliefs were centred around the male trinity of Indra, Mitra and Varuna. The Vedas also reveal that the native language of the Aryans, Sanskrit, is an Indo-European tongue related to Greek, Latin, Hittite and most European languages, including English. The Vedas also make it clear that the invading Aryans regarded the indigenous population of the Harappan culture as physically and mentally inferior to themselves, despite the obviously advanced cultural achievements of the Harappans as compared to the nomadic life of the Aryans. References to these claims of superiority suggest that the dark skins, smaller stature, and religious and social beliefs of the Harappans lay at the core of these claims—which were used to justify and explain the institution of the caste structure. Most pertinent to the study of Goddess reverence in India are the Vedic passages that refer to the people of the Harappan culture as *Danavas,* people of Danu—and an account in the *Rg Veda* that describes the murder of Mother Danu by the Aryan god Indra.

It is not too surprising that early Vedic writings do not include images of Goddess figures as powerful, or even as especially important. Certain aspects of nature are perceived as female spirits, but these personifications are relatively insignificant in comparison to the descriptions of the male deities. The names of Ushas as the dawn, and Sarasvati as a river, both appear in the Rg Veda, but the important cultural and spiritual aspects later associated with these names are not mentioned in the Rg Veda. The most dynamic female image included in the Vedas is that of Aditi, the Mother of the Aryan gods. This name is especially interesting in that the name Diti, like the name Danu, is associated with the Mother Goddess of the Harappans. The name Aditi literally means 'not Diti'. The use of this name raises the question of whether the importance, or even the image, of Aditi existed among the Aryans prior to their invasion of India. A legend in the much later *Ramayana* describes Indra's destruction of an embryo in Diti's womb. The account explains that all of the other children of Diti had been slain, and that Indra feared that the embryo might be a child who would eventually kill him.

At about the sixth century A.D., two bodies of writings began to emerge, texts that are filled with detailed and dynamic images of the Goddess. These are known as the *Tantras* and the *Puranas* (Ancient Lore). The Brahmanic leaders long resisted recognition of these texts, finally accepting them as writings of a much lesser sanctity and importance than the Vedas. It is in the Puranas, and even more so in the Tantras, that we find the accounts of Goddess as powerful, even as the dynamic force of the universe. This late emergence of Goddess imagery is generally attributed to a survival of ancient beliefs among non-Aryan groups that had been less affected by Brahmanic teachings. We should not underestimate the probability of changes and transformations in much of the material, as it may have been retained over a very long period of time, but the Goddess images and rituals of the Puranas and Tantras may offer some clue to ideas about the Goddess that may be as old as the Harappan period.

One of the areas of India that remained relatively non-Aryan is the Malabar coast of the southwest. Among many of the villages of the Malabar area, worship of the *Ammas,* the Mothers, is still the primary religious concern. Over the last two centuries, the social structure of the Malabar areas has been recorded as matrilineal and matrifocal, while polyandry (one woman having several husbands) was observed among the Nayyars of Malabar in the nineteenth century. It is interesting to note the presence of many woman poets in the collections of Tamil poetry from the Madura area of Malabar, dated to about 100 B.C. Along with women's poems about the feelings of a nursing mother during famine, the feelings of a young girl when a neighborhood boy destroys her sand castle and the joys of palm wine at a village festival—lesbian love appears to have been included as a non-controversial topic. The poetess Avviyar, author of many poems in the Tamil collections, wrote, "O Bee, fair of wing...among all the flowers you have known, is there any more fragrant than my lady of the lovely hair and perfect mouth? Graceful as the peacock she dwells, rich with love for me." (*Koruntogai 2*)

Other areas that remained relatively unaffected by Aryan Brahmin influences are Bengal and Assam, to the northeast of India. Matrilineal and matrifocal customs still exist in these areas as well, while Goddess names such as Kali, Candi and Chamunda originate in Bengali beliefs. The shrine at Kamrupa in Assam is regarded as one of the most important seats, *pithas,* of Tantric rituals which centre upon the Goddess as the ultimate Shakti. Tantric Yoga groups reveal a quite different attitude towards women in practice, as well as in their theological beliefs. They are one of the few religious orders that include women in the highest positions of clergy. They were the first to speak out against the Aryan custom of *suttee,* a wife being burned upon her husband's death pyre. It is also interesting to realize that caste discrimination is discouraged at Tantric rituals as well as in Tantric beliefs. In contrast to other Hindu tenets, the Tantric texts list 'pride in family' and 'pride in caste' as two major obstacles that must be overcome before enlightenment can be achieved. Tantric sexual rituals, *Maithuna,* are certainly to be compared to the sexual rituals of Sumer and Babylon. In exploring the possible links between the sexual rituals of Sumer and those of India, it may be significant that the sexual rituals of Sumer were enacted by priestesses who lived together in the temple, while contemporary Tantric Maithuna is most often enacted between wife and husband.

In the more narrative Puranas, many Goddess names appear, each associated with specific traits and symbols. They are understood to be aspects or incarnations of the Great Goddess Devi. Devi, in turn, represents the concept of the ultimate Shakti. To fully describe and discuss each of the enormous number of Goddess names and aspects would require several volumes, but some of the better known aspects are included as part of the account of Devi, while a separate account of Kali is included in this section. For those interested in further reading or study, other aspects of the Goddess are: Candi, the fierce; Chamunda, the demon slayer; Annapurna, she of the abundant food; Gauri, the golden one; Jagad Amba, world mother; Ambika, little mother; Kulakatyayani, intuitive wisdom; Bhuvanesvari, earth—to list but a few.

One interesting image that appears in the Puranas is that of the Submarine Mare who holds the fiery ambrosia of passion and anger in her mouth. This image invites comparison with the Celtic imagery of the Goddess as the great mare whose mane can be seen in the foam of the waves of the ocean. Although actual connections between the spiritual beliefs and images of the Celts and the Indians may be remote, and certainly highly speculative, it is interesting to note that the name of the Mother Goddess as Danu occurs in the literature of both India and Ireland.

Wherever a deeper exploration of Goddess imagery and reverence leads, there is no question that the beliefs of India offer us a wealth of information about the nature of life creating deity as female.

SHAKTI

Knowledge of Shakti, literally power, occurs primarily in the Tantric texts. Descriptions of the nature of Shakti might well be used by modern physicists in attempts to describe the nature of pure or primal energy. Shakti reverence is known to this day, especially among the non-Aryan peoples of Bengal, Assam, Nepal and the southern Malabar coastal area. The four most important shrines of Shakti worship are Oddiyana, Jalandhara, Purnagiri and Srihatta, though many other sites of Tantric worship exist throughout India. The concept of Shakti as the serpent of Kundalini Yoga may be linked to the Naga serpent deities of the Dravidian south. The image of the Shakti serpent rising to the Ajna Chakra of the forehead may well be compared to the symbolism of Egypt, in which the Cobra Goddess Ua Zit emerges from the forehead as the Third Eye of Wisdom.

She who holds the Universe in Her womb,
source of all creative energies,
Maha Devi who conceives
and bears and nourishes
all that exists—
She is the ghanibuti,
the massed condensed power of energy;
She is the sphurana,
the power that burgeons forth into action;
She is purest consciousness and bliss,
inherent in the manifestation of all being.

Never can She be known
in Her perfect completeness,
for Her omnipotence is in all
that She continually does.
Do they not say
that even Shiva is unable to stir,
lies as a corpse,
until She grants him Her energies?
In the form of the coiled serpent,
the Bhujangi Kundalini,
She unwinds Herself through the chakras,
through the lotuses of the body,
as She creates Her cosmic serpent spiral
through the lotus chakras of the Universe.

At Her sacred shrine of Kamrupa,
they drink the kula nectar
that is the blood that passes from Her
as the moon passes from the sky,
while those who reach out to know Her
sit in Her circle of worshippers,
the sacred Shakti Cakra Pravartika,
knowing that if they worship Her with full devotion,
She will appear and give what is requested,
as She maintains the many beings of the world.

Some say that there are many worlds,
each ruled by a goddess or a god,
but that there is just the One Great Mother,
the Jagad Amba, the Makara,
Shakti of all existence,
She to whom even the gods bow down
in reverent worship and respect,
anxious for even the dust of Her feet
to touch their waiting heads—
for it is Shakti who is the ultimate source,
the infinite Cosmic Energy of all that occurs,
Maha Devi of the thousand petalled lotus.

DEVI

The word *deva,* or the feminine *devi,* is the Sanskrit word that means deity, cognate with the English word divine. It literally means 'glowing with brilliant illumination'. Though the name Devi is from the Aryan Sanskrit, Her image encompasses many of the names and aspects of the Goddess as known in non-Aryan beliefs. The names included in this account; Kali, Parvati, Sati, Laksmi, Tara and Durga occur primarily in the Puranas. The description of Devi that comprises the first paragraph of this piece is adapted from the *Saundaryalahari,* Flood of Beauty. The account of the defeat of the evil buffalo demon, Mahisa, is drawn from several of the Puranas, including the *Markandeya* and the *Skanda.* Though probably coincidental, it is interesting to note that the colours of the eyes of the Goddess, and the colours of the guna strands of matter, are red, black and white—the three colours used in the cone mosaics of Goddess temples in Sumer.

Whose feet can it be that form the image of the holy crest upon the sacred writings? Who is it that is Supreme Intelligence, second to none? Who is it that is earth, air, fire, water, and yet is the ether of all energy, and yet again is Pure Mind? Who is it that owns the gunas, the very threads of matter of all that mortals see and touch? Who is it that has three eyes, one red, one white, one black, the colours of the eyes the same as those of the guna strands? Who is it that is many sided love, the protection and guidance of a mother who speaks with loving kindness to each and every child that calls out to her in need, yet at the same time is the feelings that bring the body to desire—the sight of the sun and the moon as breasts upon the perfect body arousing the lover to passion? Who is it that daily battles all that is harmful? By whose permission do all other deities have access to their stations? Name Her! Name Her! Luminous with energy, magnificent in Her brilliance, it can be no one but Devi! If She were to close Her eyes for an instant, the entire cosmos would disappear.

Upon the desire for divine wisdom, or safe childbirth, or a healthy infant—She is called upon as Sati. Upon the mountains where She takes Shiva as Her consort, and finds that She must listen to him curse the very one She wants to bless, yet provides Shiva with Her Shakti power so that unless he is united with Her, he cannot move—She who was once known as Sati, She who then lived again as Uma—She who is the daughter of the Mountain Himalaya, She is called upon as Parvati.

Upon the need for special luck, blessings and good fortune, when one turns to She who came forth from the primeval churning of the Ocean, sees Her seated upon the lotus, ever fresh with the cool of the water from the trunks of Her attendant elephants, knowing that She was once the patient Sita, knowing that She returned again as Radha, knowing that She sometimes answers to the name of Sri—She is called upon as Laksmi.

Upon the struggle of each swimmer caught in the tangled waters of the ocean of the world and the contemplation of the

One who will lead each swimmer from the confusion of the wild currents of the sea of life, so that each may rise and blossom as a lotus blossoms on the surface of the waters, upon thoughts of the One who is the Mistress of the Boat of Salvation, the One who guides the shipwrecked to safe shores, the One who is the knowledge, the wisdom, the guiding star, the Prajnaparamita, protecting, rescuing, redeeming Saviour—She is called upon as Tara.

Upon the need for courage, when one considers the righteous conquest of evil by awe inspiring majestic powers that lead the way—She is called upon as Durga. Upon consideration of the passage of time, the span of this life, when asking who is it that takes life only to give it back again, and sees the skin that is like the petals of a blue lotus at night covered with a tigerskin around Her loins, a garland of heads hanging about Her neck, knowing that She sometimes answers to the name of Mahacinatara—She is called upon as Kali.

Long ago in lifetimes past, the name of Durga passed to Devi. But long before that time Durga was the name of the force of evil, the wicked one, the Mahisa Buffalo, who drove the deities from their home in heaven, making them seek refuge in the forests upon earth. Durga destroyed all that was sacred, smashing the holy places where the beings of heaven had once been welcomed. The Buffalo Demon stole the heat from hearth fires, pushed great rivers from their paths, sent rain when rain should not have fallen, held rain back when it was needed most, struck the ocean with his horns, uprooted mountains with his horns, dusted himself with the precious powder of the minerals of the mountains —and dragged off every Goddess of perfection, forcing them to do his housework.

The people cried to Shiva, praying to him, begging him to destroy the evil demon. But the powers of the Buffalo were greater than those of Shiva. Against the evil demon, Shiva was weak. Thus Shiva went to Devi, who sat as golden Gauri, knowing that She was Shakti, knowing that She was the power and energy of the world and that She could succeed where he had failed. But Devi had much to do and thought to rid Herself of yet another task, so She sent the dark Kalatri, guardian of the night, to confront the Demon Durga. It was not long before the truth was clear. Kalatri too was helpless before the powers of the Buffalo. If the Demon Durga was to be stopped, only one could do the job—so to halt the evil Durga, mighty Devi then rode forth upon Her lion.

The demon was prepared for battle. One hundred and twenty million elephants, one hundred and twenty million war chariots, one hundred and twenty million horses, and troops beyond number—all these lay in wait to battle Devi. Mahisa Durga had made them all. A storm of arrows hailed upon Devi's body, but as if they were raindrops, they slipped off without harm. The army of the demon hurled great rocks, as the Buffalo gored Devi's troops with his horns. The demon's breath stirred up hurricanes, tearing trees from their roots. The demon hurled these uprooted trees at Devi, but they fell from Her unscathed body as sand falls from the crevice of a cliff in a strong breeze.

The Buffalo Durga lashed the ocean with his tail, so that great waves fell upon the land. Devi's one thousand arms were each busy with battle, shooting aside one thousand arrows sent by Durga's troops. Angered at the demon's attack upon the lion that She rode, Devi threw a lasso about the Buffalo's tail, only to find that the demon Buffalo itself became a lion. Though She plunged Her sword through the neck of the lion, it then took the form of a man, sword and shield in his hands. Seeing this, Devi pierced his heart with arrows, only to find that the evil demon Durga had become an elephant.

So it was that the evil being continued to ravage the land. He created a mountain of wickedness, hurling this at Devi who cut through its density with Her sword, slicing it into seven smaller hills. Battle after battle, no one won and no one lost, until the time that the evil Buffalo took his true form, revealing himself as the manifestation of all evil. Stripped of all that he had used to hide, without elephants, without chariots, without horses, without troops, Durga showed himself as Durga—and he too had one thousand arms.

The battle was fierce. Arms matched arms, as each wicked hand of Durga challenged each perfect hand of Devi. And then in the heat of the battle, Devi pulled back in silence. Worrying that She had admitted defeat, the world watched as Devi stopped to drink the blood red wine. With surprise, they heard Devi call out to the evil Buffalo, telling him to roar with laughter, for that would be his final roar. The world watched as Devi drank the celestial wine, finishing the last drops. They saw Her place Her

mighty Devi
then came forth

foot upon the demon's neck and heard the roar of Devi's laughter as Her trident pierced the body of the Buffalo—until it lay dead.

Thus the world rejoiced. People shouted 'Victory' and 'Saviour'. And in memory of the time that Devi saved the world from the evil Buffalo, they took his name of Durga and gave it to the Goddess Devi, so that those who speak of Durga know that Durga is but one part of Devi, while remembering the cosmic struggle She fought so long ago.

KALI

Kali, literally meaning Time, is a Goddess name that is traced back to early Bengali beliefs and may be related to Korravai, a Dravidian name of the fierce warrior aspect of the Goddess. Although Kali is worshipped in many shrines and temples of India, literature and general practice make it clear that Kali is yet another aspect of the great Devi. The material concerning Kali is found primarily in the Puranas, both the *Skanda* and the *Harivamsa* used for this account. It is vital to be conscious of the inherent racism in certain accounts of Kali, especially those that state that Her blackness reveals a lesser level of spiritual development, e.g. *Skanda Purana*. Such statements must be seen in the context of Aryan Brahmanic attitudes imposed upon Dravidian peoples, and the caste system in which Aryans assigned the darkest Dravidians to the lowest caste. This aspect of Indian beliefs should not be ignored. It demands that an examination of its presence and intent be made at greater length—if what is truly spiritual, and what is political, are ever to be understood in Indian belief systems.

Black as the petal of a blue lotus at night,
black as the night touched by the light of the moon,
Kali is the essence of Night,
She who is called Sleep,
She who is named Dream,
She who is the joyous dancer of the cremation ground,
She who chooses from among the corpses
which souls shall be released
from the bonds of existence—
to know eternal bliss.

She is Maha Kali, Great Mother Time,
She is Nitya Kali, Everlasting Time,
She is Raksa Kali, Goblin yet Protector
during earthquake, famine or flood,
She is Smyama Kali, the Dark One who dispels fear,
She is Smasana Kali, Ever Joyous Dancer
on the corpses of the cremation grounds,
surrounded by wailing female spirits,
a garland of heads about Her neck,
a belt of human hands about Her waist,
blood upon Her lips.

Yet others say that She lives in the triple heaven,
wearing a bodice of gold,
and a string of pearls that glisten like moonbeams,
Her four arms of darkest iron
holding a trident and a sword,
holding a perfect lotus and a pot of honey,
and that Her banner is the peacock's gracious tail,
as peacock feathers adorn Her wrists and ankles.
It is this Kali who dwells forever
on the summit of Mount Vindhya,
born again from the womb of Yasoda,
murdered as an infant girl
by the wicked coward Kamsa,
who seeing Her take Her place in heaven
saw his own violent death—
while She lived on Vindhya, eternal and divine.

Daughter of the Ocean, Mother born of Anger,
wet nurse to invincible warriors,
though they say that death
lingers in the waters of Her womb,
still, full devotions are made to Kali
on the ninth day of each month,
and those who worship with full heart
receive all that they desire.
For who does not know that this is the Kali Yuga,
the Fourth World of bitterness and sorrow,
and that when the Yuga finds its natural end,
Kali shall be there to gather the seeds—
to create the new Creation.

ANASUYA

This most surprising account of the woman Anasuya, literally 'free from envy', is from the *Bhavisya Purana*. As with most Purana dating, estimates on this text vary greatly, ranging from 500 to 1200 A.D.

Woman among women, seldom do they speak of her or her great wisdom and the Goddess powers that dwelled within her, for she spoke of herself as mortal as she sat upon the banks of the Ganges, deep in meditation, calling upon the holy deities.

Yet there are a few who did remember that as she sat there, deep in deepest mind, suddenly three gods appeared before her, those of whom she had long heard, and long been taught to trust. But great was her surprise when Shiva approached upon his Nandi Bull, holding his phallus in his hands. And great was her surprise when Vishnu appeared on his Garuda Bird, thinking only of his physical desire for her. And even greater was her surprise when Brahma appeared, telling of being in the power of Kama's passion and that he thought only of possessing her body.

When she heard their unexpected speeches, of their bodily cravings for her, despite the fact that her husband Atri sat close by her side, she held her silence, for so long had she been taught to hold these gods in great respect. But in response to her respectful silence, the three gods fell upon her with violent attack, determined to take her body forcefully, to use it to satisfy their own desires.

Thus astonished by their actions, her anger raged and rose against them. Though they were the ancient gods that she had learned to worship and revere, she cursed their very existence, hurled insults at their being. Calling them 'The Phallus', 'The Head' and 'The Two Feet', she warned them that all worshippers would laugh at them unless they realized that they were as sons to her, as to any mortal woman. With wisdom, she explained that their uncontrolled desires grew from their ignorance at not recognizing that they were but children to her, and if they desired to be revered as worthy holy beings, they must learn to know her as their mother.

SARASVATI

In the *Rg Veda,* Sarasvati appears as the spirit of the Sarasvati River, a river that once flowed from the Himalayas into the Indus. Early sites of the Harrapan culture once flourished along its banks. Today the river bed lies along the edge of the Thar Desert. In the later *Brhaddharma Purana,* She takes an anthropomorphic form, presenting the knowledge of writing to the son of the Goddess Parvati. Her name occurs in many later prayers and rituals, each providing some of the material included here. At times described as the wife of Brahma, She is also known as Vac and revered as the presiding deity of the arts: music, painting, carving and especially associated with the acquisition of writing.

The echoes of the lovely notes
that She strums upon Her vina lute,
and the clear resounding words
that She plays upon the strings of Her voice,
float across the waters
of the river Sarasvati,
as it flows from the melting snowcaps
of the heaven touching Himalayas.
How fortunate are those who watched
and saw the gracious Sarasvati
seated upon the downy back
of the great white swan,
as the crescent of the moon
glowed from Her perfect brow.

Who was it that remembered
that it was She who brought the gift of language,
the poetry and the words of ancient knowledge,
designing the very letters
of the sacred Devanagari script
whose alphabet forms the garland
from which the holy mantras are picked?
Thus memories were carved in stone—
Sarasvati's holy arms holding the tablets,
Sarasvati's holy hands holding the stylus,
so that none would forget
The Mother of the Written Word.

THE GODDESSES OF ASSAM

Assam, the land of the Khasi peoples, is located at the far northwestern edge of India, on the southern ridges of the Himalayas. This particular account was recorded by Mrs. M. Rafy, who spent many years of her life in Assam, eventually publishing her studies as *Folktales of the Khasis.* The structure of the divine family, as described in this account, appears to reflect evidence of the matrifocal customs that have been observed among many groups of Assam. The image of the moon as brother to the sister sun recalls the Inuit (Eskimo) legend of Sun Sister (see Native American section). Both legends explain the dimmer light of the moon as the result of a brother's sexual attack upon his sister. The details of the funeral rites for the Mother, Earth, is as much a creation story as one of death—one that may be better understood in the context of the topography of the area of Assam.

High in the Khasi Hills, along the banks of the River Brahmaputra, not far from Kulhakangri of the rising Himalayas, ancient stories of the holy family who guide the people are remembered still. For who can forget Mother Earth and Her four children— Goddess Ka Um of the waters; Goddess Ka Ding of the fire; Goddess Ka Sngi of the sun; and their brother U Bnai who shines as the moon.

Thus it is remembered that when Earth's children were very young, the moon shone as brightly as the sun. Young Sun Goddess Ka Sngi appeared faithfully each day, to be the light for Her Mother, resting only when Her day's work was done. But Brother U Bnai was selfish, caring little for the needs of others, seldom doing his family chores. Often, he disappeared for days at a time, staying out late at night accompanied by loose companions, leading a life of indulgence and wasteful pursuits. It was no wonder that Mother Earth was filled with worry, and each time he returned his sisters scolded him, only to find that their words fell upon ears deaf to their concerns.

As adulthood came upon him, U Bnai wandered ever further, often descending to the caverns deep beneath Earth, cavorting there with evil beings who encouraged him in his thoughtless, lazy life. In the darkness of U Bnai's absence, time continued to pass. So long had he been gone from his home in the heavens that a day came upon him that was filled with a longing for the lovely home and family he had nearly forgotten. Deep in memories of home, U Bnai once again flew up into the vast blue heavens.

Though he soon reached the home that he had longed for, his mind was still filled with the wrong thinking and selfishness he had known in the caverns. And upon seeing his dear sister, the glowing Ka Sngi who filled the world with Her brilliant beauty, instead of the brotherly devotion he should have felt in his heart, it was his body that gave him greatest concern—as he looked upon the lovely Ka Sngi with thoughts of lust and desire.

No sooner did he greet Her in the heavens, than he spoke of his desire for Her. He danced about, trying to tempt Her with his own glowing beauty. He bragged of all that he had seen in his travels, of the nights of abandon he had known, thinking this would win Her interest. And seeing that She did not respond, he then compared Her to all others he had met, telling Ka Sngi that no one in heaven, no one in the caverns beneath Earth, was as beautiful as She was in Her perfect radiance. Though his compliments were kind, Ka Sngi filled with astonishment as U Bnai then stated that Her beauty was equalled only by his own, and further added that She would be foolish to spurn the offer of his passions.

Ka Sngi was patient with Her brother, though She knew that what he said was filled with wrong thinking. With gentleness, She explained that he must not think of Her with passion, but only with brotherly concern. Despite Her reassurances of the sisterly love She felt, despite Her reassurances that he would someday find a better suited mate, U Bnai grew angry that his pleasure was being denied. So long had he done just as he pleased, he could not believe that he would not have his way, and determined that he would take whatever he desired, he then fell upon Ka Sngi in violent assault.

Rage filled the heart of the patient sister, for this insult was more than She would bear. So it was that She reached deep into Her own brilliant radiance and filled Her hand with the cooling ashes of Her fire, hurling these at U Bnai! As the dry grey ashes landed upon his face, the fire of U Bnai began to dim, smothering the light of the brother, as it smothered his wrong thinking passions. In shame, he left the presence of Ka Sngi, the scars left by the ashes scarring his arrogant vanity, so that from that day on he seldom appeared in the light of the day.

Many eons later, when Mother Earth grew old, Her three daughters looked down from the heavens and sorrowed when they saw their Mother lying still in death. In the deep grief they felt, they sought to show the respect that daughters give their mothers when they have finished with this life. Thus the daughters spoke together. Earth's body was vast. How could they perform the funeral rites that would free their Mother's soul from Her body?

Trying to decide how this might best be done, the three sisters agreed that Ka Sngi, the youngest, should perform the sacred rites. The Sun Goddess then sent down great waves of heat, trying to burn the body so that the soul could be free. The forests and meadows of Earth were soon scorched and grey but the body did not truly burn. After many days of trying, Ka Sngi returned to Her sisters, tired and discouraged. 'I have done all that I could, but still our Mother's body retains its shape of life and Her soul cannot depart.'

It was then that the second sister, the Goddess of Water, Ka Um, thought to make a flood. This would at least cover Earth's body so that it would not lie exposed. Ka Um then sent Her heaviest rains, pouring water from the heavens until the rivers and lakes overflowed their banks and the ocean fell in great tides upon Earth. The body of Earth lay deep beneath the flood. But when the waters began to slowly drain away, Ka Um returned to Her sisters, tired and discouraged. 'I have done all that I could, but still our Mother's body retains its shape of life and Her soul cannot depart.'

The eldest of the three, Goddess of Fire, Ka Ding, then understood that it must be Her task to free Her Mother's soul. With Her mighty powers, She burned the scorched forest until the intensity of Her heat caused Earth's body to burst into flame, to boil as heaving lakes of lava, so that great blisters formed into mountains, leaving deep valleys between. When the waters that remained from Ka Um's flood flowed into the valleys and formed rivers where they had not been before, Ka Ding knew that She had finally performed the sacred rites. It was in this way that Earth's body was changed enough to free the soul within Her.

RANGADA

This is another little known account of a mortal woman, this one from the great epic work known as the *Mahabharata*. Although Hindu tradition suggests that this 90,000 stanza work is from about 3000 B.C., most scholars of Indian literature date it to about 900 B.C., some to as late as 300 B.C.

High upon her horse she rode, courage shining clearly in the gleaming darkness of her eyes. Her hunting arrows sent straighter than any of the village, her fearlessness in driving off an enemy imitated but never equalled by those who followed her, Rangada led her people through hunt and battle.

Knowing little of modesty and coy behavior, Rangada spoke easily of what was on her mind. Thus when she found the youth Arjuna sleeping in the woods beneath a tree, she dismounted from her horse and walked closer to see the lovely lad who wakened from the sound of the forest leaves that crackled beneath her feet. In fear, he reached for his arrows, until Rangada spoke of her enjoyment of his beauty, explaining that she had drawn close only to better admire each fine feature of his face and the structure of his lean brown body, saying that for him she could feel love and that she would enjoy knowing his body in this way.

Arjuna, confused by her open speech, spoke quickly of his vow of celibacy, that which he had taken not many days before, and meant to keep throughout one year. But he then added to this reason for refusal that even should he desire to break his vow, he would surely not do so with a woman so outspoken, one whose quiver of arrows told of a life that he did not regard as womanly, at least not as he believed a woman should be.

Hurt deeply by the words he spoke, confused in heart and mind yet still filled with wanting to know Arjuna better, Rangada put away her hunting clothes, discarded her bow and arrows. In their stead, she wrapped herself with silks, slid bangle bracelets upon her arms, slipped bangle bracelets upon her ankles, hung golden loops upon her ears, rubbed sweet smelling oils upon her cinnamon skin—and made her way to the tent of Arjuna. Entering without a word, as Arjuna sat in holy meditation, Rangada lay down upon his mat, so that when his eyes did open she beckoned him to come and lie beside her.

So it happened that Arjuna broke his vow of celibacy, for though she said her name was Malha, Arjuna thought that the woman who had appeared so mysteriously in his tent was the nymph or Goddess, woman as perfect as woman can be. In the months that then passed, Malha and Arjuna wandered joyfully along the banks of rippling mountain streams, made love on the soft ferns of the forest, as Arjuna hunted for what food was needed and Malha prepared it to suit his taste.

Thirteen moons had grown large and disappeared when a group of villagers riding by Arjuna's tent stopped to ask Arjuna if he had seen their leader. They spoke of a woman just twenty-two years, a woman of most perfect aim, a woman whose body blended perfectly with the rhythm of her horse's gallop, a woman whose heart was brave, whose courage any man would want to follow. The villagers then told Arjuna of how their homes had been attacked and how though they had battled fiercely, they could not drive the invaders from the land. Again they spoke of their leader Rangada, agreeing upon her brilliance in both hunt and battle, explaining their days of constant troubles since her disappearance. Arjuna, thinking to help them in their plight, knowing of his own prowess in battle, offered to ride with them. As he waited for their answer, he thought of the brave woman leader, imagining the pleasures of riding alongside such a remarkable woman.

Within the darkness of the tent, Rangada heard the speaking and recognized the voices of her comrades of the past. Unable to remain quietly inside, as she heard the reports of their troubles, she came forth to greet her friends, to offer her help—daring Arjuna's wrath at the game she had played as Malha. Cries of joy greeted Rangada's appearance, each village comrade reaching out to grasp the hand of the leader who had so long been missing. Some fell upon their knees with gratitude that she had finally been found, but none was more astonished than Arjuna.

Even as Arjuna saw his gentle Malha mount a great black steed, her arms strong enough to calm its excitement, her legs strong enough to soothe its great body, still he did not trust his eyes. But when from her seat high upon its back, Rangada invited Arjuna to join them in the battle, he mounted the horse by her side, ever puzzled by the feelings of unexpected joy that came from riding alongside Rangada Malha.

USHAS

The name of Ushas, and her identification with the dawn, occur in the *Rg Veda*. Her image is definitely of Indo-European origin, to be regarded as much the same deity as Eos of Greece and Aurora of Rome. In accordance with most of the female deities of the Vedic writings, She is young, lovely and somewhat nymphlike. The association of Ushas with the dawn led to references in later texts that call upon Ushas to arrive as the dawn of spiritual awakening.

Holy Spirit of the morning light,
Her golden glow rises in the eastern sky
as Her chariot drawn by seven cinnamon heifers
passes through the celestial gates,
followed by one hundred golden chariots.
Her gauzy veils of many colours,
each embroidered with threads of gold,
float behind Her in the gentle breeze,
revealing the smile upon Her face.
Riding upon Her path in the heavens,
She arrives as the dawning of the day.

Sun before the sun,
as old as the time
when the sun first rose
on the first morning,
Ushas is forever young,
causing some to wish
that She would not arrive each day,
for Her eternal youth only serves to remind
that each time that She appears,
the rest of us grow older.

Yet those who embrace
the joys of knowing many dawns,
call upon Her to bring the light of dawn
into the inner night of the mind,
asking that She shed Her rays of morning light
not only to awaken each body,
but to awaken each mind.

Of Sea and Star and Serpent
Sumer

umer, the most ancient literate civilization on record, left a legacy of Goddess imagery and reverence that gleams with the rich patina of five thousand years. As Creator of heaven and earth, as giver of the laws of life, the concept of writing, methods of agriculture and much more, images of Goddess reverence in Sumer allow us to glimpse into the dawn of civilization.

After several millenia of Goddess worshipping Neolithic cultures in the Near East, such as those of Jericho, Catal Huyuk, Hacilar, and the Hassuna and Halaf periods, a culture began to develop along the southern banks of the Tigris and Euphrates Rivers. This culture, known as Sumerian, appears to have been the first in the world to have developed a system of writing. The Sumerian culture is associated with a slightly earlier culture known as Ubaidian, formed by peoples who had entered Mesopotamia shortly before the Sumerian period. Some of the people of the Ubaidian culture are known to have settled at the site of Eridu, close to the Persian Gulf. Although Ubaidians are most often credited with initiating Sumerian development, lesser known cultures in the Eridu area probably played a part in the initiation of this ancient civilization. None of the evidence has so far provided scholars with knowledge of the racial or linguistic identity of the ancient Sumerians.

The Sumerian language confuses the identification of the Sumerian peoples even further, in that their language was neither

Semitic nor Indo-European, the two major language groups of the area. One of the foremost scholars of Sumerian culture, Professor S.N. Kramer, described the Sumerian Language as "...reminiscent to some extent of the Ural-Altaic languages." These languages are best known among groups of northern Siberia and among the Finns, the Turks and other north Asian groups (see Japanese section). One must be careful not to draw conclusions from such a statement, but consideration of this possible link certainly suggests the need for further research.

Thus the racial identity of the Sumerians is still quite open to question, but there is no question that from about 3500 B.C. onwards, Sumer was well into an astonishing cultural flowering. The development of the culture reached a high point in the Jemdet Nasr period (about 3200 B.C.) with the invention of writing. From 3200 B.C. until shortly before 2000 B.C., writing appears to have been used primarily for keeping temple records of land assignments and the gathering and distribution of crops and livestock. One early law code (Urukagina) is dated to about 2300 B.C. But except for a few fragments and the temple records, most of the epic poetry, law codes, hymns and ritual texts of Sumer are from slightly before 2000 B.C. and afterwards. The Sumerian system of writing, wedge shaped marks (cuneiform) pressed into clay tablets while they were still damp, evolved from the initial use of pictorial symbols to those of an increasingly abstract nature. This major contribution to history was then adopted by the Semitic Akkadians, and through the Phoenicians of Canaan was eventually passed on to the Greeks, the alphabet symbols undergoing considerable changes and development throughout the many centuries in which this occurred.

It is vital to realize that our current knowledge of the Sumerians is based upon the chance fortune of what has so far been discovered and the condition in which it has been found. The artifacts that provide us with information about Sumerian life and religious beliefs are those that were in use from about 3200 to 1700 B.C. Excavations are continually adding to our body of knowledge about the Sumerian people. As this occurs over many decades, information is often found that confirms or contradicts scholarly theories based upon the earlier evidence. It is for this reason that I have chosen to present information that is known from specific tablets and artifacts, pointing out some hopefully interesting connections, but avoiding overly generalized analyses about what we simply do not yet know. It is important, however, to realize that what is known today about a particular Goddess image is not necessarily, or even likely, the totality of that image as it was known in the past. It is information that we know with some certainty today.

The evidence of Mesopotamia reveals that there was a close relationship between the Sumerians and the Semites who were settled slightly further to the north. This is attested by 2400 B.C. but may have existed long before that time. Many rulers of Sumer had Semitic names and at several sites evidence of Sumerian and early Semitic culture have been found side by side. One scholar even went so far as to suggest that the entire Sumerian culture was composed of Semitic people and that the Sumerian language was used only for purposes of writing, but the evidence seem to refute this hypothesis at almost every point.

It is true that the Sumerian Goddess Inanna is closely associated with the Semitic Goddess Ishtar (see Semitic section—Vol. I), Ishtar eventually replacing the name of Inanna at the great temple in Erech. But there are many differences in the imagery and symbolism of the Goddess as She appears under each of these names. Even within the Sumerian culture itself, many differences are to be noted between Goddess imagery and ritual as known in separate locations and various periods.

One location that invites further investigation is that of the city of Nippur, an extremely sacred centre of the Sumerians, and specifically connected to the bestowal of divine right to rulership. The name most often mentioned by scholars as the 'chief deity' of Nippur is Enlil, though it was his wife Ninlil who actually bestowed the divine right. Careful examination of the Sumerian account of Enlil's rape of Ninlil before their marriage, the name of Nanshebargunu given as the mother of Ninlil and as the Mother of Nippur, another text stating that the Goddess Nidaba (Goddess of Writing) was the mother of Ninlil, and the importance of the 'Laws of Nidaba' in Lagash where the Goddess was most often named as Nanshe—all exist as clues for a more careful exploration of the special sanctity of Nippur. Though Enlil's name was certainly important during the historical periods, the powers of the Goddess as Nanshebargunu, Nanshe, Nidaba or Ninlil may have preceded the importance of Enlil in Nippur.

We might also want to more carefully examine the legend of the attack upon the Goddess Ereshkigal by the war god Nergal, an account that deals with the way in which Ereshkigal lost the sole sovereignty of the Land of the Irkalla. This exploration should certainly include a careful consideration of the role of the male deity Enki (Ea) in his assistance to Nergal, as well as a study of the transformations and the continually increasing importance and power of Enki as he appears in the legends of Ninmah, Ninhursag, and Inanna.

While reading and rereading the translations of Sumerian epic poetry, it is difficult not to take notice of and to respond to the poetic use of metaphor and simile, as well as to the style of phrasing in which an idea is presented and then expanded upon. In the prayer of Enheduanna (from about 2300 B.C.), this ancient poet/priestess described her sad plight at being driven from the temple of Ningal in the city of Ur as that of being 'forced to flee the cote like a swallow'. The hymn, actually to Inanna, the daughter of Ningal, describes the wrath of Inanna as an 'attacking storm' and Inanna's voice as 'blowing louder than a howling storm...moaning louder than the evil winds'.

Another text, describing the destruction of the temple at Ur about 400 years later, is a lament for the Goddess Ningal. Here we can see the expansion of the message conveyed, as each new fact confirms and further explains the lines preceding it:

> Your city has been made into ruins,
> You are no longer its Mistress;
> Your righteous house has been given over to the pickaxe,
> You no longer inhabit it;
> Your people have been led to the slaughter,
> You are no longer their Queen...
> O Queen, your city weeps before you as its Mother.

It is not difficult to imagine Sumerian poems or hymns being recited aloud, this form of expanded repetition emphasizing and clarifying what is being said. A somewhat similar style of phrasing also occurs in Semitic literature, especially noticeable in the epics of Ugarit. It may well be that these written texts followed a long tradition of oral recitation. The poetic imagery found all throughout the Sumerian texts reveals a sophistication of thought and expression no less developed that any we have found since the days of the Sumerian people.

NAMMU

Nammu is probably the earliest recorded name of a universe creating deity so far discovered anywhere on earth. She is described in a few extremely ancient fragments as 'the mother who gave birth to heaven and earth'. The ideogram symbol used for Her name is identical to the sign used to designate the ocean. Ama or Amu is the Sumerian word for mother, and it is possible that the Sumerian *Nin* once preceded this Goddess name as it does so many others. Nammu is not only credited with being the Mother of all Deities, but also as the one who first decided that human beings should be made, an act then carried out by Her daughter Ninmah. Descriptions of the Sumerian paradise known as Dilmun, as an idyllic ancient homeland, are believed to have influenced other Near and Middle Eastern cultures and may be the source of the Hebrew account of Eden.

Ama Tu An Ki—
Mother who gave birth
to heaven and earth,
Primordial Creator of the Universe
who oversees the fashioning of life
and to each decrees their fate,
Oldest of the Old,
ancient, even among Sumerians.
Mother Primeval Sea left memories
in the land of the two rivers—
that is was She who had created all above,
that it was She who had created all below.

Memories of far off Dilmun island,
paradise where death and sickness were unknown,
perfect land where skies were always clear and blue,
where trees were thick in the orchard
and each heavy with its perfect fruit,
lingered as knowledge of the ancient homeland,
island where Sumerians had once lived,
island first created by Nammu.

NINA

Nina (Nana) also appears as a very ancient name of the Goddess in Sumer. She is most often represented as a serpent tailed or fish tailed woman, these images perhaps associated with Nammu as the Primeval Sea. The oldest artifacts identifying Nina are from the settlement at Eridu, close to the point at which the Tigris and Euphrates reach the Persian Gulf. Evidence of offerings of fish were found upon the ancient altars of Eridu, though in historical periods this city was associated with the male deity Enki. The prefix *Nin* precedes many Goddess names and some have translated it as Goddess or Lady (in its original sense as the female counterpart of Lord). There is a male deity known as Ninurta, described as a son of Ninmah but *urta* may mean ancient mother and may once have been a Goddess name itself. Since the name Nina is the most basic form of the title Nin, I have taken the liberty of including many other Sumerian Goddess names and aspects in this piece, but it should be understood that these names and the statements associated with them do appear as separate from Nina in the Sumerian tablets. It is generally thought that each of these Goddess names was originally known as that of the Mother Goddess in a specific town or community, and that later identification by specific aspects or activities in an assembly of deities may be the result of the continual centralizing of government and a subsequently more centralized theology.

From the deep waters of the Goddess Sea came the Holy One of many names, Ama Gal Dingir, Mother Great Goddess, Her mighty powers known among the people of ancient Sumer.

When they spoke of Her as She who watched over Nammu's isle of Dilmun—they said that She was Nin Sikil. When they called upon Her to tend them in their times of illness, to provide healing herbs and the magic words of cure—they said that She was Ninkarrak, Gula or Bau. When gratitude was offered for the beer and the wine that She had given for their pleasure and the libations at the holy rites—they said that She was Ninkasi. When they spoke of Her as Wild Cow of the Cattle Folds, High Priestess who sat upon the throne, offering sagacious counsel, interpreting the dreams of the people—they said that She was Ninsun or Ninsunna. When they spoke of Her as the birthgiving Mother, the one who wept at the time of the great flood, the one to whom all those who had drowned returned to at their death, the one whose temple graced the wide plains of Khafajah—they said that She was Ninti or Nintu.

When they knew Her as The Lady of the city of Lagash, the one who gave the barley of the fields so that the people could eat to satisfaction, or when She was approached in Her holy shrine and asked to untangle the threads of the images of dreams so that all could understand what had been told to them when their eyes were closed with sleep, knowing Her as The Judge of Humankind on the last day of each year, She who asked if they had comforted the orphan, She who asked if they had cared for the elderly and ill, She who asked if they had given shelter to the homeless, She who asked if they had given food to any who were hungry—they said that Her name was Nanshe.

When they spoke of who it was that formed the people of the earth with the guiding help of Nammu, and who it was that directed brother/husband Enki to feed the people She had made, and who it was that watched as Enki attempted to make people of his own and thus produced such a feeble being that it could not walk and could not talk and could not even reach its hand out to take the bread that had been offered, and who it was that seeing this cursed Enki for the sorrow he had brought by trying to fashion human life when it was not his natural work to do—they said that Her name was Ninmah.

When they looked upon Her as the holy mountain that rose from the primeval waters, the Wild Cow that came at the beginning and shattered the very air with Her presence as Regent of Earth and Heaven, and when they stood before Her shrine at Al Ubaid where the winged lioness guarded from above while images of Her sacred herd of cattle were marked in ivory on Her blue mosaic wall, and when they remembered that it was She who first gave birth to the healing plants that Enki ate in greed as soon as She had birthed them, and when they remembered who it was that then placed the gravely ill Enki by Her sacred vulva until She brought forth eight deities of healing, each born without any pain of labour, so that the greedy Enki was soon cured of his illness—they said that Her name was Ninhursag.

When they spoke of The Mother in the city of Nippur, She who owned the divine Dukug, the grain chamber of the heavens, and of the time She gave the gift of the Dukug, thus teaching the growing of the grain, how to sow, how to harvest, while in Her Tummal shrine on earth, She received the lad that She had chosen as the shepherd, and when they remembered that it was She who gave birth to the moon in the darkness of the Netherworld; and yet cannot forget the anger of the memory of Her rape by Enlil who then sat upon the throne of Nippur's First Mother, Nanshebargunu—they said that Her name was Ninlil.

When they gazed into the night time sky over the cities of Harran and Ur and saw the glowing circle of Her in the moon, and heard Her called upon by women who knew the power of Her light, and when they knew of the names of those who served as High Priestess at Her ever gifted altar as Enheduanna and Eannatum, those who had once lived in the cloistered gigparu rectory of the temple, and when they sang the songs of lamentation of the destruction of the city and called upon Her as The Mother and Queen of Ur, She who held the sovereignty while husband Nannar was Her ishib priest, and they cried because She could no longer watch over Ur and because Enheduanna who had once interpreted Her messages was no longer able to convey Her wishes—they said that Her name was Ningal or Nikkal.

Yet when they stood where the two rivers met and poured into the wide gulf that led into the sea, and knew Her at the settlement of Eridu as The Oldest One, Serpent Goddess of the Oracles, Mistress of Unfathomable Decrees, Interpreter of Dreams, Prophetess of Deities, She who assigned the destinies of lives while swimming as a fish, Her tail opalescent in the waters, the sacred sign that spelled Her name the same as the sign of the city of Nineveh—they spoke of Her as Nana or Nina and to Her they directed these prayers so many thousands of years ago:

> Hear O ye regions, the praise of Queen Nana,
> Magnify the Creatress, Exalt the Dignified,
> Hold high the Glorious One,
> Draw close to The Mighty Lady
>
> O Nina, Lady of the Holy Rites,
> Lady of precious divine decree,
> Lady who decides the fates,
> Thy word is reliable,
> it excels above all else,
> Prophetess of Deities art Thou,
> Sovereign of the lands art Thou.

NIDABA

In the artifacts of the Goddess Nidaba, She is often symbolized as serpent or woman with a serpent tail. At the towns of Nippur, Lagash, Erech and Umma, She was regarded as the tutelary deity of writing, preceding any male deities to whom this important cultural contribution was later credited. The oldest evidence of writing so far discovered—and believed to be the earliest on earth—was found at the temple of Erech and dates back to the Jemdet Nasr period (about 3200 B.C.). Throughout the historical periods this temple was consecrated to the Goddess Inanna. This earliest form of written language, once deciphered and translated, turned out to be records of land assignments by the temple. Since later Sumerian documents explained that the group of priestesses known as the Naditu were in charge of this aspect of temple activities, it appears quite likely that it was the Naditu who first developed a method of recording their accounts, thus the very beginnings of the ability to record ideas in written form. Nidaba's name also appears as the author of the sacred laws of Lagash, those by which the Goddess Nanshe judged humankind each New Year. The images of Nidaba, and the woman scribe Belit Sheri who recorded the deeds of the dead, offer interesting parallels to the images of Maat and Seshat of Egypt (see Egyptian section).

Serpent Goddess of Wisdom, Divine Serpent Lady of Life, Basmu Usum—Holy Cobra, She who made Her way through the reeds of the marshes of Sumer even before it was called by that name and from the reeds that She knew so well, She created the stylus to press into the dampness of the soft flattened clay, giving one of the most precious gifts, that of taking what is in our mortal minds and preserving for those yet to come, ideas that might once have been forgotten—yet now remain as long as clay that has been baked in fire's oven.

Most Ancient Scribe, not only did She give the stylus but Her decrees of wisdom's ways, for those who were filled with the eternal presence of Her being marked down for all posterity what She taught in the beginning. Most Learned One of the Holy Chamber, born in the ib room of Goddess temple, yet at the same time living in the starry skies, Her seven arms holding the seven tablets, She is the designer of the fifty decrees of righteousness, Her laws for living written as arrangements of the stars upon Her heavenly tablets of the darkest blue of lapis stone.

Holy Nidaba, was it not She who taught the knowledge of the written word to Belit Sheri and then appointed Her as scribe to mark down the deeds of all who live—upon the leaves of the Tree of Life? It was She who arranged the patterns of the stars so that people may choose their paths between them, thinking always of Her wisdom, calling upon Her in times of indecision, in contemplation of the messages of sleep, asking always for Her guidance in best following Her ways.

Holy One of the Reed, Holy One of Wisdom—is there a knowing mortal upon this earth who can write a line, a phrase, a word, and remember Her ancient sacred being without thoughts of gratitude?

INANNA

Inanna was probably the most widely known Goddess name among the Sumerians in the later periods of Sumer. As Erech became the centre of Sumerian culture and government, Inanna's increasingly popularized image assimilated many of the aspects and rituals known under other Goddess names in various towns and communities. The name of Inanna, often written as Innin, may be related to the ancient Goddess name Nina. As Nina was symbolized by a serpent, so Inanna's name was often accompanied by a serpent coiling about a staff. The description of Inanna as the daughter of Ninmah or Ningal (depending upon the location of the text), also suggests the rise in importance of Inanna as Sumerian theological structures were changing. It is interesting to note that whereas Enki plays the role of son or troublesome husband in the legends of Nammu, Ninmah and Ninhursag, he is given a much greater stature in the legends of Inanna. The name of Inanna's assistant Ninshuber may reveal a change of gender over the years, as other Sumerian documents include the line Ninshuber Amamu, i.e. Ninshuber is my mother.

From the ancient family of Creator Goddess Nammu, from Nammu's daughter known as Ningal or Ninmah, came the Daughter Goddess Inanna. Her Goddess powers lessened as Mesopotamian centuries passed, yet still She was called upon as Mistress of the Heavens, Sovereign Lady of the Land, Queen of the Assembly of Deities. But Inanna was spoken of as the daughter of Anu, or the daughter of Nannar, or the daughter of Enki, said to fix destinies with the help of Enlil, said to have received Her right to choose who would sit upon the royal throne from Enki. Though Nammu had created heaven and earth and Ninmah had created people, new tribes moving to the land of the two rivers made less of the nature of the Goddess, viewing Her as Daughter more than Mother, explaining Her still remembered powers as those that had been given to Her by men.

Yet the most ancient image of Creator Mother lingered in some Sumerian hearts for Inanna was still said to hold 'full power of judgement and decision and the control of the law of heaven and earth'. Her Goddess essence was called upon in the earthly form of Her High Priestess, to regulate the divine order, to fix destinies at the time of each new moon, and deepest reverence was paid to Her even by the deities of the Great Assembly of Heaven, as She announced the judgements of the land. Mortals looked upon Her holy light as the morning star that heralds each day, as the evening star that announces the arrival of each night, as the sacred planet Venus—Inanna watching over all.

It was said that Inanna's Eye was Ama Usum Gal Ana, Mother Serpent Great of Heaven, even as She was known as Lioness in Battle, lions adoring Her Goddess being carved upon a mace head at Khafajah, while Inanna sat upon Her lion throne or stood upon the lion's back, even as heifer horns adorned Her holy head in the ancient settlement of Erech. Those who spoke of moonlike Ningal as Inanna's Mother, said that Utu was the sun and now Her brother, yet many still claimed that She was The Mighty Queen, 'designer of all heaven and earth, able to make the mountains quiver, able to shake the very heavens, able to destroy the indestructible, able to make perish the unperishable.'

Some Sumerians spoke of Her tender love and of the time that She had favoured Agade, bringing peace and prosperity to that town through Her ever watchful guidance. Thus the tablets spoke of Her sagacious counsel given through Agade's elderly women and men who called upon Her as Majestic Queen, She whose decrees are supreme, Divine Mother who reveals the laws—while Her ever present symbols of the gatepost knot and loop were tied upon each storehouse filled with wheat and barley, speaking silently of the food that She gave, and of Her gift of the knowledge of the growing—as those in Nippur had spoken of Ninlil.

Along the waters of the Tigris and Euphrates and the flowing Tigris finger of Diyala, each pouring into the wide and waiting mouth of the Persian Gulf, shrines and temples to Inanna were set as rising jewels upon the desert sands. At Kish and Khafajah, at Nippur and Lagash, at Agrab and Agade, Inanna's eight petalled star glistened alongside Her gatepost loop, while at the temple at Tell Brak set deep into the Khabur Valley, even before the time of the building of the pyramids of Gizeh, symbols of the Goddess Eye were left among a multitude of beads, and eight petalled rosettes glowed with the golden light of the evening star.

Of all the towns and villages that called upon Her name and built great shrines and temples to house the essence of Her divinity, none could compare with the temple of E Anna that stood on the ancient sacred grounds of the city of Erech. Close by the waters of the Euphrates, for centuries Her worshippers had erected the new upon the old, most ancient foundations beneath the newer grandeur of red and black and white mosaic pattern, carefully formed from the tiny bases of terra cotta cones. Until, with the ever growing cluster of courtyards and buildings, they formed the great E Anna, Inanna's House of Heaven, center of protecting guidance, home of the Great Goddess who watched over all from Eshnunna to Eridu.

Great were the powers of she who was the Entu, Lady who is a Deity, living in the sacred gigparu apartments as High Priestess to Inanna, incarnation upon the earth of Her heavenly being above, presiding over temple lands, over communities of people, dispensing land and food to all. The orphan, the elderly, the weak, were each cared for with as much concern and tenderness as those who could work the land of Erech and bring the fruits of their labours to the storehouse of the temple. Priestesses carried out the Entu's work, Naditu women living together in their gagu temple home, watching over the fields and fisheries, the poultry, the cattle and the orchards, recording what had been brought in, recording what had been given out, thus helping the people of Inanna—as the Entu governed wisely as the mother of the city.

Deep beneath earth's blanket, that which covered the sanctified E Anna for over five thousand years, lay the lowest level of the Goddess shrine at Erech, most ancient temple that housed the first markings recording the assignments of the land, the apportioning of the food, the allotments of the fish, the cattle, the wheat, the fruit, that which had been gathered and distributed by the temple offices. Ancient marks of written language pressed into the once soft clay by priestesses, those who collected and distributed all that was needed by the people of Erech, bestowed upon the memory of human mind the precious gift of written reminder, milestone of cultural growth—the pragmatic genius of the women of E Anna marked forever on the passing stream of time, indelible as the brilliant gift of the Sumerian Goddess.

Lying not far from the ancient tablets, tall as a child of four years, was the alabaster vase whose ringed carvings preserved images of E Anna ritual, Goddess or High Priestess seated upon the throne, horned as the heifer of heaven, approached by naked rotund men who brought their offerings of wheat and fruit, of fish and animals, to lay before the holy feet of She who sat upon the throne, guiding the community of Erech, over five thousand years ago.

At the time of the New Year, the priestess of Inanna prepared for the yearly sacred mating, ritual from times most ancient even then, each year the High Priestess choosing for her bed the one she would appoint as shepherd, a new lad for the year, yet always spoken of as Damuzi, true son, consort of the Goddess. The priestess of Inanna made ready, wrapping her breechcloth and robes about her body freshly bathed, making her face to glow as amber, placing the kohl upon her eyes, inviting the new Damuzi to prove himself upon her bed, to test his fitness as the year's new shepherd.

The chosen Damuzi appeared before her, promising to perform Inanna's holy rites, promising to accomplish the divine pattern, stating that he had brought the presents to the sacred house of Inanna, declaring that he would follow carefully the ancient Goddess rites of the New Moon. The priestess of Inanna, though pleased with all the offerings and his promised dedication to Inanna, reminded the lad that he had not yet proved his worth, announcing to the gathered congregation:

> When on my bed he has shown his love,
> when he has given pleasure to my loins,
> when I have given pleasure to his,
> then shall I show my kindness to Damuzi,
> then shall I arrange his destiny,
> only then shall I appoint him to be shepherd
> of the flocks of my land.

Thus on the day of this holy ritual, on the day of the year's end, a bed was set for the High Priestess of Inanna, so that she might test the new Damuzi. Descending from the wide steps of the temple, she led the new Damuzi to her bed, assuring him that the fruits he brought were sweet, that his herbs and plants were tasty, and that his youthful beauty was as sweet as honey, promising that when she had enjoyed his beauty, her love would be more savoury than honey—for she would then choose him for Inanna's holy lap, appoint him as the year's new shepherd, present him with the crook and staff, touch him with the wand of shepherdship. So deep in Sumerian memory was the knowledge that the shepherd must be the lad who was chosen by the Goddess that later kings who sat upon Mesopotamian thrones spoke of themselves as Damuzi, as the beloved of the holy Inanna, king—because they had been chosen for Her holy lap.

Within Inanna's holy house lived the priestesses in the mastaku quarters, immaculate, perfect, sacred nu-gig women who made love to those who came to pray, initiating those who would gain wisdom of the sanctity of life's creative process, of Inanna's gift to mortals, welcoming those who yearned to touch divinity, to understand the miracle of the creation of life, to be in contact with the essence of existence – through love sanctified within the sacred shrine, through communion with the holiest of women, the perfect earthly reflections of She who makes all life.

Though Erech had long been a mighty city, the first where written language saw the light of day, the first where the wheel of the potter had been made to circle round, where the High Priestesses of Inanna had long sat upon the throne of guidance, there were those who had forgotten that Enki was but the son of Nammu, the First Mother who had created heaven and earth, and that Enki was the oftimes foolish husband of Ninmah or Ninhursag. Thus they told a story to explain the marvel of Erech's gains and the many gracious gifts of the Goddess to that town, claiming that its ever blossoming culture had been taken from Enki's home in Eridu, adding that Enki was a god of wisdom and that he was the father of the Goddess, of She who was still said to be Designer of all Heaven and Earth.

The tale they told was that Inanna had one day stepped into the Boat of Heaven and sailed south upon the wide Euphrates from Her home in Erech until She reached the watery abyss of

Enki's shrine in Eridu. Entering nervous Enki's home, She had been offered food and drink to appease Her possible wrath, yet it was not Inanna who grew drunk but nervous Enki who drank more than he served, and in his drunken state he had agreed to give all the gifts of culture, the precious one hundred Me's, to the mighty Goddess, so that She might take them back to Erech.

Arranging the one hundred Me's safely for the journey, back into the boat Inanna stepped. Hardly had She started north to Erech, when Enki changed his mind and sent a group of monsters of the sea to attack the Boat of Heaven of Inanna, to return the Me's to Eridu and Enki. With the help of loyal assistant Ninshuber, Inanna fought the monsters off, still piloting the boat along its course, all the while shouting angry curses at the god of Eridu for his sudden change of mind, for his daring to reclaim what he had freely given, and most of all for launching this attack upon the open waters without warning. So furiously did they defend the boat, that with Ninshuber's help, Inanna drove the monsters from their path and journeyed on towards Erech, finally docking safely at its shores.

Thus went the story that was told to explain why those of Erech spoke of the many gifts, the Me's that had been given by Inanna to Her people in the city of Erech: weaving and pottery, the sowing and harvesting of the grains, justice, truth and understanding, wisdom and the laws that guided people, eldership and the sexual rituals, the crook and the sceptre and the priestly office of Divine Lady. These gifts and many more did Inanna give to Erech—but the followers of Enki claimed that She had taken them from a drunken god of wisdom whose sagacity and decisions rang as hollow echoes in the bottom of an empty drinking jug, while they could not forget that She had brought them in Her Boat of Heaven.

Many were the tales about Inanna and Damuzi; many were the hymns of sadness sung upon Damuzi's death, mournful memories of the young lad's dying and how Inanna wept for Her son lover while the women of Inanna grieved in sympathy and lamentation:

> For the lover who slumbers,
> for the child who no longer
> brings happiness to the temple of E Anna,
> for holy Inanna who sorrows more deeply than any.

My child, the far removed,
my Damu, the far removed,
my lover who brought the plentiful food,
my lover who provided abundant drink,
my lover who is bound like the Tigris,
my lover who is captive like the Euphrates.

The mate of the Queen of Heaven no longer lives,
the keeper of the cattle stalls no longer lives,
in E Anna there is weeping,
the crying is for the plants,
for they no longer grow,
the crying is for the barley,
for it no longer grows,
the crying is for the flocks of sheep,
for no longer are the young lambs born,
the crying is for the herds of cattle,
for no longer are the young calves born,
the crying is for the great rivers,
for they no longer bring the floods.

Though the drought and famine of the land were reminders of Damuzi's death, Sumerians also remembered a time long before, when Inanna had descended into the Irkalla. Walking down the steps of the Land of No Return, arriving in the domain of the Land of the Dead, Inanna had found Herself a captive and had been freed only with Her promise that She would supply a life —in substitution for Her own. So it came to pass that Inanna once again ascended into heaven, searching for a substitute to send to the Irkalla in Her stead, accompanied and guarded by a host of Gallas, ghastly heartless demons who turned life into death.

Seeing the loyal Ninshuber waiting for his Mistress to return, the Gallas were about to take him as the substitute until Inanna stayed their pale white hands, telling of his constant, faithful service and declaring that Ninshuber was not to be Her choice as substitute. Approaching the city of Umma, the Gallas spied the god named Shara and once again stepped forward to claim him as the substitute, but Shara bowed low in the dust at Inanna's holy feet and for this act of reverence and respect, Inanna turned the Gallas from this humble god—thus sparing him from being taken to the Land of No Return. Approaching the city of Badtibera, the Gallas spied the god Latarrek and once again stepped forward to claim him as the substitute, but Latarrek bowed low in the dust at Inanna's holy feet and for this act of reverence and respect, Inanna turned the Gallas from this humble god—thus sparing him from being taken to the Land of No Return.

Finally arriving at the district of Kullab, a neighborhood upon the grounds of Erech where Inanna's temple glistened in the sunlight, Inanna was shocked to see Damuzi, the son She had appointed as the shepherd, the lover She had appointed as the keeper of the goat stalls—for no longer was he dressed in shepherd's clothes. Dressed in royal robes, he was sitting high upon Inanna's throne, and more astonishing, Inanna saw that he was rejoicing at Her disappearance, happily claiming Her position of Sovereign and Ruler of the Lands of Erech. There he sat, joyfully celebrating Her long absence, the days that She had spent in the Irkalla, hoping that She would never return.

Infuriated at his heartlessness, at his pleasure in sitting upon Her throne, while shedding not a tear at Her disappearance, or at the possibility of Her death in the Irkalla, his thoughts only upon the crook of sovereignty and the power that he had gained upon Her absence—Inanna looked upon him with the Eye of Death. Thus the Gallas claimed Damuzi as the substitute, dragging him off to the Irkalla, to the Land of No Return, for allowing his ambition to cause him to forget all love and loyalty to his mother, his mate, his Goddess.

So it came to pass that each year, at the time of remembering Damuzi's death, when the rivers grew low in the dryness of the summer, the story of how Damuzi died was told. And though Inanna grieved for the loss of son and lover, Her heart was for the welfare of the people, those who were Hers to protect and guide. Thus She banished even Her own son when he had rejoiced at taking the ancient Mother's place upon the throne, for despite the many changes in the nature of Inanna, many still remembered Her wisdom and Her guidance as those that had once been given by Her ancient Grandmother Nammu, She who gave birth to heaven and earth.

ERESHKIGAL

Although the Goddess who once held the sole sovereignty of the Irkalla, the Land of the Dead, is at times described as sister to Inanna, Ereshkigal appears to be a quite separate and perhaps more ancient deity. The legend included here was found on tablets at El Amarna in Egypt and dates to about 1400 B.C. But Ereshkigal's name appears on some of the oldest writings of Sumer. The translation of *kigal* is Great Earth, but the meaning of *Eresh* is uncertain. In this particular myth I have not only told the story of Nergal's attack upon Ereshkigal, as described on the El Amarna tablets, but also tried my hand at the unique style of Sumerian writing that made its way into my own sentence structure after so many readings of this and other Sumerian legends. It should be noted that Ea, the male deity who assists Nergal in this tragic story, was the Babylonian name for the Sumerian Enki.

Great was the feast
planned by the Annunaki,
joyous were the festivities
being arranged by this assembly of deities,
plentiful was the barley beer,
abundant was the khubuz bread.
Wine from the date, wine from the grape,
these flowed like a flooding river.
Quince and fig, pomegranate and apricot,
all of these were set beside
the overflowing baskets of fresh fish
and the mountainous platters of roasted goat.
All of the deities of the Annunaki were invited,
even the lesser deities of the Igigi
were asked to attend—
never before had such a banquet been made,
not even in heaven.

Far from the preparations of the heavenly feast,
She who was once known as the Birth Giving Mother,
She who was now Ruler of the Underworld,
She who was the Mistress of the Land of No Return,
She who was the Sovereign of the dark Irkalla,
Queen Ereshkigal—sat upon Her throne,
presiding over Her domain
of those who had passed from the living.

By Her side was the woman Belit Seri,
sacred scribe of the records of the dead,
She who wrote each human deed
upon the leaves of the Tree of Life.
By Her side was the righteous Nungal,
She who judged the essence of each life,
daughter of the Queen of Souls, Ereshkigal.

So busy was Ereshkigal
when the messenger of the Annunaki arrived,
when Kika had descended the steps of heaven,
and passed through the seven gates of Irkalla,
when Kika told Ereshkigal of the coming party—
that great was Her sadness when She had to refuse
the tempting invitation.
Too demanding were Her duties—
chaos would creep into the Netherworld
without Her constant presence.

Thus She chose Namtar,
he who followed Her every word,
Her most loyal assistant,
to ascend the steps of heaven,
to attend the great Annunaki banquet in Her stead,
there to join the feast as Her ambassador
and upon leaving, to bring the portion of Ereshkigal
back to the Land of No Return—
Ereshkigal's share would be brought to Her by Namtar.

When the proper time had come,
when the banquet was about to be given,
Namtar made his way through the seven gates of Irkalla,
one by one, he ascended the steps to heaven
and so awesome was the respect for Ereshkigal,
so great the fear and wonder
at Her Queendom of Dead Souls,
that each deity stood and bowed low when Namtar arrived,
for who in the Annunaki,
for who in the Igigi,
was not humble in the presence
of even a messenger of Ereshkigal?
Though only Her assistant,
Namtar was treated with esteem and honour.

Thus each deity paid respect to the Mistress of the Dead,
that is, all except one,
a young god, a warrior god,
a god that revelled in destructive storms
and stirred up pestilence and disease.
It was Nergal who would not stand.
It was Nergal who would not bow down.

Upon Namtar's return to Irkalla
the story of Nergal was told.
He described the astonishment
on the faces of the other deities at the feast
at the rudeness of the young god.
Namtar told how some had shouted 'ignoramus',
how others had pressed Nergal to courtesy,
but how none of these had prevailed.
Nergal had remained seated
while all the others stood and bowed
to the ambassador of Queen Ereshkigal.
'Can he be so young or so foolish
that he is ignorant
of the powers of the Mistress of Irkalla?
He shall see the Land of the Dead for himself.
He shall know that I alone
rule this mighty Queendom.
Namtar, bring him to me
so that he may extend his apologies.'

A second time Namtar ascended the steps of heaven.
A second time he entered the realm of the Annunaki.
There he announced the words of his Mistress,
that Nergal must descend to dark Irkalla
to offer his apologies to Ereshkigal.
Not a deity defended the young god's rudeness,
for all were in great awe of the Sovereign of the Dead
but Ea took Nergal aside and gave him warning,
he who thought to undermine
the powers of Ereshkigal
gave advice to the god of war and destruction,
'Refuse any bread that might be offered,
refuse any meat that might be given,
refuse any drink that might be served,

refuse any seat that might be set for you,
refuse any bathing water poured,
and most important,
refuse to be taken to the couch of the Goddess,
should She desire your body.'
Ea warned that if he accepted any of these,
Nergal might be forced to stay in Irkalla.

Thus Nergal descended to the Land of the Dead.
Nergal followed Namtar to the Land of No Return.
Down the long staircase of heaven did he follow him.
Through the seven gates of the Netherworld
did Namtar lead the god of war and disease
until they stood before the mighty Ereshkigal,
stood before the throne of the Mistress of the Dead.
All warnings flew from Nergal's mind,
so powerful and magnificent was Her being.
Mother of Mothers.
Was there a woman in heaven or on earth
who could compare with Ereshkigal?
Was there any whose strength was as mighty,
any who possessed greater wisdom of existence,
any as filled with the eons of experience,
any who through knowing death so well
better understood the essence of Life?
Overwhelmed by Her presence,
Nergal fell to his knees
and kissed the ground before Her,
and as docile as a young lamb,
he soon followed Her to Her couch of pleasures.

So long alone had She been through all eternity,
so busy with Her work had She been kept,
that the Mistress of the Netherworld
kept Nergal on Her couch of pleasures
for six full days,
kept Nergal on Her couch of pleasures
for six full nights.
But on the seventh,
Nergal asked permission to return to heaven,
requested that he might go home,
to assure the others of his well-being,
promising that he would soon return.

Though not pleased at the thought
of his absence from Her couch of pleasures,
Ereshkigal agreed to his departure.

Once returned to heaven,
once reappearing at the abode of the Anunnaki,
Nergal was again taken aside by Ea.
He who had warned Nergal before
now spoke again, saying
that though Ereshkigal might be difficult to resist,
should Nergal become Her lover
would he not fear for his other pleasures,
his desire to make great and bloody wars,
his delight in dealing out disease and pestilence,
his satisfaction in stirring up turbulence and storm?
Surely if he returned to this powerful Goddess
and became the lover of the Mistress of the Dead,
She would keep him on Her couch of pleasures
and there he would be forced to spend his life,
foregoing all his former pleasures.

Nergal then thought anxious thoughts,
Nergal feared the truth of what Ea had said
but just as he was thinking upon
the breaking of his word to Ereshkigal,
Namtar arrived in heaven,
the messenger of Ereshkigal
ascended heaven's steps yet a third time
and soon conveyed the words of his Mistress
that Nergal was now Hers,
that Nergal must be returned
to the Land of the Dead,
that Nergal must be sent back
to the Ruler of the Irkalla.

But Ea thought to defeat the mighty Queen,
took sides with Nergal against Ereshkigal,
by arming him with fourteen warrior demons,
by instructing him to make a sword
of the mesu, hashurru and supalu trees,
by supplying him with false tokens
for the seven gates of Irkalla,

Was there any whose strength was as mighty?

so that Nergal would not be naked and unarmed
when he arrived before Her throne,
as were the others who entered the Land of the Dead.
The god of the Anunnaki, Ea,
encouraged Nergal
to defy the powers of the Queen of the Irkalla.

Nergal followed Namtar down the steps of heaven,
as if accepting the word of Ereshkigal,
as if concerned about Her loneliness,
but at each gate of the seven
he passed out the false tokens of Ea,
at each gate of the seven
two of the warrior demons he planted,
so that when Nergal entered into Her presence
he was in a mind for war.
He stood before The Mighty One,
he stood before the Queen of the Nether world,
but once again he felt Her magnificence,
once again he desired to lie with Her
upon Her couch of pleasures,
and in the confusion of his desires
he wondered if he could have both—
Queen Ereshkigal
and the freedom to do all that he wished?
Surely not as long as Irkalla was Hers to rule.
Surely not as long as She held such power.
Surely not as long as She truly did not need him,
but only desired to have him
for the pleasures of Her couch.

The mind of the god of bloody war,
the mind of the god of disease and pestilence,
the mind of the god of destructive turbulence and storm,
soon thought of a plan
that was most comfortable to his mixed desires.
He thought of marriage—
and roughly grasping the hair of Ereshkigal's head,
he pulled Her from Her throne
and threw Her hard upon the ground,
threatening to cut off Her head—
unless She agreed to be his wife.

He demanded that he should sit upon the throne
and that She should sit beside him.
He demanded that in his hands,
She must place the Tablets of Destiny,
that which had been Hers alone.
He demanded that he be master
of the land of the Irkalla
and that She be his dutiful consort.
Lying upon the cold stone floor,
seeing the warrior demons fending off all aid,
seeing the sword of mesu, hashurru and supalu
close upon Her throat,
Ereshkigal realized the alternative
would be Her violent death—
and thus She agreed to the proposal.

The records of Assyria and Egypt
tell us this is how
Nergal took control of the Land of No Return
from the ancient Sumerian Ereshkigal.
They tell us that upon Her acceptance,
upon Her agreeing to his 'proposal of marriage',
he then kissed Her.
They do not say how She felt.
They tell us that he then wiped away Her tears.
They do not tell us what was on Her mind.

Yet one small prayer,
more ancient even than the stories of Nergal,
remind us of the omnipotence
that Ereshkigal once knew,
remind us of a time
when death was but a part of life,
a return to the Great Mother:

> "I will praise the Queen of Humankind,
> I will praise Ereshkigal,
> Queen of Humankind.
> Among all the many deities,
> Ereshkigal is merciful."

She Who Makes the Universe Spin Round

Egypt

The magic powers of the uraeus serpent that emerges as the Third Eye, the broad winged vulture who protects in death, and the nurturing cow upon whose belly the stars of heaven shine—remain as symbols of the Goddess from the lands that lie along the Egyptian Nile.

Small clay statues created by the people of the neolithic cultures of the Badarian, Tasian, Gerzean and Amratian periods have been unearthed at numerous sites of pre-dynastic Egypt. The similarity of these statues, formed between 4000 to 3000 B.C., to those of the following dynastic periods, reveal that they were images of the Goddess in those earliest periods of developing Egyptian culture.

At about 3000 B.C., Upper Egypt (the south) and Lower Egypt (the Delta area) were brought together under a centralized government. Primarily accomplished through martial conquest, this amalgamation of The Two Lands is most often associated with the arrival in Egypt of a group known as the Shemsu Hor, people of Horus. Before the consolidation of these two areas, which differed both culturally and topographically, each was symbolized by an important Goddess figure. Upper Egypt was known as the land of Nekhebt, whose image was the wide winged vulture, while Lower Egypt was the land of Ua Zit, the Cobra Goddess whose image was retained in the sacred Uraeus head dress. Despite all political events, Goddess reverence remained deeply ingrained in the hearts and minds of the people of ancient Egypt.

For the three millenia generally referred to as the time of ancient Egypt (3000 B.C. until the Roman period), the culture of Egypt was relatively self contained. Yet there were contacts, some through war, most through trade, between Egypt and the nations of Crete, Cyprus, Canaan, Anatolia and Sumer. Certain images and theological concepts of Egypt invite comparison with those of these other ancient cultures. Although there is no evidence of direct contact between Egypt and India, artifacts do reveal trade connections between Egypt and Sumer, and between Sumer and the west Kulli area of India. The appearance of the serpent, the lotus and the cow as sacred symbols of the Goddess in both Egypt and India may provide the start of an interesting study, one which should not fail to take the presence of Australoid people both in Arabia and in India into consideration.

Egypt's relationships with its neighbors to the south and west are more obvious, Egyptian references to the Goddess in Nubia and Libya confirming these connections. Yet little research has been done on these relationships, despite specific references to the Egyptian Goddess Hathor as a lioness in Nubia. In any study of these relationships, it is of paramount importance to examine the passages in Herodotus which reveal that *all* of Africa (with the exception of Egypt) was once referred to as Libya (see African section—Vol. I). Egyptian references to the Goddess as The Fiery One, the Cobra or the Heavenly Cow invite interesting comparisons to beliefs that still exist in Zaire. Accounts of the Alur people include images of a divine celestial cow that provides the rain, while Nkundo lore includes a description of the magical serpent Indombe who, when angered, emanates a blazing heat and light from Her body. Egyptian ideas about the site of Creation as a flaming island in the waters may reflect images not unlike the still fiery lava pit of Mt. Nyiragongo in Zaire, as it once stood in the waters that extended from Lake Kivu. Geologists have found that the present land mass north of Lake Kivu, the site of the flaming volcano Nyiragongo, was part of a vast lake during periods of human habitation.

The religious ideologies of ancient Egypt are complex. Contradictory accounts of Creation, each from a different area, reveal that each one claimed the status of prime mover for their own local deity. As a result of this complexity and multiplicity of

Egyptian materials, many contemporary texts on Egyptian beliefs may be misleading in that large bodies of information may be completely ignored or mentioned so briefly that they are overlooked or assumed to be of little importance.

Although most scholars describe Amun, the ram or goose deity of the town of Thebes, as male, they often neglect to mention that several early documents refer to Amun as father and *mother*. The most oft ignored body of evidence is that which was found in the town of Khemmenu (Hermopolis). In the Khemmenu material, the female Nuneit and the male Nun who were both regarded as the Primeval Sea, were described as the first deities to exist. The more familiar but later accounts from Thebes reveal the influence of the Khemmenu beliefs, but cite Amun as the prime mover, thus lessening the importance of Nuneit. Some contemporary studies mention Nun only, explaining that he was regarded as the one who made the Nile rise. These same studies neglect to mention that, according to the Khemmenu material, it was Nuneit who first created the Nile. Another difference in the Theban and Khemmenu accounts is the role of the female Amunet. The Khemmenu texts specifically state that Amunet alone attended the great Cosmic Egg, the egg from which the sun god Ra was said to have been born. Since, in other texts, Ra is most often described as the son of the Goddess whose body was the heavens, Nut or Net, the reference to Amunet in this context may be extremely significant. Not only is the figure of Amunet absent in the majority of studies of Egyptian culture, but many scholars state that the Cosmic Egg was laid by the male Amun, who, strangely enough, is identified as a goose, rather than a gander. It is interesting to note that the hieroglyph for the Cosmic Egg was the same sign that was used to designate an embryo in a woman's womb.

Another area in which subjective choice of material distorts the reader's understanding of Egyptian beliefs is the general emphasis on the male Thoth, and the exclusion of material concerning the Goddess Seshat (Sefchet). In very early dynastic writings, Seshat was described as the Goddess of Writing and the Ruler of Books. Yet nearly all contemporary studies discuss Thoth as the singular deity associated with the scribal arts, while passages concerning Seshat, and the fact that they were earlier than those concerning Thoth, are simply ignored.

One rather astonishing practice of many scholars of Egyptian religion is the stated perception of *Maat* as an abstract principle, rather than as a deity. Numerous images of the Goddess Maat show Her in the form of a woman. The many verbal references to Her as the manifestation of truth, justice, moral law, and cosmic balance give us some idea of the extreme importance of Her image, but these attributes do not define Her as any more or less of an abstraction than Jehovah, Allah or Brahma.

Should the reader feel that the above perhaps reveals the limitations of space, rather than a male-oriented bias among many scholars, we must still confront the most oft used translation for the word *roemt* whose sign includes specific images of a woman and a man, the word that a few scholars have translated as 'people' or 'humankind', but most have translated as 'man' or 'men'.

Aside from these problems of bias, upon reading the vast body of literature on ancient Egypt, most especially the direct translations of specific documents, an endless wealth of material on Goddess images in Egypt may be discovered. From birth to death, and even after death, the Goddess was perceived as a sacred essence that played a vital part in the life of every Egyptian. From the time of the nameless statues of the prehistoric period until the time that the temples of the Goddess Isis were closed by the Emperor Justinian in the fifth century A.D., Goddess reverence in Egypt provided images of womanhood that may rise to the surface of our woman mirrors of today.

UA ZIT

The image of the Cobra Goddess Ua Zit, who was revered on the Nile Delta of pre-dynastic Egypt, was retained for three thousand years as the Uraeus serpent, The Eye, ever present on the foreheads of other Egyptian deities and royalty. The ancient Ua Zit may well be the origin of the serpent imagery so closely associated with Goddess reverence on Crete. Ua Zit was also associated with images of Au Set (Isis) who was linked to the star known as Set, Sept and Sothis in Egypt (Sirius in Greece). The name and concept of Ua Zit may have been connected to the Sumerian belief in *Ama Usum Gal Ana,* Great Mother Serpent of Heaven—*zit* or *zet,* the Egyptian word for serpent; *usum,* the Sumerian word for serpent. The image of Ua Zit may also have survived in the Arabian Goddess Al Uzza who was regarded as either Venus or Sirius. The most sacred centre of the worship of Ua Zit was the Delta town of Per Uto (the Greek Buto) that is thought to lie beneath modern day Dessuk. Buto was regarded as one of the most important oracle sites of Egypt at the time of Classical Greece. Although the Greeks spoke of the Cobra Goddess as Buto, they dedicated the Buto shrine to the Goddess Lato, mother of the sun and the moon. The placement of the Ua Zit Cobra on the forehead, invites comparison of this image to the Indian concept of the Shakti Kundalini serpent rising to the Ajna Chakra (see Indian section).

Deep beneath the ever accumulating silt
of the Delta lands of the mighty Nile
lies the holy place of the ancient Cobra,
Goddess known as Ua Zit, Ua Zet, Uatchet, Wazit,
Wadjet, Uadt, Udot, Edo, Edjo, Uto,
Uterus womb that rose between the reeds
on the secret Khemmis isle that floated
on the lotus marshes of the Delta,
great Zet serpent of the wadi canals,
who took the holy Au Set in as daughter,
who protected holy Au Set in childbirth,
who protected the child that Isis bore.

Ua Zit spread Her cobra hood
at the Buto site of oracles
where the future was foretold,
so that Buto gained renown throughout the world.

Ua Zit wound Her serpent body
about the royal sceptre of cosmic sovereignty,
as She coiled about the sacred lotus,
as She twisted about the waz reed of the Delta,
the reed of the marshes
taken to form the first stylus of Egypt,
the pen that marked both idea and event
upon papyri, bone and clay.

Uniting with Her sister Nekhebt,
to create the power of all Egypt,
as Isis united with Her sister Nebt Het, Nepthys,
Ua Zit emerged from holy forehead
as the Third Eye, the Eye of Wisdom,
as the venom that She spit forth
with fiery red tongue
gave Her the name of The Lady of Spells,
The Lady of Flame,
The Lady of the Flaming Waters,
The Lady who shed Her skin
to be born again and again and again,
for Ua Zit had existed before Egypt was born,
had existed before the Creation.

MAAT

Although Maat is most often described by contemporary scholars as an abstract concept, images of Maat in both murals and sculptures depict Her as a woman, the ostrich feather upon Her head, a sceptre in one hand, the life symbol of the ankh in the other. Somewhat like Huruing Wuhti of Hopi beliefs, Maat is at times depicted as twin sisters, though a singular Maat is the more general image. Egyptian texts refer to Maat as The Eye, much like Ua Zit, but Maat is associated with the heart as the place where moral judgements were made. The name and images of Maat occur in many Egyptian writings, most significantly in the various versions of the Egyptian Book of the Dead. The ostrich symbolism associated with Maat, alongside references to Maat's role in the Creation, suggest that any study on the concept of the Cosmic Egg should include a more careful examination of how the image of Maat may have been connected to this primeval event. It may be of interest to note that discs of ostrich eggshell have been discovered in the burials of pre-dynastic cultures, while the hieroglyph for the *Ba,* soul, is almost identical with the sign that designates the ostrich. The imagery and concepts associated with Maat may be the foundations for later Greek images of the Goddess Themis who holds the Scales of Justice, and perhaps the early Greek Goddess of Wisdom, Metis.

> The Eye of Heaven,
> Sister twins who judge what is right,
> Ever present Maat,
> Guardian of the justice and truth of the universe,
> Guardian of the rhythm and order of the cosmos,
> Sovereign of the Council of Maat
> where the assembly of deities, the great Ennead,
> rule by Maat's decrees.
>
> Great is Maat
> who gave the unalterable laws of life,
> who insisted upon truth and kindness,
> who took the ostrich feather
> that She wore upon Her head
> and placed it in the balance,
> to test the weight of each heart
> that lay in the other bowl of the sacred scales,
> the heart of each who died
> to be weighed against the lightness of Maat's feather,
> as Maat tied a cloth about Her eyes
> so that no prejudice
> might fault Her word.

Heavy is the heart
that has not given bread to the hungry,
that has not given water to the thirsty,
that has not given clothing to the naked,
that has not given a boat to the shipwrecked.
Light is the heart
that has lived a life of good deeds,
as it lies in the bowl of the balance
in the Hall of Double Maat
where Maat announced the judgement
to be recorded on the leaves
of the Tree of Life.

In hopes of achieving the Maa Kheru,
the true voice, the light heart
light as the first day
when it was given by the mother,
the reverent submerged themselves in the waters
that were the Pool of Maat,
the place where the Flame was buried,
where the crystal tablet was transformed into water,
the place where the sceptre of flint
lies upon the shore,
flint known as the Giver of Breath,
flint scythe that reaps what has been sown.
as the soul reaps the deeds of its heart,
as it balances against all that Maat decreed.

Maat watches as the Morning Star,
the Eye that sees each day begin;
Maat watches as the Evening Star,
the Eye that sees each day come to an end,
Her double light a constant reminder
of the Scales in the Hall of Double Maat.

THE LADY OF THE AMENTA

The *Amenta* of Egyptian texts is the heaven that could be attained by those who led lives of righteousness. According to the Egyptian Book of the Dead, the soul went through a period of arduous testing and judgement before it was allowed into the Amenta. Upon finally arriving, the soul was welcomed by the sight of the Lady of the Amenta who stood upon the summit of the heavenly mountain. The final hieroglyphs of the Book of the Dead associate the Goddess as Hathor, Methyer, Au Set and Maat with the concept of the Lady of the Amenta. *Amn, Amen* or *Amun* literally means hidden in the sense of invisible or secret. What appears to be a multiplicity of names and images of the Lady of the Amenta may have been understood to convey the multi-faceted nature of the Goddess who was hidden by the profusion of names and traits, yet inherent in all. References to the role of Amunt (Amunet, Ament) in the Khemmenu accounts of Creation may be yet another aspect of the identity of the Lady of the Amenta.

I have chosen this particular account of the Goddess as the one in which the many other Goddess names and aspects are described. It should be understood that each of these names do appear as separate deities. Some are associated with a specific community or town and may have been drawn into theological structures that incorporated various beliefs, as populations came to live under increasingly centralized governments. Though a total synthesis may never have been made, to the extent of the perception of aspects of Devi in India, it should not be forgotten that the Goddess as Au Set (Isis) was known as 'Mother of One Thousand Names'.

It was the Lady of the Amenta who stood upon the holy mountain of heaven, waiting for those who had passed the rigours of the Hall of Double Maat, waiting for those who had recognized the Ladies of the Pylons of Testing, waiting for those whose hearts were light enough to allow their souls an everlasting peace.

They said that She was Au Set, and also Maat, while at the same time She was Hathor, and yet Meh Urit. Still She was Taurit, and at the same time She was the perfect face in the boat of one million years. Lady of the Amenta, might She also have been Amunet, She who existed on the Isle of Flame that rose out of the primeval waters and helped all life to come forth from the great Cosmic Egg? They said that She was Amn, invisible as the air that we breathe, yet as real as the breeze or the wind. And it was said at Khemmenu that it was Amunet who helped the Egg of Life to open, the Egg that some said had been laid by a serpent, the Egg that some said had come from the womb of a feathered bird.

They said that She was the Lady of One Million Ka, the Lady of all spirit bodies, the Great Magician, She who had come forth from the primeval waters, green as the frog that explored the bank of the river, remembered in Nubia and Sudan as She who attended each woman in birth, midwife as Amunet was midwife—but they gave Her name as Heqt or Hekit.

When Her work was apparent in the bountiful harvest and in the flow of abundant good fortune—they said that She was Renenti. When She blessed the future of each child that was born—they said that She was Meshkenti. When She filled the rivers and the lakes with the fish that satisfied all appetites—they said that She was Mehiti. When the waters of the river surged so full that they overflowed upon the land, helping the new crops to grow tall and full—they said that She was Merit.

When in the town of Bubastis, where lives were filled with joyous pleasure and graceful feline beauty, as the women and the men arrived in barges, clapping and singing, playing upon flute and sacred sistrum, where Her people honoured Her in festival, as Her catlike head sat upon Her womanly body while She protected the souls of cats that had died and had been wrapped in the linen of the afterworld—they said that She was Bast. When She roared as the powerful Lioness who excelled in the hunt, and was known for Her strength in rage as She aimed Her perfect arrows from Her bow, conquering all enemies that challenged the safety of Her town of Memphis—they said that She was The Powerful Mother Sekhmet.

When She appeared as the kindly, mothering cow whose udders provided the milk of good fortune—they said that She was Methyer or Meh Urit. When She was known as the oldest of the old, the Mother who gave birth to all other dieties as She took the form of a Hippo who roared wildly as She cooled Her body in the waters filled with brown earth—they said that She was Ta Urt or Taurit. When She appeared as the ancient vulture who was once known as Nekhebt, and made Her home in Thebes where She gave birth to the Moon, Khonsu, and as the Mistress of Heaven She possessed nine mighty bows, and was known by the picture of the wide winged vulture that was the very word for mother—they said that She was Mat or Mut.

When She appeared as the silent serpent who slid among the tombs in the moonlight, Her womanly head upon reptilian body —they said that She was Mertsegret. When She was known by the sign of the many legged scorpion—they said that She was Serkhit. When She appeared as the two holy ones who came forth from the Sudan, one as the Lady of Life, the other as the Serpent of Rebirth—they said that She was Ankhet and Satet.

Yet even without a name, the Goddess of ancient Tamera, the land that we now know as Egypt, came forward in the testing of each soul so that the dead one of the still heart recognized and acknowledged each: first, The Lady of Terrors, the Sovereign Mistress of Destruction who protected those who travelled on the right paths; second, the Lady of Heaven, Mistress of the World, who devoured with fire and was greater than all humankind; third, The Lady of the Altar, the beloved of every other deity, She to whom all offerings were made; fourth, The Lady of Knives, Mistress of the World, She who protected the needy from their foes; fifth, The Lady of Breath, She whose presence could not be known; sixth, The Lady of Light, The Mighty One, the one whose height and breadth were beyond knowing; seventh, The Lady of the Linen, who wrapped the bands about the one who had died; eighth, The Lady of the Tongues of Flame; ninth, The Lady that is Highest Chief, Lady of Power who was robed in emeralds; tenth, The Lady of the Great Voice, She who might terrify all others, but feared none; eleventh, The Lady Who Burned all Evil; twelfth, The Lady of Splendour as brilliant as fire; thirteenth, Au Set, She who blazed as the light that made the Nile waters rise and overflow, as She reached out to all; fourteenth, The Lady of the Knife who danced in blood on the Day of Judgement; fifteenth, The Lady who trapped all evil in its own lair; sixteenth, The Lady of the Rain Storm; seventeenth, The Lady of the Knife and the Ankham Lotus of rebirth; eighteenth, The Lady of the Temple who purified all sinners; twentieth, The Lady of the Deep who gives drink to the thirsty; twenty-first, The Lady who is the Knife known as the Giver of Breath.

Thus when the heart, that was first given by the mother, recognized and acknowledged each of the many natures, and after many years of life the heart was found to be as light as the feather of Maat, the soul was free to enter into heaven, there to look upon the Holy Hidden Mother—the Lady of the Amenta.

SESHAT

Seshat (Sefchet), appears in Egyptian documents as early as the First to the Third Dynasties. In them, She is referred to as the Goddess of Writing and Ruler of Books. Although Seshat's attributes are reminiscent of the Sumerian Nidaba, Seshat might also be compared to the Sumerian Belit Sheri, both Seshat and Belit Sheri depicted as scribes who record the deeds of the dead upon the leaves of the Tree of Life (see Sumerian section). In some references, Seshat was associated with the more familiar male deity of the scribal arts, Thoth. This relationship may be of interest in that other documents link Thoth with the Goddess Maat—in this same activity of the judgement and recording of the deeds of the dead.

Sacred Seshat, Holy Sefchet,
It was She who designed the hieroglyphs
so that words could be recorded,
She who invented numbers,
so that the barrels of barley could be measured,
so that even the stars of heaven
could be counted.
Divine Architect of the first temples,
it was Seshat who first stretched the cord
to decide upon the width and length,
to decide upon the placement,
of ancient Egypt's shrines.

Sacred Seshat, Holy Sefchet,
Divine Inventor of the scroll of papyri,
the sheet of tchama,
held the ink palette
that She so wondrously devised
in one perfect hand,
held the reed stylus pen
that She so wondrously devised,
in the other.

What is equal to the wonderment of Her work,
for it is Seshat who stood before the Tree of Life
in the great Hall of Double Maat,
marking down for all eternity
that which was done in each life,
writing upon the multitude of tiny leaves
that grew from the branches of the holiest of trees,
recording for memory eternal
the sum total of each life,
recording them no worse than they had been—
and no better.

Sage were Her words of advice:
Enjoy your life,
before the heart that your mother gave you lies still.
Death arrives sooner than expected,
and all the grief and mourning
will not bring the still heart back to life.
Earthly treasures will be left behind,
possessions decay with time,
but your daily deeds, both good and bad,
are truly what you own forever.
Give bread to those who have no field
and a good name is yours for eternity.

HATHOR

The cow of the heavens, known as Neit, Methyer or Meh Urit, was best known by the name of Hathor. There is no question that this last name was one assigned by the worshippers of Horus, since Hat Hor literally means House of Horus. But images and concepts of the holy heifer seem to have preceded this name. Some texts describe Hathor as the wild cow upon the primeval hill that emerged from the waters. In the Book of the Dead, this image was also known as Meh Urt. Hathor's association with the lioness of Nubia and Her title as the Lady of Punt suggest that reverence for the celestial cow may have come to pre-dynastic Egypt from groups that had lived on the more southerly stretches of the Nile in Sudan. It is interesting to note the image of the celestial cow that still exists among the Alur people of Zaire, as well as the fact that the Dinka people of Sudan long revered lions as their totemic ancestors. As the Cow that is the heavens, and as the Lady of the Sycamore, Hathor is closely linked with images of Neit. The uraeus cobra so often shown on the forehead of Hathor also links Her to the Goddess Ua Zit.

Wild Ox, Fierce Lioness, Gentle Cow of Heaven, like ancient Neit, Hathor is the sacred cow who provides the milk of life. Was She not known since the days of those who first came to dwell along the Nile's fertile banks when the land was new, those who drew Her image on the rocks of Naquada and at the settlements of Girzeh some seven thousand years ago?

Like ancient Neit, She nestled in the foliage of the Great Sycamore, waiting to welcome the souls of those who would no longer live on earth, ready to supply them with food and with drink, Her ripening figs that grew upon the Sycamore known as the food of eternity. Lady of the Sycamore, Living Body of Hathor upon Earth, this holiest of trees is blessed by the Goddess who sits within its branches. Many are the natures of Her mysteries, for some say that She is Seven Hathors, as Au Set is the seven stars that shine in Sothic constellation.

Yet who, in all the great lands of Egypt, ancient Tamera, did not learn when but a child that it was Hathor who first taught the sweet sound of song, the graceful movement of the dance that follows the rhythm of the jingling of the sistrum rattle that bears Her image? And who did not learn that it was Hathor who first taught the mining of the malachite, the sacred blue green stone that lay in the earth, though some say it fell as powder from the emerald stars that glistened upon the vastness of Her belly? And who did not learn that it was Hathor who taught of love and first explained to mortals the way in which new life was made, and gave lovers to the lonely.

She was the Mother who gave happiness; She was the Mother who gave joy; She was the Mother who exulted in all that was good. From the chambers of Her temples, they carried Her image each morning, setting it upon the sunlit terraces, so that She might look upon the dawn. Her name was called upon from Byblos to Somali, from Nubia to Sinai, from Edfu to Ombos, from Deir el Bahri to Thebes, from Heliopolis to Denderah, still She was known as The Lady of Punt, the land of cone roofed huts that could be sailed to by following the ocean coastline to the south, the Land of Ebony and Ivory.

Ancient priestesses stood before Her altars, women known as Sepi and Nisedger Kai, Matmuti and Demiosnai. They called upon the ancient cow of heaven as Lady of the Stars, the One who Shines as Gold, Mistress of the Desert, Lady of Heaven, Sovereign of Imaau, Hathor who gives the breath of life to the nostrils with Her sacred ankh symbol, Hathor who heals with Her celestial milk that soothes the torn body, Hathor who sends the wind for the sails so that the boats may glide along the waters, Hathor who appears as the Sacred Seven who come to the birth of each infant to prophesy the destiny that each will come to know.

Each year, the joyous Feast of Hathor was celebrated with the sweet music of the sistrum, as all of Egypt danced to please the Goddess. But most important at this greatest feast of the year was the drinking of the red barley beer, the beer that flowed like the river when it overflowed, dizzying the mind until it forgot all else but thoughts of the power and the wisdom of the Goddess. Two stories were told to explain the reason for this day, both relating why it was the first day of the New Year, and why it was dedicated to Hathor. The Book of the Cow of Heaven told of the sun god Ra calling to Hathor for help. Calling upon Her as his Eye, he told Her of the men who had gone to the mountains, there to plot a conspiracy against him in his weakened period of great age. As he begged for Her protection, She took the form of the angry lioness Sekhmet, and in this form She went forth to slay his enemies. Easily conquering those who had plotted the harm to Ra, Sekhmet Hathor began to enjoy the taste of blood. Now even more afraid, for Sekhmet Hathor did not stop and it seemed that She might destroy all humankind, Ra mixed the red ochre of the ground into great vats of barley beer and poured this on the ground so that it might appear as blood. Sekhmet Hathor began to drink and drink and drink, until She grew so drunk that She returned to Her gentle form of Hathor. According to the people of Ra's Heliopolis, this is why red beer flowed like water at the Festival of Hathor.

But a second tale was told by those in Denderah, where images of Hathor stood tall about the temple, as the joyous day of the New Year, the Feast of Hathor, was celebrated in the Nile town not far from the most ancient rocks of Naquada. Here they said that Hathor had grown angry, and threatened to destroy the universe that She had created. Roaring with fury, Hathor threatened to wash the very earth back into the primordial sea and to return to Her ancient form of the great serpent. In Her rage, She took the form of the lioness and made Her way back to the land of Nubia. In Hathor's absence, grief and chaos came to the land of Egypt. The land of the Nile knew only confusion and disorder. So desperate was the situation that Hathor's brothers, Shu and Thoth, also took the forms of lions and followed Hathor into the land of Nubia. After many months of searching for the Powerful One, they came across Her sitting upon the Mountain of the Sunrise.

Tragic tale after tragic tale came forth from the brothers, each ending in words of persuasion, asking, begging, pleading for Hathor to return to Egypt. Hathor filled with compassion for the people that She loved. Though Her heart was filled with reservations, Hathor once again returned to Egypt, bringing peace and harmony back to the land of the overflowing Nile. So it was that as the river began to swell, as the constellation of Sothis rose with the morning sun, Egyptians celebrated the Feast of Hathor, knowing a new and better year was coming, honouring the Great Mother of Heaven with song and dance, and beer that flowed as water. Hathor had returned and with Her came the goodness of life.

NEIT

Even upon a casual reading of Egyptian documents, one will find a multitude of references to the Goddess in Egypt as Nut, Net, Nit, Neit and Neith. Although many scholars discuss the first three names as those of one Goddess, and the last two as another, both Neith and Nut were described as emerging from the primeval floodwaters and as The Mistress of Heaven. Later texts do generally identify the name Neith with the worship of the Goddess in the town of Sais, while the names Nut, Net or Nit are most generally used when referring to the Goddess as the divine woman or heavenly cow who *is* the heavens. To some extent, this confusion results from the lack of vowels in Egyptian hieroglyphs, many scholars making educated guesses and inserting vowels to ease the pronunciation. All the above names may be related to the Egyptian word meaning deity, *neter*. A good part of the material included in this account is drawn from the early *Pyramid Texts* of Unas, Pepi and Teti.

Most ancient Mother,
Great Radiant One,
Lady of the Stars,
Mistress of the Celestial Ocean,
Highest Judge,
Fiery One who rose from the Primordial Floods,
It is Neit who reaches down from the heavens
to take the hand of each who dies,
taking them into Her arms
to place them as stars of the universe,
each to light Her perfect body
with an emerald light,
sowing mortals upon Her heavenly self,
as others sow the green plants of the fields.

Some say that She is Nuneit,
the primeval waters that once covered all earth;
some say that She is Tefneit,
Giver of the moisture and the sunlight;
Some say that She is the Lady of the Loom and Shuttle,
and Lady of the Arrow and the Bow,
the Lady whose image stood at the most ancient shrine
of Sais upon the Delta lands
the most sacred image marked:
I am all that has ever been,
I am all that is,
I am all that shall ever be,
yet never have mortal eyes
perceived me as I am.

Ascending from the primeval waters,
Her body became the vast heavens,
Her perfect toes and fingertips touching the earth
as She arched over it in cosmic beauty,
the tear from Her eye creating the Nile,
the stars glowing with emerald light
set into Her very body,
the single word 'beauty' marked as glyph
between Her sacred horns.

The earth nestles between Her thighs,
as daily She gives birth to the sun,
each evening accepting him back into Her body,
just as each mortal returns unto Her
when the span of life is over,
Her holy image painted on the ceilings of each tomb,
Her holy image painted inside the inner lid
of the wooden casket in which dead repose,
as She leans forth from Her celestial sycamore
to quench the thirst of afterlife.

Joyous was the festival of Lamps
when all Sais glowed with flames
in honour of Her mysteries,
each small dish of oil and salt,
with woven wick afloat,
burning brightly through the night
in memory of the great fire upon the waters,
in memory of the Fiery One,
The Great Magician Neith.

Though if Her anger was provoked
She might cause the sky to crash upon the ground,
still She was the Mother of All,
broad winged Goddess who protects from evil,
who defends the good with bow and arrow,
as She once defended those ancient priestesses
who took Her name:
Neit Hotep,
Meryet Neit,
Her Neit,
priestess queens who ruled when Egypt was young,
when only women served at Neit's altars,
each knowing throughout her life
that she would one day glisten as a star
upon the measureless body of the Mother of Heaven.

AU SET (ISIS)

Although the name of Isis is most often used to designate the most well known image of the Goddess in Egypt, the name Isis, literally Ancient Ancient, was the Greek interpretation of the name of the Goddess that Egyptians spoke of as Au Set or Au Sept. Au Set was identified with the star best known as Sirius; the Egyptian names for this star were Sothis, Sept and Set. The constellation Canis Major, which includes the very bright star Sirius, appeared on the horizon just before sunrise at the time of the year that the Nile began to swell (approximately mid June). This seven star constellation may account for the idea of the seven Hathors, so closely related to Au Set, as well as images of the seven headed serpent. The horns on images of Au Set were directly drawn from images of Hathor as the celestial cow, the sun disc between the horns explaining the role of the Goddess as the mother of the sun. Later ideas that Au Set or Isis was associated with the moon were not known in early Egypt which regarded the moon as the male Khonsu, son of the Lioness Sekhmet. Au Set was linked to the Goddess as Neit who was regarded as Au Set's mother, and also to the Goddess Ua Zit who was so closely associated with Au Set giving birth, the uraeus cobra nearly always shown on the forehead of images of Au Set. Au Set's connection to the seaport of Byblos in ancient Canaan (Lebanon) may be better understood by a reading of the Goddess as Ashtart (see Semitic section—Vol. I).

Sirius, Sothis, sacred star that was first known as Sept or Set, the seven lights of heaven known as Au Set, She arrived to herald the time of longest light and brought with Her the gift of the abundant soil, as She raised the waters of the Nile, the waters that She had created from the tear of Her eye. Thus She commanded the blessed months of the Sothic inundation to begin.

Many names had the wondrous Au Set: Mistress of the Cosmos, Ruler of the House of Life, Sovereign of all that is Miraculous, Almighty Lady of Wisdom, Mother From Whom All Life Arose, Primeval Lotus Nefertim, Establisher of Justice, Champion of Righteous Law, Giver of the Gift of Abundance, Inventor of Agriculture, Designer of the First Sail, Planter and Harvester of the First Flax, Inventor of the Loom, Source of the Healing Herbs, Owner of the Throne, Magistra of Fate, The One Who Separated Heaven and Earth, Roadmaker of the Paths through the Stars, Controller of the Wind and Thunder, Restorer of Life, She Who Makes the Universe Spin 'Round. What in heaven or on earth was not of Her making?

At the procession of the harvest, they remembered that it was beloved Au Set who first understood the ways of the seeds and the planting, bringing the abundance of the stalks of wheat and barley which were so proudly carried at Her sacred festivals, in honour and commemoration of what She so ingeniously discovered in the beginning. And from Mother Au Set came the knowledge of justice and the law of the heart, so that no one needed to fear insolence or violence, nor excessive punishment. For as Au Set dispensed justice to all people, She taught that they must dispense it to each other. Declaring that righteousness was more valuable than gold or silver, Her very name sanctified an oath of truth.

Through Her dedicated daughters who cared for Her many sacred shrines, She gave the medicines of healing, protecting women in childbirth, restoring sight to those who could not see, returning the use of a damaged arm or leg that would not move, delighting in helping those who called upon Her to regain their strength and health. Often, She visited even during the depths of sleep, gently brushing Her wings in healing incantation over ailing bodies until health came once again. It was Au Set who gave the recipes for birth and non-birth and explained the magic of the shepen seeds that soothed the constant crying of an infant. It was Au Set who gave the gift of knowing the future of the womb, explaining that if the seeds of barley grew quickly in the waste water of the fullbellied woman, she would surely be blessed with a daughter, while if the seeds of wheat grew first, it was a boy that would be born. It was Au Set who taught of the jasper and carnelian made into the image of Her holy tie, symbol once made of woven loop whose loose ends told of separation, while the loop above the knot revealed the oneness. It was Au Set who taught how to dip the sacred knot into the water of the ankham lotus flower of rebirth, and how to then press it into the wood of the sycamore fig, while reciting these words of incantation: Holy Blood of Au Set, Holy Splendour of Au Set, Holy Magic Power of Au Set, please protect the wearer of this amulet and halt those who would do this wearer harm.

Even in the time of the still heart, the time of being wrapped in bands of linen, when the sacred loop of Au Set was seen by those who judged, the wearer was rewarded with fertile acres in the Sehket Aaru of the Amenta. For wearing it announced the understanding that all people come forth on earth to do the will of their ka, and if the ka of the heart was as light as the feather of

Maat, Au Set would then breathe the air of divinity into the nostrils of the still heart, air more pure than any ever known, while the ever burning flame that blazed behind Her protected the body that remained on earth.

Though wiser than all people, though wiser than all deities or spirits, the followers of Ra said that there came a time when Au Set knew all—except the secret name of Ra. Though Ra was each day born from Mother Neit who had once held the holy Au Set in Her heavenly womb, still Au Set did not know this name and was determined to know of it. Thus Au Set formed a serpent made of the earth and of the spittle of the sun and when Ra walked across the serpent's path, Au Set's powers were so deep in the venom that Ra was paralyzed by the serpent's bite.

The jaw bones of Ra, they clattered. The limbs of Ra, they shook and trembled. Ra could not move, but finally he found his voice. "Never has there been such a pain.", he said. "There is a fire in my heart and water in my limbs." He called to all the holy ones but none knew how to help. Then Au Set appeared, She whose mouth held the breath of life, She whose magic banished pain, She whose word was capable of restoring life even to the still heart. Au Set appeared before Ra and offered to help, knowing full well Her plan and goal. Ra told Her of how a serpent came into his path and had bitten of his body. He told Her of the pain that he felt, hotter than fire, colder than water. He told Her that his vision was so badly blurred that he could not even see the sky. Tears streamed from his face. Perhaps with compassion, perhaps with guilt, Au Set carried out Her plan, telling Ra that if he would trust Her with his secret name, She would heal him of his pain.

But the name did not come easily from the tongue of Ra, for instead he began to boast of his royal ancestry, to describe his privileges and powers, rambling on and on about what he could do. Listening with patience, Au Set then reminded him that he had not yet told Her what She needed to know; Ra had not yet revealed his secret name. Despite his ancestry and powers, the pain of Ra was great. So it was that, reluctantly, he bid Au Set to enter into his heart where She would learn his secret name. And in this way, Au set gained this last knowledge; adding it to Her omnipotent wisdom, She began the cure.

Seeds of coriander She took, seeds of the khasit She took, the leaves of the saam She took, seeds of the shammis She took, juniper berries She took—and grinding these into a fine paste, mixing it with honey, She soothed the ointment upon the injured Ra. As She did so, She spoke the secret name that She alone had learned, until the pain of Ra disappeared. Some say that Au Set was not all wise until She learned the secret name of Ra, yet others say that She was wise enough to know how to discover it.

Another time so long remembered was when Au Set first discovered the planting of the seeds, receiving this knowledge at the very moment that She had placed offerings upon the holy altars of those who had engendered Her. Upon receiving this gift of the knowledge of renewable abundance, Au Set spoke of it to Her brother who was known by the name of Au Sar or Osiris. In his excitement at what Au Set had learned, Osiris ran off to tell all the others, only to be murdered by his jealous brother Seth who sealed the body of Osiris in a perfectly measured coffer and placed this box of wood on the river so that it floated out to the Great Sea.

When news of the murder reached the ears of Au Set, She set out to search for the body of Osiris, and thus began Her long journey. It was not until She reached the far off port of Byblos, on the northeastern edge of the Great Sea, that She found the temple pillar built of the wood of a tamarisk tree, its branches still entwined about the coffer that held the body of Osiris. Thus retrieving it from the Temple of Ashtart in Byblos, Au Set brought it back across the waters to the sacred site of Per Uto, planning to give it proper Egyptian burial.

It was there in the marshes of Per Uto that with the help of sister Nepthys, Au Set made the breath of life enter into the body of Osiris though his heart was still, the sisters patiently fanning the air with their great wings—until Au Set conceived a child within Her womb. It was in Per Uto that She stayed, consoled in Her grief by the holy Cobra Ua Zit, until the child Horus was born. Thus it was said that Ua Zit helped Au Set in Her childbirth among the reeds of Per Uto, safe upon the isle that floated in the marshy waters. But when Au Set left the safety of Per Uto, leaving the child to the caring wisdom of Ua Zit, Seth came again and stole the body of Osiris.

This time he cut the body into fourteen pieces which he scattered along the lands of the Nile, so that Osiris would not be honoured by burial place or tomb. But Au Set was determined to give Her brother proper burial, thus She made Her way in a barge among the marshes of the Nile, burying each part where She found it. Though the backbone of Osiris found peace at Busiris and the head came to lie at Abydos, never did Au Set find the fourteenth part, the childmaking organs of Osiris, while fishermen gave witness that this part had been fed to the oxyrhynchus fish of the Nile. So it happened that Au Set ruled upon the throne, ever holding the child Horus upon Her holy lap.

Great shrines and temples were built to honor Her magnificence, Her holy spirit living at Edfu and Bubastis, at Saqqara and at Memphis, at Busiris and at Pharos, at Philae and at Byblos, even as She lived in the heavens, shining as the astral Sothis. For over three thousand years Her ominipotence was known, spreading across the Great Sea to Sicily and Pompeii, to Palermo and Campania, and throughout the widespread lands of the Romans. But the Roman consuls sometimes thought to abuse Her sacred altars until Aurelius Caracalla defended Roman reverence to Her name, saying that She was one with mighty Ceres. Thus Romans erected a great temple to Isis, one that glistened on the Hill of Capitoline, not far from where the Tiber flowed.

The Roman festivals of Isis celebrated the joyous blossoming of springtime, as devotees moved along in sanctified procession, celestial sounds of pipe and flute patterning the rhythm of the white robed followers who called upon Her name. But there came a time of sadness when Justinian silenced the music in the streets, emptied the sacred houses of Her worship. Still many remembered the image of the Perfect Mother with the holy child upon Her lap, the woman whose body had been adorned with the stars of heaven, though Her mother essence gained yet another name, Maria.

ISIS (after Apuleius)

Altars to Isis have been discovered as far from Egypt as the banks of the River Thames in London, many of these dating to the Roman period. The worship of Isis was well known in the Roman Empire and the images and rituals from Egypt generally well accepted and familiar to the Roman population. This particular piece is based upon passages of the Wm. Adlington translation (1566) of the book written by the North African born

Ruler of the House of Life

from a tapestry by Jenny Stone

Roman writer Apuleius, originally entitled (like Ovid's) *Metamorphoses,* later popularized as *The Golden Ass.* The very specific imagery and speeches are included in the story of Apuleius' travels during which he finds himself trapped in the form of a donkey. His search for the help of the Goddess leads to the passages in which the following descriptions and statements occur.

Brilliant from the sea, She rose, flower garlands crowning Her abundant hair that fell upon Her perfect neck. Set upon Her forehead was the circlet of mirror, attended by a serpent on each side, as the sheaves of wheat that rose from the circle shone in the moonlight. Her cape as dark as the night gathered in folds beneath Her left arm, flowing over the shoulder of Her right, all but covering the linen that lay white upon Her golden body, the weave of finest linen adorned by the crocus of yellow, the rose of red and the flame of brightest orange. Stars glittered along the edges of the blackness of the cape; stars circled on the cape of night around a mid-month moon. And upon the lowest hem that fell upon Her perfect ankles, the ripest fruits and the brightest of flowers wreathed in abundant border.

Encircled by the fingers of Her right hand was the sistrum rattle adorned with the face of the mighty Hathor, its thin copper discs moving along upon narrow rods in bell like tones. Encircled in the fingers of Her left hand was the golden cup that formed the boat, its handle rising as uraeus cobra leading the fore. Her palm sandalled feet were scented with the finest incense and spices of Arabia, as Her voice resonated with these words:

> I am Nature, Mother of All,
> Ruler of the Elements, Progenitor of Worlds,
> Chief of All Deities,
> Mistress of the Living,
> Mistress of the Dead,
> The Sole Manifestation
> of all goddesses and gods.
> It is my will that controls
> the planets of the sky,
> the helpful winds of the sea,
> and the grievous silence of the dead.
> Though revealed by diverse customs and rites,
> and called upon by many names,
> my omnipotence is respected throughout the world.

To the Phrygians of Pessinus,
I am Mother of All Deities.
To the Athenians,
I am the wise and valiant Athena.
To those of the Cyprian Isle,
I am Aphrodite or Venus,
born of the foam of the Paphian coast.
To those of Crete who use the bow,
I am Dyktynna, Artemis or Diana.

To those of the island of Sicily,
I am called Persephone or Proserpina.
To the Eleusinians,
I am Mother Demeter, Mother Ceres,
or simply Mother of Wheat.
Some call upon me as Hera or Juno,
Bellona or Hecate.
But both of the Ethiopian peoples,
those who live in Egypt
and those who dwell further to the East,
understand my ancient wisdom
more than any others,
for they know the ceremonies that are dear to me
and call me by my true name—
Almighty Isis.

Upon seeing Her perfect image, upon hearing Her perfect voice, Lucius Apuleius began to pray: O Holy Blessed Lady, constant comfort to humankind whose beneficence and kindness nourish us all, and whose care for those in trouble is as a loving mother who cares for all her children—you are there when we call, stretching out your hand to put aside that which is harmful to us, untangling the web of fate in which we may be caught, even stopping the stars if they form a harmful pattern. All other deities, whether bountiful or merciless, do reverence to Thee. It is Isis who rules the world, stamping out the powers of evil, arranging the stars to give us answers, causing the seasons to come and go, commanding the winds to move ships, giving the clouds to water the growing seeds so that we may have food. If I had one thousand mouths and one thousand tongues within each, still I could not do justice to your Majesty. Yet I will forever remember your help in my time of need and keep your blessed image deep within my heart.

To Walk the Trail of Beauty
Native Americans of North America

rom the Athapascans to the Zuni, Native American accounts of mother as creator, earth as mother, woman as nature, woman as ancestral mother of tribe or clan, and woman as teacher of culture—emerge in a vast diversity of images and legends.

This diversity is quite understandable when one considers the immense number of different cultural groups that inhabited the continent of North America long before Euro-Caucasians arrived; scholars of linguistics have discovered some 550 different languages spoken by Native Americans. Yet integral to many of the accounts of origins and spiritual beliefs of Native American groups separated by thousands of miles is a sense of deep personal connection to earth and a oneness with the beings and processes of nature.

The people we today refer to as Native Americans are descendants of groups of people who entered the North American continent in waves of migrations that occurred over many millenia. The most generally accepted route of these migrations is that of the land bridge that once stretched across the Bering Strait, connecting the Chukchi Peninsula of Siberia with Alaska. Although there is a great deal of scholarly debate about the earliest dates of these migrations, and some would state a cautious 10,000 B.C., many others claim that they began some 40,000 years ago. Whatever the dates, the racial links between Native American peoples and the Proto-Mongolian groups of Asia are noted with almost universal agreement.

One of the earliest recognizable cultures of North America is the Sandia of New Mexico, arguments on the dating of this culture ranging from 25,000 to 10,000 B.C. Following the Sandia were the Clovis, the Folsom, and the Cochise cultures among others, each revealing specific stages of Native American development. Although cave dwelling is not generally associated with Native American groups, very early sites such as Danger Cave in Utah, Gypsum Cave in Arizona, and Bat Cave in New Mexico reveal that some Native American peoples did make use of caves as habitations. These particular cave sites occur in the southwest U.S., but this does not imply that caves in other areas of North America may not have been used in a similar manner. The name Cherokee, derived from *Chiluk-ki,* literally means cave dwellers.

The knowledge of cave habitations in the southwest is especially interesting in that cave dwellings of the southwest may be connected to Pueblo concepts of the Womb of Mother Earth. The generally round, often subterranean, Pueblo shrines of rituals and ceremonies, the *kiva,* contains a central opening in the ground, a hole known as a *Sipapu* or *Sipapuni.* This opening in the kiva is regarded as the Womb of Mother Earth and symbolic of the Place of Emergence, the sacred site at which Pueblo people came forth into the Fourth World, the world in which we now live. The transfer of humanmade substitutes for ritual caves, such as the crescent trench for Kunapipi in Australia and the Inna shrine of the Cuna in Panama (see Vol. I), suggests that a further exploration of possible links between the significance of the kiva and the use of caves might result in some interesting studies.

The pueblo dwellings built by Native Americans are admirable feats of structural engineering, often containing hundreds of rooms built on high rocky cliffs (such as Mesa Verde in Colorado) or set deep into massive caves (such as Betatakin in Arizona). The pueblos were constructed by a group of people known as the Anasazi, The Ancient Ones, members of a culture that flourished from about 300 A.D. to about 1300 A.D. The Pueblo people of today, primarily the Hopi and Zuni (the sources of the accounts of Huruing Wuhti and Spider Woman that are included in this section), have retained beliefs and customs that may survive from the Anasazi period.

Other clues to early Native American cultures were left by what is known as the Hohokam culture, literally 'Those Who Have Vanished'. Sites near Phoenix, Arizona reveal a well developed network of irrigation reservoirs and canals built by the Hohokam people some two thousand years ago. Several aspects of the Hohokam culture suggest that it was deeply influenced or even initiated by groups of Native Americans that had moved north from Mexico during the early Classic Period of that area. Connections between Native Americans of North and South America may be further noted in the Uto-Aztecan languages. These languages, known among the Comanche, Utes, and to some extent the Hopi of North America, also include the Nahuatl language of the Aztecs. The Corn Mother of the Hopi and Chicomecoatl of Mexico (see Vol. I) may be more closely linked than the apparent association of the Goddess with maize as an important food.

The great Mound Builders of the area that is now Ohio, Kentucky and West Virginia created earthworks that rise as high as seventy feet and often stretch for miles. These burial mounds are attributed to the Adena and successive Hopewell culture, the Hopewell extending as far as the areas known as Minnesota, Florida and New York. Objects found in these mounds reveal an early Native American knowledge of working with copper and quarrying stone, and a mobility or trade network that allowed the Mound Builders to acquire stone from Wisconsin, mica from the Appalachians and obsidian from the Rocky Mountains. The culture of the Mound Builders initially appeared at about 1000 B.C. and flourished for some 1500 years. Archaeological evidence suggests that the decline of this culture may have been the result of a widespread invasion or violent attack at about 500 A.D.

The Iroquois language reveals the connections between the Oneida, Onandaga, Cayuga, Seneca, Mohawk, Tuscarora, Huron and even the more southerly Cherokee. The League of Nations formed by the Iroquois who lived in the area of the Great Lakes may well have been an important influence in the formulation of the concepts of U.S. democracy, concepts generally attributed to Classical Greece or Magna Carta England. Those stating this premise point out that ancient Greece was not truly a democracy since slavery existed, while England still supports a royal family. Those who disagree with the importance of Iroquois influence upon Euro-Caucasian ideas about democracy argue that the system of the Council of Sachems, the governing body of the Iroquois League, was not truly democratic either. The Iroquois *women* chose the sachems and had the power to remove them if they did not perform their duties satisfactorily. If many aspects of a democratic system were adopted upon observation of the Iroquois government, we may, in hindsight, conjecture upon the effects of the rejection of this particular aspect of the system. Another interesting aspect of Iroquois social structure was the control that Iroquois women had over the food supply, even the results of hunting. This particular area of control enabled the women to decide on whether or not to supply food to men preparing for war, the refusal to supply food staples cancelling many a battle. Incidentally, Iroquois women were also responsible for appointing the religious clergy, both genders represented equally among the Iroquois 'Keepers of the Faith'.

Another major group of Native Americans linked by their languages are the Athapascans (Athabascans). This grouping includes many of the tribes of Alaska, Canada and the northwest U.S. It also includes the Apache, Kiowa and Navajo of the southwest. The Athapascan peoples appear to have been relative late comers to North America and the fact that Athapascan languages are tonal has caused some scholars to compare it with Chinese. Accounts of Changing Woman and Asintmah, included in this section, are both of Athapascan origin, though Changing Woman is spoken of by the Navajo of the southwest, while the account of Asintmah is told in western Canada. The accounts of origins of cultural knowledge, such as the legends of Pasowee of the Kiowa and Wild Pony of the Jicarilla Apache are also representative of Athapascan peoples.

One important aspect of spiritual beliefs that exist among many diverse Native American groups is the significance of dreams and visions. Cultural information, spiritual knowledge, and prophesies of the future, are often attributed to dreams or trance visions. The accounts of Pasowee and Wild Pony provide some idea of the part that dreams played in the receiving of wisdom. The respect for dreams as a source of useful information has been known in many cultures, including Sumer, Babylonia, Australia, Greece, China and Africa, thus the existence of this view of dreams is not unusual. Yet the degree to which Native American peoples have valued dreams as a vehicle of both cultural and spiritual wisdom should certainly be considered in any exploration of this most puzzling and fascinating experience of humankind.

The legends included in this section are but a small portion of the accounts and images of woman as sacred and/or heroic among the Native American peoples. Those interested in further research may find the following to be of interest. The Three Kadlu Sisters, known among the Inuit (Eskimo) of Baffin Island, are said to cause thunder and lightning by rubbing their bodies together. Sedna is known among the coastal Inuit as the Goddess of the Dead and as the Sovereign of the Ocean, ruler over the sea mammals and fish so vital to Inuit life. Along with the accounts of Huruing Wuhti and Spider Woman that are included in this section, the sacred rituals for the Deer Mothers and the Corn Mother are important in Pueblo spiritual beliefs. Buffalo Cow Woman is remembered as the Ancient Mother who gave the wisdom of the peace pipe to the Lakota (Sioux). The Cree people of the Algonquin speaking tribes (which also include Cheyenne, Blackfoot, Naskapi, Arapaho, Micmac, Penobscot, Chippewa and Ojibwa) speak of the Grandmother of People, Messak Kummik Okwi. This primal grandmother was understood to be in charge of all the food on earth, an image similar to that of mother as earth, explaining the Algonquin custom of placing a small portion of each meal upon the ground—to thank 'Our Grandmother'.

The changes in Native American cultures and customs caused by the continually increasing occupation of North America by Euro-Caucasians are obviously enormous. It has only been through the most dedicated and tenacious persistence that what we know of Native American beliefs has been retained. Yet despite all that has occurred to weaken or erase these ancient beliefs, the concept of earth or nature as Mother emerges into contemporary thought with a deep significance. Facing threats of partial or total destruction of the planet by radiation, pollution, toxic chemicals and the abuse of resources, a perception of earth as our Mother may well be one of the most viable paths towards preserving life. And those among us who heard the term 'trespassing' used to remove Native Americans from Alcatraz Island might well consider the irony and arrogance in Euro-Caucasians accusing Native Americans of trespassing on any part of North America, certainly this westernmost outpost of the lands regarded for thousands of years as Mother.

SPIDER WOMAN

Accounts of Spider Woman as Creator are known among many of the Pueblo people of the southwest of North America. One of the most detailed accounts of the Creation by Spider Woman is from Sia, a pueblo of the Keres. Although Sussistanako is the most often mentioned name of Spider Woman, She is also spoken of as Tsitsicinako and Kokyangwuti. Her daughters, Ut Set and Nau Ut Set, are also known as Itsictsiti and Nautsiti. The account presented here is an adaptation drawn from several sources, with special acknowledgement to the not yet published work of Judith Todd.

In the beginning there was nothing but Spider Woman, She who was called Sussistanako, Thinking Woman, Thought Woman. No other living creature, no bird or animal or fish yet lived. In the dark purple light that glowed at the Dawn of Being, Spider Woman spun a line from East to West. She spun a line from North to South. And then She sat by these threads that stretched to the four horizons, these strands that She had drawn across the universe, and sang in a voice that was exceptionally deep and sweet. As She sang, two daughters came forth: Ut Set, who became the mother of the Pueblo people, Nau Ut Set, who became the mother of all others.

Following the directions of Spider Woman, these two daughters formed the sun from white shell, red rock, turquoise and pearly abalone shell. When it was ready, they carried the sun to the top of the highest mountain and dropped it into the sky so that it would give light. But when they saw that it was still dark at night, they then formed the moon, putting together pieces of dark black stone, yellow stone, red rock and turquoise. Still things were not quite right, for when the moon travelled far, there were many nights when they could not see. It was for this reason that with the help of Spider Woman, Ut Set and Nau Ut Set created the Star People, giving them sparkling clear crystal for eyes so that there would never be complete darkness again.

Once the lights of heaven were in place, Spider Woman used the clay of the earth, the red, the yellow, the white and the black clay, and with this She made people. Upon them She placed a covering of creative wisdom, that which She spun from Her own Spider being. To each, She attached a thread of Her web. It is for this reason that each person has a delicate thread of web connected to Spider Woman, connected to the doorway at the top of the head. Those who do not know this, allow the door to close, but it is only when we keep the door open by chanting through it, that we may draw upon this link to the creative wisdom of Spider Woman.

Many forgot about the door. Many people grew cruel and corrupt. They forgot the ancient wisdom. Three times over people forgot and three times over they were washed away in great floods. But each time Spider Woman saved those who did remember, those who had kept the door at the top of their heads open. These were the people that She brought to the place of hollow reeds. Teaching them to use the reeds as boats, those whose doors were still open floated upon the waters until the time they might enter into the new world, the Fourth World. The floating was long. The waiting was long. The travelling was very far. And when it was over, they emerged into the new world, climbed up through the Sipapu hole that was the Womb of Mother Earth.

Ut Set provided them with corn, explaining that it was the milk of Her breasts. Nau Ut Set gave them prayer sticks and stones for grinding the corn. Spider Woman provided them with eagle feathers for their hair, so that they might travel safely forever after. But only those who remember to keep the door open, to draw upon the wisdom of Sussitanako, know which way to travel, for they can see and feel the thread that is part of the Web of Destiny that Spider Woman weaves.

HURUING WUHTI

This legend of Creation from the Hopi people of southwestern North America presents a double image of Creator that is puzzling, yet perhaps related to the two daughters of Spider Woman. The mysteries involved in the idea of two separate deities with the same name, or two aspects of the same deity that dwell in separate locations, are certainly of interest, as is the belief that the creation of earth and life was accomplished by Sister Goddesses. It is also interesting to note that the Hopi account states that the first woman was created before the first man.

Sister Mothers of the World, as old as the time when all the universe was the Great Sea, Mother Huruing Wuhti lived in the House of the Ocean of the East, Mother Huruing Wuhti lived in the House of the Ocean of the West. So it was that they created the land in the waters between them, created the earth on which we live.

Soon they wondered if there was any life upon the earth. They met upon the bridge that was the great rainbow that stretched between them, the bridge that reached from east to west. And there on the rainbow bridge they created a tiny bird, a bird to fly over the earth to see if any life existed. When the bird returned, bringing the message that there was no life to be found, the Two Mothers, Huruing Wuhti, then together formed the animals and birds that now live on earth.

Pleased with what they had done, they then formed a woman. Naming her Tuwabontums, they placed her on the earth. When this was done they formed a man. Naming him Muingwu, they placed him on the earth. So it happened that Tuwabontums and Muingwu became the first parents of the Hopi people. It is for this reason that Hopi people remember the Mothers Huruing Wuhti as creators of the earth and the life upon it.

CHANGING WOMAN

Although Changing Woman is regarded as an anthropomorphic figure, the beliefs and customs associated with Her allow us to understand that She is the processes of Nature. This Navajo concept of female deity may well be compared to the accounts of Nu Kwa and Mother Nature (Tao) (see Chinese Section–Vol. I). The extremely important Navajo concept of walking in the Trail of Beauty certainly brings the concept of Tao (The Way) to the mind of any student of spiritual thought.

Creator of the Navajo people, Changing Woman, Estsan Atlehi, is the Mother of All. She is the Holy Woman who brings each season, Mother Earth who is the seasons, Iyatiku who Brings All Life, Mother Nature in all that She unfolds.

Some say that She was born at the foot of the Mountain Around Which Moving Was Done, born on a bed of flowers, a delicate rainbow arching as coverlet over Her infant body. From Her body grew the four mountains of the compass points, the mountains that mark the East and West, the mountains that mark the North and South. This day of birth was a day of joy, a day of brilliance and thus the memory of it is kept in the ever joyous song of The Blessing Way. For if Changing Woman had not been born, She would not have rubbed the skin of Her perfect body—and in this way brought forth the Navajo people.

It is Changing Woman who teaches the flow of life, the restlessness of the sand as it flies with the wind, the wisdom of the ancient rocks that never leave their home, the pleasure of the tiny sapling that had risen through them. So it is into the House of Changing Woman that each young girl enters, as her blood begins to flow with the moon, as she passes into womanhood.

It is Changing Woman who teaches the cycles, the constant round of hot and cold, of birth and dying, of youth and aging, of seedling to corn, of corn to seedling kernel, of day to night, of night to day, of waxing moon to waning moon—and thus She gave the sacred songs that help to ease all in their passage. For is it not Changing Woman who each year sleeps beneath the blanket of snow as Grandmother who walks with a turquoise cane, but then each year awakes with the flowers of Spring, awakes as the young Mother of us all?

It is to Changing Woman that we look as we search for the wisdom of life. While some may believe that they can defy Changing Woman's patterns to make their own, wise people know that this cannot be done, for to try to change the ways of Changing Woman, is to destroy all life. But those who understand the ways of Changing Woman, forever walk The Trail of Beauty.

WHITE SHELL WOMAN

This Navajo account of the birth of White Shell Woman, Yolkai Estsan, not only offers an explanation of how we came to have light on earth but strongly suggests the spiritual importance of both the birth and the event. The interpretation of the identity of White Shell Woman has been both as sister to Changing Woman and as an aspect of Changing Woman, rather than as a separate deity. The concept of double female or sister deity may be compared to Huruing Wuhti of the Hopi people and to Ut Set and Nau Ut Set of the Pueblo. It may also be of interest to compare this concept with that of the triple Goddess images as known among the Celts, Greeks and Scandinavians.

Yolkai Estsan, White Shell Woman,
uttered the cry of infancy,
made Her first sound of life,
as She lay at the foot of Mount Tacoli,
as She lay in a cradleboard
formed of two rainbows,
the thin red lines of the rising sun,
the fingers of dawn, touching Her tiny feet.

Four coverlets were wrapped about the baby girl,
each blanket woven of misty cloud,
one black, one yellow, one blue, one white,
four blankets trimmed with loops of lightning,
dawn's sunbeams woven carefully through each loop,
while over the small brown face
the arch of a rainbow could be seen.

Thus White Shell Woman came into the world,
on a day when the world
had long been sad and troubled,
had long been dark with cloud,
on a day when the light of dawn
touching the light of the rainbows
glowed in immense but silent promise.

Soon feeling the darkness,
Yolkai Estsan formed a circle,
shaping it of turquoise and white shells.
Over this She held a rock of crystal,
held it until a fire burst forth,
a blaze that grew so hot, so bright,
that with the help of the Holy People,
White Shell Woman pushed it further and further away,
higher and higher into the spaces of heaven.
So it happened that Yolkai Estsan,
She who had been born at the time of trouble,
She who had arrived attended by rainbows,
brought light to the Earth.

ASINTMAH

The idea of Earth as Mother is one that is found in the religious beliefs of many Native American groups. This account of Mother Earth and the first woman of the world is from the Athapascan people of western Canada. The Athapascan language is used by Native American peoples who inhabit Alaska, western Canada and the northwestern United States. It is this language that links the Kiowa, Apache and Navajo people to these northwestern tribes, for despite the great migrations southwards, the languages are still similar enough to reveal the connections.

When Mother Earth was very young, the mountains and the rivers of Her proud body blossomed in the springtime of Her being. She was more than fair to look upon, but Her greatest beauty of all was that part of Her that became the homeland of the northern Athapascan peoples.

It was here on this most perfect part of Earth that She adorned Her body with caps of crystal snow and glistening ice that melted when She grew warm. From this snow and ice came streams of clear blue water, feathered with bubbling foam, racing over granite boulders across Her beloved body that held the trees whose tips grazed against the heavens.

It was on this most perfect part of Earth that Asintmah, first woman of the world, appeared at the foot of Mount Atiksa near the Athabasca River. The holy Asintmah walked among the forests that grew upon Earth, gathering branches that had been discarded by the trees, careful not to tear or wrench away any that might still be growing on the body of Earth. Joining these branches together, Asintmah built the first loom. And upon it she wove the fibers of the fireweed, the willow herb that Earth so favoured, weaving them into The Great Blanket of Earth.

Once the weaving was completed, Asintmah began her long walk to spread the sacred blanket across the vast body of Earth. Securing one corner to Sharktooth Mountain, she tied another to The Pillar of Rock, the third to Levelhead Mountain and the fourth to Mount Atiksa. Then sitting down beside the edge of the blanket, Asintmah began to weave threads of music, singing of all the beauties of Earth, singing songs of how Earth would soon give birth to new lives, beings as perfect as Herself.

Asintmah's songs soon changed to those that would soothe the pangs of labour, that would ease the birth for She who lay under the fireweed cover, as Earth's contractions made the Great Blanket heave and fall—in Her efforts to give Her children life.

Suddenly all was quiet. Earth lay still and calm once again. It was in this way that Asintmah knew that the children born of Earth's womb had been delivered. Reaching carefully beneath the blanket, Asintmah felt the moving life that lay between Earth's thighs. Bringing it out into the light, Asintmah saw a small grey body with four tiny feet and a long string for a tail. It was Mouse.

Excited by this little creature, Asintmah again slipped her arm beneath the blanket and found another life, this one all covered with soft fur, its ears tall with pride. It was Rabbit. So pleased was Asintmah with these two new beings that she continued to search about, her arm reaching ever further under the great blanket that still covered Earth. In this way she soon brought out Cougar and Caribou, Wapiti and Moose, and all the other beings that now walk about on Earth.

So it was that with the help of the holy Asintmah, the woman who existed before all others, Maiden Earth became Mother Earth. And although this all happened a very long time ago, Athapascan people remember that even now they must care for their aging mother, the one who gave them life, and revere the memory of the woman Asintmah who was with Her in the beginning.

AWEHAI

This explanation of how the earth was formed is from the Iroquois people of northeastern United States. The Iroquois Nation was composed of five tribal groups which had formed the *Hodenosaunee,* The League of Five Nations. A similar account is known among the Huron people who also spoke an Iroquois language, but did not belong to the Hodenosaunee. Some versions of the story of Awehai (Atansic) state that the earth was built on the back of the Great Turtle, an image that brings to mind the Chinese account of Nu Kwa using the legs of the turtle as the four columns that hold up the universe. Records of early Iroquois laws and customs not only reveal a system of matrilineal descent but a great deal of political and economic power held by the Iroquois women.

In the days before the Onandaga, the Oneida and the Seneca, the Cayuga and the Mohawk, were separate peoples, in the days even before people came to live upon the earth—there were other beings, in other worlds.

One of these was the woman Awehai. Another was Awehai's husband. The third was a man that Awehai's husband thought she loved, more than she loved him. Thinking this drove the husband into such a jealous frenzy that he uprooted the tree that was at the very center of the world. And into the great chasm left by the uprooted tree, the husband threw the innocent woman to her death.

Falling, falling, through the great dark hole, Awehai grasped at the life around her. Her fingers curled about seeds of vegetables and flowers. As she continued to fall through the great space, she gathered beavers, otters and toads into her arms, clutching them to her breasts. Further and further she fell, as if there would never be an end—until the vast waters of another world spread out below her.

As her body grew closer to the water, creatures with broad feathered wings flew to the place where she would land, making a soft feathery cushion. Gathered under and around her, they carried Awehai until she was safely atop the Great Turtle. The otters, beavers and toads that she had carried with her, scurried about, gathering the dirt that had been shaken from the roots of the great uprooted tree. Pressing this dirt together, they formed it into an island—the one that we now know as Earth.

Once Earth was made, Awehai scattered the seeds from the plants, those she had gathered as she fell. Soon the Earth was covered with green sprouts of nourishing abundance. When Awehai saw this New World, she brought forth children to live upon it. So it happened that the Iroquois people came into being, children of the woman Awehai who had made the new land in the great waters, the woman whose heart had refused to surrender, the woman whose arms had reached out for life.

SOMAGALAGS

The stories of Somagalags are from the Bella Coola people who live along the coastal areas of British Columbia. Though the latter part of the story presented here appears to be based upon social concerns, the brief references to the birth of the three mountains suggest that Somagalags may once have been the name associated with Earth as Mother.

Down from the heavens that stretch over the lands of the North Pacific waters, in the land of the river known as the Skeena, came Mother Somagalags.

There by the waters where she descended, she found a man and taking him to her, she soon grew great with child. Greater yet, she grew, until she gave birth to Kuga Mountain. Again she took the man and again she laboured. This time she bore Zaychisi, not quite as high as Kuga. Yet a third time she took the man and thus brought forth the Mountain Segos, even smaller than the others.

When the mountains were fully grown, Somagalags left the Skeena River and made her way to the smoothest of beaches. Once there she went from beach to woods, from woods to beach, again and again, until she had carried out all the dry fallen cedars that she needed to make a home. Cleaning off the branches, smoothing off the bark, she built herself a fine cedar cabin in which to live.

There upon the drifting sands that lay by the great ocean waters, in the cabin of cedar, Somagalags once again gave birth.

This time she bore four young wolves, cubs that howled for food and warmth. Placing the infant cubs in the warmest corner, she walked to the water's edge, filling her basket with the tasty clams that had been sleeping in the ocean waters. When she returned to the cabin with her basket of clams, she was surprised to hear the laughter of human children coming from inside. But when she entered through the doorway, all she saw were four cubs, deep in newborn sleep. So Somagalags made the fire, and over it she cooked the clams to feed her hungry wolves, trying to forget the puzzle of the voices.

The ocean waters glistened red in the light of the sun that was bringing an end to the day, as Somagalags once again made her way across the sands from shore to cabin. She held her digging stick in one hand, her clam filled basket in the other. Wearily, she recalled how long it had been since the birth of the cubs, how many times she had fetched the clams, how many times she had made the fire, how many times she had fed her young. But upon reaching the great cedar tree that stood near the cabin, the sound of voices and laughter brought a halt to her thoughts.

In silence, she drew close to the window. Peering inside, she was astonished to see four nearly grown young men—in place of her four wolf cubs. Anger rose in her heart. Fatigue filled her body. She thought of the entire day, the many long days that she had spent standing in the waters in hopes of finding a new bed of clams, the many times she had carried the basket full and heavy with the clams that she had found, the many times she had gathered the fire wood and carried it home so that she might feed and warm the four young cubs.

Furious, digging stick in hand, she climbed through the window. With it she chastised the four young men for tricking her into believing that they were only cubs, that they could not gather their own food, that they could not fetch their own wood, that they could not make their own evening fire. Though quick to protest and offer excuse, the young men finally admitted that they had wronged their mother. Each agreed that if she would teach them how to care for themselves, they would pay her back for all that she had done for them.

So it happened that Somagalags took them to the beach to teach them the secrets of how to find the clams. She took them into the woods where she pointed out the straightest cedars and told them how they could be felled, could be used to build new shelters that would keep them from the cold sea winds. She showed them which trees could be used to carve the sacred totem, so that they and their children would never forget that they were from the Clan of Somagalags. She taught them how to carve the totem form of Somagalags, First Mother of the Clan, She who gave birth to Kuga, Zaychisi and Segos mountains, She who still watches over Her children who live upon the land of the North Pacific waters.

QUESKAPENEK

The Okanagan Valley in southern British Columbia is even today known for its fertile soil and the excellent food that it produces. This explanation of the abundant growth of food in the land that borders the Okanagan River is told by the Salish tribe of that area. The account describes Queskapenek as a mortal woman but the results of Queskapenek's efforts may well reveal this account as a derivation of an earlier image of Earth as Mother.

Along the blue waters of the Okanagan River, to the south of Chu Chua and Pukaeshun Mountain, the Okanagan people of the Salish tribes remember the Mother Queskapenek. They remember her as the Chieftainess, the First Woman, the one who gave them the abundant Okanagan lands.

Many, many years ago, Queskapenek was a young woman who spent long and pleasurable hours by the waters of the Okanagan. It was there that she gave birth to children. It was there that her children gave birth to their children, as the autumn skin of Queskapenek grew rich with wisdom lines. Her face, then carved with the intricacies of the art of the finest sculptor, told of she who had seen much, she who knew the many secrets of life.

There came a time when Queskapenek knew that she had little time left to spend with the family that she had created, with the tribe that now knew the Okanagan Valley as their home. She worried about what might happen to her children, wanting to be able to provide for them, wanting to be able to mother them, even after her departure from earth.

It was with this concern deep in her mind that Queskapenek put her basket on her arm and walked into the woods. There she sought out the tastiest of roots and plants that she could find, placing each in her basket until it was full. In much the same way, she walked along in the grassy meadows, gathering the seeds of fruits and vegetables, the tastiest that she could find. Each time the basket was full, Queskapenek took the riches in her basket to the place where the soil was most nurturing to growth, where the clear mountain waters made the earth most fertile—and in this land she planted all that she had gathered.

It was in this way that the lands of the Okanagan Valley soon became known for their abundance of fine foods, for this was the legacy left by the Mother Quescapenek. It is for this reason that Salish people remember the ancient Queskapenek, the mother who still provides for them, still cares for them, even though naught but her spirit is to be seen in the Okanagan Valley.

SPIDER GRANDMOTHER

In the account of Spider Woman included in this section, the image of Spider was perceived as Primeval Creator. But there are numerous accounts from the Pueblo peoples of a somewhat less omnipotent image of Spider, as Spider Grandmother. Although some scholars of Native American religion claim that connections between Spider Woman and Spider Grandmother are purely coincidental, the events associated with Spider Grandmother suggest a more careful examination of the links between the two images. The following account is from the Kiowa people. The Kiowa are not Pueblo, but perhaps through contact with the Pueblo people they include some of the accounts of Spider Grandmother in Kiowa legend and belief.

The council of the animals met in the eternal darkness with hopes of finding a solution to the constant night—and to the difficulties of seeing the very ground on which they walked. Many tried to solve the problem. Rabbit dreamed up a plan—that didn't work. Fox devised another—that ended in failure. Eagle tried to find light—only to throw his wings up in discouragement. Woodpecker thought he could do better—only to find that the new world still remained in darkness.

After each had bragged in loud voices, and after each had failed, there was silence. Then from the darkness came a voice, a little voice that sounded very old. It was Spider Grandmother, suggesting that she might be able to remedy the problem. The others responded with laughter and challenging jeers. Surely this old grandmother could not do what Fox and Eagle could not do. But the wisdom of patience made her deaf to their answers. In hope of helping her people out of the blinding darkness, Spider Grandmother set off towards the East, set off towards the land of the Sun People.

The walk was long and arduous. Over vast dry deserts, over perilous mountain trails, across wide rivers and around wide lakes, Spider Grandmother continued to walk—the thread of her webbing spinning out behind her. In the darkness, she came upon a bed of soft wet clay and from it she fashioned a bowl. Once again, she began to walk, now carrying the new bowl in her hands. Many nights of darkness passed. Many days of darkness passed. And then a glow of orange appeared before her in the distance, telling her that she had reached the land of the Sun People.

Fatigued from the long walk, she rested, not far from the blazing fire that wondrously lit the night—hoping that she would not be noticed. As the evening went by, closer and closer she drew to the great fire that lit the land of the Sun People. And then, so quickly that no one saw, she pinched off a small piece of the bright orange flame, popped it into her bowl, and walked quietly away.

Following the strand of web that she had spun behind her, Spider Grandmother began the long walk home. She carried the bowl with great care, so that the piece of fire would not fall out. But much to her surprise, the fire grew brighter and larger as she walked, until its brightness and its heat became so unbearably intense that she flung the blazing fire ball into the air. Tiny and old as she was, she flung the fire so high up into the heavens that it

After each had bragged
in loud voices

stayed there and became the sun. So it was that Spider Grand-mother brought light for her people, ending the darkness that had been in the New World.

Yet even at the moment that she tossed the sun into the sky, Spider Grandmother thought to keep a small piece. This she placed in the bowl and brought back to her people, giving them this second gift of fire for the cooking of the food, for the baking of the clay and for the light of the evening campfire. It is no wonder that when people, even today, sit about the council fire, they tell these and other wondrous stories of the ancient Spider Grandmother.

SUN SISTER

The following account of how the sun and the moon came to be in the sky is generally simply designated as Eskimo. But it is important to realize that so called Eskimo people are a group that is spread from Siberia, through Alaska and Northern Canada, and on Greenland. Within this group are separate peoples such as the Tahagmiut, Chugach, Netsilik, Aleut, Iglulik, Nunamuit, and many others. It is also worth noting that the word Eskimo was applied to these people by a Jesuit. So called Eskimo groups refer to themselves as *Inuit*, the plural of *inuk*, which simply means human, as Inuit means The People. Though the legend of Sun Sister is known among many Inuit groups, there are several variations of it.

In the singing house, the voices of young women, the voices of young men, sing and laugh together as the snow falls outside. By the soft light of the whale oil, they watch one another as a great wind blows across the whiteness. The wild wind grows wilder, angrily whipping the snow up into its own path until, even fiercer than before, it forces its way into the singing house—blowing out the lamps.

Dark as when one's eyes are closed, the singing house was silent. And then from the silence, a muffled sound came forth, a frightened crying. Who could it be? And where, in the invisible room? Only two people knew. Sister, and he who attacked her in the darkness, afraid to show his face. What kind of man could this be? Sister rubbed her palms in the soot on the floor and when the lamps were once more lit, Sister knew—from the handprint of soot on his back.

'My brother, my own brother', Sister thought, as disbelief turned into shock. The pain of betrayal joined the pain of violation. From the corner of her eye, Sister saw the whale light flicker on a knife. In hatred, in outrage, in shame, she seized the knife and thrust its blade deep into the chest of her brother!

With her heart pounding heavily, pounding loud inside her own chest, Sister pulled a log from the pile. Lighting one end of the log in the fire, Sister ran towards their home, her log torch lighting the way, cold tears chilling her cheeks. But Brother too took a log and tipped the end with fire. Determined that Sister would not tell what had happened in the singing house, he followed her, making a path of bloodstained footsteps in the snow. Though he tried to run, his steps became ever slower, the ache in his chest ever greater. Finally, when his legs could no longer hold him, he fell upon his torch, lay there upon the blazing heat of the small fire, upon the icy cold of the snow, lay dying on the great flat whiteness.

Glancing behind her, hoping to see the distance between them grow greater, Sister saw the light go down. She saw it dim. Though the handprint of soot and the blood on the knife were clearer to her than the torch that went down, Sister turned to help Brother.

Almost before she had a chance to move towards him, she felt her cold and tired body being lifted from the ground. Higher and higher she rose, until she knew that she was in the highest heavens. Still she held her blazing torch, still she held the log tipped with fire, for now as she took her place in heaven, She became the sun. And to this day, Her torch glowing brightly, we know Her as Sun Sister.

Brother too was lifted into the heavens. But Brother had fallen on his torch and his light was dim. Thus his half extinguished light became the moon, placed in heaven to remind all men of the terrible wrong that he had done, so that none would follow his ways.

So it came to be that in the singing house, young voices can still be heard, telling the story of Sun Sister and Moon Brother—and how they came to be in the heavens.

POHAHA

Although this account of Pohaha is based upon an actual woman, the association of the story with the Mask of Valour has helped it to remain as a legend among the Cottonwood Clan of the Pueblo people. Beyond existing as a record of a woman's courage in combat, Pohaha's insistence upon being recognized as a woman as she entered battle, offers a mythic symbolism that speaks of more than the specific events described.

Among the people of the Cottonwood Clan who lived in the great houses set into the massive pink rock cliffs, young Pohaha laughed and played, fished in the streams, climbed the mountains, hunted small animals for dinner—but seldom stayed home to help her mother grind the corn.

The uncles would often tease the young Pohaha, telling her that what she did was the way of boys. But Pohaha went about her day, explaining that if she did what she did, then this must be the way of girls—since this is what she knew herself to be. Even after nineteen summers of life, Pohaha continued to roam the woods, bow and arrow in her hand, refusing to marry, refusing to be kept at home to grind the corn to feed the children they wanted her to have.

When an enemy raid fell upon the people of the Cottonwood Clan, her teasing uncles challenged that such an able hunter should perhaps ride forth and help to drive out the enemy. Much to her uncles' surprise, Pohaha answered their challenge by reaching for her bow, reaching for her arrows, reaching for the war rattle that hung upon the wall—and joining the young men who rode to battle. Her courage and determination shining so brightly, Pohaha soon found herself leading all the others. Though some mocked from behind, even they followed Pohaha to the camp of the enemy.

Along the open stretches of rock and river, Pohaha led, while singing chants of victory to give the others courage. Approaching the enemy campsite, seeing those who had so mercilessly attacked their village, she pressed her horse to move faster. But just before she loosed her first arrow, she raised her deerskin skirt waisthigh. Four times she lifted her skirt, so that neither comrade nor enemy would have a doubt that this brave leader was a woman. Then in-to the intruder's camp, she led the youths of her village. With war cry and arrow, with command and strategy, it was not long before those who had attacked their homes—and camped only to repeat the slaughter—fled before the angry archer.

Riding home, certain that the attackers would not soon return, Pohaha now sang songs of peace, as those who had fought behind her, now followed with joyous pride replacing their earlier doubts in the one who led them.

When the members of the Cottonwood Clan saw that the protectors of the village had returned victorious, they chanted in relief and celebration. They danced the dance of weapons laid to rest. They feasted upon the food of safe living. And then the great moment arrived, the moment for the presentation of the Mask of Valour, the sacred face that would be given to the one most courageous in protecting the people of the village. Four long teeth jutted from its wide mouth. One side was the blue of deep waters; the other was the golden yellow of sunshine. It was the mask of magical properties, the mask of bravery and daring—and it was about to be presented.

There was never a question of who the new owner of the mask would be. The elders of the village called the brave Pohaha forth and in the light of the evening fire, they placed the sacred mask of courage in Pohaha's hands. Even the uncles agreed that Pohaha must be Potai, Chief Defender of the Clan.

From that time on, for all the summers of her life, for all the winters of her life, Pohaha kept the Mask of Valour of the Cottonwood Clan of the great Pueblo people. In a year of great age, Pohaha returned the mask to her village, saying, "This mask contains my spirit. May it protect you always and be with you forever." And then, deep in sleep that very night, Pohaha went to the land of the ancestors, leaving the mask and the memory of her woman courage as legacy to her people.

PASOWEE, THE BUFFALO WOMAN

The story of the woman Pasowee is from the Kiowa people, an Athapascan tribe related to the Athapascans of Alaska and Canada. The
Kiowa are believed to have lived in the Wyoming area before their later
settlements in Kansas and Oklahoma. Although it is not mentioned in this
account, the story of Pasowee may be connected to one of the sacred
societies of the Kiowa, the Buffalo Women. This sacred society is especially associated with ritual dance and healing.

Stolen from her family in the middle of the night's darkness,
Pasowee lived for many years in the stranger's campsite. So torn
was she with longing for those she had once known that one day
she ran into the woods, escaping, only to find herself lost in a
place that she did not know at all.

There, lying before her at the end of the day's flight, was the
hide of a long dead buffalo, a shelter for the night. Creeping in
under the heaviness of the fur, Pasowee slept, as strange dreams
flowed as rippling water through her mind. The buffalo had come
to life. It spoke to Pasowee in a tongue that she understood. It
told her of cures that could be found within its body and how they
should be used to heal the ill. It told her that its skin could be used
for shelter, just as it had kept her warm throughout the night. It
whispered the wisdom of the ages into her sleeping ears. And
then, just before the dawn, it told her of the campsite filled with
the people from whom she had been taken so many years before,
and which brooks and streams to follow to reach them again.

When the morning light lifted her eyelids, she did not forget
the night of dreams. Sitting for a moment upon a nearby hill, she
watched two wolves kill another buffalo, just as the spirit of the
long dead buffalo had prophesied. Gnawing upon the buffalo
they had killed, the two wolves then appeased their empty
stomachs just as the spirit of the long dead buffalo had foretold in
her dreams. Now trusting the spirit of the buffalo, Pasowee
waited until the wolves had had their fill and then cut off enough
meat for herself. When the meat was dry enough to eat along the
way, she started upon her journey.

Following the fast running waters described by the buffalo,
Pasowee rejoined her people. With joy, they welcomed the

woman they had not seen since her childhood and asked her to tell of her time since she had first been taken. In silent answer, Pasowee showed a piece of buffalo hide that she had carried with her. Then she dried it over stones that were still hot from the fire. Everyone watched as Pasowee then stitched a circle of the buffalo hide to a circle of deer hide, carefully tying the hoof and tail of the buffalo to this leather pouch. Into this pouch she put the medicine that had been made known to her in the buffalo dream.

The miracle of the buffalo medicine brought joy and good health to the Kiowa people. But there was still more wisdom that the spirit of the buffalo had given to Pasowee to pass on to her people. So it was that she led the young women and the young men of the camp into the forest where the great trees lived. Circling about a grove four times, they entered the grove as Pasowee chose a tree, a cottonwood, upon whose lowest branch she hung a cloth. There in the grove the young people stayed until the sun disappeared. There they stayed all through the night of stars that glistened between the leaves of the highest branches.

When the light of the morning came, Pasowee sent the young men to find a buffalo. Then surrounded by the women, she stood before the tree which held the cloth, an axe held tightly in her hands. Three times she swung the axe towards the tree and on the fourth swing she began to cut. When the great tree toppled to the ground, Pasowee showed the women how to paint a carbon black upon its trunk, a clay red upon its branches. Then stripping the red branches from the black, the women made the first *deodogiada*, the first central post of a tipi.

Pasowee then chose the site upon which the tipi was to stand and taught the women how to tie the ropes, so that by pulling upon them the circle of women made the deodogiada stand as tall and as straight as it had done in the forest. Around the central post, the women then placed smaller posts, twenty-two in number. And close to the base of the deodogiada, they placed the small red branches, whistles, feathers and pebbles, and a bowl of cedar shavings—as Pasowee instructed them to do.

The smell of the burning cedar welcomed the young men as they returned with the buffalo. Ten suns passed as the skin was dried and joined and fastened into place. So it happened that from the spirit of the buffalo, Pasowee taught the Kiowa people how to build their homes. It is for this reason that Pasowee is long remembered as Buffalo Woman, Medicine Woman, she whom the spirit of the buffalo chose as teacher of the Kiowa.

WILD PONY

This legend of primeval times, as explained by the Jicarilla Apache people, is especially interesting in that it includes a description of the origins of a ritual for young Jicarilla girls. This account of the First Woman, Wild Pony, offers some insight into the value placed upon dreams as a manner of gaining knowledge, a value also evident in the Kiowa account of Pasowee. The Jicarilla Apache, though related to the Athapascan peoples of Canada, are now settled primarily in the northeastern area of New Mexico. The name Wild Pony and the part of this account that concerns the use of horses can date no further back than about 1600 A.D., the period that horses brought by the Spanish first became available to Native Americans.

In the days when days began, an old woman and an old man appeared upon the plains. The woman called the man Smoke. The man called the woman Wild Pony. As they walked upon the new Earth, a magic being, a hatsin, came to join them. This hatsin greeted them with welcoming words and then explained their future to them.

'You shall be the parents of a great and noble tribe. It is for you to learn to live upon this land, for one day the Jicarilla Apache people will remember you as their first ancestors.' Wild Pony and Smoke were astonished by this prophesy. Still they heard the hatsin's words about the greenblue rocks in the distance and the shining silver metal that was to be found in them. They turned to look at the rocks, following the direction of the hatsin's pointing finger. By the time their eyes returned to where they stood, the hatsin had disappeared.

'The silver in the rocks is all very interesting,' Wild Pony said, ''but how shall we become ancestors of a great tribe when we cannot even find enough food for the day?' They searched about the rocks and looked across the plains but there was no food to be found. As they found themselves growing closer to despair, the magic hatsin returned as suddenly as it had left.

'You must go to the South. There you will learn of the corn and the grain. There you will learn how to plant seeds so that Earth will feed you and your people forever.' It was for this reason that Wild Pony and Smoke went to the South. There they came to understand the corn and the grain that would feed the tribe they would bring into being.

When their stomachs were full, the hatsin appeared for a third time. This time it came to speak to Wild Pony alone. The woman and the magic being walked out upon the plains. As they walked they saw wild horses galloping across the plains, moving faster than any person could walk or run. 'Now I shall tell you of the horses', the hatsin said. 'They have strong backs and can travel great distances. But remember, these horses shall help you only as long as you treat them as your friends.'

After these words had been spoken, Wild Pony expected the hatsin to disappear as it had done before. But the hatsin stayed, continuing to walk by her side. Further and further they walked, until they came upon a stretch of soft red ground. And it was there that the hatsin told Wild Pony about the clay. It kneeled upon the ground, scooping a handful of the soft wet earth into its hand. It was this clay that it rubbed upon Wild Pony's hands, saying, 'This clay is yours to use. With it you can make bowls to hold the corn and grains. And when you find water, you can carry the water in the clay.'

Encouraged by the hatsin, Wild Pony sat by the stretch of soft red ground and formed some of it into a bowl. It was the first bowl ever made on earth. She looked up to show the bowl to the hatsin, but once again it had disappeared. Sitting alone on the ground, Wild Pony decided to make another bowl, and another, thinking how pleased Smoke would be when she brought them back.

Tired from the events of the long day, four clay bowls by her side, the sky red with the sun's descent, Wild Pony fell asleep. The sleep was deep and as heavy as the red hills of rock that lay close to where she slept. And in this deepness, in this heaviness, Wild Pony's mind slipped into dreams. She felt the red clay in her hands. She pressed and pushed. She rolled it and smoothed it. Soon she held a large round red bowl in her hands. She took the bowl to a stream of clear water that raced over small rocks and there she filled the dream bowl with water. But suddenly the bowl began to grow soft in her hands. The water trickled out over the collapsing sides, until she held only the soft red clay that had been a bowl for but a moment.

Wild Pony stared at the clay, deep disappointment filling her heart. It was in this sleep, in this dream that Wild Pony had by the clay bed, that the hatsin appeared for the fourth time. It told the dreaming Wild Pony how to make a bowl so hard that it could hold water and never again return to soft clay. 'First, you must dry the bowl in the sun. When it is dry and hard, wrap it in the bark of the pine tree. Seal the bark with the resin of the pine. When this is done, place the bowl in a fire that smoulders for three days.' With these instructions, the hatsin taught Wild Pony how to make bowls that would hold all the water that she needed.

Years blew across the wild grasses. Horses found by Wild Pony and Smoke became their friends and carried them to far places. Corn and grain kept them from hunger. Silver was hammered into rings for arms and necks. Wild Pony and Smoke were happy upon the Earth. Children came to Wild Pony and children came to her children.

It was many years later that Wild Pony decided to teach her daughter's daughter how to form the clay, how to make the fire and keep it smouldering for days. I shall not live forever, thought Wild Pony. I shall teach the child of the clay and the pine bark so that she may have bowls even after I am gone. Wild Pony rolled the clay and pressed it into shape, explaining to her grandaughter of eight years how a bowl was made. But when the girl tried to form a bowl, the clay cracked and slipped apart. The girl could not turn the clay into a bowl.

As Wild Pony fell asleep that night, she felt the sadness of realizing that the knowledge of the bowls would be forgotten. Her heart was again filled with disappointment, as it had been when she was young and the bowl had grown soft in her hands. And as she remembered that dream, the hatsin again appeared to her, though it had not visited her since that time.

This time it reminded Wild Pony of how it had rubbed the clay upon her hands and told her that is was hers to use. 'This you must do for the young one, as I did it for you. When you have passed along this gift, she too will be able to make bowls.' Wild Pony smiled and nodded in her sleep, remembering the day of that precious gift. Again the hatsin remained. For even as Wild Pony's dreaming mind was on that day so many years ago, the hatsin said, 'I have one more gift of knowledge for you. It is perhaps the greatest gift of all and when I have told you about it, you will know all there is to know.' It was in this dream that the hatsin told Wild Pony how to make the sacred pipe of peace and the wisdom of using it. Once the words had been said, the hatsin vanished, never to appear again.

When the morning sun brought the light, Wild Pony took her grandaughter to the place of the red clay. There she took a handful of the clay and rubbed it into the small hands of her daughter's daughter. As she did this, she said the words that have been repeated to Jicarilla Apache girls ever since that day, 'Now the clay is yours to use.' But when they sat down together alongside the red clay, they did not make a bowl. Instead they made a peace pipe. Together the grandmother and the daughter's daughter made the very first peace pipe on Earth.

When the time came to take the sacred pipe from the smouldering fire, they allowed it to cool in the air. It was this pipe that they filled with the tobacco leaves that they had gathered in the hills. And sitting side by side, Wild Pony lit the pipe, drew upon it four times and then passed it to her grandaughter. The grandaughter too drew upon the pipe four times, making four puffs of smoke in the air. Grandfather Smoke watched the women and tried to imitate what he saw. Rolling a leaf of a yucca plant, he filled it with tobacco. But after four puffs on the yucca pipe, the pipe turned to ashes. Smoke took a branch of sumac wood, and from this he carved yet another pipe. The sumac was not much better than the yucca and Smoke was soon surrounded by more smoke than he intended.

Feeling sorry for her grandfather, the grandaughter asked Wild Pony if she might give the clay pipe to Smoke. And so the custom came into being that each girl of eight years has her hands rubbed with clay and makes a sacred peace pipe, each reciting the story of Wild Pony, the First Mother, as she presents the sacred peace pipe to her people.

The Golden Mirror of Ise
Japan

rom the blazing fires of volcanic Fuji and the brilliant golden light of Amaterasu to the misty nearly forgotten images of the female spirits of the sea, Goddess imagery in Japan is as varied as the many peoples who came together to form this island culture on the western edges of the great Pacific.

Despite a lack of material on Upper Paleolithic habitation in Japan, the evidence of Upper Paleolithic cultures in Siberia, China and Indonesia suggest that Japan may have been inhabited since Upper Paleolithic periods. We do know that the Jomon culture of later Neolithic periods left numerous small statues of women that are similar to the Neolithic Goddess figures of other areas, as well as stone circles that resemble those of the Near East and Europe.

To understand the sources and the eventual synthesis of Goddess reverence in Japan, one must consider the evidence of migrations into Japan of: Ural-Altaic peoples from eastern Siberia, Sino-Monogolian peoples from China and Korea, and Polynesian peoples from the South Pacific. Yet even as Japanese records reveal continuous confrontations between these various cultural streams, they also reveal an astonishing willingness to synthesize diverse beliefs into a composite perception of life and existence.

It is generally accepted that the Neolithic Jomon culture was developed by the ancestors of the Ainu peoples who once inhabited nearly all of the islands of Japan. The greatly diminished population of Ainu is today centred primarily on the northern island of Hokkaido. The Ainu appear to have migrated from eastern Siberia and to have spread from the island of Sakhalin into the islands of Japan, through the Ryukyu islands immediately to the south of Japan, and into parts of Melanesia. Ainu people have even been associated with a group of indigenous Australians known today as the Gippsland people.

The Ainu have been most closely linked to the Tungus people of Siberia, an Ural-Altaic group whose reverence for the polar bear as deity and/or ancestral totem may offer some insight into Ainu beliefs. Similar beliefs concerning the Samoyed dog occur among other Ural-Altaic peoples of Siberia. Affinities between Ural-Altaic languages reveal the widespread habitation of the Ural-Altaic speaking peoples, including those of northern Sweden, Finland, the Samoyedic groups of the arctic tundra, the Tungusic groups of eastern Siberia, and inhabitants of Manchuria, Mongolia, Turkey and Hungary.

Much more study on the various groups of Ural-Altaic speaking peoples is needed to clarify the similarities and the differences, but from the existing Ainu of Hokkaido we have learned of their reverence for mountains, especially volcanoes, and their association of Mount Fujiyama with the Goddess Fuji. Ainu beliefs about the North Star may have resulted from observations on the nomadic travels of many Ural-Altaic peoples, the seemingly stable North Star perhaps important in establishing direction and position on the tundra lands of Siberia.

Although most material suggests that the general movement of Polynesian peoples was continually eastwards, there is evidence that reveals that many Polynesian peoples also migrated to Japan and became part of the general population. Information on the Goddess as the volcanic Mahuea of New Zealand and on the volanic Pele of Hawaii raises the possibility that the concept of the sanctity of Fuji arrived with the Polynesians. Yet Ainu reverence for Fuji may actually be the source of this spiritual concept, later spread by Ainu peoples who migrated at least as far as Melanesia and were absorbed into the Polynesian population (see Polynesian section—Vol. I).

The later influx into Japan of peoples from Korea and China may have brought Confucianist attitudes towards ancestor worship, along with an emphasis on a male-oriented rule of states that were forming at about 500 A.D. Similarities between Chinese ideas and those of Japan surface in the accounts of Amaterasu, as well as in the legends of sea serpents and sea princesses. There is no question that the Chinese Goddess Kuan Yin (see Chinese section—Vol. I) was the origin of the Japanese Goddess Kwannon. Still revered in a temple in the Asakusa district of Tokyo (Edo), Kwannon's association with the sea is evident in the portrayals of Her riding upon a dolphin or fish.

In studying the Goddess imagery of Japan, it is extremely important to realize that none of the written records of Japan are earlier than the eighth century A.D. It is perhaps even more important to know that nearly all of the early material was recorded by scribes who had been commissioned by the Imperial Dynasty or other important ruling families. It is also helpful to note that at the time of the initial recording Japan did not possess a method of writing. Thus the records of Japan were recorded in Chinese characters, at times even in the Chinese language. What we today refer to as *Shinto*, a major religio/political system in contemporary Japan, was actually the *Kami No Michi* of Japan, written in Chinese as *Shen Tao* (Shinto), literally The Way of the Spirits.

The most important texts of ancient Japan are the *Kojiki* and the *Nihongi*. These books were initially commissioned by the Emperor Temmu, ruler of the state of Yamato on the island of Honshu. Temmu's stated intention was to collect the ancient beliefs of the land, and to do so he selected the writer Yasumaro to record the words of Hieda No Are, a member of the royal guild of reciters. Yasumaro completed the Kojiki in 712 A.D. He then presented the Emperor with the more varied Nihongi, a work that includes slightly different versions of the more linear account in the Kojiki. Most studies of the ancient beliefs of Japan are based upon these two major works. There is some additional material from that period and slightly afterwards: the *Kogushui*, the *Manyoshu*, the *Engi Shiki* and the *norito* (the ritual prayers). The Kogushi and the Engi Shiki were also commissioned by ruling families, those who felt slighted by Kojiki and Nihongi biases towards the Imperial Dynasty.

Though political biases are obvious, biases concerning female imagery are seldom discussed by scholars of Japanese literature. It is true that the major deity of the Kojiki and the Nihongi is the Sun Goddess Amaterasu. Yet the emphasis on the secondary status of the female in the accounts of Izanami, and the lineage of Amaterasu that leads to the claim that the rulers of the

Imperial Shinto Dynasty descended from Amaterasu's grandson Ninigi, whom Amaterasu is said to have appointed to be in charge of Japan, not only reveal state biases but perhaps masculist ones as well.

Even in comparisons of the Kojiki and the Nihongi, certain conflicting accounts are apparent. The Kojiki, and some versions in the Nihongi, describe the birth of Amaterasu from the eye of the male Izanagi, the mate of Izanami. Yet one version in the Nihongi clearly states that Izanami gave birth to the sun as one of Her first children. Since this occurs in only one version, it would be difficult to claim that this was the original account of Izanami—as mother to Amaterasu—yet in nearly all Kojiki and Nihongi versions, Amaterasu does refer to Izanami as Her mother. The idea of the sun being born from the eye of a primeval deity may have been derived from a Chinese account of P'an Ku, literally Ancient Serpent. In the Chinese account, the sun is born from the eye of P'an Ku. The possibility of the image of Izanami once having been regarded as a serpent is further suggested by Kojiki and Nihongi passages about Izanami first giving birth to Yebisu (Hiruko), a water serpent.

The possibility of early ideas of a divine serpent of the sea may help to explain the rather puzzling repetition of the number eight in many of the images and symbols of Japanese beliefs. Both the Kojiki and the Nihongi state that at the original Creation by Izanami and Izanagi, eight islands were made—despite the fact that Japan has four major islands and an almost infinite number of smaller islands. The sacred mirror that is the symbol of the Sun Goddess Amaterasu is described as the eight handed mirror. Eight pairs of deities are said to have preceded the existence of Izanami and Izanagi. The Japanese idiom meaning great or massive, as used in the ancient records, is 'eight fathoms deep'. In the Kojiki version of the slaying of the serpent (the account so similar to the one of Yakami included in this section and the Chinese account of Li Chi) the serpent is described as having eight heads and eight tails, and it was said that eight daughters of one family had been sacrificed to it. In the account of Li Chi, the sacrifices were made in the eighth month of each year. (Each of these legends is told to explain the conquest of the serpent and thus who brought an end to this practice.) As a purely speculative guess, may I suggest the possibility that the number eight may be related to very early ideas of a sea creature, such as the octopus, holding up the islands.

Similar ideas are found in Chinese accounts of the earth resting upon the back of a great turtle, an idea that is also known among the Iroquois (see Awehai—Native American section). Aztec accounts include images of a massive alligator holding up the earth. It may be relevant that in one Nihongi account a divine princess who lives in the sea takes her true form—as a crocodile. Legends still linger in Japan, of a great fish *namazu* who lies beneath the islands, its movements and wriggling said to be responsible for the many earthquakes in the area. In the effort to see past the conscious and intentional recording of Goddess imagery in eighth century Japan, the speculation of an ancient Sea Goddess linked to the image of Izanami, and the repeated use of the number eight, may provide a direction in understanding the many Japanese accounts of female spirits of the sea.

Echoes of ancient *miko* priestesses in the Japanese texts suggest that female clergy once held a much greater role in the religious affairs and rituals of the numerous shrines, than was known in later periods. *Noros*, shamanesses who acted as prophets, much like the Chinese women known as *wu*, may have been the origin of the more structured role of miko. Relatively recent evidence of sexual rituals at Shinto shrines may reveal vestiges of a form of worship that was similar to that of the Goddess as the Tantric Shakti in India and the worship of Inanna, Ishtar, and Ashtart in Sumer, Babylon, and Canaan (see Indian, Sumerian and Semitic sections).

One aspect of Japanese Goddess imagery that is rather puzzling in its strong resemblance to images of the Scandinavian Goddess Frigga is that of the celestial weaving house of Amaterasu. It would be difficult to think of two more strikingly contrasting peoples than the Japanese and the Scandinavians. Yet both Amaterasu and Frigga (see Scandinavian section) are described as living in celestial palaces surrounded by semi-divine women of the weaving room in the palace. It is tempting to consider the Ural-Altaic connections between Japan and northern Sweden, but realizing that most of these Ural-Altaic peoples relied upon furs and skins rather than the weaving of textiles, this uncanny resemblance may be purely coincidental, perhaps each drawn from early communal weaving houses as they developed within their own cultural millieu.

Along with each specific image of Goddess reverence, it is important to understand that inherent in nearly all legend and ritual of Japan is a perception and experiencing of the natural environment: mountains, rivers, sea, rocks, trees, flowers, birds, animals, fish—that may best be compared to the Tao of China or Native American concepts of Mother Earth. The one word most important in understanding this perception of the world is *kami*. Defined as spirit or spiritual essence, it is the acknowledgement of the kami in each manifestation of natural life that endows the perceiver with an understanding of the spiritual dynamics of the world. This concept, often associated with the later Zen Buddhism of Japan, probably originated with the indigenous Ainu. The Japanese word kami is derived from the Ainu word *kamui*. The Ainu people of Hokkaido still consider the process of climbing mountains as spiritual pilgrimage.

The following accounts of Izanami, Amaterasu and Ukemochi offer some idea of Goddess imagery as it was known in Japan during and after the eighth century A.D. Yet glimpses into earlier beliefs may emerge from these mirrors of womanhood, even as one stands on the coastline of these great mountains that jut out from the sea and is warmed by the golden glow of the reflection of the morning sun, as She rises from the vast Pacific waters to look first upon the islands of Japan.

FUJI

The Ainu, the indigenous inhabitants of the islands of Japan, paid homage to the Goddess of Fire as Fuji (Fuchi, Huzi). The site most sacred to those who revered Her was the volcanic Fujiyama located on the main island of Honshu. The Ainu population diminished as migrations of peoples from Korea, as well as from the Pacific Islands, formed the population we today refer to as Japanese, most of the Ainu retreating to the island of Hokkaido. The image of Fuji is extremely similar to images of Mahuea of New Zealand and Pele of Hawaii. The concept of Goddess as a volcano may have formed from observations of the spreading of volcanic lava in ocean waters, such lava creating new islands or adding new areas to existent land. The Ainu association of the bear with the North Star offers a puzzling similarity to the Greek account of Kallisto as the bear constellation that includes the North Star.

Guardian of the Fire
upon the blazing mountain
that stands not far from ancient Yedo,
Her sacred throne floats in the flames
so that all may know of Her sovereign power,
of Her sacred place upon the Eternal Mountain,
towering rock that touches earth as it touches heaven,
as Fuji looks upon Her own beauty
in the mirror surface of the lakes
that lay about Her feet.

Some say that She descended from the heavens
as the woman Turesh who lived upon Mount Fuji,
first woman of the world
who brought the knowledge of existence
to those on earth,
for though it is the mighty Goddess Fuji
who governs from the mountain of flame,
it is Her daughter who is the spirit of the hearth,
the one who taught of warmth from the cold,
the one who taught of the fire beneath the pot.

Ancestress of the once mighty Ainu people,
was it She who lived as Mother Bear,
great white furry being
who lived upon the guiding light that never moved
from the ancient Ainu home in heaven,
polar star where souls may rest
before returning once again to earth?
Each year, at the time of the Iyomande,
the messenger cub was sent to heaven
by those who lived in the caves
upon the islands that floated in the waters,
to remind the Mother of the constant star
that they would one day return home.

IZANAMI

Both the *Kojiki* and *Nihongi* accounts of Creation described Izanami as
the divine woman in the eighth pair of deities that arrived at the beginning
of time. Little is said of the other seven, but Izanami is credited with most
of the activities associated with the formation of land and life. What is
especially interesting in these eighth century A.D. records, is the specific
emphasis on the female acceptance of secondary status. This emphasis
raises the question of the possibility that this aspect of the account of
Izanami was added to justify a role reversal from the customs of earlier
periods. The eventual placement of Izanami in a castle in the land of the
dead may be connected to this effort to justify role reversal, or perhaps
was intended to explain the double role of Izanami as Creator, as well as
Goddess of the Dead. The eighth century descriptions of Izanami's first
child as an ugly and unacceptable water serpent may indicate an earlier
image of Izanami as a deity of the sea, perhaps comparable to the fish
tailed Chinese Goddess Nu Kwa, or to the Goddess of the Sea and of the
Land of the Dead known among the Inuit (Eskimo) under the name of
Sedna. Remnants of images of a Sea Goddess occur in the accounts of
Urashima and of Fireshade, as told in the *Nihongi*. Several scholars have
suggested that the small island of Awaji was the sacred centre of reverence
for Izanami, associating this island that lies between Honshi and Shikoku
as the Onogoro of the Creation accounts.

Holy Izanami, She Who Invites,
once stood upon the Floating Bridge of Heaven,
once stood on the Ama No Uki Hashi.
In those ancient days when Izanami was young,
She decided to take brother Izanagi as Her mate,
thus the sister and the brother
circled about the Pillar of Heaven,
She from the left,
he from the right,
and upon meeting as agreed,
She spoke of Her desire for him,
suggesting that they mate.
From this mating came the child,
the Water Serpent Yebisu,
the one She sent off in the Boat of Heaven.

But those who wrote for Emperor Temmu of Yamato
regarded this offspring as a tragedy,
claiming that a breach of courtly etiquette
had caused the birth of such an unseemly child,
thus explaining that it was the male who must speak first—
and that the woman should answer only in compliance.
So it was said that the two had once more circled
around the Pillar of Heaven,
the brother then speaking first of his desire,
Izanami echoing his words.

From the mating of the two
came forth the islands of Japan—
as the two moved together like the wagtail,
like the bird of perfect song
that Ainu people had said made the islands
by the wagging of its tail in the waters,
even as others spoke of the tail of the great fish
that stirred up the waters
until the lands came forth.
The island of Onogoro was the first,
and from this home on the waters,
eight great islands came forth from Izanami.

From Izanami came the sun and the moon,
the sea and the rivers,
the mountains and the valleys,
the trees and the herbs,
thirty two beings She brought into existence,
thirty two beings filled with sacred kami spirit.
But upon the birth of the thirty third,
the male that was the kami of fire,
the one known by the name of Kagu Tsuchi,
the womb of Izanami was so badly burned
that She was forced to leave
all that She had created
and to retire to the Land of Yomi,
The Land of the Dead.

It was in the land of Yomi
that Izanami built Her castle,
thus living peacefully among the dead,
but there came a day
when Izanagi thought to visit Izanami,
and ignoring Her request that She not be seen in death,
Izanagi entered the Land of Yomi.
The reunion was far from joyful
for when Izanagi saw Izanami in a state of death
he fled in repulsion and fear.
Enraged by Izanagi's actions,
Izanami sent the Shikome after the fleeing man,
these angry female spirits of Yomi
causing Izanagi to run even faster,
until the terror stricken man
placed a great boulder between the Yomi
and the land above,
and from behind the massive rock
spoke words of divorce
to the divine woman who had died
bearing his son—
as She had borne all existence.

AMATERASU OMIKAMI

The *Kojiki* relates that the Sun Goddess Amaterasu was born from the left eye of the male Izanagi, *after* the death of Izanami. Yet a *Nihongi* version of the Creation mentions that Izanami gave birth to the sun and the moon *before* giving birth to the water serpent. The *Kojiki* also states that brother Susanowo was born from Izanagi, but includes passages in which both Amaterasu and Susanowo speak of Izanami as their mother. These conflicting accounts reveal the existence of at least two separate bodies of beliefs, and the attempt to create a composite statement of origins. In examining the process of the amalgamation of religious beliefs, we are fortunate in having access to information about the intentional synthesis of Buddhist and Shinto imagery in eighth century A.D. Japan. Initially based upon the writings of Kobo Daishi in 774 A.D., Pure Land Buddhism developed the idea that Amaterasu had returned as the Amidha Buddha, a concept that bears comparison to the Buddhist idea that the Chinese Goddess Kuan Yin was a reincarnation of the male boddhisatva Avalokitsevara. The symbol of the mirror of Amaterasu, regarded as a sacred Shinto object even today, may be associated with the ancient Ainu idea that the volcanic Goddess Fuji enjoyed looking down upon Her image—as reflected in the lakes at the foot of the mountain. Images of the sun as female and the moon as male are echoed in the accounts of the Khasis of Assam and the Inuit Sun Sister (see Indian and Native American sections). Several lines of the Icelandic Volupso reveal that the sun was once regarded as female among Scandinavians as well. Shinto is still a major religion in Japan, an interesting synthesis of a deep reverence of nature alongside what may be viewed as the political structure based upon beliefs in a divine heritage from Amaterasu, as confirmation of the royal family—not unlike beliefs in divine right as long expressed in Christian nations of Europe

On the banks of the Ise Wan, near the town of Uji Yamada in the district of Mie, stands the Ise Shrine of Amaterasu Omikami, holiest Shinto shrine in all Japan, humble wooden temple that houses the Most Sacred Mirror, eternally reflecting the shining glory of the gracious sun, She who chooses to shine upon Japan before all others, She who is the Divine Ancestress of those who rule Japan.

Heaven Shining She is called, Great Woman Who Possesses Noon, She who reigns over The Plain of High Heaven, Her sacred five strand necklace made of the magatama beads that call upon the spirits adorning Her golden throat, as She watches over all on earth, guiding the building of the canals of irrigation, guiding the fields of growing rice, guiding the silken threads left by

Ukemochi, guiding the great Weaving Hall of Heaven, the Imino Hataya, where women live and spin in Her celestial palace.

Her brother Susanowo was assigned the dominion of the sea, and displeased that his sister held greater power, he formed a scheme to take that power as his own. With cunning, he announced that he planned to visit their mother Izanami, She who lived in the Land of the Dead. Thus he gained the right to approach the domain of Amaterasu, pretending to tell Her of his plans, but he arrived with such loud and crashing noises that Amaterasu suspected that he intended to challenge Her higher rulership. Swiftly, Amaterasu prepared Her defense, taking up three swords and Her quiver of one thousand arrows that She placed upon Her back; She held Her bow in one hand and five hundred arrows in the other. Arming Herself in this way, She planted Her great legs upon the ground, so firmly that She could not be dislodged.

But upon his arrival, Susanowo denied his intention to cause harm, denied any intention of challenging the power of Amaterasu. And as a gesture of good will, he suggested that they mate, stating that to have children together might mend their loyalties and trust in each other. So it was that Amaterasu mated with Susanowo, and became the mother of the three daughter goddesses, Oki Tsu Shima, Tagi Tsu and Ta Giri Hime.

Yet it was not long after this claim of honorable intention that Susanowo blocked the canals of irrigation, the canals so dear to Amaterasu. He piled them with mounds of dirt so that the waters could no longer flow to the thirsty waiting plants. Still not satisfied with this attack upon what was dear to Amaterasu, he then entered the places in which the rice plants grew and stomped upon each and every plant until the rice paddies lay in muddy chaos. As if he had not already caused enough destruction, and fully proven Amaterasu's original suspicions, Susanowo then thought to smear the celestial weaving house in the palace of the Goddess with the excrement of animals and humans. Finding that his patient sister had been willing to overlook these hostile deeds, excusing Susanowo's acts of destruction by saying that he had swallowed too much saki wine, which often was his habit— Susanowo then murdered a piebald colt and heaved its body into the celestial weaving house. It was then that Amaterasu filled with rage, for as the weight of the horse struck the looms and tables of the hall, they fell upon the women who wove the tapestries in the sacred weaving house, sending several to the Land of the Dead.

The Goddess of the Plain of High Heaven, She Who Is Heaven Shining, filled with anger, but refusing to fight on such a demeaning level, She decided to announce Her rage by the absence of Her warmth and light that brought the goodness of life. Thus She retired to the Cave of Heaven, the Ama No Iwayato, from which Her light would not shine, and pulled the great door tight behind Her—so that the world was in darkness.

No longer was there day and night. No longer did the golden light help the rice to grow. Life was impossible. The deities of heaven assembled on the banks of the celestial river to discuss what might be done to restore the treasured presence of Amaterasu Omikami. They decreed that Susanowo would be punished and fined, and then banished him from the heavens. But how to tempt Amaterasu from the cave? How to let Her know that Her brother had been sent away?

It was for these reasons that the plan was conceived. The playful Goddess Ama No Uzume would dance by the entrance of the cave, making motions and faces that would bring such a laughter from those who watched Her that the curiosity of Amaterasu would be aroused enough to open the door and peer out.

Thus the wild dance of Ama No Uzume took place before the Rock Cave of Heaven and when the golden Goddess was tempted to discover what caused such joy and laughter, She found Herself facing the mirror of eight hands that had been hung upon the sacred Sakaki tree of Mount Kagu. So intense was Her brilliant image, so beautiful the reflection upon the polished bronze surface, that She stepped further out to take a closer look, while those who watched quickly closed the door to the cave that had been Her home of anger.

Some say this story was told each year as the days that had darkened earlier each night reversed into the mirror image of each day's light lasting moments longer, the winter solstice remembered by the Sakaki tree laden with jewels and the mirror that would shine with the light of the returning sun. But most remember the mighty Amaterasu as She who shines on the Land of the Rising Sun, Divine Ancestress from whom all rulers were born, She whose mirror now rests in sacred wrappings in the holy place of Ise, She who won not by confrontation but retreat, She who still shines from the Highest Plain of Heaven.

UKEMOCHI

The association of the Goddess Ukemochi with all food, whether found in the sea, planted in the fields or hunted in the mountains, as well as with the silk used for clothmaking, suggests that this deity may once have been revered as the Goddess of a particular community or area. This explanation of Her death and the transfer of Her attributes to a deity appointed by the Shinto Amaterasu may again reveal the efforts of the writer of the *Kojiki* and the *Nihongi* to formulate a centralized theology. The language and concepts in the material concerning Ukemochi suggest that Her image may have been derived from early Korean beliefs. The account also includes yet another explanaton of the understandable idea that the sun and the moon avoid each other as a result of personal antagonism. This idea, which is present in the accounts of the Khasis of Assam and the Inuit of Alaska and northern Canada, even appears in the Mayan account in which the moon is regarded as the Goddess Ix Chel (see Native Americans of Mexico—Vol. I).

From the Goddess Ukemochi came the abundance of the rice fields, the fish of the rivers and the sea, and the animals of the mountains. Long had She been revered as the Goddess who provided all until there came a day when the moon god Tsuki Yomi, brother of Amaterasu, was sent to Ukemochi to serve within Her heavenly palace, to help Her feed the people of Japan.

Arriving at Her home in the heavens, Tsuki Yomi was offered the rice, the fish and the meat that poured forth from Ukemochi. But Tsuki Yomi refused the food that appeared upon the table as a great banquet to welcome his arrival and chose to view Ukemochi's gracious hopsitality as insult to his pride, claiming that She had vomited these foods from Her own body.

Already angered at the humility of his assignment, further angered at what he regarded as insulting, Tsuki Yomi drew his sword and murdered the Goddess who had provided for Her people. Yet even as She lay in death, Ukemochi left a legacy of much that was of value, for from Her stomach the rice still came, and from the black silk of Her eyebrows came the threads of silken cloth, and from Her divine head came the horses and oxen, while the wheat and the beans, that were the staple foods of those who tilled the land, continued to come forth from Her womb.

When Amaterasu heard of the murder, She filled with rage and indignation that Tsuki Yomi should have committed such a crime. It was at this time that She appointed Ogetsu Hime to tend the work that Ukemochi had once done but in anger at Her brother, She banished him from the heavens. Filled with shame, he dimmed with the dishonour of his act, shrunk with the knowledge of the evil that his pride had instigated, and from that time on Tsuki Yomi was careful not to show his face in heaven when he knew that his sister was awake.

Some say that when Ukemochi died, it was the Goddess Tamiyo who was appointed to to do the work of Ukemochi, but that Amaterasu put the silkworms into Her own mouth, so that the strands of radiant colours poured out from the mouth of the brilliant Amaterasu.

YAKAMI

The Buddhist tale of the heroine Yakami, still known along the southern coastline of the island of Kyushu, bears some resemblance to a Kojiki account of an eight headed, eight tailed serpent that was slain by Susanowo —a serpent to whom young girls were sacrificed. The resemblance of the two accounts is all the more puzzling in that Yakami is the name of a divine princess mentioned in other Kojiki accounts associated with the island of Kyushu. It is possible that the young woman Yakami was substituted for Susanowo in this legend, but also possible that the original story was altered upon being recorded in the *Kojiki*. The possibility that the image of the young heroine, as the slayer of the serpent to whom young girls were sacrificed, is the original account is further suggested by the ancient Chinese legend of the young woman Li Chi. The valour of Li Chi is still celebrated in ballads of the Fukien province of China, an area whose coastline lies across the East China Sea from Taiwan and the Ryukyu Islands that are stepping stones to Japan. It is quite possible that the Li Chi legend was absorbed into Japanese culture, just as Buddhism and so many other aspects of Chinese culture have been. The Shinto Kojiki account that credits Susanowo with the slaying of the serpent states that he then married the young woman whose life was saved, thus revealing the importance of this legend in Shinto records. The Li Chi account, somewhat like the Chinese legend of Gum Lin, describes how the serpent was lured to its death by tempting rice and malt cakes, Li Chi afterwards remarking to the remains of the previous sacrifices that the sorrow was that they were punished for their gentleness and timidity.

On the southernmost tip of Japan, where the waters of the Pacific flow gently in and out of the inlets along the coastline of Kyushu, there lived the brave Yakami. Golden in the daily sun, almost a being of the sea, she spent her childhood years diving in the waters filled with oyster beds, her young legs firm with muscle, her heart as calm and fearless on the floor of the deep ocean as upon the mat in her own cabin.

Happy young voices could be heard along the rocks of the shore when a perfect pearl was found or when baskets of fish were so full that parents would be pleased. But at times there was the sadness of the loss of a dear friend to the great shark or an illness that could not be cured, and all the sunshine and the sea would not be enough to drive away the quiet grief. Yet for all the events of her young life, never had Yakami been more full of sorrow than when the news came that her parents had been sent to the south, exiled to a prison on a far off island for speaking out against those in power.

There was little work done that day. Young women who usually spent the days diving down to the sea floor now sat around Yakami, their eyes filled with compassion for their comrade—she who had helped them carry their baskets on days when she found little of her own, she who had offered some of what she had on days when others had found none. But royal rulers were not the dangers of the sea, and despite the fearless and courageous lives they led, all felt weak and powerless to lift the heaviness from Yakami's heart.

Her grief too great to search for oysters, Yakami wandered by the wharves, wove her way in and out among the fishing boats, watched the masts lean and sway on the rocking waters of the cove, watched the repairing of the rope nets, staring at the fishermen who climbed from the wharf to deck—from deck to wharf. Surely these boats could travel further than she could swim. Looking out at the open waters, she wondered just where, just how far away her parents might be. 'Do you go to the islands of the south?', she asked an old fisherman, as he sorted his fish on salty wet boards. He nodded, as he threw two smaller fish into a basket.

'I would like to go with you', Yakami ventured. 'I can help with the sorting and I know how to tie the knots when the nets are damaged.' The elderly man smiled in assent, helping Yakami feel some of the heaviness lift from her heart as she knew what she must do. 'My parents have been put into prison', she explained. 'Perhaps on Tenega, peraps on Yaku. They may be even further south. But I must begin to search.' Although no word had passed from the old man's lips until that moment, his eyes then began to dart from side to side, anxious to see that no one was in sight. And then he whispered to Yakami, 'I cannot. My family might suffer. No one will take you on such an errand.'

By the time that Yakami asked the others, all seemed to know the purpose of her trip. Young or old, rough or gentle, all refused and moved away from where she stood, as if afraid of an illness. How strange, she thought. Daily these people risk their lives among the coral and the shark. Daily they risk their lives against the chance of typhoon winds and the tsunami waves that could come upon them like moving mountains. Yet all were afraid of the rulers and those who did their bidding. It seemed that the perils of humans held more terror than all the perils of nature. But more determined than ever, Yakami waited until the dark blanket of night kept the secret, as she untied the ropes of a small unguarded boat. In silence, she slipped the oars through the waters until the mainland was out of sight, raising two small sails in the grey of a dawn of endless waters.

Twice, the sun rose to her left. Twice it arched over her. And twice it slipped into the waters until the time that Yakami saw the island. The moon had reached the top of the heavens by the time she tied the boat to a rock at the island's edge. But when daylight came again and she made her way among the people of the island, all she learned was that prison was not a subject for conversation. Knowledge of her mother and her father was as distant as on the day they were first taken. With half the sun in the sky and the other half floating on the waters, Yakami noticed a holy place set upon the top of a hill, the craggy grey rocks along the side of the hill making an inviting stairway to the summit. Though exhausted from all that she had done, Yakami felt that if she could climb to the shrine, all would be well. As if the very wind carried her on its currents, Yakami floated past the yellow and orange flowers that sprung from the rocks, so that she soon found herself on the top of a cliff that hung out over the ocean below. And there, not far from the small shrine of cypress wood, she lay beneath a wind-blown tree, smelling the familiar salt of the waters, listening to the familiar roar of its ever falling waves as the surf licked against the wall of rock below, and closed her eyes in sleep.

When her eyes opened to strange sounds, the stars were gathered about a top heaven moon. The sleep had been long and heavy, but now her eyes opened wide to see two figures standing at the very edge of the ocean cliff. The taller one recited the norito prayers, while the smaller figure's sobs were caught in the wind. The hems of the white cloth robes they wore blew behind them like sails on a fine day. And then, as if in a bad dream, Yakami saw the taller one reach out, as if to push the smaller one from the cliff. With almost no thought in mind, Yakami leaped to where they stood, grasping the arm of the little one, surprised to see the face of a girl even younger than herself.

The other, a priest grey with many years, gave no apologies but instead explained that the girl had been chosen as the sacrifice to the dragon of the sea, the evil god who lived in these waters and stirred up tai fung winds that played havoc with the boats of these waters if he were not appeased by the yearly sacrifice of a young girl. Yakami, thinking that with the loss of her parents she had little for which to live, insisted that she take the place of the sobbing one, and taking the white robes from the girl, she put them on her own body. Still the fires of hope had not gone completely from her, for as she stood upon the edge, waiting to meet her death, she slipped her diving dagger between her teeth, as she had done so many times before.

As the priest and the young girl watched from the cliff, Yakami's body slid silently into the icy ocean waters. Even as the priest said the prayers of death, Yakami's strong legs swam between the creatures of the sea, pushing deeper and deeper until she saw the skates and rays that hovered on the ocean floor. It was not long before she found the glowing entrance to the rocky cavern so deep beneath the sea. And there she saw the pearly scales, the eyes

Still the fires of hope had not gone out

as red as rubies, the body as great as a fallen tree—the evil dragon of the sea. But though the great thing moved towards her, Yakami quickly circled about its head, and from above she plunged the dagger so that green blood flowed from its eyes. Blinded by its own blood, the dragon stirred the waters into such a rage that Yakami fought the tow of a whirlpool. Then raising her arm with all the force that she could summon, she drove the dagger deeper into the dragon's chest. Suddenly all was calm, as the life fluid of the dragon seeped into the sea.

Astonishment was clear upon the faces of the priest and the young girl who still prayed for the dead Yakami, as they saw her surface upon the water. It was not long before the entire island heard the joyous news and of the courage of the fearless young Yakami. Amidst the cheers of celebration, they again heard the story of why she had come. The word of what had happened sailed off to all the other islands, until it reached the officials of the prison where Yakami's parents had been kept. In gratitude for what she had done, orders were given for the parents release so that they joined Yakami in joyous reunion.

Though Yakami left the island, never was her memory forgotten, as each year at the time of the ancient sacrifice all families gave thanks to Yakami that their daughters would be safe. Never forgotten at the hilltop shrine, her name was called upon as The Brave One, The Good One, as voices floated over the waters singing the story of her courage.

In the Land of Elves and Giants
Scandinavia

rom the misty fjords of Norway, from the
steamy frost of volcanic Iceland, from the dense
forests of Finland, from the lakes and rivers of Sweden, from the
peninsula of ancient Jutland, come accounts of ancient Goddess
reverence that linger in the nature spirits and the magic chants of
Scandinavia.

In any exploration of Goddess imagery in Scandinavia, there
are two important yet seldom mentioned factors that should be
considered. The first of these is that the population of most of
central and northern Sweden and Norway, and all of Finland, was
initially composed of people known as Finns, a Mongolian, Ural-
Altaic speaking people. Related to the Arctic Siberians, the Finns
were quite physically different than the tall, light haired, blue eyed
Teutonic/Germanic groups we generally think of as Scandinavian
today. As northern Germanic tribes such as the Norse, the Danes,
and the Swedes, pressed further from central Europe into the
north, the Finns retreated even further north, many remaining in
the area known as Finnmark or Lapland. Each group left reminders of their encounters with the others in ancient lore and legend.
It has been suggested that accounts of small dark elves and
dwarves, the beings of Svart Alfaheim (Dark Elf Land), may have
emerged from northern Germanic perceptions of Finnish peoples.
Since Finland is regarded as a Scandinavian country today, Finnish Goddess images are included in this section, but the reader
should be aware of the existence of these two diverse cultures that

were the foundations of pre-Christian Scandinavian beliefs. It is for this reason that I have referred to the accounts of northern Germanic peoples as Nordic, rather than Scandinavian, reserving the designation of Scandinavian to encompass both Nordic and Finnish cultures.

The second factor that is often ignored in studies of early Scandinavian beliefs concerns the specific passages within early Nordic records which clearly state that the deities of the Nordic peoples had come from ancient Turkey (Anatolia). According to the thirteenth century A.D. *Prose Edda* of Iceland, the Assembly of Deities known to the Nordic peoples as the *Aesir* came from Troy on the northwestern coast of Turkey. This idea may have developed during the period of 800—1000 A.D. when Norse Vikings were known to have travelled as far as Russia, Turkey and even to Jerusalem. But it is possible that a Nordic connection with Turkey was much earlier, possibly related to the Indo-European speaking groups that entered Anatolia in the second millenium B.C. The province that included the area of Troy at about 1500 B.C. was known as Assuwa. This was the province that became known to the Romans as Asia, the name Asia later used to refer to all of Turkey. (When the use of the name Asia was extended to the Asian continent as we know it today, Turkey then became known as Asia Minor.) The Nordic references to Troy are especially interesting in that they refer to the early Nordic deities as—'The Asians'. This possible link between the people we later know as Nordic and the people of the ancient province of Assuwa may explain the name of the area in which the Nordic deities were said to dwell—*Asgard*, the Land of As or Asa. The Norse storm god Thor, often referred to in the Nordic literature as Asa Thor, was said to have been one of the first deities 'born' in Troy. The name and image of Thor may be related to the Anatolian storm god known in the fourteenth century B.C. as Taru, Tarhund or Tarhuis.

This possible relationship may also help to throw some light on the name of the Queen Goddess of the Aesir—Frigga. Though some scholars link the name of Frigga with the Sanskrit *prija*, meaning love, the name Frigga (and the variations of Freyja and Frija) may have been based upon concepts of the Goddess as known among one of the Indo-European speaking peoples of ancient Turkey, the Phrygians. Just as Aphrodite on Cyprus was spoken of on the Greek mainland as Cypria, and Artemis of Mt.

Cynthus as Cynthia, the Phrygian Goddess most widely known as Kybele (Cybele) and as the Mother of All Deities, may have been remembered by Nordic peoples as Phrygia—Frigga. (Tacitus wrote that the Germanic Aestii tribe revered the Goddess as The Mother of All Deities.) It is truly unfortunate that we have so little material concerning Nordic beliefs until some two thousand years after the Phrygians inhabited Anatolia.

The material that provides us with most of the information about Goddess reverence among the Nordic people is drawn from: the Icelandic poetry of about 900 to 1100 A.D., referred to as the *Elder Edda* or *Poetic Edda*; a compilation of ancient Norse beliefs and traditions brought together by Snorri Sturluson of Iceland in the thirteenth century A.D., referred to as the *Younger Edda* or *Prose Edda*; some records by Saxo Grammaticus of Denmark, a contemporary of Sturluson; and the *Germania* of the first century A.D. Roman writer, Tacitus. One of the most interesting and informative Eddic poems is the epic known as the *Voluspa*. literally *Wise Woman's Prophecy*, sometimes referred to as *The Sibyl's Vision*. This epic takes the form of the words of a *volva*, the Icelandic term for prophetess or sibyl. It is in the Voluspa that the volva not only reveals her knowledge of the past—from the very beginning of time—but foresees the future and the time of Ragnarok, Doomsday. The Norse account known as *Eirik's Saga*, dated to about the twelfth century A.D., provides a detailed account of the physical appearance and actions of such a prophetess, and her use of magic chants that invoked the spirits that provided her with prophetic knowledge. (This incident, which takes place on Greenland, and may reveal Finno-Lapp influences, was clearly regarded as pagan by the new Christians who had quite mixed feelings about gaining information about the future in this way.)

From the Eddic materials we learn that the sun, Sol, was regarded as female, while the moon, Mani, was thought of as male. Although this gender identification of sun and moon differs from Greek, Roman and other Indo-European beliefs, it does agree with the Indo-European Hittites of fourteenth century B.C. Anatolia (see Anatolian section—Vol. I). The Eddas also reveal that the Nordic people believed that there had once been a war between the Aesir and another group of deities known as the *Vanir*. The Vanir were described as living in *Vanheim*, the Land of Van. It has been suggested that the Vanir may have been the deities revered by the people who lived in the area of Vannoy in northern Norway (Lapland). An even more speculative suggestion is that Vanheim may be associated with the Lake Van area of eastern Turkey. When the war was over, some of the deities of the Vanir were taken into the Aesir. One of these Vannic deites was the Goddess Freyja. Despite this account of the late adoption of Freyja into the Aesir, She was apparently an extremely popular image of the Goddess among the Nordic people. Sturluson commented that at the time he was writing, two centuries after Christianity had been made the official religion of Iceland, 'only the Goddess Freyja is still alive'.

Aside from the Goddess images included in this section, other names and images of divine or magical women appear briefly in the Nordic records. Gollveig, which may mean Golden Witch, is mentioned in the Voluspa as the major victim of the 'first war on earth'. The volva explained that Gollveig had been burned in the Hall of Hor three times over, smitten with spears, yet still lived and would live eternally. The volva also mentioned Heitha or Heartha as a 'far seeing witch', 'wise in magic'. Most interesting are the few Eddic lines referring to a divine cow who existed before all else. Her name Audhumla, may mean Creator of Earth. Four rivers came forth from Her udder. Described as The Cow of the Abyss, living in the land of flame and frost, She disappears from Nordic record after She creates the first human. One can only wonder about possible connections between Audhumla and the bovine images of the Greek Goddess as Hera, and the sacred cow as Hathor of Egypt (see Egyptian section). The name of the Goddess Ostara appears in southern Germanic record, associated with spring festivals. The reference is late and may be derived from the Semitic Ishtar or Ashtart.

There are many Eddic references to *Jarnved,* Ironwood, as the homeland of Giant Women. One of the most intriguing and puzzling statements about the Giant Women is the line in the Prose Edda, "That age was called the Golden Age before it was spoiled by the arrival of the women who came from Giantland." The Voluspa mentions three Giant maidens who arrived shortly after the world was created, at the time when no lack of gold was known. The concept of giants among a people as tall and large as the Norse is certainly puzzling. Any attempt to gain some understanding of this may well begin with ancient Greek accounts of Giants who lived in Thrace, accounts thought to have been associated with the Celtic tribes to the north of Greece.

Sources of early Finnish beliefs are even more sparse than those of the Nordic people. The primary sources are the collections of chants known as *Magic Songs*, and the epic poem *Kalevala*. Although we are fortunate in having the information preserved in the Kalevala, it is unfortunate that this compilation of Finnish lore by Elias Lonnrot was made as recently as the nineteenth century A.D. Fragments of names and ritual have also been found in the sacred chants of Finnish groups that settled in Estonia where the Earth Goddess was known as Maa Ema, and among the Votyaks of Siberia where She was known as Muzjem Mumi. The Goddess names that were preserved in Finland were Ilmatar, Mielikki, Maan Emoinen and Rauni. The name Rauni was associated with the ronn or rowan tree, the mountain ash. It is difficult to say whether the Finnish peoples adopted the sanctity of the rowan from the Nordic peoples or vice versa. Throughout many parts of Scandinavia, the rowan became the centre of rituals on Rowan Witch Day, May 1st. The tiny orange berries of the rowan were used to ease childbirth, which probably led to its alternate name of quickbaum (life tree). The rowan was long considered to be a protection against evil in Scandinavia, twigs and branches kept as amulets, the berries also said to restore youth.

Finnish spiritual beliefs reveal similarities to other Finno-Ugric/Ural-Altaic speaking peoples of the Arctic regions. The early Finns were related to Samoyedic and Siberian groups, as well as to Eskimo groups of North America and Greenland. The twelfth century A.D. Vinland Sagas describe a people on what may have been Newfoundland as much the same people as the Lapp or Eskimo groups of Greenland. Although the possibility is seldom if ever discussed, it does seem likely that some Native American peoples may have entered North America from Greenland. The concept of Earth as Mother, as well as the reverence for the bear as ancestor, spiritual ideas that occur in both Finnish and Native American cultures, may be more than coincidental.

Evidence of the Chancelade people of Upper Paleolithic periods of France, whose remains exhibit Eskimoid or Mongolian features, suggests that Proto-Finnish peoples may once have lived as far south as the caves of France. Eventually retreating to the most northerly regions of both the eastern and western hemispheres, many Finns were assimilated into Nordic groups and settled into agrarian societies, while others continued to follow a nomadic way of life, building only temporary shelters, moving as the reindeer moved.

It may well have been some of the early Finns who were described by Tacitus as the Fenni tribe. Tacitus placed them to the northeast of the Germanic tribes, explaining that among the Fenni the women did as much hunting as the men. There is still too little known about these Arctic peoples who may well have given us snow shoes, skis, sleds and kayaks. Perhaps their ability to do what astonishes us most, survive in the most frigid zones on earth, is what has protected them from our prying questions. (Most scholars prefer to do their research in sunny Greece or Italy.) Yet stories of the ancient Creatress Ilmatar, Mistress of the Forest Mielikki, and the ancient Sacred Chants that call upon the spirits of nature, flow south with the sparkle of snows melting in clear blue northern rivers.

It is evident that Goddess imagery in Scandinavia is a complex study of both Nordic and Finnish beliefs, and the synthesis of these two diverse groups of people. Images of women as Divine Mother, as Queen of the Witches, as Queen of the Elves, and as the one endowed with knowledge of the future, linger in Scandinavian perceptions of nature, as surely as the foggy mist so often veils both forest and fjord, transforming what is solid and tangible into that which is hidden, ethereal and *myst*erious.

ILMATAR

Ilmatar, literally Sky Mother, is most often referred to as Water Mother in the *Kalevala*. Her image bears comparison to Inuit accounts of the Goddess Sedna, Nuliajuk or Nerrivik. Since the written records of Finnish beliefs are from such a recent period, it is difficult to ascertain the age of this image or how much influence Nordic groups may have had upon it. The Kalevala presents Ilmatar as a passive being who creates the earth almost by accident, yet at the same time describes Her as Creator and as possessor of immense powers. The account of the teal's eggs, and the later Creation by Ilmatar, suggest that Lonnrot may have combined two quite separate creation legends in his compilation of the Kalevala.

Descending upon the billowing waters
of the never ending ocean,
Ilmatar was rocked in the waves of the wild sea,
blown along in the foamy tempest
of winds from the East.
Carried for centuries upon the swelling waves,
She floated to the East,
She floated to the West,
She floated to the South,
She floated to the North.
Feeling only cold and dreary,
Ilmatar began to regret
that She had left Her home of gentle breezes.

In the deepest moment of Her sadness,
a lovely teal came flying over,
seeking land on which to rest
seaching for a nesting place—
and finding only moving waters.
It was then that gracious Ilmatar
lifted Her great knee from the sea
creating the first hill of land established.
It was on that knee the teal soon built her nest.
Knee as green as spring's blossoming,
held the teal's nest up high,
held the six eggs of gold,
held the seventh one of iron.

But how long could the Water Mother
hold the stillness of Her knee?
Thus Ilmatar moved to find comfort,
causing the eggs to fall into the waters,
causing them to shatter into fragments.
From the lower shells the earth took form,
from the upper shells came the arch of heaven,
from the yolk came the lustrous sun,
from the white part came the moon,
and from all that was speckled in the eggs—
the stars came forth.
Still Ilmatar floated on the waters,
now peaceful and serene.
For ten more years She floated,
until the day when She raised Her head
from beneath the waters—
and thus began Creation.

Pointing with Her fingers,
She formed the fjords along the ocean.
Her toes created the underwater caves
where fish might lay their eggs in safety.
With the deepest part of Her body,
She formed all that was on the ocean floor.
Her feet created beaches.
Her head made the long curving bays.
Even the craggy rocks that stood in open water
were formed by the ancient Water Mother—
She who made all earth.

Oldest of all women,
loveliest of all women,
first of all mothers,
then formed the pillars
that held the sky in place
and upon the rocky cliffs
She engraved the forms of figures.
Still Ilmatar remained in the ocean waters,
owner of powers too numerous to count,
possessor of magic too deep to comprehend—
and perhaps She lives there still.

FREYJA

According to Snorri Sturluson, author of the thirteenth century *Prose Edda*, of all the ancient Scandinavian deities only one was still 'alive' at the time he was writing—the Goddess Freyja. The name Freyja, cognate with the Sanskrit word *prija* which is translated as love or friendship, was used in the Eddic accounts to mean Lady—as the counterpart to Lord. Freyja, often referred to as Freyja Vanadis, was known as the Queen or Mother Goddess of the group of deities known as the Vanir. The legends of Freyja's relationships with the elves of Svart Alfaheim may be purely mythical or perhaps revealing of some connection with the Finnish peoples. Sturluson gives alternative names of Freyja as Mardoll, Horn, Gefjon, and Syr, stating that these were the names She was known by among other peoples. The golden boar on which Freyja and Her twin brother Freyr rode through the forests was identified by Tacitus as a major emblem of the Mother of All Deities, as known among some of the Germanic tribes. The account of the Goddess as Gefjon (Gefion, Gefn), which occurs in the beginning of the Prose Edda, bears some resemblance to the image of the Goddess as Nerthus in Her cow drawn wagon, perhaps suggesting Gefjon's island of Sjaelland (Zealand) as the one on which the image of Nerthus was kept.

Proudly did She ride about, Freyja, Queen Mother of the Vanir, Her chariot drawn by cats as dark and sleek as the night, until just at the moment one might catch a closer glimpse, She would be off through the forest, mounted upon the back of Golinborrsti, golden boar charging between the trees. But if one chanced upon Freyja in the woods, She would gather up Her falcon wings and soar past the tops of the highest pines, the tips of Her vast wing span brushing against the clouds.

In the arrival of the spring greening, one might see Her eyes peering out from the very centres of the wildflowers of the field, Her silky hair glimmering between the branches of the trees, as the sun angled in the sky. And when night's darkness veiled the meadow, one might spy the wondrous Freyja as She stayed to watch the faerie folk, the dark and tiny elves who danced upon the golden ribbons that fell from the moon, perhaps even fortunate enough to see Freyja tossing fragrant flowers to applaud the graceful dancers or to watch Her gather honey to feed the little ones.

Many sides had Mother Freyja, as familiar with the battlefield as with the field of wildflowers. How often did She ride across the battleground, choosing from among the slain those She wished to keep with Her forever, those who would then dwell in Her heavenly castle of Folkvanger. It was they who saw the war helmet on Freyja's head. It was they who saw the sword and spear in Her hand, while others spoke of mounted Valkyrie maidens taking the slain to Odin at Valhalla.

Some said that She was one with Gefjon, for it was She who did the giving, and in this form of ancient Woman Giant She drove Her wagon through the land, speaking to the oxen four that pulled the yoke, as if they were Her sons. As Gefjon, She ploughed so deep into the earth that She pulled it with Her to the sea, thus creating the great island of Zealand and the Kattegat Sea as a moat of protection. Though some say that the hole that was left behind became Lake Malaren, others say that Zealand clearly came from the place where Lake Vanern now stands. Yet all agree that it was Gefjon who formed this island in the sea and remember Her by the Gefjon Fountain that graces the city of Copenhagen.

It was Freyja who taught the magic songs of the mystic Seydur, taught them to the women whom She chose to look into the time of what was yet to be. Sitting high upon a seat before the people of each village, the chosen women would chant of what was to come, foretelling the lives of newborn babes, imparting knowledge of the summer's crops. The holy Volva, blessed women prophets, sang to Freyja in ecstatic trance, exchanging answers for questions, providing the Nordic people with a knowledge of the future.

And when people were in need, Hindluh the Sorceress was there by Freyja's side. Some tell the story of the time when Ottar called upon Freyja in his argument with Angantyr, claiming that it was his land that Angantyr used as a home. Thus Freyja devised a scheme, arranging that each would speak in the assembly and that the one who could recite the longest list of ancestral names —that one would have the land.

As the good but simpleminded Ottar lamented about the few names that he knew, Freyja transformed Ottar into a bear and upon his back She rode into the deepest woods, to the cottage of Hindluh. There, life by life, Ottar heard of all who had owned the land, all who had used the name that was now his. Though Hindluh took him back through time, Ottar fretted more than ever. Freyja felt ever more certain that She could not trust the memory of this man. It was for this reason that She bade Hindluh to brew a potion for Ottar, so that upon drinking it, he would not forget all that he had heard. When the day came that Ottar's case was heard in the assembly, and each name tumbled from his mouth with ease, Ottar dropped upon his knees in gratitude to the compassionate Freyja.

There came a day when, deep in the northern forest, Freyja wandered into Svart Alfaheim, the Land of the Dark Elves. Close by the great oaks She saw a cave, and the four little men who lived there. Hard at work by a glowing forge, their tiny hands held the pieces of glistening gold that were soon to be parts of the most perfectly formed necklace ever seen by mortal or deity, the necklace we now know as the magic Brisingamen, made of the brilliant jewels known as The Brisings.

Watching in silence until the work was done, Freyja grew in determination that the necklace would belong to Her. She brought forth handfuls of silver, as if from the air, but the elves refused Her offer. She brought forth handfuls of gold, more than anyone had ever seen, but again the little men refused to sell the necklace. 'What do you ask?' She declared in growing impatience, and was not a little surprised when they asked for a night of love—for each. Four days and four nights Freyja spent in Svart Alfaheim, so pleased with the four little men that She nearly forgot the necklace. But on the fifth morning, true to their word, the four led Her out into the morning sunshine and there in the greenest of meadows they placed the precious Brisingamen on the Queen Mother of the Vanir.

As the clasp was fastened about the neck of the Goddess, the rainbow appeared in the sky. From the necklace came blazing fire. From the necklace came brilliant light. It brought the glow of the dawn and the dancing lights of the setting sun upon the waters. It glistened with a light that created the morning star. And most precious of all its magical presents, it brought the heat of the forge on which it had been made and the knowledge of forming gold as if it was as soft and pliable as clay. Leaving the land of Svart Alfaheim, the treasure of the Brisingamen about Her neck—Freyja brought these gifts to the people of Scandanavia.

NERTHUS AND URTH

The rituals for the Goddess as Nerthus are known from the *Germania* of the Roman writer Tacitus. He explained that Nerthus was revered by the north Germanic tribes known as the Reudigni, Aviones, Angles, Varini, Edoses, Suarines and Nuithones. These first century A.D. references to Nerthus have been compared to the thirteenth century A.D. passages about Urth, the eldest of the three Norns. Thus, I have combined the available information about both Nerthus and Urth in the following piece, but it should be understood that these two images appear in texts separated by some twelve centuries. The Norns are most often associated with the Greek Moirae, the Roman Fates, who in turn have been linked to the Anatolian sister deities who spun destiny. Hallfred Ottarson, writing in Iceland at about 1000 A.D., told of shunning the rites for the Norns for the new Christianity.

Mother of the Northern Earth,
called upon as Holy Nerthus,
dwelled upon an island in the Northern Sea,
Her image deep within a sacred grove
hidden beneath protective veil.
Yet each year She came forth,
as those who joined in joyous festival
greeted and welcomed Her appearance,
as Nerthus rode by in a wagon of finest timber,
drawn through the streets by sacred cows.
All weapons were put aside,
all iron objects locked away,
in hopes that Nerthus would bring prosperity and peace.
Though none were there to know,
they say Her image was then bathed
in the waters of a secluded lake upon the island—
and that those who bathed Her
then met their death beneath those waters.

Freyja, Queen Mother of the Vanir

Those who tell of ancient Urth
do not forget Her sacred Well,
the spring pond of magic waters
that bubbled above the white clay beds.
It was by these waters
that Urth lived with Her sisters,
for as Urth had all knowledge of the past,
so Sister Skuld foretold the future,
as Verthandi understood the vastness of now.
Three Norns they were,
living beside a root of Yggdrasil,
the root of the World Tree
that was closest to the home of the Aesir,
the dwelling place of all goddesses and gods,
the root that was kept alive
by the magic waters of the Well of Urth.

So powerful were the Three,
it was they who appeared at each birth,
allotting the fate, decreeing the future,
for each new born babe,
spinning the threads of destiny,
weaving the golden fibers of what would be,
even as they carved the laws of humanity
upon the root of Yggdrasil,
making laws so wise and righteous
that even the deities of the Aesir
held their daily court of justice
at the dwelling place of the Norns—
The Three Sisters who knew all there was to know.

IDUNA

Iduna's primary role is that of the possessor of the golden apples of immortality. Her image is one of eternal youth and springtime. The golden apples that kept the deities of the Aesir eternally young may be linked to beliefs about the orange berries of the rowan tree, the rowan berries thought to restore youth as well as to ease the pains of childbirth. The Finnish Earth or Forest Mother known as Rauni was regarded as the essence of the rowan tree, perhaps suggesting that the Nordic image of Iduna may be much the same as that of the Finnish Rauni. This account of the Nordic Iduna is drawn from the *Prose Edda* and from the tenth century poem *Haustlong* of Thiodolf of Hvin, a Skaldic poet of southern Norway.

Into the land of Asgard walked the ever young Iduna, born of the spring air, birthed from the flowers of the field, Goddess of the fruit of the orchard. With Her came Her golden treasure chest, Her gracious gift to the deities of Asgard, the glowing box containing that which so many mortals yearn to gain but is reserved only for the holy ones of the Aesir—the golden fruit of immortality.

In Her voice they heard the music of ever running brook and stream, the lovely quiet that follows the roar of thunder, that stays the din of late winter storm. As She walked among the deities of Asgard, presenting each with a golden apple, each deity became as youthful as Iduna—even as the treasure chest remained as full as when She first arrived. Delighted with Her presence, a great feast was spread in Asgard, with more than mead enough for all, each drinking horn filled to overflowing. And at this joyous celebration, Iduna took each deity to Her fruitful, loving body, so that none knew a lack of the abundant love of Iduna. Throughout this wondrous evening, Iduna's mate, he who had arrived in Asgard with Her, Bragi of the delicate features and gentle disposition, sang sweet verses that harmonized with the golden strings of his harp—verses of the miracle of the eternal youthfulness that Iduna had given to those of Asgard.

But springtime cannot last forever, and when Thiassi of snowy Thrymheim heard of the eternal springtime of life that had been given to those of Asgard, his resentment and envious desire grew. So it happened, that with the help of evil Loki, Thiassi swooped with snowy eagle wing upon the unsuspecting Iduna and took Her as a captive to the land where all is cold and dead with

347

winter. The deities of Asgard once again grew old—as all that grows in summer dries and dies with autumn wind to lie silent and dead beneath the winter snow—as prisoner Iduna shivered in the Thrymheim cold.

Sadness fell upon the holy Aesir as they watched themselves grow older with each day, their faces gaunter, their hair greyer—each day that Iduna did not appear. In the sorrow of looking upon Iduna's empty seat, the deities of Asgard cried to Frigga, asked the Queen of the Aesir who knew all— what had happened to Iduna, and how they might restore Her presence at the table. How they missed Iduna's tasty golden fruit, the warmth and gentleness of Her springtime being, the juices of eternal life. How they missed the sound of harp strings and the lilting voice that Bragi, in his grieving for Iduna, could no longer offer to the Aesir.

Frigga looked deep into Her knowing mind and saw the sad Iduna held prisoner in Thrymheim, now guarding the apples of eternal life from Thiassi, even as She fought to repel his efforts to mate with Her springtime being. Thus Frigga ordered Loki, he who had put Iduna in this peril, to now rescue Her from Her winter plight. Loki then dressed in Freyja's falcon coat, perhaps a reminder of a time when it was Freyja who brought Iduna home to Asgard. Flying north to Thrymheim, Loki arrived to find Iduna all alone; Thiassi was flying over the ocean waters searching for fish. Quickly transforming the ever young Iduna into a seed of springtime, Loki took Her up in Freyja's falcon beak—and in this way they flew across the heavens to Asgard.

But Thiassi, with the eagle sharpness of his eyes, spied Iduna leaving. With his wide eagle wings, Thiassi flew to intercept the falcon, drawing close above the mountains close to Asgard—in clearest view of those who wished Iduna to return. In their anger at the bold Thiassi, the deities of Asgard made a great fire on the mountain top. Unable to stop his flight before his wings touched the leaping flames, Thiassi met his death in the blazing fire. So it was that the great eagle of Thrymheim died, as precious seed Iduna returned to the deities of Asgard—once again giving them youth and immortality.

MIELIKKI

The evidence of Mielikki as Goddess of the Forest occurs in the *Magic Songs* of the Finns, and in the *Kalevala*. The image of Mielikki bears a surprising resemblance to the Greek Goddess Artemis, as the protector of animals of the woods and as the Goddess of the Hunt. The references to Mielikki nurturing the young bear may be associated with the ancient Finnish custom of placing a bear skull in the forest as sacred totem. This reverence of the bear appears all across Ural-Altaic speaking regions of the Arctic and raises questions about the bear rituals for Artemis, and the relationship between Artemis and the Bear Goddess Kallisto (see Greek section).

Mistress of the Forest,
fair and bountiful Lady,
nurtured the bear cub
with the honey of the bees,
yet it is Mielikki who allows the woods
to grow grey and shabby
when the snows of winter melt away,
even as the skull of ancestral bear
sits high upon a branch in the forest,
facing the rising sun,
in the hollow where light pierces
through the roof of heaven touching leaves.

Delighted by the magic sound of flute,
Mielikki then dons Her golden bracelets,
slips golden rings into Her ears,
threads golden beads around Her throat
and takes Her seat
in the mansion of golden windows
where She watches over the creatures of the woods,
providing game only to the worthy,
directing the maiden spirits,
the fleet metsanhaltija of the forest,
to open the mansion doors—
only to those
who know that Mielikki dwells within.

FRIGGA

The attributes of the Goddess Frigga are so similar to those of Freyja that the two names are often thought to refer to the same Goddess image. The major differences between the two are Frigga's much closer relationships with Her husband Odin and with Her son Balder. Since both Frigga and Freyja are associated with the magic Brisingamen necklace, the account of Odin's attempts to steal it may help to point out some of the differences. The idea of a sacred necklace was also associated with the Greek Goddess Harmonia, Aphrodite's daughter. It is interesting that the amber used in Mycenaen Greek jewellry (at about 1500 B.C.) is believed to have been imported from Jutland, ancient Denmark. Tacitus wrote of the Germanic Aestii tribe, both as worshippers of the Mother of All Deities and as the only ones who gathered amber for the Romans. The account of the death of Frigga's son Balder has been compared repeatedly to the accounts of Attis, Adonis, Osiris, Tammuz and Damuzi, the dying son/lovers of the Goddess in the Near East. Although Frigga is continually referred to as the wife of Odin, She is described as living in a separate palace, Fensalir, surrounded by other goddesses or divine women. Sturluson lists one of these women as Gefjon, the Goddess image earlier described by him as the creator of the island Sjaelland, and the name he gives as a variant of Freyja.

High upon Her throne in the Palace of Celestial Marshes, in the women's hall of mist and sea, in the fabled Castle Fensalir, sat the Goddess Frigga, Queen Mother of the Aesir. It was She who spun the golden threads of fate, weaving universal design of past, of present, and of future.

With Her were the holy women who dwelled with Her at Fensalir. Gracious Fulla was friend and confidante, advisor whose ears were always open to mortals as they prayed on Midgard, especially to women who asked for ease in childbirth, or asked Fulla to prevail upon Frigga to weave fine destinies for little ones whose lives were waiting to be spun. And there was wise Gna who rode upon the swift steed Hofvarpnir, to learn all that had occurred so that She might convey these messages to Frigga, causing many to say that Frigga said little—but knew all.

In the Hall of Fensalir lived Eira of the magic herbs, skilled physician always willing to aid those who suffered from disease or wound, and Hlin who protected those in danger, while Syn acted as the counsel for defense of any innocent who was wrongly accused. Sjofn turned the minds of mortals to thoughts of love, while Lofn helped those whose love was forbidden. Var watched over vows and contracts, wreaking vengeance on those who did not keep their word, while Gefjon cared for all women who chose to live their lives without a husband.

In the midst of all these holy women, Frigga sat upon Her throne, clad in long white robes that darkened with the coming of each night, the feathery plumes of the sacred heron rising from Her royal crown, so that many said that Frigga flew as the heron flies, ascending straight up into the heavens, but others said that it was the wings of the falcon that She wore. The golden girdle of heaven's arch circled about Her holy waist, as the belt of stars circle in the sky, yet some say that this jewel encrusted girdle was the magic necklace, the brilliant Brisingamen.

Memories of Mother Frigga of more ancient days drew visions of delicate young Balder, who died leaving his holy Mother to mourn, though Frigga had begged all living things on earth to spare the life of Her gentle son when She heard that Hella, Divine Queen of Nifhelheim, wished to take him for Her own. But the evil giant Loki, he who thwarts all that is good, hearing that Frigga had not spoken to the tiny mistletoe that grew at the foot of the great oak, used the hand of Balder's blind brother to shoot a dart of mistletoe into Balder's chest. Thus was Balder sent to Nifhelheim in deathly sleep.

Learning of the tragedy, Frigga sent Hermodar to the Underworld of Hella, the dark and gloomy Nifhelheim, to arouse compassion for the grieving Frigga. Though Hella thought to keep the gentle lad for Herself, She promised the return of Balder—if all living things on earth would weep as Frigga wept. Once again, Frigga travelled far and wide, speaking to each thing that lived on earth. From each She received a promise that they would mourn for Balder, and would weep as Frigga wept. But evil Loki, this time posing as the Giant Woman Thiokk, refused, and once inside his cave he only laughed at the trick he had played on Frigga. Thus Balder remained with Hella, and shall until the day of Ragnarok will come—they day of doom and final battle that will bring to an end to Midgard as we know it.

Frigga not only mourned for Her son but was often saddened by Her marriage, for husband Odin thought so much of himself that he had little time left for thoughts of Frigga. Thus Frigga chose the company of the elves or the brothers of Odin, Vili and Ve, to join Her in Her bed at Fensalir. So unloving was Her husband Odin that he took the golden necklace that had been Her most prized treasure. When Frigga saw it on a village gate above Her, adorning a statue that Odin had made in his own image, She filled with righteous anger and demanded its return.

Odin with arrogant refusal, recited magic runes over the statue, thus empowering it with speech so that it could name the name of any who might try to remove the precious necklace. Perhaps Odin would have kept it always, had gracious Fulla not cared so deeply for Mother Frigga. So it was that Fulla made arrangements with a friendly elf, and with him laid the plan to place a magic spell of sleep upon the guards of Odin who watched the gate. With this done, the elf climbed upon the arch and pushed the statue to the ground. In this way the shattered statue told no tales, while Fulla retrieved the necklace for Queen Frigga. Thus the ancient Brisingamen, that which Freyja had once earned , was reclaimed as the possession of the Goddess.

SKADI

The image of Skadi is as the Goddess of Winter. Although descriptions of Skadi mention Her robes of white fur and Her icy crystal arrows, the name Skadi (cognate with the Greek *scotos*, the Gothic *skadus*, and the Norse *skadi*) literally means the Dark One. As hunter with the bow and arrow, the image of Skadi may be compared to the Finnish Mielikki. Her name and image have been compared to Scathach of Scythia who appears in Celtic accounts as 'wise in weaponry'. The accounts of Skadi were later incorporated into Hans Christian Andersen's story of The Snow Queen.

Though some said that Skadi was dark and full of harm, the ancient Mother of the North taught Her people how to make the skis and skates and sleds to slide across the miles of whiteness of Norwegian winters. Great woman of Thrymheim, it was Skadi who stirred up the snowflakes of heaven so that they swarmed like bees around Her white fur robes and boots. Even upon the broadest snow shoes that She invented for Her people, Skadi remained fleet and agile, as She used Her bow and arrow in the snowy woods.

They say She came to Asgard upon hearing of the fiery death of Thiassi, eagle father of wintry Thrymheim, his feathered wings burned to ashes when he had tried to keep Iduna from the deities of Asgard. Standing before the deities of the Aesir in Her snow white fur and crystal armour, Her arrows sparkling with the frost, Skadi demanded a life for a life. Thus the deities of Asgard, seeing Her determined anger, offered Her a husband in Thiassi's stead.

Though in Her mind delicate young Balder was the object of Her fancy, those of Asgard insisted that Her choice be blind and wrapped a linen cloth about Her eyes so that She could see no higher than the ankles of all the men who stood about Her in a circle, waiting for Skadi to make Her choice. So it was that Skadi had to pick, almost as if with eyes shut tight, as so many women are wont to choose their mates, thinking that the feet most perfect, most delicately formed, were those of Frigga's sweetest son, the gentle Balder. But when the blinder was removed, it was Njord of the foggy seacoast, he who had come from the Vanir, that She had taken as Her husband.

All went rather well as long as they remained in Asgard. But when the time arrived that they should choose a marriage home, Njord insisted that Skadi join him in his home along the mild misty beach where the sounds of gulls pierced the air, while She insisted that he return with Her to the snow covered mountains of Thrymheim, where the call of wolves was music more familiar to Her ears. Trying to devise a plan that would be suitable to both, the year was evenly divided, so that half the time was spent in Njord's Noatun home, dwelling then in snowy Thrymheim for the remainder of each year.

What seemed such a fair and reasonable solution ensured that one of them always would be saddened, whichever place was taken as their home. Though She had won him fairly, Skadi finally announced to Njord that they must part. Some who tell this tale say that She left with love and friendship. But others claim that She flew into a rage and breaking up the timber of their marriage bed, She strapped the boards upon Her feet and thus invented skis. Walking flat upon them until She reached the hills of sliding snow, She then skied across the mountains and the valleys—back to Her Thrymheim home.

Once again in the land of constant snow, Skadi found Uller, he who liked the winter. Some say Uller's mother Rind was the Mother of the northern forests who some call upon as Rauni. Those of northern Norway, who say that Skadi and Uller were their parents, tell of calling upon Skadi in blinding blizzards, asking Her to help them in their plight. And some say they see Her hunting in the moonlit snow, Her arrows glistening with ice, or see Her riding in Her sleigh of icy crystal, its ski runners almost floating over the packed whiteness, as great white furry dogs pull Her to Her palace built of bricks of ice.

Those who later came to Norway with stories of a holy child born to a virgin in Jerusalem, spoke of Skadi as the evil Snow Queen who tempted innocent children from their homes, keeping them as captives who had lost their souls. But there are those who say that one day Skadi left the land of Thrymheim and skied across the waters of the great Norwegian Sea, landing on the shores of the island to the west—where She was called upon as Scota—Great Mother of the Scots.

HELLA

Hella, the Goddess who ruled Nifhelheim, the land of the dead, appears in the Eddas only in this connection. It is quite likely that Nifhelheim was associated in early Norse minds with the island of Iceland, the volcanic Mt. Hekla and the nearby town of Hella probably named in this way. Hella was described as treacherous and frightening, yet quite human in Her desire to have the beautiful Balder join Her in Nifhelheim. Germanic material on the Goddess as Holla and Holda may indicate that the most ancient nature of Hella had been much more complex. The connection between these two Goddess images, Hella and Holla, is made clear by the German word for Hell, *Holle*. The German Goddess Holla was later regarded as Queen of the Elves or Queen of the Witches. The name Holla, which may have been a title, is extremely interesting in that it is not only cognate with the term hell, but also with holy, heal, hallow, hello, whole, all, halo and holly. The name as Holda is probably related to the various names given to elves, witches, Valkyries and Giant Women—as Hild, Hulda, or Hilda. It is somewhat ironic that Holla, initially the Goddess of the hearth fire of each home, was later associated with the burning fires of Hell. The imagery associated with Hella and Holla is reminiscent of the Goddess Hecate as known in Anatolia (see Anatolian section—Vol. I), though Her name may be linked to the Greek title of Hellotia. Holla too was woven into later Germanic fairy tale, as the witch Frau Holle described by the Grimm brothers.

Riding on the dark and moonless night,
Her hounds barking at Her horse's heels,
Mighty Holla, Queen of the Elves,
Mistress of Witches,
made Her way through the Black Forest,
blessing what was righteous,
laying spells on those who had done wrong,
causing the hellebore to grow
for the essential herb of Her cauldron,
called upon by the mysteries of the alfablot rite,
so that dead souls could rise
on the sacred hallowed day of late autumn,
the highest day of Holla.

Those who spoke of Holla as the mighty Hella
said She was the daughter
of the Giant Woman Angroboda
and that Her body was alive on one side,
blue and corpselike on the other,
for it was Hella who ruled the land of Nifhelheim,
living in the great hall of Eljudnir,
served by Ganglati and Ganglot.
It was in this land of Nifhelheim
where fields of shrouded dead
lay beside the root of Yggdrasil,
ash tree at the center of the world,
while serpent Nidhogge gnawed upon the root.

To enter the domain of Hella,
one rode through northern glens,
each gloomier and darker than the one before
until the waters of the Gjoll
brought an end to the path.
Over the water stretched the bridge of gleaming gold
the bridge that hung upon a single hair,
guarded by the maiden Modgud
of the white and bloodless skin
who took her toll of blood
from all who passed her way.

Nine regions made up Nifhelheim,
surrounded by walls taller than any other,
as the rust red bird crowed as sentinel
before The Gates of Hel.
Therein rested the departed of the earth,
in fields of bliss for the righteous,
in caves of icy streams of venom
for those who had lived lives of evil.
And for the worst, their bones were washed
in the cauldron of Hvergelmir
and fed to ever hungry Nidhogge,
while their flesh and blood dripped from ferocious jaws
of hounds that bayed and howled for more.

Though Norse memories of Hella
were filled with fear and terror,
still the Goddess Holla shook Her feather bed
causing the snowflakes to fall in the northern woods
as Her image could be seen in the halo of the moon,
and Her presence could be felt
in each sacred grove or hollow
where the hidden people danced about
bringing joy to She who sat upon the throne,
to Holla who protected all souls
and all spirits of the forest lands,
perhaps those who had once roamed Finnish Forests
as the mystical Haltija.

The Primeval Prophetess
Greece, Crete, and the Aegean

he names, images and symbolism associated with Goddess reverence in ancient Greece are so much more familiar to most of us than those associated with the Goddess images from the many other cultures of the world, that this has truly been the most difficult chapter to present.

On the one hand, many of the names and legends are so well known that, in a sense, they need not have been included in these two volumes at all, since my primary intention in this study has been to reclaim what has long been relegated to obscurity. On the other hand, the source materials concerning Goddess images in ancient Greece are so numerous, both in the area of Classical literature and accounts of archaeological evidence, that lengthy volumes, not only on individual Goddess figures but on their specific temples, have been written in recent times, e.g. *The Argive Heraeum* by W. Waldstein and *Eleusis and the Eleusinian Mysteries* by G. Mylonas. Comprehensive studies on ancient Greek religion, such as the works of L.R. Farnell, M. Nilsson, H.J. Rose, A.W. Persson and J.E. Harrison are widely read, while the writings of Bulfinch and Hamilton are even more so.

Yet to research and write two volumes on our worldwide Goddess and heroine heritage, but exclude the wealth of material about the Goddess images of ancient Greece, seemed unthinkable. The solution I arrived at in dealing with this problem, one that I hope readers will regard as reasonable, was to cite the familiar aspects of the most widely known Goddess figures of Greece but to also include lesser known details of shrine sites, rituals, and symbols, that are generally not included in popular studies of Greek religion. Thus drawing directly from the extensive works of Homer, Hesiod, Herodotus, Aeschylus, Euripedes, Pausanius, Plutarch, Strabo, Diodorus Siculus and several other ancient Greek writers, I chose statements that I felt would be of particular interest to the readers of this study. It is true that these classical sources are less easily available and therefore less widely read than the books mentioned above, but for any reader interested in further study of any or all of the Goddess images of Greece, it is these primary sources that must be studied, along with the accounts of the archaeological excavations of Greece, such as the work of H. Schleimann, S. Casson, S. Marinatos, B. Petracos, A. Evans and L. Drees.

Even as I tried to keep this chapter from requiring many more pages than any other in these two volumes, it did eventually emerge as one of the longest sections included in this study. Added to this problem of preferring an egalitarian spacial allottment, I had to deal with my personal feelings about retaining the account of Athena in the form in which I first wrote it. That is, the entire two volumes had originally been written in what some have referred to as 'staggered prose', the form in which many of the shorter accounts still appear. When I made the decision to transpose the longer accounts into the more usual prose form, I hesitated to change the account of Athena. I do hope that the reader will forgive my self indulgence in this decision, or will, upon reading the final paragraph, at least understand my reasons.

In considering Goddess reverence in ancient Greece, it is important to be aware of the numerous influences upon early Greece: Anatolian, Cretan, Cyprian, Canaanite (Phoenician), Egyptian and Thracian. Archaeological excavations have revealed the existence of Neolithic Greek cultures such as the Sesklo and the Dimini, as well as the Cycladic of the Aegean Islands, each of these producing numerous Goddess statues, and each believed to have been influenced, if not originated, by cultures from Anatolia.

The earliest written records from Greece, and minimal they are, are the partially deciphered Linear B tablets of the Mycenaeans of the fifteenth century B.C. It was not until some seven hundred years later that the works of Homer and Hesiod appeared, and with these two writers came the beginnings of the continuously literate Greece that has provided us with the written records of

Greek ideas about the world, including their religious beliefs and customs. The important books of Herodotus did not appear until about 425 B.C., and most of what we refer to as the Greek Classics are from the time of Herodotus onwards, the valuable books of Pausanius written as late as the second century A.D. Thus our knowledge of ancient Greece is a patchwork quilt drawn from the literature of some nine hundred years, while what we know of the periods before the eighth century B.C. relies on archaeological finds and the sources that Hesiod, Homer, and other writers drew upon.

It is clear that as the historically known groups, such as the Achaeans and the Dorians, gained power in specific areas of Greece, religious beliefs and practices that were known to the earlier inhabitants were affected accordingly, e.g. the superimposition of an Apollo temple on the shrine of the Goddess Gaia at Delphi, and the increasing importance of Zeus at Olympia where, archaeologists explain, a temple to Hera long preceded even the smallest altar to Zeus.

By studying the evidence produced by archaeological excavations, alongside the words of the writers of ancient Greece, we can see that over a long period of time, divine attributes were often absorbed under various names, some elaborated upon, some pared down. Family trees were constructed to explain the relationships of one deity to another, for Greece was filled with a multitude of names and images of the divine, many drawn from the cultures that were the Greek's neighbors in trade and war. Thus the Goddess Dione of the dove oracle at Dodona in northern Greece (described in detail by Herodotus, Bk. II) was said to be the mother of Aphrodite who, according to Herodotus in Book I, was brought to the Greek island of Cythera by Phoenicians from the dove oracle at Ascalon. The pomegranate as the symbol of death and rebirth not only occurs in the rituals for Demeter and Kore but also in those of the Goddess Kybele in Anatolia, while it is found in the hand of a statue of Hera at Argos, and in one of Aphrodite at Sikyon. Shrines to different deities often stood side by side in most Greek towns and cities, while the rituals and symbolism at temples, said to be in honour of one particular deity, were often quite different from those for the same deity in a different area, e.g. Demeter the Healer at Patrai, Demeter of the Underworld at Hermione, and Demeter the Law Giver at Drymaia.

Greece was a nation of religious eclecticism, drawing from east and west, north and south. Despite the many efforts to form a centralized theology, Greek writers reveal that this was never truly accomplished. Yet classical Greek culture, occurring well over two thousand years after writing was known and used in Mesopotamia and Egypt, is not only presented to us as the foundation of western culture, but as if it arose out of a cultural vacuum. Reading of the Goddess images of Greece, in the context of these two volumes, we find many of the images beautiful and inspiring, yet we can also see that they are but a part of the treasures in our wealth of ancient mirrors of womanhood.

NIKTA

Nikta (Nichta), literally Night, is known from passages in Hesiod's *Theogyny*. Her association with the Hesperides and the Gorgons, both described as living far to the southwest of Greece, may indicate that the image of Nikta was drawn from ancient beliefs of northern Africa. Perhaps associated with Nut or Nekhebt of Egypt, or Neith of Libya, Nikta does not appear to have had any shrines or temples during the time of Classical Greece, though Her image was an important one in the Orphic Mysteries.

Possessing powers greater than all other deities,
Nikta came forth from primordial chaos,
black as the midnight heavens,
and then gave birth to day,
and then gave birth to all of airy space.

From Nikta came forth the Sister Gorgons,
Sthenno, Euryale and Medusa.
From Nikta came forth the Sister Hesperides,
Aigle, Erytheia and Arethusa,
those who guard the golden apple trees
that grow in an orchard of the westernmost lands,
yet are owned by Mother Gaia,
who gave them as a wedding gift to Hera.
From Nikta came forth the Sister Fates,
Klotho, Lachesis and Atropos
those who allot life's destiny
and punish those who go against life's laws.

Her black wings sheltering Her nest,
Nikta brought forth the Egg in the Wind,
the egg from which Erotic love, Eros,
came into the world at the beginning of time—
so that the race of mortals might begin.

GAIA

Descriptions of Gaia as Creator appear in Hesiod's *Theogyny*. Though revered throughout the land of Greece, the best known shrine of Gaia lay beneath the later temple at Delphi. The image of Gaia, literally Earth, was closely associated with the sacred serpent variously known as Delphyna, Python, and Typhon. This serpent symbol also appears in accounts of Hera and Athena, both of whom absorbed many of the attributes of Gaia. The presence of Mycenaean artifacts at the shrine of Delphi suggests that the image of Gaia may have been linked to Goddess reverence on Crete.

Primeval Prophetess, most ancient Earth, came before all else and brought the world into being. They lit fires to Her on the mountain tops. They entered the depths of Her oracular caverns set deep into the mountains, to hear Her tell of what was yet to come. Alone, She created the heaven, and naming him Uranus She took him as a lover—thus giving birth to the deities of heaven. Alone, She created the sea, and naming him Pontus She took him as a lover—thus creating the deities of the sea.

Her shrines were known across the lands of ancient Greece, at Tetrapolis and Claros, at Patara and Patrai, at Aegira and Argos, at Erythrae and Kyme, at Athens and Tegea, at Salamis and Phyle, and at Gaios where the most ancient wooden images stood in Her sanctuary. There they celebrated the ancient rites, at these holy places where they called upon Her name, on sacramental ground enlightened by the words of Her priestesses, sacred Sibyls, wise Pythias, devout Mellisae.

But intruders came from the northern lands, claiming Her sacred shrines for their own, daring to diminish Her ancient majesty, yet unable to deny Her primacy—so that when speaking of their own god Zeus, they said that She must have been his grandmother, so long had She been known. Even Achaean adoring Homer, centuries after the intrusion, could not forget Her as he sang, "I shall sing of Gaia, Universal Mother, firmly founded, Oldest of all the Holy Ones".

At the site of Olympia, She was called upon as Gaia Olympia, oldest deity of that divine mountain, site where they later said Zeus reigned, as they changed the mountain's name to the masculine Olympus. Yet long before Zeus was born, Gaia had been known in the deep cleft that faced the southeast, the one where a laurel stood sentry at the entrance, where Her knowing priestesses sat dispensing Her wisdom, reciting Gaia's law on each decision.

Tales of Gaia's serpent child Typhon lingered, each telling of the battles that Typhon faced from the assaults of Zeus. First in the Corycian cave in far off Cilicia, the Anatolian home where Typhon had been born. Then at Mount Casius in the land of Syria, and later yet upon the fiery Aetna on the isle of Sicily. Do these long held memories of Zeus attacking Typhon tell of the many shrines that those who worshipped Zeus had stolen from Grandmother Gaia—and claimed to be their own?

Where shall we know Gaia best? Surely at the foot of Mount Parnassus, the site of ancient Pytho, sacred Delphi, that place of holy oracles of divine word given by prophetic tongues. These were the words that were heard throughout the world, Gaia's mystic cavern held in highest repute by both the poor and the powerful, as holy Pythian priestess spoke of what Gaia had placed inside her mind. Though men of Zeus had taken Olympia, Dorian priests claimed Pytho for Apollo. And though they still spoke of it as Delphi, Womb, Apollo spoke in louder voice—so that the gentle voice of Earth no longer could be heard.

But deep beneath the sanctified land, Gaia left silent proof of Her ancient ownership—Gaia sitting upon Her throne, the divine lioness that spoke of Ashtart and even of Sekhmet of the Nile, and much that told of dwellers from the isle of Crete, perhaps those who once knew Knossos and left its memory in the name of Parnassus. Yet even as the treasures of the Mother of Crete lay at the deepest level of Delphi, Dorian Greeks claimed that Apollo had taken the form of a dolphin and stopped a boat of merchants who had sailed from Cretan Knossos. These were the men, they say, that he appointed to control the Delphian rites, to teach the Pythian priestess to call upon Apollo—and ignore the word of Gaia.

Some say that Delphi's priestesses were as young as the leaves of springtime, innocent of the great knowledge they conveyed. But other memories speak of long white hair and faces creased with lines of wisdom that only many years of life can bring. Each crowned with laurel wreath, sitting upon the ancient tripod, they threw the barley, hemp and laurel, into the fire on which the sacred cauldron burned—though some say the fumes of Delphi were natural vapours pouring from a fissure in the deep rock secretness of the subterranean chamber that was Earth's Holy of Holies.

Those who came with questions, confused in heart and mind, purified themselves in the water of Her flowing Castalian Spring, as it cut deep into the pink earth. There they called upon the names of the divine woman spirits of the Corycian cave, perhaps in honour of those who had once attended Typhon's birth. Deep in cavern shrine, the Pythia quaffed the waters of the bubbling Cassotis that ran into the holy chamber—and once in touch with Earth, the Pythia began to speak of what she heard, answering questions in riddles of allsense, ordaining the law as she told of the future.

Some say that Dionysus, the one Egyptians speak of as Osiris, was buried deep beneath the stone in the heart of Gaia's Delphi cavern—and that this sacred rock was the navel of the centre of the earth, the core of Gaia's being—holy omphales of Pytho, knitted bout with woven fillet. Yet they also said that it was the grave of slaughtered Python, murdered Typhon, Gaia's virgin born serpent child who was once known as Delphyna. But all of these tales are memories of bygone days, as long ago as when women built the first small shrine at Delphi.

Homer sang that young Apollo, finding the site of Pytho to his liking, decided to take it for his own. But upon seeing Gaia's priestess Delphyna blocking his path to the holy chasm, Apollo used his torches and his arrows and dropped Pythoness Delphyna in untimely fiery death—thus declaring the ancient shrine as his own. Yet centuries later, Aeschylus wrote that the holy shrine had not been stolen by Apollo, but was given as a gift, placing these words in the mouth of a player upon Hellenic stage.

> First in my prayer, before all other deities,
> I call upon Gaia, Primeval Prophetess,
> Next Themis on her mother's oracular seat
> sat, so men say. Third by unforced consent,
> another Titan, another daughter of Gaia,
> Phoebe, gave it as a present to Apollo,
> and giving it, gave her name as well.

Euripedes tells yet another version, writing that a serpent, a child born alone of Gaia, guarded the cave of Gaia's oracle. Apollo then struck the serpent dead, and Gaia in Her wrath at the brutish thing that Apollo had done, sent nightmares to the men of Apollo, laying bare the past, the present and the future, so that they would know what penance they would someday pay. And who can help but wonder at the memory that Apollo once tried to rape the maiden Daphne so that the young woman was grateful to be transformed into a laurel, for Pausanius wrote that Daphne was the name of the most ancient Pythian priestess that Gaia chose to prophesy at Her Delphi shrine. Though we know little of the young Creusa, what shall be made of the tale that she was raped in a cave near Delphi—by that same Apollo—who is said to be the fountainhead of Hellenic logic and rational thought? Were these memories of the time when Gaia lost the shrine, the time that Boio spoke of when she said that Delphi had been claimed by sons of the remotest North?

Still more we know from what they tell of Apollo's attempt to heal his guilt, for they say that after he murdered Python he went to Tempe Valley to purify himself by working as a shepherd. Yet each eight years thereafter, at the time of the Septerion, a hut was built upon the halos circle, not far from the Delphian stone of the Sibyl Herophile, the site where that ancient prophetess from Anatolia once spoke the sacred prophecies. Described as the dragon's lair, each eighth year women marched with young lads to this hut, the boys overturning the tables within, setting fire to the tiny shrine. And as the fire blazed in grievous memory of what had happened so long ago, they called upon one lad as young Apollo, and afterwards pretended that he must leave for Tempe to atone for the evil he had done.

Even at the time when Pythian priestesses had learned to call upon Apollo, and the shrine grew from a tiny sanctuary to a temple rich with treasures of silver and gold, the sibyls held vague memories of ancient days. For when a plague struck four centuries before the days of Roman Caesar, the Delphic priestess decreed that the worship of the Mother of All Deities must be brought from Pessinus in Anatolia, that the rites for Mother Kybele must be brought to Athens. Two hundred more years had gone by when the Sibyl then called for the holy black stone of Kybele, insisting that it must be installed in Rome, and that all religious procession and custom for Kybele must take place in the heart of Rome.

Sacked for its treasures by the Celts, claimed by the Roman empire, looted by Christian Constantine who took the treasures to Byzantium, Delphi remained as holy oracle. But Emperor Theodosius closed the holy site as a danger to Christianity, and Arcadius, succeeding to the throne of early Christendom, took an axe to the ancient bricks and stones—until the ancient temple lay in silent ruin.

Diodorus said that the written records of Delphic prophecies and the Delphic laws known as Sibylline were written in the hexameters of familiar Delphic rhythm, and that these Sibylline records were the source of Homer's stories, the font from which his tales came forth. Rumour upon rumour grew about the final resting place of the Oracles Sibylline, nine books in all they said—once kept in stringent secrecy in Rome. Destroyed by Stilicho? Burned at Alexandria? Yet can we help but wonder if they do not still exist, perhaps hidden away in library sacrosanct, available only to those who qualify by intent—and gender—for Roman ordination? For just one century ago, the Cardinal named Mai revealed the presence of ancient Sibylline verses that he had drawn from the dust of Vatican shelves. Thus the voice and wisdom of ancient Gaia may still lie deep within Her own body—the knowledge of Earth kept hidden within earth—kept from the light of day by those who have forgotten the primacy of Mother Gaia.

THEMIS AND DIKE

Both Themis and Dike are defined as Justice. The survival of the name Dike emerges in the modern Greek word for judge, *dikasta*. Though Themis was regarded as the daughter of Gaia, Dike was said to be the daughter of Themis, one of the Horae, the Seasons. The image of Themis bears a strong resemblance to the very ancient Greek Goddess of Wisdom, Metis, while the Scales of Justice so often shown in the hands of Themis suggest a connection to the Egyptian Maat (see Egyptian section). Although references to Themis appear in many of the Greek Classics, Dike was a much lesser known figure, appearing primarily in the work of Aristos and Ovid.

Ancient Themis, She who held the Scales of Justice, righteousness, and moral law, was She not first known as Metis who tried to teach Achaeans the rules of fairness to all? Hesiod said that Metis was wed to their wrathful Zeus, claiming that She was the first bride of his youth. Yet when Zeus could no longer bear the wisdom and good counsel that came from Her womanly wisdom, he swallowed Her whole—explaining that he then received Her sagacious words from inside his bloated belly.

Thus they spoke of Themis, in vague memory of Metis, perhaps hoping that by inverting the pronouncement of Her name, Her womanly justice might be inverted too. Still Themis spoke of what was right, still She held Her scales up high, above prejudice, above bribery, Her word protecting the innocent, punishing the guilty. And though Achaeans once again announced Her wed to Zeus, this time as Themis, and his second bride, they soon forgot the marriage, realizing that Her indomitable strength, Her independent voice, were not the makings of an Achaean wife.

Hopes of entrapping Themis in marriage frustrated and forgotten, Greeks then spoke of Themis as the aunt of Zeus, sister to his mother Rhea, both daughters of the ancient Gaia. But Aeschylus confessed that he thought of Themis and Gaia as 'One with many names'. Themis birthed the Horae, thus creating the daughters of time, those who made the seasons come and go, those who were known as the Seasons, Eunomia, Eirene and Dike. Themis birthed the Moirae, though some said Nikta was their mother, three sister Fates who wove the future of each life, Klotho who spun the threads of life's destiny, Lachesis who allotted each year's portion, and Atropos who clipped the thread when life was done. But though they said these were the Seasons and the Fates, and that they were the daughters of Themis, were they not the many sides of Ancient Mother Justice?

Euripedes remembered that Gaia was Her mother, and that for Themis, Gaia tried to save the ancient shrine at Delphi, so that the daughter might carry on the mother's work. At Olympia too, the name of Themis was revered, long before the men of Zeus claimed that Olympia was theirs. But when the evil deed of usurpation at Olympia was done, the men of Zeus set aside a portion, an altar very small near the mouth of the sacred cavern of prophecy, not far from the tiny altar that was set aside for Mother Gaia —altars for those who could not forget the ancient days when the Mother and the Daughter had taught the ways of right. Their family share was meagre, after having owned it all, still the memory of Themis was endless large for even now we see Her as the brave Olympia, Liberty, Justice, Goddess of the scales of righteous judgement, ancient Themis, more ancient Metis, perhaps most ancient Maat.

Diodorus told us that it was Themis who first taught of the

peace that comes with divine and moral law among a people, and that it was Themis who first revealed that argument and doubt could be settled by Her ancient priestesses, those who could hear and understand the words of Themis, those who served at Her ancient shrines, those who spoke Her words and decrees aloud—so that in this way the written laws were formed, the ordinances we know as Themisteuin.

Though Themis was honoured at Troezen and Tanagra, at Athens and Aegina, at Olympia and Thebes, Pindar claimed that Themis sat upon Mount Olympus, directly next to Zeus, holding a branch of laurel and a cup of invocation in one hand, Her scales of justice in the other. They say that it was Themis who announced when the holy ones of Olympus should join together for discussion, calling each from wherever they might be, thus sharing Her words of wisdom with those who stole Olympus. Yet they listened carefully to each word of advice that She gave, wise enough, at least, to know true Wisdom's voice.

Yet one might doubt the truth of Pindar's claim, for some say that Themis sits at greater heights, missing nothing, as Her starry Scales of Justice light Her Libran home in heaven. And many say that daughter Dike sits by the side of Themis, Virginal Justice once known as Astraia, for though Dike too once lived on earth when the world was in a Golden Age, She fled to the mountains in the time of Silver, and finally escaped to heaven when those of the Bronze Age created sword and spear. Joining Mother Themis in the heavens, Dike still glistens—as the stars of ever virgin Virgo.

DEMETER AND KORE

The image of Demeter, which is best known from the accounts of the important temple at Eleusis, was also revered in many other temples and shrines throughout Greece. Though it is clear from statues and references that Demeter had a daughter, Kore, who each year descended into the Land of the Dead, the name Persephone as Queen of the Dead may have been a quite separate image in earlier periods. Persephone's Latin name of Proserpina, First Serpent, may indicate that this earlier image was linked to images of the serpent child of the Goddess, perhaps even associated with the Egyptian Ua Zit (see Egyptian section). Several of Demeter's shrines were also built on Mycenaean foundations, further suggesting a possible connection with the beliefs and rituals of Crete. Both Hesiod and Diodorus directly link Demeter with Crete, while Diodorus also mentions that Isis of Egypt was much the same deity as Demeter, provider both of law and agriculture. Upon reading the material for this account, the desire to unravel the meaning of the Mysteries was intense, but the more I read, and learned upon my visit to the site of Eleusis, the greater was my understanding that even if understood—they should not be described in so public a manner.

Abducted from the garden of earth and thrown into a chariot, the Maiden was carried off through the dark crevices of earth's chasm, to the depths of the Land of the Dead, leaving Mother Demeter to sorrow at Her death. Holy Maiden, Sacred Kore, She had only meant to find a perfect flower and instead, this blossom of young womanhood was forced to become the wife of Aidoneus Hades, Queen Persephone of the Land of the Dead, as Mother Demeter searched for Her by torchlight, wandering about the earth in Her grief.

In the month of Boedromion, when the crops of Demeter were harvested all through the land, and the autumn chills and winds began, it was the time of the Sacred Mysteries, the Thesmophoria of Syracuse, the nine days of the Greater Mysteries of Eleusis, the time to remember the abduction of the daughter, the time to remember the sorrow of the mother who searched for nine days, the time to retell all that occurred in that most ancient of times.

Near Eleusis, the initiates bathed together in the sea at Phaleron, cleansing the piglets that absorbed all sins, before they started, upon the Sacred Way from Eleusis to Athens, from Athens to Eleusis. Returning with the sacred images of Demeter and the Maiden, they passed the holy fig tree that was given by the Mother, they paid homage to each shrine along the way, and bathed the images in the sea as they had bathed themselves. Some say that when the sky protected them with its dark cover, they lit their torches and wandered over the sand and the rocks of the beach, as if in search of the missing Maiden—as Demeter had once searched along the shore.

The Mysteries of Demeter were known throughout the land. Some tell of winding passageways that the waters had cut deep into the rocks, and women making their way through these damp caves filled with unknown terrors—to recall the darkness that the Maiden must have seen, to recall the fright that the Maiden must have felt. Some speak of the opening at the other end of the darkness, the green and gold of the fields, where wreaths of flowers and myrtle leaves were placed upon each woman as she once again emerged into the wondrous sunshine, to dance and sing on the Rarian Field, the first field in Greece ever to be ploughed and sown, near the Well of Kallichoros where women first danced for Mother Demeter to bring the harvest.

So the memory was kept alive, the memory of the time that Death took the young Maiden to a land beneath the earth, and the Mother grieved and searched for nine days long. But when Demeter heard from Hecate and Helios that the Maiden had been abducted by Aidoneus Hades, only to serve as his wife and queen, to become the feared Persephone, Demeter's rage became manifest. Holding back the rain, parching the summer's crops, Demeter caused the land to lay in unproductive drought. So frightened were the deities of Olympus that Aidoneus Hades was finally prevailed upon to let the Maiden go, to return Her to Her Mother, so that the threshing floor might once again be covered. Thus the Maiden returned to be reunited with Her Mother, and those who loved Demeter joined Her in joyous song and dance to celebrate the coming home. Yet even this joy was dampened by the knowledge that the Maiden had partaken of the pomegranate seeds, some say four, some say six, and for the seeds that were eaten, the Maiden was to return each year to the Land of the Dead—one month for each seed.

So it came to be that the women carried sacred molloi cakes, the honey and sesame that was shaped and baked in the image of that sacred part of the body from which each and every human life emerges, that which is possessed only by women. Carrying the sacred molloi that symbolized the arrival upon earth, each year it was remembered that the Maiden must part from Her Mother, yet each year She would return—in the midst of laughing, dancing, singing, celebration.

Yet deep in the Eleusis shrine of the Telesterion, from which only the sounds of laughter could be heard, were enacted the Greatest Mysteries, that none have revealed until this day. The Mysteries. The Mysteries. Shall we ever know? Did they tell of Demeter as Thesmophorus, the Giver of the Law, and explain that it was She who first established the law of the land? Did they speak of the gift that She gave, the knowledge of the seeds and the growing of the wheat, so that the fruits of Demeter's harvest might feed the people of the world? Some hint at cups of barley water, mushrooms, and poppies, and accounts of Triptolemus. Some speak of resurrection, new incarnations, and the rising of the Phoenix from its ashes. Did they enact the abduction of the Maiden, or tell of how She sat upon the throne as Queen of the Dead, as mighty Persephone?

Some say that the Mystery was that the story had been turned around and that it was Adonis who had been kept by Queen Persephone for four months of each year. For even as Aphrodite begged for the return of Her son/lover, Persephone claimed that he belonged to Her, and thus was his time divided throughout each and every year.

The Mysteries. The Mysteries. Who was it that ever said that women cannot keep a secret? Yet Diodorus claimed that in times more ancient still, for those at Cretan Knossos the sacred rites were open to the eyes and ears of all who wished to know. And was it not Cicero who said that the Mysteries of Eleusis mellowed people's hearts, transformed barbarian natures into beings truly human. And even before Cicero it was said that the Mysteries for Demeter softened the dread of death. For although each year the Maiden descended to the Land of the Dead, in payment for the pomegranate seeds, always She returned, to be greeted by Her Mother Demeter, She who moved heaven and earth until She succeeded in bringing Her daughter back into the sunshine of alive.

At Patrai, they came as pilgrims to be healed by Demeter of the Mirror on the Lake. And at the Mysaion near Pellene, Demeter was honoured in the sacred grove of abundance, among the fruit laden trees and clear spring waters. Though the days of the Pellene festival were numbered as seven, on the third day all male beings were excluded from the sanctuary, as women performed the rites for Demeter throughout the night, just as they did at the shrine of Demeter in Pyraia, just as Roman women did for the Goddess Bona Dea, those whom Plutarch said 'played amongst themselves' throughout the night. Near the Corinthian grave of the Sea Women who died in battle against Perseus and his men, stood the shrine of Demeter of the Pelasgians, the first of the peoples to inhabit Greece. It was there that they dropped burning torches into the pit, hoping to light the way for the Maiden beneath the earth. At Lerna on the sea near Argos, Lernians claimed that theirs was the site at which Persephone had been taken to the Land of the Dead, yet others said that the Maiden was abducted near the River Erineos that runs by Eleusis. Megarians pointed out the Calling Rock where Demeter had called out to the Maiden, and each year the women of Megara called to the Maiden, as Demeter had done. And though they speak of the Mother as Demeter Europa at Lebadeia, and Demeter Chthonia at Hermione, and Demeter Thesmophoria at Drymaia where they said the Mother first gave the law, at the town of Potniai they simply called the Mother and the Daughter—Potniai, The Goddesses— knowing that there was never one without the other.

Was the secret known to early Christian emperors who so despised the Mysteries that Byzantine Theodosius banned them from the land, forbade the baking and the carrying of the sacred molloi cakes, silenced the singing, halted the dancing, doused the torches of the searchers—and brought about the end of the reverence for the Mother and the Daughter? What was it, Theodosius, that made you close the temple at Eleusis until the day that its lands were taken as a Christian graveyard—and the knowledge of the rebirth of the Daughter was all but forgotten?

HERA

By the time of Hesiod and Homer, the Goddess as Hera was linked to Achaean Zeus. Yet references to Metis and Themis, as earlier wives of Zeus, perhaps reveal the continual transitions in Hellenic beliefs as Achaeans gained a firmer foothold over the indigenous peoples of Greece. As with Gaia and Demeter, the symbols of Hera are linked to Crete, but also to the western coast of Anatolia and the Ionian island of Samos, where many Cretans had settled.

Shrines of the Holy Mother Hera once bejewelled the lands of the blue Aegean Sea, for though She was born on Samos near the coast of Anatolia, Mycenaeans made a home for Her at Argos, at

Tiryns, and Mycenae, yet long was She remembered on the isle of Samos, and known as the great one on the isle of Lemnos where She birthed Her son Hephaistos. Yet they say that She had been known as Mother upon the land of Crete and that at the Cretan temple of Phaistos, Her son was called upon as Velchanos, he who lived to die each year.

Some say that She was one with Gaia, though Gaia's daughter Rhea was said to be Her mother, yet She was heir to Gaia's sacred tree of golden apples that was guarded by the serpent Ladon, serpent child of Typhon who was born from ancient Gaia —though others whispered that Hera was its mother. Holy Hera, Cow Eyed Hera, was She not once known as Io, for though Achaeans said that Io was Her priestess, serving at Her great Argolian shrine, Io was the Holy Heifer of the heavens who reigned o'er all of Egypt. Thus came the tale that it was Hera's fault that Io was turned into a heifer, yet Io's wanderings reveal Her sanctity as the lands of Ionia took Her name, Ionia where the isle of Samos rose from the waters. Still they say that Io reached the land of Egypt where She took the name of Mother Isis, even as they spoke of Hera as bovine, naming the sacred hill that lay close by Her Argos temple as Euboia, rich in cows.

Thus were the holy heifers moulded from the clay, and left as evidence of votive reverence deep beneath the earth of Argos, of Tiryns, of Mycenae, homes where Mycenaeans had first settled. And at Mycenae lay the bovine head of hammered silver and golden horns, the rosette of the Holy Mother shining upon its forehead, just as the bovine head of darkest marble, crowned by golden horns was once held sacred at Cretan Knossos. Though some would see these heads as bulls, those who first found them in the ancient ruins wrote of them as images of the Holy Heifer of Egypt, horned as Nut, as Hathor, as Isis long had been—horned as the cows that still roam upon Aegean lands.

Yet more than Mother's milk was Hera, for carefully hammered plates of gold formed the double axe between Her sacred horns, and upon the Samian isle armed women ran in contest for the sacred shield of Hera. At Greek Sicyon, Hera wore the helmet and the spear. Was it for these reasons that they said that warlike Ares was Her son, and that warlike Eris was Her daughter, declaring a twinship between the two? How can we forget that it was Eris who possessed the golden apple, that which must have come from Hera's tree, the apple that rolled the Greeks into the Trojan

War? And what is to be made of the tales of Ares' temple in Papremis, that shrine of Ares on Egyptian Delta lands, for Egyptian priests of Ares each year enacted Ares' first attack upon the temple, citing memories of times long ago. And was it not these priests who said that the temple had first belonged to Ares' mother, and when he, unfamiliar to those who served at Her temple altars, had been refused entrance to Her door, forced his way into the holy place with violent assault—so that it now was known as his?

Various are the stories of Hera's early childhood, for some say that She was raised by Titan Tethys in times ancient even then, when Olympian deities fought the Titans for supremacy, yet others claim that She was nursed by the three women, Euboia, Prosymma and Akraia, at the site where the great Argive temple then was raised. It was Callithoe, so they say, who first served as priestess at this fabled Heraion of Argolis, and they add that at that time all Argive time was reckoned by the names of Hera's priestesses, as each in turn spent their years as guardian of the temple rites. Leading festival processions, holding sacred branches as they walked, these priestesses of Hera paid honour to the ancient Mother, as Founder of Civilization, Goddess of Battle, She who taught Her people to sow and reap the crops. And to the image of Hera that dwelled within the sacred Argive walls, Argive women purified in the nearby Eleutherion stream, those who had wreathed their heads with Hera's wild marjoram rigani — brought the sacred plant as offering of deepest reverence and honour. It was then that they saw the image of the Mother, a sceptre in one hand, a pomegranate in the other, so that they understood that Hera ruled in death—as She did in life. For was She not both Mother and Virginal Maiden, bathing in the clear waters of the Spring of Kanathos each year, forever renewing Her youth, infinite in Her cycles?

Those who thoughtlessly repeat that Heracles, emblem of the Dorian invasions, was the Glory of Hera, surely do not know of what they speak, for Heracles was he who quelled Hera, and the tales of the labours and life of Heracles make this all too clear. Was it not Hera's golden apples that Heracles stole after striking Hera's serpent Ladon dead, just as Zeus had murdered Typhon, just as Apollo murdered Python? And did Heracles not destroy the children of Typhon too, the serpent that some said had been born to Hera? And were these evil deeds not done at Lerna where

Typhon's Hydra was laid to rest, and at Nemea where Typhon's lion was laid to rest, towns that lay so nearby Hera's home at Argos. And was it not Hera who warned the Amazon women at Themiscyra, when Heracles came to take their Queen Hippolyta? And did Heracles not steal the cattle from Hera's sacred isle of Erytheia, and when Hera tried to fend him off, did he not shoot an arrow deep into Her breast? There are those who say this deed was done after Heracles told Molorchus to pray to him—in Hera's stead. Was it not for all these reasons that foresighted Hera had tried to prevent Heracles from ever being born, and when he had been birthed against Her will, that She sent two serpents to strike him dead? Yet even then Zeus had slyly tricked Her by bringing the infant Heracles to Her breast, placing him there while She lay deep in sleep, so that unwittingly Her milk had gifted Heracles with some of Her immortal essence. Thus they spoke of Her outrage when She awoke and found the infant Heracles at Her breast, and how She had thrown him aside so angrily, so fiercely, that Her milk spurted across the heavens—and became the Milky Way. It was said in ancient times that Heracles first took his name when he was told that from Hera he would have undying fame, and would no more be known as Alkaeus, but remembered ever after as Heracles, Hercules. But fame is gained in many ways, and as the Queller of the faith of ancient Hera, so did the prophecy for Dorian Alkaeus come true.

There are many ways to make a Goddess seem less than She might be. For even before the time of Alkaeus, Achaeans spoke of Hera as the wife of Zeus. Yet there were few who did not understand what marriage meant to an Achaean who set out to conquer many lands that had long known the worship of the Mother. To those who questioned the appearance of a father god, rather than a delicate young consort, Achaeans promised the fidelity of their father god of thunderbolts to the long beloved Mother, in each place that She dwelled. Thus was Zeus pledged in marriage, or assigned seducing role, to many woman names of power, and in this way the conquering Achaeans gathered up the names of Alkmene, Aegina and Anaxithea, of Callisto, Calyce and Hesione, of Danae, Demeter and Dione, of Metis, Maia and Mera, of Leda, Lato and Semele, of Eurynome, Eurymedusa and Europa, of Themis, Taygete and Persephone, of Io—and even his own mother Rhea. For these are but some of the women with whom Achaeans said that Zeus had had his way, as they thought it doubly useful to paint an image of ancient Hera as fraught with petty jealousy. For had Her name not been chosen as the most important wife of Zeus, only to ring in hollow echo of diminished ancient memory of She who had been sovereign, almighty Mother in Aegean lands?

Was it chance that appointed Hera as the best known wife of Zeus, or was it that when Achaeans claimed Olympia as the home of Zeus, they came upon the sacred temple of Hera, ancient before Zeus had even a tiny altar in the town? Thus was Hera wed to Zeus, though some say that he spent three hundred years courting Her upon the isle of Samos, where She had long been known as Parthenos. Yet they spoke of a child being born to Hera beneath the willow on the bank of the Imbraxos River that runs through the island of Samos, and some say that She was one with the Holy Mother of the nearby Ephesian temple. Still Achaeans said that She came to live upon Olympus, Her throne then set beside the one of Zeus.

Even then, those who remembered earlier days when Hera had been Queen alone, told of the time that She grew so great with rage that She bound Zeus to his couch with thongs of leather, threatening to push him from Olympian throne. But Acheaen weaponry aborted the rebellion and once Zeus had been untied, he threw Hera's loyal son Hephaistos, perhaps Her consort of more ancient days, down from the heights of Olympus for aiding and abetting Her. Thus was Hephaistos lamed, as the faith of Hera had been lamed. Still Zeus' vengeance was not yet satiated, for he then tied Hera's wrists to heaven, and hung the heavy anvils of metalsmith Hephaistos as weights about Her ankles, so that thoughts of further revolution were crushed beneath the weight of torture—as Achaeans then said that Hera was the Goddess of Marriage—for was She not the wife of the mighty Zeus?

APHRODITE

According to Herodotus, the worship of Aphrodite was introduced to Greece by the Phoenicians of Canaan. In turn, when the Greeks colonized areas of Canaan, they referred to the shrines of Ashtart as those of

Aphrodite Urania, literally, Aphrodite, Queen of Heaven (see Semitic section—Vol. 1). Initially revered as a more multifaceted deity concerned with oracular prophesy and with battle, the Hellenic Greeks came to regard Aphrodite primarily as the essence of erotic love. This attitude may have developed in response to the sexual rituals, so closely associated with the Goddess as Ashtart and Ishtar in Canaan and Babylon, continuing in the Greek temples of Aphrodite, especially at Corinth. The Romans knew Aphrodite as Venus, the star that had been sacred to Aphrodite, Ashtart, Ishtar and Inanna.

White bird of the heavens, dove wings gliding over the sea, Aphrodite Ourania, Queen of Heaven, came from ancient Phoenician Ascalon in the land of Canaan to the nearby isle of Cyprus. Landing at Kition, landing at Amathus, landing at Paphos, those who saw Her shake the water from Her wings upon the rocks of Petra Tou Romiou thought that She had been born of the sea, the whiteness of Her feathers blending with the whiteness of the aphros foam.

They say Phoenicians carried Her to the Cyprian isle, even to the Holy Island of Cythera that Homer spoke of as divine. Still some say that Her home is on the Holy Hill of Corinth in the land of Greece. Once called upon as Ashtart, Queen of Heaven known throughout Canaan, Her April festivals continued along the coast of Cyprus. Her sacred essence was in the milkwhite marble stone, Galatea stone that Pygmalion adored, stone anointed with the oil of olives by pilgrims who travelled from far across the sea, to receive a phallus and a lump of salt on the first day of the month of Nisan. In this way they paid their respect at the holy shrine of Paphos where Aphrodite Ourania, Queen of Heaven, had chosen to make Her new home.

With Her came the memories of Adonis, he who had been Her son/lover Tammuz in Canaan, the sweet young shepherd of the myrtle tree whose gentleness and beauty were lost in untimely death, his blood escaping from the wild boar wound, colouring the poppies of the Cyprian Troodos Mountains, so that women in their sorrow at Aphrodite's loss, wove poppies and myrtle leaves in wreathes about their heads. Lamenting with Aphrodite, the women carried the pomegranates of Persephone, Queen of the Land of the Dead, and planted basket gardens of seeds that would die as Adonis died, before full maturity could come. Such were the sacred rituals for Aphrodite, enacted only by the women, for

Lucian complained that these were the mysteries from which all men were excluded. And in his anger, Lucian claimed that they were lascivious orgy, mere corruption of the mind.

Holy women, sacred women, served Aphrodite in Her temples, taking lovers from among those who came to pay respect and honour to Aphrodite Who Gives Life, to Aphrodite who blessed Her devotees with eternal youthful vigour, to Aphrodite who took Her bodily pleasures from both deities and mortals. Many were the men She had possessed—gentle Adonis, rocklike Hermes, warlike Ares, royal Anchises, watery Poseidon, delicate Dionysus, metalsmith Haephaistos, and oar pulling Butes. Thus the women who served at Her temples, both princesses and peasants, followed the ways of Aphrodite, burning myrrh and frankincense in sacred invocation, while bedding any they desired within Her holy shrines. Those who worshipped Aphrodite kept the love of women in their hearts, as poet Sappho of the isle of Lesbos, who called out to Cypria, Queen of Paphos, Golden Crowned Aphrodite, wrote of the blessing of 'sleeping on a tender girlfriend's breast' and of 'girls who lay upon soft mats with all that they most wished for beside them'. To those who entered the holy places of Aphrodite, love was love. Thus at Her Oschophorian rites, young boys dressed as girls. And at the Argive feasts for Aphrodite, men put on the robes of women, while women donned the clothes of men.

Yet some remembered Aphrodite as the Mother, First Mother of the Race, She from whose body the first Thebans had sprung. Essence of Love, essence of Motherhood, Oldest of the Fates inscribed upon Her shrine at Athens, Aphrodite was known as Goddess of the Spear at Paphos, She Who Battles in Mylasa, and as Armed Aphrodite on Cythera and at Akrocorinth. Thus when Her broken image was raised from the sea at Milos, perhaps it spoke not of perfect female body, but of arms that had been wrenched away.

At Sikyon, even then the ancient site of Mekone, Aphrodite held the sacred mekon poppy in one hand, the pomegranate in the other. It was here they say that Demeter first discovered the poppy. And at Hermione, where the shrine of Demeter Chthonia stood, a shrine for Aphrodite was the site where all virgins came to sacrifice to the Queen of Paphos, before accepting the love of a man.

Though some would say that Aphrodite thought only of physical pleasures, Aeschylus heard Aphrodite say:

> I am the Goddess Cypria, mighty among people.
> They honour me by many names.
> From the tides of Pontus to the Pillars of Atlas
> These lands are mine to rule.
> To those who acknowledge my power,
> I give honours and rewards.
> But those who dare to defy me,
> I shall swing them by their heels.
> For how can I be joyous in my heart,
> If I am not honoured by my people?

Though many centuries have passed, and churches have been built upon the ancient sites, echoes of Panagia Aphroditessa linger in the Shrines of Maria, as the ancient corner stone of Paphian church is anointed with the oil of olives, and a candle lit before the ancient stone—in honour of Holy Aphroditessa—as the Maid of Bethlehem.

HESTIA

Primarily associated with the fire of the hearth, and the eternal city flame that was carried by torch to colonies to indicate their acquisition, the image of Hestia appears to have arrived in Greece at an extremely early period. Though Her name was known on Mycenaean Crete, Her presence among the Scythians may reveal a northeastern origin. Hestia was described as sister to Demeter and Hera in Hesiod's Theogyny, but She had few shrines in Greece. Yet Romans, who spoke of Her as Vesta, regarded Her as an extremely important deity. In Plutarch's account of the early Roman leader Numa Pompilius, the temple of Vesta and the roles of the vestal priestesses are described in some detail. The reverence for Vesta may have survived in Celtic Britain and Ireland in the worship of the Goddess as Bridget.

Banding together by the light of lava
bursting from volcanic heights,
Scyths once gave Her name as Tabiti Vesta,
though Greeks came to know Her as Hestia,
whose name was used to seal each oath,
as spiritual communion rose from Her flame,
kept bright by the women of the mountains.

Some left the land where fires burned brightly
upon Caucasian mountains,
and roamed along the Black Sea's northern coast,
passing through Thrace and Thessaly,
entering the lands of Greece,
carrying Her eternal flame,
everburning heart of tribal light,
blazing core of council meetings
which one may borrow to start the hearth,
or carry to ever distant lands,
planting as a memory of home
that which can be taken
and at the same time left behind—
Mother Flame whose children grow
and yet She never dies,
while sacrifice and incantation
pay honour to Her name.

Hestia of the Hearth,
given a family seat upon Olympus,
was spoken of as one most ancient,
yet almost forgotten by Hellenes
who preferred to think of mountain fires
as the property of Zeus.
Yet Hestia's flame burned brighter
in the air of ancient Rome
where gracious marble temple
circled about Her constant light,
and Vestal priestesses of pure and perfect being,
those who were called upon to judge,
for their voices could speak nothing but the truth,
lovingly tended Her ancient light,
now glowing upon the Palatine Hill of Rome,
and offered cakes of Mola meal

to the many women who came to pray
and to celebrate the June Vestalia,
at this most sacred of temples,
where Hestia was called upon as Vesta.

ARTEMIS

Though the names of Themis and Artemis bear a puzzling similarity, the descriptions of these two images of Goddess are quite different in both imagery and symbol. As if to further confuse a comprehension of the nature of Artemis, we find Artemis of Anatolian Ephesus as a sedate Mother Goddess, though clearly associated with Amazons, while Artemis in Greece was regarded as the fleet young huntress and protector of the animals of the woods. The worship of Artemis is often linked with Crete (as Dyktynna and Brito Martis), and may be compared to images of Libyan Neith, but the Artemis symbols of bear and stag, and Her association with Bendis of Thrace, may reveal a northern European origin. Her role, both as hunter and as protector of the animals, may well be compared to Mielikki and Skadi (see Scandinavian section). Romans regarded Her as the one they called upon as Diana, this name perhaps linked to the Greek Dione of the Dodona Oracle, and to the Greek word *diania*, meaning intelligence.

Numerous were the stories of the women of the mountains of western Anatolia, and Amazon troops coming to the aid of Troy near the waters of the Sangarius, and how these women had once come from far off Libya to found the Anatolian towns of Priene and Prusa, Smyrna and Sardis, Pergamon and Kyme, Myrina and Mitylene, Astyra and famed Xanthos, and the most honoured site of Ephesus where the Mother of the Amazons was called upon as Proto Thronia, First Upon the Throne—and as the mighty Artemis. So sacred was the Mother known at Ephesus that it caused Pausanius to say, "All cities worship Artemis of Ephesus, and individuals hold Her in honour above all other deities. This is due to the renown of the Amazons, those who first consecrated the land of Ephesus, those who dedicated the first image of the Goddess, long before Ionian Greeks arrived."

Though Amazon murals adorned the Anatolian temple sites of Artemis at sacred Magnesia upon the waters of the Meander, and at long remembered Halikarnassos where priestess Artemisia called upon Her name and built great walls of stone that were carved in honour of the valour of the Amazons, Artemis also travelled far from Anatolia. They spoke of Her as fleet Dyktynna of the Cretan isle, and Crete's sweet maiden Goddess Britomartis. Yet did not Strabo speak of Her as Artemis Bendis who carried spear and torch, as She rode Her swift steed throughout the lands of Thrace. Others told the story of the maiden Iphigenia, at Chersonese on Lake Maeotis, at the northern edges of the great Black Sea, and how Iphigenia brought the ancient sacred statue of Artemis to the town of Brauron in the heart of Greece. Yet Hesiod claims that Iphigenia was transformed into the threefold Hekate, the mighty Artemis as known among the Taurians.

Perhaps confused by Her allness, as She who was at one with the animals, the bear, the stag, the wolf, the lioness, while at the same time The Mighty Huntress, the Birth Easing Nurse, Protector of Girls, Fleet Maiden Daughter of the Woods, giving life, taking life—Hellenic Greeks, masters of dualities, perceiving in opposites, divided Artemis in two. Thus naming the rocky isle of Delos as the birthsite of holy Artemis, they declared Her Artemis name of Lato to be Her own mother, while Her Artemis name of Eilythia was said to be the midwife—at the birth of the Artemis who had existed always. For on the ancient isle of Delos were the offerings of silver labia and silver vulva—that had so long before been dedicated to Mother Ashtart by Phoenicians.

Though Greeks spoke of Artemis as the Daughter of Lato, who some describe as Dark Robed Night, the daughter was known as Artemis Eilythia still, as many remembered that the Mother and the Daughter were but one and the same, and that giving life and living life are inextricably entwined, and that the multitude of epithets of the Goddess were merely the many names and titles of the Holy One. Thus they spoke of Artemis as Pheraia, Aphaia Aegina, Kurotrophos, Opis, Agrotera, Brito Martis, Dyktynna, Bendis, Aritimi, Limnaious, Lady of the Lake and Lioness. Even as She was being born on Delian Mount Cynthus, they pointed to the moon and said Her name was Cynthia. Pausanius gave Her name as Artemis Astratia, explaining that each month holy rites were held for Her at the time of the new moon, even as such rites were held for Her at Anatolian Halikarnassos.

But at Greek Pyrrichos, the temple of Artemis was built to honour Amazons who had fallen there, while inscriptions in the temple spoke of Artemis Ashtart.

Was there a province in all of Hellenic Greece that did not see by the light of the flames of the great bonfires built in Her honour, and by the light of torch processions that celebrated Artemis all through the land. Young girls dressed as bears at Brauron, at the temple of the Taurian Artemis image that had been brought from the Black Sea, while at Patrai the priestess of Artemis rode in a wagon drawn by deer, to celebrate Her festival in wide and glorious procession.

In Sparta, at the festival of Tithenedia, the goat was sacrificed to keep young women 'safe from marriage', as the young lads held tight to an image of Artemis, the willow branch upon bare skin reminder of the rage that Artemis might feel towards any who defied Her laws.

Memories of Kallisto lingered, though some said that this was but another name of Artemis. Yet long was the story told that Zeus had taken the form of Artemis, and in this form had tricked the nymph Kallisto into love. It was for this reason that Kallisto was turned into a bear and placed in the northernmost heavens, perhaps remembered by the girls who dressed as bears at the festival of Artemis in Brauron. Yet the island that held the great temple of Artemis, so close to the volcanic mountain, the island Greeks later spoke of as the lovely Thera—was once known as the Isla of Kallista.

Many were the legends of Artemisian nymphs, the women who ran with Artemis in the woods and forest, spoken of as nymphs for they were as fleet and nimble as the deer that were sacred to the swift Artemis. Yet when their strong legs and the perfect aim of their arrows could not match the ones from whom they might have need to flee, they called upon Artemis for protection, even as the Pleiades of heaven felt safety by the side of Artemis.

Daphne, running from Apollo, in fear of being captured and abused, cried out to Artemis for help and found herself transformed into a laurel, able to whisper her gratitude to Artemis only in the rustling of her leaves. Arethusa, a woman of the woods, fled from Alpheus, who thought to violate Arethusa in the forest, and merciful Artemis changed her into the clearest of spring waters so that she might flow along in safety, yet still roam through her beloved woods. Atalanta, swiftest runner of all Boetia, nursed in infancy by a bear, kept her vows of independence by the fleetness of her legs, thus spurning all who mentioned marriage by challenging suitors with races that she always won. But when tempted by the gold of an apple, laid as lure upon her racing path, she entered into tragic marriage, sorrow and misfortune. Yet even after her mistake, Atalanta was rescued by watchful Artemis who transformed her into a mighty lioness so that she might still run side by side with Artemis.

Some say that the hunter Orion dared to violate a woman of Artemis and that for this he was severely punished by the perfectly aimed arrows of the Mighty Huntress. Hunter Aktaon paid the penalty for arrogantly spying upon the unclothed Artemis as She bathed in the stream of a cloistered morning forest. So enraged was Artemis at this impudence that the Goddess made of him a stag, so that the very dogs with whom he hunted, tore him limb from limb.

Artemis Parthenos they called Her, parthenos so long defined as virgin, only revealing the strange nature of patriarchal mind. For parthenius was the child of a parthenos, and parthenos was simply one apart, one free to follow the wind, one free to follow the beds of streams and rivers, one free to enjoy the company of the women of the woods. So was the world a better place when both men and women knew that the spirit of Artemis was close by, forever ready to help, forever ready to punish any that broke the laws of parthenos. For still She came to the side of the mother and eased the pains of childbirth, as She came to the side of the lioness that was bringing forth her cubs. And as provider of the juniper and hellebore that could be used for healing, Artemis taught of the medicines of the woods.

Romans called upon Her as Diana, Huntress Moon who sent Her perfect arrow beams down from the night time skies, She who rode in great procession upon the isle of Sicily, Her chariot drawn by lions. For as they say the lion is the sun, so must the lioness, mightiest hunter of the jungle, be the moon. Far did She travel, on earth as in heaven, for Trojan Brutus told the story of how his ship landed upon a silent island in Mediterranean waters and there, kneeling before an altar of Diana, She told the Trojans of the island in the waters far to the west. In gratitude for these words of Diana, when these Trojans landed upon the isle of Albion that later took the name of Britain, altars were built for the

so must the lioness be the moon

ancient Diana whose women may still be seen dancing upon the heath, with only the stars lighting their celebration of the monthly return of each new moon—the eternal return of Artemis Diana.

ATHENA

How much clearer
the riddle of your Athena being grows,
when first I think of Metis,
'wiser than any deity or mortal',
Metis, full with child,
prophesied as danger to Achaean Zeus,
who in his cowardly fear
swallowed the wisest one—whole,
and later on the shores of Tritonis,
from his then pregnant head,
split apart by the axe of Hephaistos,
brought you forth full grown,
Goddess image made in male fantasy mold,
gestating in his arrogant warrior mind,
umbilically attached
to placental thunderbolts of wrath—
yet not untouched by the genes
of She who filled his cowardly belly.

No Olympian I,
for what faith could I follow
that tried to deceive me
into thinking that life comes forth from man,
when no male being ever known
has carried a child to birth
and from his body pressed life forth.
I might be fool enough to think the earth was flat,
or that the sun moved round it,
but what child does not notice
the swelling of the belly of the woman
that precedes the emergence of new life?

Yet, dear Athene, how to find the threads
of your true Goddess being,
searching for loose strands
that were later woven
into Achaean invader design?
I search on Crete, in Libyan Africa,
at Troy and Canaanite Ugarit.
I dig about in the oldest stones and bones of Athens,
but if I miss a thread or two
of your true essence,
or mistake a recent one for old,
I beg your forgiveness, Ancient Weaver,
for I am but a novice
at the craft you taught,
a mere mortal attempting to disentangle
the threads of your usurped divinity.

I look for threads
at your Libyan festival among the Auses people,
inhabitants of the lake known as Tritonis,
so long ago by Herodotus described,
two teams of women young and strong
in ritual combat with sticks and stones,
enacted among a people
who did not believe in marriage,
and lived with whom they pleased,
worshipping the brave Athena,
though once they called upon you
as Mother Archer Neit,
your sacred aegis
but the common dress of Libyan women,
fringed goatskin thonged with leather,
as yours is fringed with snakes.
And was it not the Machlyes,
the Auses' closest neighbors,
who remembered the time of Jason's visit,
and the tripod that he coveted,
the one that would give Libyan lands to Greece?
Was it during that same time
that Perseus murdered Queen Medusa,
Ruler of the Gorgons of Tritonis Lake,

a murder possible only with your help,
Perseus beheading Medusa by looking into the mirror
the mirror that you gave him,
Her image in the mirror now seen upon your breast—
so that looking at you, do I see the dim reflection
of the slaughtered Libyan Queen?
O Wise One, O Brave One,
are you Medusa, Metis, or Athene?

I look for threads
upon the silent isle of Crete,
whose voice is hidden in undeciphered text,
for they say it is your birthplace,
and that the serpents
twisted bout the arms of priestesses
travelled with you
when Mycenaeans brought your holiness
to the land of the Hellenes.
Cretan Goddess of the double axe,
Lady of the Labyris,
known in dark oracular caves,
were you once called upon as Hella
and remembered thus in torch races
of Mycenaean founded Corinth,
known there as Athena Hellotia,
with memories of a maiden Hellotia
who hid within your temple,
seeking sanctuary from invaders
and there was burned alive—
for who can forget that beneath the foundation
of your splendid Athenian shrine,
crown of the Acropolis,
lie the fragments of Mycenaean structure,
walls and sacred images
that we know so well from Crete.

I look for threads in Troy,
fabled city of coastal Anatolia,
for it was there, from your Trojan temple,
that your famed Palladium was stolen,
your sacred image of olive wood

that bore the name of one you slew in Libya,
by the shores of Lake Tritonis
where Queen Medusa died,
but this memory was spoken of as accidental slaying
of sister playmate Pallas,
she who died when but a maiden,
she whose name you took
in agonizing memory of sister lost,
or does your title Pallas, Pallados,
speak of your pallium, your mantle,
goat skin aegis of protection?
Yet I wonder if I should match
the colours of the threads
of your Palladium in Troy
with those I found in Libya,
threads that speak of accidental death,
among the women who fought in teams among the Auses,
as revelation that she had lain with a man
and was thereby weakened for the combat.
Is it for this reason
that you take the name of Parthenos,
knowing that your strength
would fade to weakness
should you take a male to your Athenian bed?
Still more tangled threads
lie about your Trojan temple,
terrorized Cassandra, fleeing to your altar,
clinging to your sacred image
to escape Achaean Ajax,
yet raped within your sanctuary,
violated before your very eyes,
Cassandra driven over the edge of sanity's cliff.
But when Achaean Odysseus,
comrade of Ajax in Trojan battle,
stole your image from the desecrated shrine—
you saw fit to see him safely home.

I look for threads upon the isle of Cyprus,
for there at Larnaca Tou Lapithou
inscriptions bear your name,
honouring you as Anat Athena,
while Sanchonthion of ancient Berytus,

city now spoken of as Beirut,
speaks of you and Anat as one and the same.
Truly Anat wore the helmet and the shield,
Her strength in battle well known in Ugarit,
northern coastline city of Canaan,
home of Mycenaeans who had once lived on Crete.
But Anat was also known among the Hyksos
who called upon Her name in Egypt,
drawing Her image with helmet and with shield,
with battle axe in hand,
speaking of Anat as Mistress of the Heavens,
Domina of Deities.
But there are some that say
the Hyksos, once expelled from Egypt,
fled to the isle of Crete.
Would they not have known you there
as Cretan Goddess of the Double Axe,
Lady of the Labyris,
Warrior Goddess Anat,
Holy Neit, so long known as Mistress of the Arrow,
Lady of Sais upon the Delta—
ancient owner of your temple at Sais?

Following these threads of unpatterned,
yet intricate design,
again they lead me back to Lake Tritonis,
Libyan homeland of ancient Neit,
site, they say, where Zeus pulled you from his head.
For Diodorus tells of Amazons,
mighty bands of women,
who came from Hespera,
island in the fabled Lake Tritonis,
women led by gallant Myrina and Mitylene,
courageous generals, sisters, queens,
who brought the worship of their Goddess,
The Mother of All Deities,
to mountainous Anatolia,
settling the nearby island of Lemnos,
naming its capital for Myrina,
settling the nearby island of Lesbos,
naming its capital for Mitylene.

You wear the battle of the Amazons
upon your shield in Athens,
in memory of the women warriors' battle
in that most noted city of Attica.
Was it then that you were taken captive
and imbued with the values of Achaean men—
or do you still remember your sisters
who fell in tragic defeat,
their blood soaking deep into Athenian soil?

Lady of Wisdom, Lady of Battle,
a rich tapestry of you I could weave,
born in the home of Libyan Amazons,
daughter of digested Metis wisdom,
inheritor of Neit who ruled the Libyan heavens,
sister of the helmeted Anat—
are these all one and the same,
diverse voices echoing from you
as Mother Courage Wisdom of us all,
for when I bring my unfinished weaving north,
strangely enough, I find you at Delphi,
revered at your shrine as Athena Pronaia,
most ancient spot in all of Delphi,
where, says Aristides, it was you
who was guardian of the oracles of prophecy,
and that your serpent Erechthonius
was Gaia's Python, Gaia's Typhon,
and that you were one with Gaia,
and that at the oracle of Erythrae,
you took the seat of Themis,
offering Themis counsel to Olympians—
yet answering only to the name of Athene.

Yet still I cannot weave the pattern
before I add the colours of your inventiveness
to my armful of scattered threads,
for they tell me that it was you
who first invented the wheel for the potter,
that it was you who built the first bridle,
and first tamed wild horses
so that they would pull the wheels of wagons,
even yoking the winged horse Pegasus

that grew from the drops of Medusa's blood,
that you taught the arts of medicine and healing,
carved the first flute to ever sing sweet sounds,
and, of course, Ancient Weaver,
it was you who designed the first weaving loom,
taking great pride in the tapestries you wove.

In and out of these threads,
your serpent Erechthonius slides.
Rumour has it that the serpent was born
when you fought off rape
and the semen of Hephaistos fell upon the earth,
thus birthing Erechthonius.
Though most say that the serpent of wisdom
was the child of Gaia,
Delphyna, Python, Typhon,
yet many times I have seen the serpent
hiding behind your mighty shield,
and have heard that it lives
on the great hill of Athens,
in your temple that was built
on ancient Mycenaean shrine,
the temple known as the Erechtheum,
the one guarded by Caryatid women,
though once the serpent dwelled in your own temple,
as Homer long ago explained,
causing me to wonder if it was not the Erechtheum
that was your holiest of shrines,
long before the Parthenon was built.
They tell me that it was for your serpent of wisdom
that the errephorai women brought the cakes of honey,
the young women who tended your eternal fire,
those who wove your holy peplos shirt,
so that each month the sacred serpent was fed,
and though I know your serpent lived in Athens,
I cannot help but think of the sacred serpents of Crete,
and even ancient Ua Zit of the land of the Nile.

Close by the Erechtheum,
they built your holy Parthenon,
one time jewel of Athens upon the city summit—
Parthenon for Parthenos—

woman who will take no husband,
finding strength in womanhood alone.
Was it your continual refusal to mate with men,
whether deity or mortal,
that allowed you the strength
to defeat the Giant Enceladus,
and to grasp the reins of Diomedes' chariot
so that you could pin arrogant Ares to the ground
with your everpresent spear?
Yet driving chariots was not unwomanly
for in the marble memories of your Panathenian Festival,
Parthenon images of late summer days in Athens,
I see that it is Amphitrite
who controls the reins,
while husband Poseidon sits by Her side,
as they draw close to the greatest of celebrations,
to join the horse and chariot races,
to join the procession of the torches,
to celebrate your birthday.

Standing here at the foot of the Acropolis,
I wonder, shall I hang my tangled threads in Athens—
yet I know your shrines were spread so far and wide.
Well were you known in the Rhodian city of Lindos,
and on Mount Pontinius in Argolis your temple stood;
in Sicily they called upon you as Athena Napkaia,
while Athene Alea was your title in Arkadia.
At Archarnae and Sunium, Colonus and Phyle,
at Thebes and Alalcomenae,
in Boetia and northern Thessaly,
at Mycenae and Tiryns, Delphi and Megara,
in each were you known and held in high esteem.
Yet it is to Athens
that I bring this armful of still unpatterned fibers,
and on this hot summer day
I climb the long ascent to your great Parthenon temple,
now as confused in architect design
as this tapestry that I have tried to weave—
once usurped as Christian church,
once blown apart by ammunition
stored within its sacred walls,
now background picturesque for visitors

who climb upon the broken blocks,
shouting, laughing, smiling for cameras,
and yet as I stand here in the tiring sun,
this tangled mass of threads
filling my arms, my head, my heart,
I see you sitting upon a broken stone,
your helmeted face resting upon your hand,
and I approach, explaining,
that truly do you trouble me Athena,
for though I say that you have not been born of man,
neither are your words or actions
of woman's heart begot,
for when you say that the child
is the child of the father only,
and the mother but the vessel of containment,
I ask which part of you is from man's mind—
and which of woman born.

You answer, Ancient Weaver,
with threads of your own,
telling me the story that untangles my threads,
as you take them to weave in clearer design—
the tale of how you won this sacred site,
contesting watery Poseidon
who could only bring forth a well of salt water,
while you produced the olive tree
for food and fuel and shade,
but how hollow was the victory
for it angered the Achaean men of Athens
who outnumbered the women—by one,
and thus, forced to accept your presence
as the Holy One of Athens,
since the contest had been fairly won,
in angry revenge, they voted
that women could no longer have their vote,
and from that time, the names of children
would be taken from the father's clan,
reducing the import of motherhood
to carrying vessel and nurse.

Yes, now I remember this last story,
and sit beside you on this dry and broken rock,
that was once part of your glorious Athenian temple,
and hear you say, 'What else could I do?
Forgive me, but try not to forget
that when first you learned
such a word as *Goddess,*
not long after you first began to read,
and images in books filled your growing mind,
it was I whose image went beside that word,
Athena, proud in my helmet of Valour,
Athena, proud in my name of Wisdom—
reaching out to you from the page,
filling you with a woman strength
that no one else would give.

BIBLIOGRAPHY

Note: The sources listed here have been divided by cultural area, while sources that include several areas are listed in the final 'general' section. This bibliography has been compiled with two aims in mind. The first is to list the principal sources, both primary and secondary, employed in researching the Goddess and heroine images included in each of the fourteen sections of *Ancient Mirrors of Womanhood*. The second aim, and the major one, is to supply a list of source materials for the reader interested in further research on a specific area or topic. Most of the sources listed have extensive bibliographies of their own which, in turn, can lead the reader to further information on the specific subject of their interest.

Since *Ancient Mirrors of Womanhood* is intended as an introductory text, aimed at encouraging further research, and reclamation of important images of womanhood as known in the past and among the many cultures and racial groups of the world, it is my hope that this volume will stimulate such studies, and eventually bring long ignored information into the mainstream of our culture. This volume is intended as a stepping stone, to encourage interest, to point out what has existed, and to act as a germinal source for further research. Whatever one's religious or spiritual inclinations — or lack of them — the information and evidence concerning the images of woman included in this volume should be known and familiar to any truly educated person.

CHINA

Barondes, R. *China, Lore Legends and Lyrics* Philosophical Library 1960
Birch, Cyril. *Chinese Myths and Fantasies* Oxford University Press 1962
Bodde, Derk. "Myths of Ancient China" in *Mythologies of the Ancient World* ed. by S.N. Kramer Doubleday 1961
Chen, Ellen. *Tao as The Great Mother and the Influence of Motherly Love in the Shaping of Chinese Philosophy* Religious Heritage Series University of Chicago Press 1972; Paper presented at 25th annual conference Association for Asian Studies Chicago March 1973
Nothingness and the Mother Principle in Early Chinese Taoism International Philosophical Quarterly Vol. 9 No. 3 September 1969
De Bary, W.T. *Sources of Chinese Tradition* Columbia University Press 1960
Eberhard, Wolfram. *Folktales of China* Routledge & Kegan Paul 1965

Ferguson, John. "Chinese Mythology" in *The Mythology of All Races* ed. by MacCulloch, J.A. Boston 1928

Giles, H.A. *Chuang Tzu* London 1889

Karlgren, Bernhard. "Legends and Cults in Ancient China" *Bulletin of the Museum of Far Eastern Antiquities* No. 18 1946

MacKenzie, Donald. *Myths of China and Japan* Gresham London n.d.

Maspero, Henri. *The Mythology of Modern China* Asiatic Mythology London 1932

Nai, Hsia. *New Archaeological Finds in China* Peking 1972

Roberts, Moss. *Chinese Fairy Tales and Fantasies* Pantheon 1979

Tao Teh King of Lao Tzu translation Bahm, A.J. Ungar 1958

Van Gulek, R.H. *Sexual Life in Ancient China* Brill, Leiden 1964

Werner, E.T.C. *Myths and Legends of China* Harrap 1922

_____ *A Dictionary of Chinese Mythology* Julian Press 1961

CELTS

Bromwich, Rachel. *Medieval Celtic Literature* Toronto 1974

Chadwick, Nora. *The Celts* Pelican 1970

_____ *The Druids* Cardiff 1966

Cross, T.P. & Slover, C. *Ancient Irish Tales* Dunn 1969

Dillon, Myles. *Early Irish Literature* University of Chicago 1950

Dillon, M. & Chadwick, N. *The Celtic Realms* Weidenfeld & Nicolson 1967

Dunn, J. *Tain Bo Cuailnge* London 1914

Evans, J.G. *The Book of Taliesin* Llanbedrog 1910

Ford, Patrick. *The Mabinogi and Other Medieval Welsh Tales* University of California Press 1977

Foster, J.C. *Ulster Folklore* Belfast 1951

Fox, C. & Dickins, B. *Early Cultures of North West Europe* 1950

Guest, Lady Charlotte. *The Mabinogion* Cardiff 1977

Hatt, J. *Celts and Gallo-Romans* Nagel 1970

Hubert, Henri. *The Rise of the Celts* Kegan Paul n.d.

Jones, Gwyn & Thomas. *The Mabinogion* Dent 1950

Kennedy, P. *Legendary Fictions of the Irish Celts* London 1891

MacCana, Proinsias. *Celtic Mythology* London 1970

MacCulloch, J.A. "Celtic Mythology" in *Mythology of All Races* ed. by MacCulloch, J.A. Boston 1928

Murphy, Gerard. *Saga and Myth in Ancient Ireland* Dublin 1955

O'Rahilley, C. ed. *Tain Bo Cuailnge from the Book of Leinster* Dublin 1967

O'Sullivan, S. *Folktales of Ireland* London 1966

Piggott, Stuart. *The Druids* Praeger 1968

Pinchin, Edith. *The Bridge of the Gods in Gaelic Mythology* London 1934

Rees, Alwyn & Brinley. *Celtic Heritage* Thames & Hudson 1961

Rolleston, T.W. *Myths and Legends of the Celtic Race* Harrap n.d.

Ross, Anne. *Pagan Celtic Britain* Routledge & Kegan Paul 1967

Severy, Merle. "The Celts" *National Geographic* May 1977

Spence, Lewis. *The History and Origins of Druidism* Aquarian 1949

Squire, Charles. *The Mythology of Ancient Britian and Ireland* London n.d.

Thurneyson, R. *British Druids* Halle 1921

Trevelyan, M. *Folklore and Folk Stories of Wales* London 1909

Wood-Martin, W.G. *Traces of the Elder Faiths of Ireland* London 1902

NATIVE AMERICANS—CENTRAL AND SOUTH AMERICA

Braden, C.S. *Religious Aspects of the Conquest of Mexico* Duke University Press 1930

Brenner, Anita. *Idols Behind Altars* New York 1929

Burland, C.A. *The Gods of Mexico* Putnam 1967

Caso, Alfonso. *The Aztecs, People of the Sun* University of Oklahoma Press 1958

Clark, J.C. *Codex Mendoza* 3 Vols. London 1938

Coe, Michael D. *The Maya* Thames and Hudson 1966

Covarrubias, M. *Indian Art of Mexico and Central America* Knopf 1957

Dibble, C.E. & Anderson, A.J. *Florentine Codex* University of Utah 1957, 1959

Emmart, E.W. *The Badianus Manuscript, An Aztec Herbal of 1552* Baltimore 1940

Gann, T. & Thompson, J.E. *The History of the Maya* New York 1931

Goetz, D. & Morley, S. *Popul Vuh* University of Oklahoma 1952

Horcasitas, F. & Heyden, D. *Book of the Mayan Gods and Rites by Fray Diego Duran* University of Oklahoma 1971

Joyce, Thomas A. *Mexican Archaeology* London 1914

_____ *South American Archaeology* London 1912

Keeler, Clyde. *The Secrets of the Cuna Earth Mother* n.d.

Kingsborough, E. *Antiquities of Mexico* 9 Vols. London 1830-48

MacNeish, R.S. "Early Man in the New World" *American Scientist* Vol. 64 1976

_____ *The Prehistory of the Tehuacan Valley* University of Texas 1967

Mason, J.A. *The Ancient Civilization of Peru* Penguin 1957

_____ "Mirrors of Ancient America" *University of Pennsylvania Journal* Vol. 18, No. 2 1928

Means, P.A. *Ancient Civilizations of the Andes* London 1931

Meggers, B.J. "Transpacific Origins of Mesoamerican Civilization" *American Anthropologist* Vol. 77 1975

Morley, Sylvanus. *The Ancient Maya* Oxford University Press 1946
_____ *An Introduction to the Study of Maya Hieroglyphs* Bureau of American Ethnology Bull. 57 Washington 1915
Spence, Lewis. *The Gods of Mexico* Harrap 1932
Steward, Julian and Faron, Louis. *Native Peoples of South America* McGraw-Hill 1959
Thompson, Eric. *Maya Hieroglyphic Writing* Oklahoma 1960
_____ *The Rise and Fall of Maya Civilization* Oklahoma 1954
Vaillant, George. *The Aztecs of Mexico* Doubleday 1962
Von Hagen, Victor. *World of the Maya* Mentor 1960
Special acknowledgement to Yvonne Retter for information on Colombia.

SEMITES

Albright, Wm. F. *Recent Discoveries in Bible Lands* Funk & Wagnalls 1936
_____ *Archaeology and the Religion of Israel* John Hopkins 1942
_____ *The Archaeology of Palestine* Penguin 1949
_____ *Yahweh and the Gods of Canaan* Athlone 1968
Anati, E. *Palestine Before the Hebrews* Jonathan Cape 1963
Baramki, D. *Phoenicia and the Phoenicians* Beirut 1961
Barnett, R.D. *Catalogue of the Nimrud Ivories* British Museum 1957
Bermant, C. & Weitzmann, M. *Ebla* Quadrangle 1979
Bertholet, A. *A History of Hebrew Civilization* Harrap 1926
Budge, E.A.W. *The Babylonian Story of the Deluge and the Epic of Gilgamesh* British Museum 1920
Cassuto, U. *Anath* Jerusalem 1951
Contenau, G. *Everyday Life in Babylon and Assyria* Arnold 1954
Cook, Stanley. *The Religion of Ancient Palestine in the Second Millenium B.C.* Constable 1908
_____ *The Religion of Ancient Palestine in the Light of Archaeology* Oxford 1930
Delaporte, L. *Mesopotamia* Routledge & Kegan Paul 1925
De Vaux, Roland. *Ancient Israel* London 1965
Dossin, G. "Un Rituel du Culte d'Istar Provenant de Mari" *Revue d'Assyriologie* Vol. 35 1938
Driver, G.R. *Canaanite Myths and Legends* Allenson 1950
Farnell, L.R. *Greece and Babylon* Clark 1911
Gordon, Cyrus. *Ugaritic Literature* Rome 1949
_____ *Ugaritic Manual* Rome 1955
Gray, John. *The Legacy of Canaan* Leiden 1957
_____ *Archaeology of the Old Testament World* Nelson 1962
_____ *The Canaanites* Thames & Hudson 1964
_____ *Near Eastern Mythology* Hamlyn 1969

Hooke, S.H. *Origins of Early Semitic Ritual* Oxford 1935
_____ *Babylonian and Assyrian Religion* Hutchinson 1953
Jacobsen, Th. *Toward the Image of Tammuz* Harvard University Press 1970
Jastrow, M. *The Religion of Babylon and Assyria* Atheneum 1898
Kapelrud, A.S. *Baal in the Ras Shamra Texts* Copenhagen 1952
Landes, G. "The Material Civilization of the Ammonites" *Biblical Archaeologist* September 1961
Langdon, Stephen. "Semitic Mythology" in *Mythology of All Races* ed. by MacCulloch, J.A. Boston 1928
_____ *Tammuz and Ishtar* Oxford University Press 1914
_____ *Babylonian Liturgies and Hymns* Oxford n.d.
Layard, A.H. *Nineveh and Babylon* British Museum 1853
Luckenbill, D.D. *Ancient Records of Assyria and Babylonia* Greenwood 1927
Macalister, R.A.S. *Bible Sidelights from the Mound of Gezer* Hodder & Stoughton 1906
_____ *Gezer Excavations* London 1912
Moscati, S. *Ancient Semitic Civilizations* Elek 1957
_____ *The Semites in Ancient History* University of Wales 1959
_____ *The World of the Phoenicians* Weidenfeld & Nicolson 1968
Olmstead, A.T. *A History of Palestine and Syria* Chicago 1931
Parrot, A. *Nineveh and Babylon* London 1961
Patai, Raphael. *The Hebrew Goddess* Avon 1978
Rowe, Alan. *The Topography and History of Beth Shan* University of Pennsylvania 1930
Saggs, H.W.F. *The Greatness That Was Babylon* Mentor 1968
Schaeffer, C. *The Cuneiform Texts of Ras Shamra—Ugarit* Oxford 1939
Scholem, G. *On the Kabbalah and its Symbolism* Routledge & Kegan Paul 1965
Smith, Robertson. *The Religion of the Semites* Black 1894
Strong, D. & Garstang, J. *The Syrian Goddess* Constable 1913
Vieyra, M. "Istar de Nineve" *Revue d'Assyriologie* Vol. 51 1957

AFRICA

Arnott, K. *African Myths and Legends Retold* Oxford University Press 1962
Bleek, W.H. & Lloyd, L.C. *Specimens of Bushman Folklore* Allen and Unwin 1911
Crowther, S. & Taylor, J.C. *The Gospel on the Banks of the Niger* London 1859
Forde, D. *African Worlds* Oxford University Press 1954

Harden, D. *The Phoenicians* Thames & Hudson 1962
Heidel, A. *Babylonian Genesis* University of Chicago 1951
Hitti, P. *The History of Syria* Macmillan 1951
Herskovits, M.J. *Dahomean Narrative* Northwestern University Press 1938
Hollis, Claude. *The Nandi* Oxford University Press 1909
Itayemi, P. & Gurrey, P. *Folk Tales and Fables* Penguin 1953
Knappert, Jan. *Myths and Legends of the Congo* Heinemann 1971
Krige, E.J. *The Realm of a Rain Queen* Oxford 1943
Ladner, Joyce. *Tomorrow's Tomorrow, The Black Woman* Doubleday 1971
Little, K.L. *The Mende of Sierra Leone* Routledge & Kegan Paul 1951
MacDonald, Duff. *The Heart of Africa* Aberdeen 1882
Marvel, Elinore & Radin, Paul.. *African Folktales and Sculpture* Bollingen Series Pantheon 1952
Parrinder, E.G. *West African Religions* Epworth London 1949
Rattray, R.S. *Ashanti Religion* Oxford 1923
_____ *Religion and Art in Ashanti* Oxford 1927
_____ *Akan—Ashanti Folk Tales* Oxford 1930
Torrend, J. *Bantu Folklore* Routledge & Kegan Paul 1921
Wagner, G. *The Bantu of North Kavirondo* Oxford 1949
Werner, Alice. *Myths and Legends of the Bantu* Harrap 1933

OCEANIA

Andersen, J.C. *Myths and Legends of the Polynesians* London 1928
Basedow, H. *The Australian Aboriginal* Adelaide 1925
Beckwith, M. *Hawaiian Mythology* New Haven 1940
Berndt, R.M, *Kunapipi* Melbourne 1951
Cowan, J. *Legends of the Maori* Fine Arts Ltd. Australia 1913
Danks, B. *Melanesians and Polynesians* London 1910
Dawson, J. *Australian Aborigines* Melbourne 1881
Dixon, Roland. "Oceanic Mythology" in *Mythology of All Races* ed. by MacCulloch, J.A. Boston 1928
Elkin, A.P. & Berndt, R. and C. *Art in Arnhem Land* Chicago 1950
Emerson, N.B. *Pele and Hiiaka* Honolulu 1915
Gill, Wm. W. *Myths and Songs from the South Pacific* London 1876
Grey, George. *Polynesian Mythology* Whitcombe and Tombs Ltd London 1965
Handy, E.S.C. *Polynesian Religion* Bulletin 34 Bishop Museum Honolulu 1927
Hiroa, Te Rangi. *The Coming of the Maori* Wellington, N.Z. 1950
Howitt, A.W. *The Native Tribes of South East Australia* London 1904
Izett, J. *Traditions of the Maori People* Wellington, N.Z. n.d.

Layard, J. *Stone Men of Malekula* London 1942

Lewis, A.B. *The Melanesians* University of Chicago Press 1951

Mullins, J. *The Goddess Pele* Tongg Publishing   Hawaii 1977

Smith, P.S. *Hawaiiki, The Original Home of the Maori* London 1921

Smith, Ramsay. *Myths and Legends of the Australian Aboriginals* Harrap n.d.

Spencer, B. & Gillen, F.J. *The Arunta* London 1927

Strehlow, T.G.H. *Aranda Traditions* Melbourne University Press 1947

Williamson, R.W. *Religion and Social Organization in Central Polynesia* Cambridge 1937

ANATOLIA

Akurgal, Ekrem. *Art of the Hittites* Thames & Hudson 1962

Bennett, F. *Religious Cults Associated with the Amazons* Columbia University Press 1912

Bittel, Kurt. *Hattusha, the Capital of the Hittites* Oxford 1970

Blegen, Carl. *Troy* Princeton 1950

Cadoux, C.J. *Ancient Smyrna* Blackwell 1938

Esin, U. & Benedict, P. "Recent Developments in the Prehistory of Anatolia" *Current Anthropology* 1963

Frankfort, H. *Asia Minor and the Hittites* Pelican 1954

Garstang, J. *The Land of the Hittites* Constable 1910

——————— *The Hittite Empire* Constable 1929

——————— *Prehistoric Mersin* Oxford 1953

Garstang, J. & Gurney, O.R. *The Geography of the Hittite Empire* London 1959

Goetze, A. "Cilicians" *Journal of Cuneiform Studies* Vol. 16 1962

——————— *The Hittite Ritual of Tunnawi* American Oriental Series New Haven 1938

Gurney, O.R. *The Hittites* Penguin 1952

——————— "Hittite Prayers of Mursili II" *Annals of Archaeology and Anthropology* No. 27 Liverpool 1940

Guterbock, H.G. *Hittite Religion* New York 1949

——————— "Hittite Prayers to the Sun" *Journal of American Oriental Society* 1958

Hardy, R.S. "The Old Hittite Kingdom" *American Journal of Semitic Languages* 1941

Haspels, C.H. *The Highlands of Phrygia* Princeton University Press 1971

Laroche, E. "Tarhunda" *Revue Hittite and Asianique* 1958

Lloyd, Seton. *Early Anatolia* Thames & Hudson 1961

——————— *Early Highland Peoples of Anatolia* Thames & Hudson 1967

Mellaart, J. "Anatolian Chronology in Early Middle and Bronze Age" *Anatolian Studies Journal* 1957

_____ *Anatolia* Cambridge 1962

_____ *Earliest Civilizations of the Near East* Thames & Hudson 1965

_____ *Catal Huyuk* Thames & Hudson 1967

_____ "Excavations at Hacilar" *Anatolian Studies Journal* 1961

_____ "Excavations at Catal Huyuk" *Anatolian Studies Journal* 1964

Ramsay, W.M. *Cities and Bishropics of Phrygia* Clarendon 1895

Ransome, H. *The Sacred Bee in Ancient Times and Folklore* Allen & Unwin 1937

Sakir, Cevat. *Asia Minor* Ismir 1971

Sayce, A.H. *The Hittites, Story of a Forgotten Empire* London 1892

Schleimann, H. *Troy* London 1884

Van Loon, M.N. *Urartian Art* Istanbul 1966

Vieyra, M. *Hittite Art* London 1953

INDIA

Avalon, Arthur. *Shakti and Shakta* Madras 1929

_____ *Hymns to the Goddess* Madras 1953

_____ *Principles of Tantra* Madras 1955

Banerjea, J.N. *The Development of Hindu Iconography* Calcutta 1946

Basham, A.L. *The Wonder That Was India* Grove 1954

Bharati, Agehananda. *The Tantric Tradition* Rider 1965

Bose, D.N. & Haldar, H.L. *Tantras—Their Philosophy and Occult Secrets* Calcutta 1956

Brown, Norman O. *Saundaryalhari* Harvard Oriental Studies Vol. 43 Cambridge, MA. 1958

Clayton, A.C. *The Rg Veda and Vedic Religion* Madras 1913

Crooke, W. *Popular Religion and Folklore of Northern India* Westminster Press 1896

Dikshitar, V.R.R. *Studies in Tamil Literature and History* London 1930

Farquhar, J.N. *Outline of the Religious Literature of India* Oxford 1920

Hoffmann, H. *The Religions of Tibet* Allen & Unwin 1961

Hopkins, E.W. *Epic Mythology* Strassburg 1915

Konow, S. & Tuxen, P. *The Religion of India* Copenhagen 1949

Langdon, Stephen. *The Script of Harappa and Mohenjo Daro and its Connection With Other Scripts* London 1934

MacDonell, A.A. *Vedic Mythology* Strassburg 1897

_____ *Hymns from the Rg Veda* London 1922

MacKay, Ernest. *The Indus Civilization* London 1935

MacKenzie, Donald. *Indian Myth and Legend* Gresham n.d.

Marshall, Sir John. *Mohenjo Daro and the Indus Civilization* 3 Vols. Probsthain 1931

Muir, J. *Original Sanskrit Texts on the Origin and History of the People of India* London 1874

Muller, F.M. & Oldenberg, H. *Rg Veda Hymns* Oxford 1897

O'Flaherty, W.D. *Hindu Myths* Penguin 1975

Piggott, Stuart. *Prehistoric India* Penguin 1950

Pillai, M.S.P. *Tamil Literature* Tinnevelly 1929

Rafy, Mrs. M. *Folktales of the Khasis*

Renou, L. *Religions of Ancient India* London 1953

Roy, P.C. *The Mahabharata* Calcutta 1935

Sastri, H. *Origin and Cult of Tara* Archaeological Survey of India n.d.

Thompson, E.J. & Spencer, A.M. *Bengali Religious Lyrics* Oxford 1923

Whitehead, H. *The Village Gods of India* Calcutta 1916

Wheeler, Sir Mortimer. *The Indus Civilization* Cambridge 1953

Wilson, H.H. *The Great Mother* Oriental Translation Fund 1840

Zimmer, H. *Myth and Symbols in Indian Art* Bollingen Series 1946

SUMER

Braidwood, R.J. *Prehistoric Investigations of Iraqi Kurdistan* University of Chicago Press 1960

Chiera, Edward. *Sumerian Religious Texts* Upland, Penn. 1924

Cornwall, P.B. "Two Letters from Dilmun" *Journal of Cuneiform Studies* No. 6 1952

Crawford, O.G.S. *The Eye Goddess* Phoenix 1957

Delougaz, P. *The Temple Oval at Khafajah* University of Chicago 1940
_____ *Pre-Sargonic Temple in the Diyala Region* Chicago 1942

Evans, G. "Ancient Mesopotamian Assemblies" *Journal of American Oriental Society* No. 78 1958

Frankfort, H. *Cylinder Seals* Macmillan 1939
_____ *Archaeology and the Sumerian Problem* Chicago 1932

Handcock, P. *Mesopotamian Archaeology* Macmillan 1912

Harris, Rivkah. "Naditu Women of Sippar I & II *Journal of Cuneiform Studies* Vol. 15 & 16 1962

Hinz, Walther. *The Lost World of Elam* New York University Press 1973

Jacobsen, Th. "Formative Tendencies in Sumerian Religion" in *The Bible and the Ancient Near East* ed. by Wright, G.E. Doubleday 1961

Kramer, S.N. *Sumerian Mythology* University of Pennsylvania 1944
_____ *Sumerian Myths, Epics and Tales* Princeton 1957
_____ *History Begins at Sumer* Doubleday 1958
_____ *The Sumerians, Their History, Culture, and Character* University of Chicago 1963.
_____ *The Sacred Marriage Rite* Indiana University Press 1969

Langdon, Stephen. *The Sumerian Epic of Paradise* University of Pennsylvania 1915

_____ *Tammuz and Ishtar* Oxford 1918

Lloyd, Seton. *Mesopotamia, Excavations at Sumerian Sites* London 1936
_____ *Ruined Cities of Iraq* Department of Antiquities Iraq 1942

Mallowan, M.E.L. *Twenty-Five Years of Mesopotamian Discovery* British School of Archaeology Iraq 1956

Mason, Herbert. *Gilgamesh* Mentor 1972

Moortgat, A. *The Art of Ancient Mesopotamia* Phaidon 1967

Oppenheim, A.L. *Ancient Mesopotamia* Chicago 1964

Parrot, Andre. *Sumer* Thames & Hudson 1960

Perkins, A.L. *The Comparative Archaeology of Early Mesopotamia* University of Chicago Press 1949

Roux, G. *Ancient Iraq* London 1966

Sandars, N.K. *Poems of Heaven and Hell from Ancient Mesopotamia* Penguin 1971

Van Buren, E.D. "The Sacred Marriage in Early Times in Mesopotamia" *Orientalia* Vol. 13 1944

Von Oppenheim, M. *Tell Halaf* Putnam 1931

Woolley, Leonard. *History Unearthed* Benn 1958
_____ *Excavations at Ur* Crowell 1965
_____ *A Forgotten Kingdom* Norton 1968

EGYPT

Albright, W.F. "The Early Alphabetic Inscriptions from Sinai" *Bulletin of the American School of Oriental Research* Vol. 110 April 1948

Allen, T.G. *The Egyptian Book of the Dead* University of Chicago Press 1960

Anthes, R. "Egyptian Mythology in the Third Millenium" *Journal of Near Eastern Studies* Vol. 18 1959

Apuleius, Lucius. *The Golden Ass* trans. Wm. Adlington ed. by Harry Schnur Crowell Collier 1962

Boscawen, W. *Egypt and Chaldea* London 1894

Breasted, J.H. *Ancient Records of Egypt* 4 Vols. New York 1906-07
_____ *The Development of Religion and Thought in Ancient Egypt* London 1912

Budge, E.A. Wallis. *Egyptian Book of the Dead* British Museum 1895
_____ *Egyptian Magic* Kegan Paul 1901
_____ *The Gods of the Egyptians* Methuen 1904
_____ *The Dwellers of the Nile* Religious Tract Society 1926

Cerny, J. *Ancient Egyptian Religion* London 1952

De Buck, A. & Gardiner, H. *Egyptian Coffin Texts* Chicago 1935

Edwards, I.E.S. *The Pyramids of Egypt* Penguin 1947

Emery, W. *Archaic Egypt* Penguin 1961

Erman, Adolf. *The Literature of the Ancient Egyptians* London 1927
_____ *Life in Ancient Egypt* Dover 1971
Evans, Sir Arthur. *The Early Nilotic, Libyan and Egyptian Relations with Minoan Crete* Macmillan 1925
Faulkner, R.O. *The Ancient Egyptian Pyramid Texts* Oxford 1969
Frankfort, H. *Ancient Egyptian Religion* New York 1948
Gardiner, A.H. *Egyptian Grammar* Oxford 1927
_____ *The Astarte Papyrus* Griffiths Institute Oxford 1936
Harris, J.R. *The Legacy of Egypt* Oxford 1971
Lichtheim, M. *Ancient Egyptian Literature* University of California 2 Vols. 1973, 1976
MacKenzie, Donald. *Egyptian Myths and Legends* Gresham London n.d.
Mercer, S. *The Religion of Ancient Egypt* Luzac 1949
_____ *The Pyramid Texts in Translation and Commentary* New York 4 Vols. 1952
Morenz, S. *Egyptian Religion* Methuen 1973
Murray, Margaret. *The Splendour That Was Egypt* Sidgewick-Jackson 1972
Petrie, Wm. Flinders. *Egypt and Israel* London 1925
_____ *Life in Ancient Egypt* Constable 1923
_____ *Religious Life in Ancient Egypt* Constable 1924
Piankoff, A. "The Theology in Ancient Egypt" *Antiquity and Survival* 1956
Rundle Clark, R.T. *Myth and Symbol in Ancient Egypt* London 1959
Sayce, A.H. *The Religion of Ancient Egypt and Babylon* Clark 1902
Van Seters, J. *The Hyksos* New Haven 1966
Witt, R.E. *Isis in the Graeco-Roman World* Thames and Hudson 1971

NATIVE AMERICANS — NORTH AMERICA

Alexander, H.B. "Indian Mythology" in *Mythology of All Races* ed. by MacCulloch, J.A. Boston 1928
Bancroft, H.H. *The Native Races of the Pacific States* New York 1876
Bada, J.F. "New Evidence for the Antiquity of Man in North America" *Science* Vol. 184 1974
Bandi, H.G.. *Eskimo Prehistory* University of Washington Press 1958
Beauchamp, W.M. *History of the New York Iroquois* N.Y. State Museum Bulletin 1905
Benedict, Ruth. *Patterns of Culture* Houghton Mifflin 1934
_____ *Zuni Mythology* AMS Press 1935
Boas, F. *Folktales of the Salishan and Sahaptin Tribes* American Folklore Society 1917
_____ *Keresan Texts* American Ethnological Society 1928
_____ *The Central Eskimo* University of Nebraska Press 1964

Brown, J.K. "Economic Organization and the Position of Women among the Iroquois" *Ethnohistory* Vol. 17 1970

Bunzel, R. *Zuni Origin Myths* Bureau of American Ethnology No. 47 1929

Caldwell, J.R. & Hall, R.L. *Hopewellian Studies* Springfield, Illinois State Museum 1970

Canfield, Wm. *Legends of the Iroquois* New York 1902

Clark, E.E. *Indian Legends of the Pacific North West* Cambridge University Press 1958

Curtis, E.S. *The North American Indian* Cambridge, MA n.d.

Downs, J.F. *The Navajo* Holt, Rinehart & Winston 1972

Drucker, P. *Indians of the Northwest Coast* McGraw Hill 1955

Emerson, E.R. *Indian Myths* Boston 1884

Farb, Peter. *Man's Rise to Civilization* Dutton 1968

Hagan, W.T. *American Indians* University of Chicago Press 1961

Haury, E.W. *The Hohokam* University of Arizona Press 1976

Hewitt, J.N.B. *Iroquoian Cosmogony* Bureau of American Ethnology Vol. 21 1903

Hippler, A.E. "The Athabascans of Interior Alaska" *American Anthropology* Vol. 75 1973

Jahoda, G. *The Trail of Tears* Holt, Rinehart & Winston 1975

Jennings, J.D. *Prehistory of North America* McGraw Hill 1974

Marriott, A. & Rachlin, C. *Plains Indian Mythology* Crowell 1975

McFeat, T. *Indians of the North Pacific Coast* University of Washington Press 1966

Morgan, L.H. *Ancient Society* Meridian 1963

_____ *League of the He De No Sau Nee* Corinth 1962

Opler, M.E. *Myths and Tales of the Jicarilla Apache* American Folklore Society 1938

Parsons, E.C. *Pueblo Indian Religion* University of Chicago Press 1939

Rasmussen, Knud. *The Eagle's Gift* Doubleday 1932

Spence, Lewis. *Myths and Legends of the North American Indians* Harrap London 1914

Stubbs, Stanley. *A Bird's Eye View of the Pueblos* University of Oklahoma 1950

Swanton, J.R. "The Indian Tribes of North America" *Bureau of American Ethnology* 1946

Thompson, Stith. *Tales of the North American Indians* University of Indiana Press 1929

Tyler, Hamilton A. *Pueblo Gods and Myths* University of Oklahoma 1964

Waters, Frank. *Book of the Hopi* Ballantine 1963

_____ *Masked Gods* Ballantine 1970

BIBLIOGRAPHY

JAPAN

Anesaki, Masaharu. "History of the Japanese Religion" in *Mythology of All Races* ed. by MacCulloch, J.A. Boston 1928

Aston, W.G. *History of Japanese Literature* London 1909

_____ *Shinto, the Way of the Gods* London 1905

_____ *Nihongi, Chronicles of Japan from the Earliest Times to A.D. 697* Allen and Unwin 1956

Batchelor, John. *The Ainu and their Folklore* London 1901

_____ *Notes on the Ainu* Asiatic Society of Japan Stanford 1958

Chamberlain, B.H. *Kojiki, Record of Ancient Matters* Asiatic Society of Japan 1883

Davis, F.H. *Myths and Legends of Japan* Harrap 1913

Dorson, R.M. *Folk Legends of Japan* Tuttle 1962

Eliseev, S. *Asiatic Mythology* Harrap 1932

Etter, Carl. *Ainu Folklore* Wilcox and Follett 1949

MacKenzie, Donald. *Myths of China and Japan* Gresham London 1923

McAlpine, Helen & Wm. *Japanese Tales and Legends* Oxford 1958

Phillipi, D.L. *Norito, A New Translation of the Ancient Japanese Ritual Prayers* Kokugakuin University 1959

Sansom, George. *A History of Japan to 1334* Stanford 1958

Satow, Ernest. *Ancient Japanese Rituals* Asiatic Society of Japan Vol. II. 1927

Seki, Keigo. *Folktales of Japan* University of Chicago Press

Smith, R.G. *Ancient Tales and Folklore of Japan* Black London 1908

Wheeler, Post. *The Sacred Scriptures of the Japanese* Allen & Unwin 1952

SCANDINAVIA

Auden, W.H. & Taylor, P.B. *The Elder Edda* Faber & Faber 1969

Bellows, Henry. *The Poetic Edda* American Scandinavian Foundation 1923

Brodeur, A.G. *The Prose Edda of Snorri Sturluson* Scandinavian Classics 1916

Christiansen, R.Th. *Studies in Irish and Scandinavian Folktales* Copenhagen 1959

Craigie, Wm. *The Art of Poetry in Iceland* Oxford 1937

_____ *Scandinavian Folklore* London 1896

Davidson, H.R.E. *Gods and Myths of Northern Europe* Pelican 1964

_____ *Scandinavian Mythology* Hamlyn 1969

Glob, P.V. *The Bog People* Faber & Faber 1969

Halliday, W.R. *Indo-European Folk Tales* Cambridge University Press 1933

Hollander, Lee M. ed. *The Skalds* University of Michigan Press 1968

ANCIENT MIRRORS of WOMANHOOD

Holmberg, Uno. "Finno Ugric, Siberian Mythology" in *Mythology of All Races* ed. by MacCulloch. J.A. Boston 1928

Kirby, W.F. *Kalevala* Dent 1907

Magnusson, M. & Palsson, H. *The Vinland Sagas, the Norse Discovery of America* Penguin 1965

Powell, G.E.J. & Magnusson, E. *Icelandic Legends* London 1864

Rydberg, Viktor. *Teutonic Mythology* Swan Sonnenschein 1891

Simpson, Jacqueline. *Icelandic Folktales and Legends* University of California Press 1972

Sleeman, J.H. *Agricola and Germania* Cambridge 1958

Sturluson, Snorri. *The Prose Edda* translation by Young, Jean I. Bowes and Bowes Cambridge 1954

Tacitus. *Germania* translation by Mattingly, H. Penguin 1948

Turville-Petre, E.O.G. *Myth and Religion of the North* Weidenfeld & Nicolson 1964

GREECE AND THE AEGEAN

Alexiou, Stylianos. *Ancient Crete* Thames & Hudson 1967

_____ *Minoan Civilization* Heraklion 1969

Ames, D. *Greek Mythology* Hamlyn 1963

Avery, C. *The New Century Classical Handbook* Appleton Century Crofts 1962

Bennett, F. *Religious Cults Associated With the Amazons* Columbia 1912

Butterworth, E.A. *Some Traces of the Pre-Olympian World* De Gruyter 1966

Casson, S. *Essays in Aegean Archaeology* Oxford 1927

Catling, H.W. *Patterns of Settlement in Bronze Age Cyprus* Lund 1963

Dempsey, T. *Delphic Oracle* Blackwell 1918

Di Cesnola, L.P. *Cyprus, its Ancient Cities, Tombs and Temples* Murray 1877

Dikaios, P. *Khirokitia* Oxford University Press 1953

Drees, Ludwig. *Olympia* Paul Mall Press 1971

Evans, Sir Arthur. *The Mycenaean Tree and Pillar Cult* Macmillan 1901

_____ *The Earlier Religions of Greece in Light of Cretan Discoveries* Macmillan 1925

_____ *The Palace of Minos at Knossos* Macmillan 1936

Farnell, L.R. *The Cults of the Greek States* 5 Vols. Clarendon 1896

Flaceliere, R. *Greek Oracles* Elek 1965

Gjerstad, E. *Studies of Prehistoric Cyprus* Uppsala 1926

Glotz, G. *The Aegean Civilization* Routledge & Kegan Paul 1925

Graves, R. *The Greek Myths* 2 Vols. Penguin 1955

Guthrie, G. *The Greeks and their Gods* Methuen 1950

Harrison, J.E. *Prologomena to the Study of Greek Religion* Cambridge 1903

_____ *Themis* Cambridge 1912

Higgins, R. *Minoan and Mycenaean Art* Praeger 1967

Hood, Sinclair. *The Minoans, Crete in the Bronze Age* Thames & Hudson 1971

Hopper, R.J. *The Acropolis* Macmillan 1971

Hoyle, P. *Delphi* Cassell 1967

Hutchinson, R.W. *Prehistoric Crete* Penguin 1962

Huxley, G.L. *Early Sparta* Faber & Faber 1962

Karageorghis, V. *Mycenaean Art from Cyprus* Barrie & Jenkins 1970

Karakatsanis, A. *Museums and Collections in Greece* Athens 1970

Kitto, H.D.F. *The Greeks* Penguin 1951

Marinatos, S. *Crete and Mycenae* Thames & Hudson 1960

Matz, F. *Crete and Early Greece* Methuen 1962

Miliades, Y. *A Concise Guide to the Acropolis Museum* Athens 1971

Mylonas, G. *Eleusis and the Eleusinian Mysteries* Princeton 1961

Nilsson, M. *The Minoan-Mycenaean Religion and its Survival in Greek Religion* Lund 1927

Parke, H.W. *Greek Oracles* Hutchinson 1967

Pendlebury, J. *The Archaeology of Crete* Methuen 1939

Persson, A.W. *The Religion of Greece in Prehistoric Times* University of California Press 1942

Petracos, B. *Delphi* Delphi Museum 1971

Poulsen, F. *Delphi* Glyndendal 1921

Rose, H.J. *A Handbook of Greek Mythology* Methuen 1928

_____ *Gods and Heroes of the Greeks* Meridian 1958

Sakellariou, A. *Prehistoric Collections* Athens 1970

Sandars, N.K. *The Sea Peoples* Thames & Hudson 1978

Schleimann, H. *Mycenae* London 1878

Seltman, C. *The Twelve Olympians* Pan 1952

_____ *Women in Antiquity* Pan 1956

Spretnak, C. *Lost Goddesses of Early Greece* Beacon 1984

Von Matt, L. *Ancient Crete* Thames & Hudson 1967

Willetts, R.F. *Cretan Cults and Festivals* Barnes and Noble 1962

GENERAL

Bacon, E. *Vanished Civilizations* Thames & Hudson 1963

Biggs, Robert. "Akkadian Wisdom Literature" in *Ancient Near Eastern Texts* ed. J.B. Pritchard Princeton University Press 1950

Braidwood, R.J. *Prehistoric Men* University of Chicago 1948

Brandon, S.G.F. *Creation Legends of the Near East* Hodder Stoughton 1963

Bulfinch, Thomas. *Bulfinch's Mythology* Tilton 1881

Chiera, E. *They Wrote on Clay* Chicago 1938

Childe, Gordon. *New Light on the Most Ancient East* Norton 1969

Cole, S. *The Neolithic Revolution* British Museums 1970

Colum, Padraic. *Myths of the World* Grosset & Dunlap 1930

Crossland, R.A. "Immigrants from the North" *Cambridge Ancient History* Vol. I Cambridge 1970

Daniels, Glyn. *Malta* Thames & Hudson 1957

Dawson, Christopher. *Age of the Gods* Murray 1928

Dawson, D. *The Story of Prehistoric Civilizations* Franklin Watts 1951

Ehrich, R.W. *Relative Chronologies on Old World Archaeology* Chicago 1954

Finegan, J. *Light from the Ancient East* Princeton 1946

Frankfort, Henri. *Kingship and the Gods* Chicago 1948

_____ *The Birth of Civilization in the Near East* Doubleday 1951

_____ *The Problems of Similarities in Ancient Near Eastern Religions* Clarendon 1951

_____ *The Art and Architecture of the Ancient Orient* Penguin 1954

Frazer, J. *The Golden Bough* Macmillan 12 Vols. 1911-15

Frobenius, L. *The Childhood of Man* Seeley 1909

Gadd, C.J. *Ideas of Divine Rule in the Ancient Near East* Oxford 1933

Garcia, L. & Galloway, J. & Lommel, A. *Prehistoric and Primitive Art* Thames and Hudson 1969

Gaster, T. *Thespis* Doubleday 1950

Gimbutas, M. *The Gods and Goddesses of Old Europe* Thames & Hudson 1974

Gordon, Cyrus. *The Ancient Near East* Norton 1962

_____ *The Common Backgrounds of the Greek and Hebrew Civilizations* Norton 1962

_____ *Forgotten Scripts* Penguin 1968

Gray, John. *Archaeology of the Old Testament World* Nelson 1962

_____ *Near Eastern Mythology* Hamlyn 1969

Grayson, A.K. "Nergal and Ereshkigal" in *Ancient Near Eastern Texts* ed. J.B. Pritchard Princeton University Press 1950

Graziozi, P. *Paleolithic Art* Faber & Faber 1960

Guido, M. *Sardinia* Thames & Hudson 1963

Guilliame, A. *Islam* Penguin 1952

Hall, H.R. *The Ancient History of the Near East* Methuen 1913

Hamilton, Edith. *Mythology* Mentor 1955

Harrison, R.K. *Ancient World* English Universities Press 1971

Hartland, E.S. *Primitive Society* Methuen 1921

Hawkes, J. *Dawn of the Gods* Chatto & Windus 1958

_____ *Prehistory: History of Mankind, Cultural and Scientific Development* Mentor 1965

_____ *The First Great Civilizations* Hutchinson 1973

Hooke, S.H. *Myth and Ritual* Oxford University Press 1933

_____ *Myth, Ritual and Kingship* Oxford 1958

_____ *Middle Eastern Mythology* Penguin 1963

James, E.O. *The Origins of Religion* Heritage 1937

_____ *Prehistoric Religion* Thames & Hudson 1957

_____ *Myth and Ritual in the Ancient Near East* Thames & Hudson 1958

_____ *The Cult of the Mother Goddess* Thames & Hudson 1959

_____ *The Ancient Gods* Weidenfeld & Nicolson 1960

_____ *Seasons, Feasts and Festivals* Thames & Hudson 1961

Kramer, S.N. ed. *Mythologies of the Ancient World* Doubleday 1961

Larousse. *New Larousse Encyclopedia of Mythology* ed. by Guirand, F. Hamlyn 1960

Leach, M. *Standard Dictionary of Folklore* Funk & Wagnalls 1949

_____ *The Beginning* Funk & Wagnalls 1956

Lissner, I. *The Living Past* Putnam 1957

Lloyd, Seton. *Foundations in the Dust* Oxford 1947

_____ *Mounds of the Near East* Thames & Hudson 1961

Lommel, A. *Prehistoric and Primitive Man* McGraw Hill 1966

Maringer, Johannes. *The Gods of Prehistoric Man* Knopf 1960

McEvedy, Colin. *The Penguin Atlas of Ancient History* Penguin 1967

Menan, Aubrey. *Cities in the Sand* Thames & Hudson 1972

Murray, M. *The Witch Cult of Western Europe* Clarendon 1921

_____ *The Genesis of Religion* Routledge & Kegan Paul 1963

Norbeck, E. *Religion in Primitive Society* Harper 1961

Osborn, H.F. *Men of the Old Stone Age* Scribner's 1916

Piggott, S. *The Dawn of Civilization* Thames & Hudson 1961

Powell, T.G.E. *Prehistoric Art* Praeger 1966

Pritchard, J.B. *Palestinian Figures in Relation to Certain Goddesses Known Through Literature* Kraus-Thompson 1943

_____ *Ancient Near Eastern Texts Relating to the Old Testament* Princeton 1950

_____ *The Ancient Near East* Princeton 1958

_____ *Archaeology and the Old Testament* Princeton 1958

_____ *The Ancient Near East in Pictures* Princeton 1969

Speiser, E.A. "Akkadian Myths and Epics" in *Ancient Near Eastern Texts* ed. J.B. Pritchard Princeton University Press 1950

_____ *Akkadian Myths and Epics* Princeton University Press 1957

Stephens, Ferris. "An Akkadian Hymn" in *Ancient Near Eastern Texts* ed. J.B. Pritchard Princeton University Press 1950

Spiegelberg, F. *Living Religions of the World* Thames & Hudson 1957

Spielberg, Stephen. *E.T. et al.* Hollywood, CA, 1982.

Stone, Merlin. *When God Was A Woman* Harcourt Brace Jovanovich 1978

Spiegelberg, F. *Living Religions of the World* Thames & Hudson 1957

Van Over, Raymond. *Sun Songs* Mentor 1980

Vitaliano, D. *Legends of the Earth* Indiana University Press 1973

Von Cles-Reden, Sybelle. *The Realm of the Great Goddess* Thames & Hudson 1961

Warner, Rex. ed. *Encyclopedia of World Mythology* Phoebus 1971

Wright, G.E. ed. *The Bible and the Ancient Near East* Doubleday 1961

RITUALS AND COMMEMORATIONS YOU MAY WANT TO REMEMBER

The ritual for menarche — see Mu Olokukurtilisop/Native Americans of Mexico, Central and South America and Changing Woman/Native Americans of North America.

The ritual for the joining of the twin spirits within the Goddess — see Kunapipi/Oceania section.

The rituals for the grain and corn, growing and harvesting—see Chicomecoatl/ Native Americans of Mexico, Central and South America.

The commemoration and thanksgiving for water on the 21st day of the third moon of the Chinese lunar calendar. See Gum Lin/Chinese section.

New Moon — The fixing of the destinies. See Inanna/Sumerian section and Artemis/Greek section. (Possibly related to Shapatu rites in Babylon. See Ishtar, Shekhina/Semitic section).

Dawn — The arrival of Ushas as enlightenment. See Ushas/Indian section.

The Birth of a Baby — Decreeing its future. See Nerthus — Urth (the Norns)/Scandinavian section, and Hathor/Egyptian section.

Death rituals — See Neit, Seshat/Egyptian section, and Ereshkigal/Sumerian section.

February 1st (or 2nd)—Imbolc, the Day of Bridget—especially concerned with the birth of lambs. See Celtic section.

Vernal Equinox — Spring Festival. See Kybele/Anatolian section; possibly Ashtart/Semitic section (this last is listed as the first day of Nisan, later celebrated on April 1st.). See Aphrodite/Greek section.

April 4 — The arrival of the sacred black stone in Rome. See Kybele/ Anatolian section.

May 1st — Celtic Beltane, probably originating from reverence for the Goddess as Beltis, Belit and Ba'Alat. See Ashtart/Semitic section. Celebrated in honour of the Goddess as Ostara in Germany. Rowan Witch Day, possibly related to the return of Iduna and the Celtic Beltane fires. See Iduna and introduction/Scandinavian section.

June — Vestalia in Rome, in honour of Vesta. See Hestia/Greek section.

RITUALS AND COMMEMORATIONS

New Year's Day — (mid-June) Heliacal rising of the star Sothis (Sirius), possibly related to the Festival of Lights at Sais. See Neit, Isis, Hathor/Egyptian section.

Summer Solstice — See Danu/Celtic section, and Iamanja/Native Americans of Mexico, Central and South American section.

August 1st (or 2nd)—Lugnasadh, see Tailltiu in Celtic section introduction.

August 21 — September 20 — The reign of Virginal Justice. See Themis and Dike/Greek section.

New Year's Day — (autumn) The yearly judgment of people by the Laws of Nidaba. See Nina (Nanshe)/Sumerian section.

Autumnal Equinox — possibly the original Day of the Sheepfolds listed as the 28th day of the month of Tammuz. Tammuz is known as late June and early July on the Hebrew lunar calendar, also as the month of July in Turkey. This may have been the origin of the Days of Judgement and Atonement still honoured by Hebrew people as the Hebrew New Year. In the Babylonian tablets it was the day to present a golden star and a vulva of lapis lazuli to the Goddess. See Ishtar/Semitic section. The death of Tiamat recited; see Tiamat/Semitic section.

September 20 — 30 (Greek month of Boedromion) The rituals of Eleusis and the Thesmophorias for Demeter and Kore. See Greek section.

September 21 — October 20 — the reign of Mother Justice. See Themis and Dike/Greek section.

October 31st—November 1st—The Alfablot rite for Holla (Hella) to raise the souls of the dead. See Hella, Nerthus and Urth/Scandinavian section.

November 1st—Samhain, the Celtic New Year, the day of the emergence of all souls. The day that Gwion was said to have been fished out of the waters and reborn as Taliesin after stealing the knowledge of the Goddess Cerridwen. See Cerridwen/Celtic section.

December 12 — The holy day of the Goddess at Tepeyac. See Coatlicue/Native Americans of Mexico, Central and South America.

Winter Solstice — The raising of the evergreen and the prayers for new growth and fertility. See Hanna Hanna/Anatolian section. The probable emergence of the Sun Goddess from the cave. The decoration of the Sakaki tree. See Amaterasu/Japanese section.

New Year's Day — (Dec. 21-22, Winter Solstice) Original New Year for Scandinavians.

ASTROLOGICAL CONSIDERATIONS

Have you ever wondered why nearly all of the deities regarded as ruling the astrological signs are male? Have you ever wondered why all the named deities are the deities of Classical Greece? Archaeological evidence suggests that the concept of the astral bodies of our solar system affecting character, personality and life's events, probably originated in Babylonia. Egyptian records reveal concern with astrological ideas at about the same time, or shortly afterwards. The list below contains suggestions for a revision of the deities associated with astrological signs. Drawn from various cultures, rather than relying solely on Greek precepts, each image of Goddess, as the ruler of a particular sign, is in keeping with the aspects generally attributed to it, but provides us with a woman view of astrological influences. Reading the full accounts of each of these images of Goddess, the reader may find that these Goddess images offer more insight into each sign than the Greek deities generally designated today.

ARIES	The Morrigan—Celtic
TAURUS	Hathor/Isis—Egyptian
GEMINI	Devi (in Her aspects of Parvati and Kali)— India (Vol. II)
CANCER	Ix Chel—Native Americans of Mexico
LEO	The Sun Goddess of Arinna—Anatolia
VIRGO	Nu Kwa—Chinese
LIBRA	Ishtar—Semitic
SCORPIO	Pele—Oceanic
SAGITTARIUS	Artemis—Greek
CAPRICORN	Awehai — Native Americans of North America America
AQUARIUS	Mawu—African
PISCES	Nammu/Nina—Sumerian

Index